Universalist Church of America

Church Harmonies

A Collection of Hymns and Tunes for the Use of Congregations

Universalist Church of America

Church Harmonies
A Collection of Hymns and Tunes for the Use of Congregations

ISBN/EAN: 9783337242763

Printed in Europe, USA, Canada, Australia, Japan

Cover: Foto ©Thomas Meinert / pixelio.de

More available books at **www.hansebooks.com**

CHURCH HARMONIES:

A COLLECTION OF

HYMNS AND TUNES

FOR THE USE OF

CONGREGATIONS.

PREPARED UNDER THE DIRECTION OF THE
UNIVERSALIST PUBLISHING HOUSE.

BOSTON:
UNIVERSALIST PUBLISHING HOUSE,
37 CORNHILL.
1877.

Press of Wright & Potter Printing Company,
79 Milk Street, Boston.

PREFACE.

For many years there has been a growing desire in many congregations of the Universalist Church to participate more directly in the service of singing in the public worship. The present Collection of Hymns and Tunes has been made to meet this desire; and the compilers believe they have succeeded in producing a work which will meet the needs of our people.

The tunes have been selected with reference to congregational singing only; and as there are hymns so closely associated with old tunes that they suggest one another, and could hardly be divorced, the compilers have not hesitated to insert a tune a number of times, when it seemed best adapted to give expression to the hymns. It is believed that this will be found a valuable and welcome feature of the work.

The hymns are mainly those of the fine new collection known among us as the "Portland Collection," when published without a liturgy, and as "Prayers and Hymns," when published with a liturgy. To make each page complete, it has been found necessary to make an addition of nearly two hundred hymns, all of which add value to the book.

By arrangement with Oliver Ditson & Co., Hamersly & Co., and other owners of the copyrights of tunes, we have been able to make a fine collection of tunes for congregational singing. And we publish the "Church Harmonics," believing it will be welcomed by our people as a help to Christian worship.

Boston, August 1st, 1873.

GENERAL INDEX.

CHURCH HARMONIES.

SABBATH WORSHIP.

ITALIAN HYMN. 6s & 4s.

1 DOBELL'S COLL.

Solemn Invocation.

1 Come, thou Almighty King,
Help us thy name to sing,
Help us to praise;
Father all glorious,
O'er all victorious,
Come, and reign over us,
Ancient of days!

2 Come, thou all-gracious Lord!
By heaven and earth adored,
Our prayer attend!
Come, and thy children bless;
Give thy good word success;
Make thine own holiness
On us descend!

3 Never from us depart;
Rule thou in every heart,
Hence, evermore!
Thy sovereign majesty
May we in glory see,
And to eternity
Love and adore!

2 MARRIOTT.

Let there be Light.

1 Thou, whose Almighty word
Chaos and darkness heard,
And took their flight!
Hear us, we humbly pray;
And, where the Gospel day
Sheds not its glorious ray,
Let there be light.

2 Thou, who didst come to bring.
On thy redeeming wing,
Healing and sight!
Health to the sick in mind,
Light to the inly blind,
Oh now, to all mankind,
Let there be light!

3 Descend thou from above,
Spirit of truth and love,—
Speed on thy flight!
Move o'er the waters' face,
Spirit of hope and grace,
And, in earth's darkest place,
Let there be light!

GOTTSCHALK. 7s.

3

F. H. HEDGE.

Invocation.

1 Sov'reign and transforming Grace!
We invoke thy quickening power;
Reign the spirit of this place,
Bless the purpose of this hour.

2 Holy and creative Light!
We invoke thy kindling ray;
Dawn upon our spirits' night;
Turn our darkness into day.

3 To the anxious soul impart
Hope all other hopes above;
Stir the dull and hardened heart
With a longing and a love.

4 Work in all, in all renew,
Day by day, the life divine;
All our wills to thee subdue,
All our hearts to thee incline.

4

C. WESLEY.

Seeking God.

1 Light of life, seraphic fire;
Love divine, thyself impart:
Every fainting soul inspire;
Enter every drooping heart:

2 Every mournful sinner cheer,
Scatter all our guilty gloom;
Father, in thy grace appear,
To thy human temples come.

3 Come, in this accepted hour,
Bring thy heavenly kingdom in;
Fill us with thy glorious power,
Rooting out the seeds of sin.

4 Nothing more can we require,
We will covet nothing less;
Be thou all our heart's desire,
Be our heaven, in holiness!

5

Love to the Saviour.

1 Hark, my soul, it is the Lord;
'T is thy Saviour,—hear his word,
Jesus speaks, he speaks to thee:—
Say, poor wanderer, lov'st thou me?

2 Lord, it is my chief complaint
That my love is still so faint,
Yet I love thee and adore:
O for grace to love thee more!

6

METHODIST COLL.

Invocation.

1 Father, at thy footstool see
Those who now are one in thee:
Draw us by thy grace alone;
Give, O give us to thy Son.

2 Jesus, friend of human kind,
Let us in thy name be joined;
Each to each unite and bless;
Keep us still in perfect peace.

3 Heavenly, all-alluring Dove,
Shed thy overshadowing love;
Love, the sealing grace, impart;
Dwell within our single heart.

ARLINGTON. C. M.

DR. ARNE.

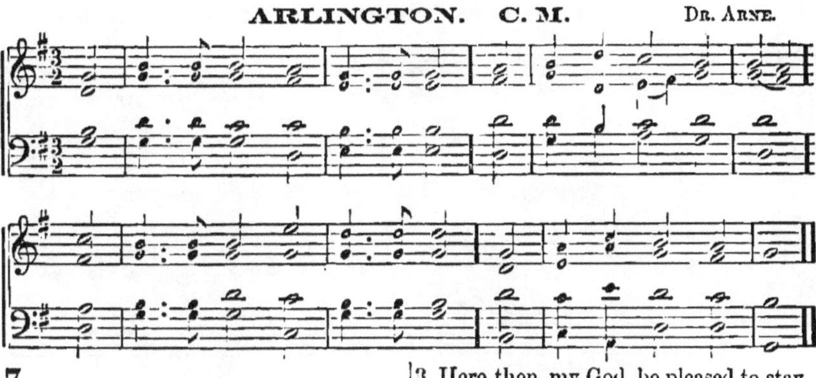

7

REED.

The Divine Spirit.

1 SPIRIT divine! attend our prayer,
And make our hearts thy home;
Descend with all thy gracious power;
Come, Holy Spirit, come!

2 Come as the light; to waiting minds
That long the truth to know,
Reveal the narrow path of right,
The way of duty show.

3 Come as the fire; enkindle now
The sacrificial flame,
Till our whole souls an offering be,
In love's redeeming name.

4 Come as the dew; on hearts that pine
Descend in this still hour,
Till every barren place shall own
With joy thy quickening power.

5 Come as the wind, with rushing sound,
With Pentecostal grace;
And make the great salvation known,
Wide as the human race.

8

C. WESLEY.

Divine Presence Implored.

1 SPEAK with us, Lord; thyself reveal,
While here on earth we rove;
Speak to our hearts, and let us feel
The kindlings of thy love.

2 With thee conversing, we forget
All toil, and time, and care;
Labor is rest, and pain is sweet,
If thou art present there.

3 Here then, my God, be pleased to stay,
And bid my heart rejoice;
My bounding heart shall own thy sway,
And echo to thy voice.

9

H. WARE, JR.

Invoking God's Aid.

1 FATHER in heaven, to thee my heart
Would lift itself in prayer;
Drive from my soul each earthly tho't,
And show thy presence there.

2 Each moment of my life renews
The mercies of my Lord,
Each moment is itself a gift
To bear me on to God.

3 O, help me break the galling chains
This world round me has thrown,
Each passion of my heart subdue,
Each darling sin disown.

4 O Father, kindle in my breast
A never-dying flame
Of holy love, of grateful trust
In thy almighty name.

10

Aid against Sin.

1 ETERNAL Spirit, God of truth,
Our contrite hearts inspire;
Revive the flame of heavenly love,
And feed the pure desire.

2 Subdue the power of every sin,
Whate'er that sin may be,
That we, with humble, holy heart,
May worship only thee.

ROCKINGHAM. L. M.

L. Mason.

11

BREVIARY.

Invocation.

1 Thou Power and Peace! in whom we find
All holiest strength, all purest love,
The rushing of the mighty wind,
The brooding of the gentle dove,—

2 Forever lend thy sovereign aid,
And urge us on, and keep us thine;
Nor leave the hearts which thou hast [made
Fit temples of thy grace divine.

3 Nor let us quench thy saving light;
But still with softest breathings stir
Our wayward souls, and lead us right,
O Holy Spirit, Comforter!

12

STENNETT.

Sabbath Morning.

1 Another six days' work is done,
Another Sabbath is begun:
Return, my soul, enjoy thy rest,
Improve the day which God hath blest.

2 O that our tho'ts and thanks may rise,
As grateful incense, to the skies, [pose,
And draw from heaven that sweet re-
Which none but he that feels it knows!

3 This heavenly calm within the breast
Is the dear pledge of glorious rest,
Which for the church of God remains,
The end of cares, the end of pains.

4 In holy duties let the day—
In holy pleasures—pass away:
How sweet, a Sabbath thus to spend,
In hope of one that ne'er shall end!

13

BREVIARY.

Creator Spirit.

1 Oh, come, Creator Spirit blest,
Within these souls of thine to rest;
Come, with thy grace and heavenly aid,
To fill the hearts which thou hast made.

2 Come, Holy Spirit! now descend;
Most blessed gift which God can send;
Thou Fire of Love, and Fount of Life!
Consume our sins, and calm our strife.

3 With patience firm and purpose high,
The weakness of our flesh supply;
Kindle our senses from above,
And make our hearts o'erflow with love.

14

WATTS.

Pleasure of God's Service.

1 Sweet is the work, my God, my King,
To praise thy name, give thanks, and [sing;
To show thy love by morning light,
And talk of all thy truth at night.

2 Sweet is the day of sacred rest;
No mortal care shall seize my breast;
Oh, may my heart in tune be found,
Like David's harp of solemn sound!

3 My heart shall triumph in my Lord,
And bless his works, and bless his word;
Thy works of grace, how bright they shine!
How deep thy counsels! how divine!

4 Lord, I shall share a glorious part,
When grace hath well refined my heart,
And fresh supplies of joy are shed,
Like holy oil to cheer my head.

DUKE STREET. L. M.

J. HATTON.

15

MONTGOMERY.

Invoking a Blessing.

1 LORD! when thy people seek thy face,
And dying sinners pray to live,
Hear thou in heaven, thy dwelling-place,
And, when thou hearest, O forgive!

2 Hear, when thy messengers proclaim
The blessed Gospel of thy Son,
Still, by the power of his great name,
Be mighty signs and wonders done.

3 But will indeed Jehovah deign
Here to abide, no transient guest?
Here will the world's Redeemer reign,
And here the Holy Spirit rest?

4 That glory never hence depart!
Yet choose not, Lord, this house alone;
Thy kingdom come to every heart,
In every bosom fix thy throne.

16

WATTS.

How amiable are thy Tabernacles, O Lord of Hosts.

1 GREAT God! attend, while Zion sings,
The joy that from thy presence springs;
To spend one day with thee, on earth,
Exceeds a thousand days of mirth.

2 Might I enjoy the meanest place
Within thy house, O God of grace,
Not tents of ease, nor thrones of power,
Should tempt my feet to leave thy door.

3 God is our sun,—he makes our day;
God is our shield,—he guards our way;
All needful grace he will bestow,
And crown that grace with glory too.

4 O God! our King, whose sovereign sway
The glorious hosts of heaven obey,
Thy willing servants may we be,
For blest are they who trust in thee.

17

C. ROBBINS.

"Speak, Lord, for thy Servant heareth."

1 WHILE thus thy throne of grace we seek,
O God, within our spirits speak!
For we will hear thy voice to-day,
Nor turn our hardened hearts away.

2 Speak in thy gentlest tones of love,
Till all our best affections move;
We long to hear no meaner call,
But feel that thou art all in all.

3 To conscience speak thy quickening word,
Till all its sense of sin is stirred:
For we would leave no stain of guile,
To cloud the radiance of thy smile.

4 Speak, Father, to the anxious heart,
Till every fear and doubt depart:
For we can find no home or rest,
Till with thy Spirit's whispers blest.

18

BISHOP KEN.

Morning Worship.

1 AWAKE, my soul, and with the sun
Thy daily stage of duty run;
Shake off dull sloth, and joyful rise
To pay thy morning sacrifice.

2 Lord, I my vows to thee renew:
Scatter my sins as morning dew:
Guard my first springs of thought and [will,
And with thyself my spirit fill.

WIRTH. C. M.

19 MRS. FOLLEN.

Love of Sabbath Service.

1 How sweet upon this sacred day,
The best of all the seven,
To cast our earthly thoughts away,
And think of God and heaven!

2 How sweet to be allowed to pray
Our sins may be forgiven!
With filial love and trust to say,
"Father, who art in heaven!"

3 How sweet the words of peace to hear,
From him to whom 't is given
To wake the penitential tear,
And lead the way to heaven!

4 And if, to make our sins depart,
In vain the will has striven,
He who regards the inmost heart
Will send his grace from heaven.

20 ANON.

The Day of Prayer and Rest.

1 EARTH's busy sounds and ceaseless din
Wake not this morning air!
A holy calm should welcome in
This solemn hour of prayer.

2 Now peace, be still, unhallowed care,
And hushed within the breast!
A holy joy shall welcome there
This happy day of rest.

3 Each better thought the spirit knows,
This hour, the spirit fill!
And thou, from whom its being flows,
O, teach it all thy will!

4 Then shall the day indeed be blest,
And send its hallowing power,
Its sacred calm and inward rest,
Through many a busy hour.

21 ANON.

A Sabbath Morning.

1 How sweet, how calm this Sabbath morn!
How pure the air that breathes,
And soft the sounds upon it borne,
And light its vapor wreaths!

2 It seems as if the Christian's prayer,
For peace and joy and love,
Were answered by the very air
That wafts its strain above.

3 Let each unholy passion cease,
Each evil thought be crushed,
Each anxious care that mars thy peace
In faith and love be hushed.

22

Friends of God.

1 UNITE, my rising thoughts, unite
In silence soft and sweet;
And thou, my soul, sit gently down
At thy great Sov'reign's feet.

2 Jehovah's gentle voice is heard,
And gladly I attend;
For lo! the everlasting God
Proclaims himself my friend.

3 By all its joys, I charge my heart,
To grieve his love no more;
But, charmed by melody divine,
To give its follies o'er.

SABBATH. 7s.

L. MASON.

(In singing hymns 23, 24, and 25, repeat last two lines of each verse.)

23

NEWTON.

Sabbath Morning.

1 SAFELY through another week
God has brought us on our way;
Let us now a blessing seek,
Waiting in his courts to-day:
Day of all the week the best,
Emblem of eternal rest.

2 While we seek supplies of grace
Thro' the dear Redeemer's name,
Show thy reconciling face—
Take away our sin and shame;
From our worldly cares set free,
May we rest this day in thee.

24

MERRICK.

"Who shall abide in thy Tabernacle?"

1 WHO shall towards thy chosen seat
Turn, O Lord, his favored feet?
Who shall at thine altar bend?
Who shall Zion's hill ascend?
Who, great God, a welcome guest,
On thy holy mountain rest?

2 He whose heart thy love has warmed;
He whose will to thine conformed,
Bids his life unsullied run;
He whose word and thought are one;
Who, from sin's contagion free,
Lifts his willing soul to thee.

3 He who thus, with heart unstained,
Treads the path by thee ordained,
He shall towards thy chosen seat
Turn, O Lord, his favored feet;
He thy ceaseless care shall prove,
He shall share thy constant love.

25

LYRA APOSTOLICA.

Vespers.

1 Now the stars are lit in heaven;
We must light our lamps on earth;
Every star a signal given
From the God of our new birth:
Every lamp an answer faint,
Like the prayer of mortal saint.

2 Mark the hour and turn this way,
Sons of Israel, far and near!
Wearied with the world's dim day,
Turn to Him whose eyes are here,
Open, watching day and night,
Beaming purest, holiest light.

3 There is One will bless your toil,—
He who comes in heaven's attire,
Morn by morn, with holy oil;
Eve by eve, with holy fire!
Pray! your prayer will be allowed,
Mingling with his incense cloud.

SILVER STREET. S. M.

26 WATTS.

The Sabbath welcomed.

1 WELCOME, sweet day of rest,
That saw the Lord arise;
Welcome to this reviving breast
And these rejoicing eyes.

2 The King himself comes near,
And feasts his saints to-day;
Here we may sit, and see him here,
And love, and praise, and pray.

3 One day, amid the place
Where my dear Lord hath been,
Is sweeter than ten thousand days
Of folly and of sin.

4 My willing soul would stay
In such a frame as this,
Till called to rise and soar away
To everlasting bliss.

27 BULFINCH.

Sabbath Worship.

1 HAIL to the Sabbath day!
The day divinely given,
When men to God their homage pay,
And earth draws near to heaven.

2 Lord, in this sacred hour,
Within thy courts we bend,
And bless thy love, and own thy power,
Our Father and our Friend.

3 But thou art not alone
In courts by mortals trod;
Nor only is the day thine own
When man draws near to God.

4 Thy temple is the arch
Of yon unmeasured sky;
Thy Sabbath the stupendous march
Of grand eternity.

5 Lord, may that holier day
Dawn on thy servant's sight;
And purer worship may we pay
In heaven's unclouded light.

28 WATTS.

Exalt the Lord.

1 EXALT the Lord, our God,
And worship at his feet;
His nature is all holiness
And mercy is his seat.

2 When Israel was his church,
When Aaron was his priest,
When Moses cried, when Samuel prayed,
He gave his people rest.

3 Oft he forgave their sins,
Nor would destroy their race;
And oft he made his vengeance known,
When they abused his grace.

4 Exalt the Lord, our God,
Whose grace is still the same;—
Still he's a God of holiness,
And jealous for his name.

LISCHER. H. M. Arr. by Dr. Mason.

29 HAYWARD.

Invocation for Lord's Day Morning.

1 Welcome, delightful morn,
  Thou day of sacred rest!
 We hail thy glad return:
  Lord, make these moments blest.
From low delights and mortal toys
We soar to reach immortal joys.

2 Now may the King descend,
  And fill his throne of grace;
 Thy sceptre, Lord, extend,
  While we address thy face.
O, let us feel thy quickening word,
And learn to know and fear the Lord.

3 Descend, celestial Dove,
  With all thy quickening powers;
 Disclose a Saviour's love,
  And bless these sacred hours;
Then shall our souls new life obtain,
Nor Sabbaths be enjoyed in vain.

30 FREEMAN.

The Seasons.

1 Lord of the worlds below,
  On earth thy glories shine;
 The changing seasons show
  Thy skill and power divine.
In all we see a God appears:
The rolling years are full of thee.

2 Forth in the flowery spring,
  We see thy beauty move;
 The birds on branches sing
  Thy tenderness and love;
Wide flush the hills; the air is balm:
Devotion's calm our bosom fills.

3 Then come, in robes of light,
  The summer's flaming days,
 The sun, thine image bright,
  Thy majesty displays;
And oft thy voice in thunder rolls:
But still our souls in thee rejoice.

4 In autumn, a rich feast
  Thy common bounty gives
 To man and bird and beast,
  And every thing that lives.
Thy liberal care, at morn and noon
And harvest moon, our lips declare.

5 In winter, awful thou,
  With storms around thee cast:
 The leafless forests bow
  Beneath thy northern blast.
While tempests lower, to thee, dread King,
We homage bring, and own thy power.

31

The Lord's Day.

1 Awake, ye saints, awake!
  And hail this sacred day;
 In loftiest songs of praise
  Your joyful homage pay:
Come, bless the day that God hath blest,
The type of heaven's eternal rest.

BERA. L. M.

ROOT & SWEETSER'S COLL.

32

NEW YORK COLL.

Sabbath Day.

1 WE bless thee for this sacred day,
Thou who hast every blessing given,
Which sends the dreams of earth away,
And yields a glimpse of opening heaven.

2 Lord, in this day of holy rest,
We would improve the calm repose;
And, in thy service truly blest,
Forget the world, its joys and woes.

3 Lord! may thy truth, upon the heart
Now fall and dwell as heavenly dew,
And flowers of grace in freshness start
Where once the weeds of error grew.

4 May Prayer now lift her sacred wings,
Contented with that aim alone
Which bears her to the King of kings,
And rests her at his sheltering throne.

33

MRS. BARBAULD.

Sabbath Offering.

1 WHEN, as returns this solemn day,
Man comes to meet his maker, God,
What rites, what honors shall be pay?
How spread his Sov'reign's praise abroad?

2 From marble domes and gilded spires
Shall curling clouds of incense rise?
And gems, and gold, and garlands deck
The costly pomp of sacrifice?

3 Vain, sinful man! creation's Lord
Thy golden offerings well may spare:
But give thy heart, and thou shalt find
Here dwells a God who heareth prayer.

34

S. S. HYMN BOOK.

Sabbath Hymn.

1 CALLED by the Sabbath bells away,
Unto thy holy temple, Lord,
I'll go, with willing mind to pray,
To praise thy name and hear thy word.

2 O sacred day of peace and joy,
Thy hours are ever dear to me;
Ne'er may a sinful thought destroy
The holy calm I find in thee.

3 Dear are thy peaceful hours to me,
For God has given them in his love,
To tell how calm, how blest shall be
The endless day of heaven above.

35

H. WARE, JR.

Supplication.

1 GREAT God! the followers of thy Son
We bow before thy mercy-seat,
To worship thee, the Holy One,
And pour our wishes at thy feet.

2 We seek the truth which Jesus brought;
His path of light we long to tread:
Here be his holy doctrines taught,
And here their purest influence shed.

36

DODDRIDGE.

The Eternal Sabbath.

1 LORD of the Sabbath, hear our vows,
On this thy day, in this thy house;
And own, as grateful sacrifice, [rise.
The songs which from thy churches

PILGRIM SONG. S. M.

MENDELSSOHN.

37

ANON.

The Hour of Prayer.

1 It is the hour of prayer:
Draw near and bend the knee,
And fill the calm and holy air
With voice of melody!
O'erwearied with the heat
And burden of the day,
Now let us rest our wandering feet,
And gather here to pray.

2 The dark and deadly blight
That walks at noontide hour,
The midnight arrow's secret flight,
O'er us have had no power;
But smiles from loving eyes
Have been around our way,
And lips on which a blessing lies
Have bidden us to pray.

3 O, blessed is the hour
That lifts our hearts on high;
Like sunlight when the tempests lower,
Prayer to the soul is nigh;
Though dark may be our lot,
Our eyes be dim with care, [not
These saddening thoughts shall trouble
This holy hour of prayer.

38

WATTS.

The Messenger Welcomed.

1 How beauteous are their feet
Who stand on Zion's hill!
Who bring salvation on their tongues
And words of peace reveal!
How charming is their voice!
How sweet the tidings are!
"Zion, behold thy Saviour, King;
He reigns and triumphs here."

2 The watchmen join their voice,
And tuneful notes employ;
Jerusalem breaks forth in songs,
And deserts learn the joy.
The Lord makes bare his arm
Through all the earth abroad;
Let every nation now behold
Their Saviour and their God.

MERTON. C. M.

H. K. OLIVER.

39

GEO. HERBERT.

The Blessing of the Sabbath.

1 BLEST day of God! most calm, most
The first and best of days; [bright,
The laborer's rest, the saint's delight,
The day of prayer and praise.

2 My Saviour's face made thee to shine;
His rising thee did raise;
And made thee heavenly and divine
Beyond all other days.

3 The first fruits oft a blessing prove
To all the sheaves behind;
And they who do the Sabbath love
A happy week will find.

4 This day I must to God appear,
For, Lord, the day is thine;
Help me to spend it in thy fear,
And thus to make it mine.

40

MRS. BARBAULD.

The Lord's Day Morning.

1 AGAIN the Lord of life and light
Awakes the kindling ray,
Unseals the eyelids of the morn,
And pours increasing day.

2 Oh, what a night was that which wrapt
A guilty world in gloom!
Oh, what a Sun, which broke this day,
Triumphant from the tomb!

3 This day be grateful homage paid,
And loud hosannas sung;
Let gladness dwell in every heart,
And praise on every tongue.

4 Ten thousand differing lips shall join
To hail this welcome morn,
Which scatters blessings from its wings
To nations yet unborn.

41

EDMESTON.

The Lord's Day.

1 WHEN the worn spirit wants repose,
And sighs her God to seek,
How sweet to hail the evening's close,
That ends the weary week!

2 How sweet to hail the early dawn
That opens on the sight,
When first that soul-reviving morn
Beams its new rays of light!

3 Blest day! thine hours too soon will
Yet, while they gently roll, [cease,
Breathe, Heavenly Spirit, Source of peace,
A Sabbath o'er my soul!

42

H. ALFORD.

Sincere Worship.

1 O THOU who hast thy servants taught,
That not by words alone,
But by the fruits of holiness,
The life of God is shown!—

2 While in the house of prayer we meet,
And call thee God and Lord,
Give us a heart to follow thee,
Obedient to thy word.

3 And, in the dangerous path of life,
Uphold us as we go;
That with our lips and in our lives
Thy glory we may show.

RAPTURE. C. P. M. Arr. by Dr. Mason.

43

MERRICK.

The Sabbath and the Earthly Temple.

1 The joyful morn, my God, is come,
That calls me to my Sabbath home,
Thy presence to adore;
My feet the summons shall attend,
With willing steps thy courts ascend
And tread the hallowed floor.

2 With holy joy I hail the day
That warns my thirsting soul away:
What transports fill my breast!
For, lo! my great Redeemer's power
Unfolds the everlasting door,
And leads me to his rest!

44

FAWCETT.

Delight in God's Glory.

1 Parent of good, thy works of might
I trace with wonder and delight:
Thy name is all divine.
There's naught in earth or sea or air,
Or heaven itself, that's good or fair,
But is entirely thine.

2 To thee my warm affections move
In sweet astonishment and love,
While at thy feet I fall.
I pant for naught beneath the skies:
To thee my ardent wishes rise,
O my eternal All!

3 What shall I do to spread thy praise,
My God, through my remaining days?
Or how thy name adore?
To thee I consecrate my breath:
Let me be thine in life and death,
And thine for evermore.

45

The glorious Works of God.

1 Thy mighty working, mighty God!
Wakes all my powers; I look abroad,
And can no longer rest;
I, too, must sing when all things sing,
And from my heart the praises ring
The Highest loveth best.

2 If thou, in thy great love to us,
Wilt scatter joy and beauty thus
O'er this poor earth of ours;
What nobler glories shall be given
Hereafter in thy shining heaven,
Set round with golden tow'rs!

CREATION. L. M. 6 ls. HAYDN.

46

MRS. STEELE.

A Prayer for Lord's Day.

1 GREAT God, this sacred day of thine
Demands our soul's collected powers;
May we employ in work divine
These solemn, these devoted hours;
O may our souls adoring own
The grace which calls us to thy throne.

2 Hence, ye vain cares and trifles, fly;
Where God resides appear no more;
Omniscient God, thy piercing eye
Can every secret thought explore:
O may thy grace our hearts refine,
And fix our thoughts on things divine.

3 The word of life dispensed to-day
Invites us to a heavenly feast;
May every ear the call obey;
Be every heart a humble guest;
Then shall our souls adoring own
The grace which calls us to thy throne.

47

WEISZEL.

Rejoice in the Lord.

1 LIFT up your heads, ye mighty gates,
Behold the King of glory waits,
The King of kings is drawing near,
The Saviour of the world is here;
Life and salvation he doth bring,
Wherefore rejoice, and gladly sing!

2 Fling wide the portals of your heart,
Make it a temple set apart
From earthly use for heaven's employ
Adorned with prayer, and love, and joy;
So shall your Sovereign enter in,
And new and nobler life begin.

48

MONTGOMERY.

Nature and Revelation.

1 THY glory, Lord, the heavens declare;
The firmament displays thy skill;
The changing clouds, the viewless air,
Tempest and calm thy word fulfill;
Day unto day doth utter speech,
And night to night thy knowledge teach.

2 While these transporting visions shine,
Along the path of Providence,
Glory eternal, joy divine,
Thy word reveals, transcending sense;
My soul thy goodness longs to see,
Thy love to man, thy love to me.

49

ANONYMOUS.

The Lord is in his Holy Temple.

1 God is in his holy temple:
 Thoughts of earth, be silent now,
While with reverence we assemble,
 And before his presence bow!
He is with us now and ever,
 When we call upon his name,
Aiding every good endeavor,
 Guiding every upward aim.

2 God is in his holy temple;—
 In the pure and holy mind;
In the reverent heart and simple;
 In the soul from sense refined:
Then let every low emotion,
 Banished far and silent be!
And our souls, in pure devotion,
 Lord, be temples worthy thee!

50

FAWCETT.

God of our Salvation.

1 Praise to thee, thou great Creator;
 Praise be thine from every tongue;
Join, my soul, with every creature,
 Join the universal song.
Father, source of all compassion,
 Free, unbounded grace is thine:
Hail the God of our salvation;
 Praise him for his love divine.

2 For ten thousand blessings given,
 For the hope of future joy, [heaven
Sound his praise through earth and
 Sound Jehovah's praise on high.
Joyfully on earth adore him,
 Till in heaven our song we raise;
There, enraptured, fall before him,
 Lost in wonder, love, and praise.

51

S. LONGFELLOW.

Vespers.

1 Now, on sea and land descending,
 Brings the night its peace profound;
Let our vesper hymn be blending
 With the holy calm around.
Soon as dies the sunset glory,
 Stars of heaven shine out above,
Telling still the ancient story,—
 Their Creator's changeless love.

2 Now our wants and burdens leaving
 To his care, who cares for all,
Cease we fearing, cease we grieving;
 At his touch our burdens fall.
As the darkness deepens o'er us,
 Lo, eternal stars arise;
Hope and Faith and Love rise glorious,
 Shining in the spirit's skies.

52

ANONYMOUS

Sabbath Morning.

1 Welcome, welcome, quiet morning,
 Welcome is this holy day;
Now the Sabbath morn, returning,
 Shows a week has passed away.
Let us think how time is gliding;
 Soon the longest life departs;
Nothing human is abiding,
 Save the love of humble hearts.

BRADEN. S. M.

53

E. TAYLOR.

Call to the House of Prayer.

1 COME to the house of prayer,
O ye afflicted, come:
The God of peace shall meet you there,
He makes that house his home.

2 Come to the house of praise,
Ye who are happy now;
In sweet accord your voices raise,
In kindred homage bow.

3 Ye aged, hither come,
For ye have felt his love: [dumb,
Soon shall your trembling tongues be
Your lips forget to move.

4 Ye young, before his throne,
Come, bow; your voices raise;
Let not your hearts his praise disown
Who gives the power to praise.

5 Thou, whose benignant eye
In mercy looks on all—
Who see'st the tear of misery,
And hear'st the mourner's call—

6 Up to thy dwelling-place
Bear our frail spirits on,
Till they outstr'p time's tardy pace,
And heaven on earth be won.

54

SPIRIT OF THE PSALMS.

The Delights of Sabbath Worship.

1 SWEET is the task, O Lord,
Thy glorious acts to sing,
To praise thy name and hear thy word,
And grateful offerings bring.

2 Sweet, at the dawning hour,
Thy boundless love to tell; [flower,
And when the night-wind shuts the
Still on the theme to dwell.

3 Sweet on this day of rest
To join in heart and voice [best,
With those who love and serve thee
And in thy name rejoice.

4 To songs of praise and joy,
Be every Sabbath given,
That such may be our blest employ
Eternally in heaven.

55

ANONYMOUS.

Evening Hymn.

1 THE day is past and gone;
The evening shades appear;
O, may we all remember well,
The night of death draws near!

2 We lay our garments by,
Upon our beds to rest;
So death shall soon disrobe us all
Of what is here possessed.

3 Lord, keep us safe this night,
Secure from all our fears;
May angels guard us, while we sleep,
Till morning light appears.

MIGDOL. L. M.

56 WATTS.

Love of the Sanctuary.

1 How pleasant, how divinely fair,
O Lord of Hosts, thy dwellings are!
With long desire my spirit faints
To meet th' assemblies of thy saints.

2 Blest are the souls that find a place
Within the temple of thy grace;
Where they behold thy gentler rays,
And seek thy face and learn thy praise.

3 Blest are the men whose hearts are set
To find the way to Zion's gate; [road
God is their strength; and through the
They lean upon their helper, God.

4 Cheerful they walk with growing strength,
Till all shall meet in heaven at length;
Till all before thy face appear,
And join in nobler worship there.

57 ANON.

The Great Temple.

1 Though wandering in a stranger land,
Though on the waste no altar stand,
Take comfort! thou art not alone,
While Faith has marked thee for her own.

2 Wouldst thou a temple? look above,—
The heavens stretch over all in love;
A book? for thine evangel scan
The wondrous history of man.

3 And though no organ-peal be heard,
In harmony the winds are stirred;
And there the morning stars upraise
Their ancient songs of deathless praise.

58 STERLING.

Praise to the God of All.

1 O Source divine, and life of all,
The fount of being's wondrous sea!
Thy depth would every heart appall,
That saw not love supreme in thee.

2 We shrink before thy vast abyss,
Where worlds on worlds eternal brood;
We know thee truly but in this,—
That thou bestowest all our good.

3 And so, 'mid boundless time and space,
O, grant us still in thee to dwell,
And through the ceaseless web to trace
Thy presence working all things well.

4 Nor let thou life's delightful play
Thy truth's transcendent vision hide;
Nor strength and gladness lead astray
From thee, our nature's only guide.

5 Bestow on every joyous thrill
Thy deeper tone of reverent awe;
Make pure thy children's erring will,
And teach their hearts to love thy law.

59 CASWALL.

Vesper Hymn.

1 Lord of eternal purity,
Who dost the world with light adorn,
And paint the tracts of azure sky
With lively hues of eve and morn,—

2 Scatter our night, eternal God,
And kindle thy pure beam within;
Free us from guilt's oppressive load,
And break the deadly bonds of sin.

MISSIONARY CHANT. L. M.

ZEUNER.

60

SALISBURY COLL.

House of God.

1 Lo, God is here! Let us adore,
And humbly bow before his face!
Let all within us feel his power;
Let all within us seek his grace.

2 Lo, God is here! Him, day and night,
United choirs of angels sing;
To him, enthroned above all height,
Heaven's host their noblest homage bring.

3 Being of beings! may thy praise
Thy courts with grateful fragrance fill:
Still may we stand before thy face—
Still hear and do thy sovereign will.

61

O. W. HOLMES.

Sabbath Hymn to the Deity.

1 LORD of all being, 'throned afar,
Thy glory flames from sun and star;
Centre and soul of every sphere,
Yet to each loving heart how near!

2 Sun of our life, thy wakening ray
Sheds on our path the glow of day;
Star of our hope, thy softened light
Cheers the long watches of the night.

3 Our midnight is thy smile withdrawn;
Our noontide is thy gracious dawn;
Our rainbow arch, thy mercy's sign;
All, save the clouds of sin, are thine!

4 Lord of all life, below, above, [love,
Whose light is truth, whose warmth is
Before thy ever-blazing throne
We ask no lustre of our own.

5 Grant us thy truth to make us free,
And kindling hearts that burn for thee,
Till all thy living altars claim
One holy light, one heavenly flame.

62

SIR J. E. SMITH.

Devout Worship.

1 PRAISE waits in Zion, Lord, for thee;
Thy saints adore thy holy name;
Thy creatures bend th' obedient knee,
And, humbly, thy protection claim.

2 Thy hand has raised us from the dust;
The breath of life thy spirit gave;
Where, but in thee, can mortals trust?
Who, but our God, has power to save?

3 Still may thy children in thy word
Their common trust and refuge see;
O, bind us to each other, Lord,
By one great tie,—the love of thee.

4 So shall our sun of hope arise,
With brighter still and brighter ray,
Till thou shalt bless our longing eyes
With beams of everlasting day.

63

MORAVIAN.

Daily Bread.

1 THY name be hallowed evermore;
O God! thy kingdom come with pow'r,
Thy will be done, and day by day
Give us our daily bread, we pray.

2 Lord, evermore to us be given
The living bread that came from heav'n:
Water of life on us bestow;
Thou art the Source, the Giver thou.

MORNINGTON. S. M.

MORNINGTON.

64

STENNETT.

Presence of Jesus.

1 How charming is the place
Where the dear Son of God
Unvails the beauties of his face,
And sheds his love abroad!

2 Not the fair palaces
To which the great resort
Are once to be compared with this,
Where Jesus holds his court.

3 Here on the mercy-seat,
With radiant glory crowned,
Our joyful eyes behold him sit,
And smile on all around.

4 To him its prayers and cries
Each humble soul presents;
He listens to their broken sighs,
And grants them all their wants.

5 Give me, O Lord, a place
Within thy blessed abode,
Among the children of thy grace,
The servants of my God.

65

J. M. NEALE.

Evening.

1 The day, O Lord, is spent;
Abide with us, and rest;
Our hearts' desires are fully bent
On making thee our guest.

2 We have not reached that land,
That happy land, as yet,
Where holy angels round thee stand,
Whose sun can never set.

3 Our sun is sinking now;
Our day is almost o'er:
O Sun of Righteousness, do thou
Shine on us evermore!

66

ANONYMOUS.

Call to Prayer.

1 Come to the morning prayer,—
Come, let us kneel and pray:
Prayer is the Christian pilgrim's staff,
To walk with God all day.

2 At noon, beneath the Rock
Of Ages, rest and pray:
Sweet is that shelter from the heat,
When the sun smites by day.

3 At evening, shut thy door,
Round the home altar pray;
And, finding there the house of God,
At heaven's gate close the day.

4 When midnight veils our eyes,
Oh, it is sweet to say,
I sleep, but my heart waketh, Lord,
With thee to watch and pray!

67

Closing Hymn.

1 We love the house of prayer,
Wherein thy servants meet,
For thou, O Lord, art ever there,
Thy chosen flock to greet.

2 We love the word of life,—
The word that tells of peace,
Of comfort in our daily strife,
Of joys that never cease.

DUNDEE. C. M.

68

Whit-Sunday. KEBLE.

1 When God, of old, came down from heav'n,
In pow'r and wrath he came;
Before his feet the clouds were riv'n,
Half darkness and half flame.

2 But when he came the second time,
He came in pow'r and love;
Softer than gale at morning prime
Hover'd his holy Dove.

3 The fires that rushed on Sinai down,
In sudden torrents dread,
Now gently light, a glorious crown,
On every sainted head.

4 Like arrows went those lightnings forth,
Winged with the sinner's doom;
But these, like tongues, o'er all the earth
Proclaiming life to come.

GOSHEN. 11s.

69

The Lord's Prayer. MRS. HALE.

1 Our Father in heaven, we hallow thy name;
May thy kingdom holy on earth be the same!
Oh, give to us daily our portion of bread;
It is from thy bounty that all must be fed.

2 Forgive our transgressions, and teach us to know
That humble compassion which pardons each foe;
Keep us from temptation, from weakness and sin,
And thine be the glory forever. Amen.

DARWELL. H. M.

70 WATTS.

Blessedness of Public Worship.

1 Lord of the worlds above,
How pleasant and how fair
The dwellings of thy love,
Thine earthly temples, are!
To thine abode
My heart aspires, with warm desires
To see my God.

2 O, happy souls, that pray
Where God appoints to hear!
O, happy men, who pay
Their constant service there!
They praise thee still;
And happy they who love the way
To Zion's hill!

3 They go from strength to strength
Through this dark vale of tears,
Till each arrives at length—
Till each in heaven appears.
O, glorious seat, [bring
When God, our King, shall thither
Our willing feet!

4 The sparrow for her young
With pleasure seeks a nest;
And wandering swallows long
To find their wonted rest:
My spirit faints
With equal zeal, to rise and dwell
Among thy saints.

71 DODDRIDGE.

Gentiles brought into the Temple.

1 Great Father of mankind,
We bless that wondrous grace
Which could for Gentiles find
Within thy courts a place.
How kind the care
Our God displays, for us to raise
A house of prayer!

2 Though once estrangéd far,
We now approach the throne;
For Jesus brings us near,
And makes our cause his own.
Strangers no more,
To thee we come, and find our home,
And rest secure.

3 To thee ourselves we join,
And love thy sacred name;
No more our own, but thine,
We triumph in thy claim.
Our Father-King,
Thy covenant-grace our souls embrace,
Thy titles sing.

4 May all the nations throng,
To worship in thy house,
And thou attend the song,
And smile upon their vows!
Indulgent still,
Till earth conspire to join the choir
On Zion's hill.

72

MILTON.

The Blessedness of the Devout.

1 How lovely are thy dwellings, Lord,
From noise and trouble free;
How beautiful the sweet accord
Of souls that pray to thee!

2 Lord God of Hosts, that reign'st on
They are the truly blest [high,
Who only will on thee rely,
In thee alone will rest.

3 They pass, refreshed, the thirsty vale,
The dry and barren ground,
As through a fruitful, watery dale,
Where springs and showers abound.

4 They journey on from strength to strength,
With joy and gladsome cheer,
Till all before our God at length
In Zion do appear.

5 For God, the Lord, both sun and shield,
Gives grace and glory bright;
No good from him shall be withheld
Whose ways are just and right.

73

PATRICK.

Te Deum.

1 O God, we praise thee, and confess
That thou the only Lord
And everlasting Father art,
By all the earth adored.

2 To thee all angels cry aloud;
To thee the powers on high,
Both cherubim and seraphim,
Continually do cry,—

3 O holy, holy, holy Lord,
Whom heavenly hosts obey,
The world is with the glory filled
Of thy majestic sway.

4 The apostles' glorious company,
And prophets crowned with light,
With all the martyrs' noble host.
Thy constant praise recite.

5 The holy church throughout the
O Lord, confesses thee— [world,
That thou eternal Father art
Of boundless majesty.

74

Christ our High Priest.

1 Come, let us join our songs of praise
To our ascended Priest;
He entered heaven with all our names
Engraven on his breast.

2 Oh! may we ne'er forget his grace,
Nor blush to bear his name;
Still may our hearts hold fast his faith;
Our lips his praise proclaim.

75

LOGAN.

Guidance and Protection.

1 God of our fathers, by whose hand
Thy people still are blest,
Be with us through our pilgrimage;
Conduct us to our rest.

2 Through each perplexing path of life
Our wandering footsteps guide;
Give us each our daily bread,
And raiment fit provide.

DALLAS. 7s M. Arr. by Dr. Mason.

76 Bowring.

Pious Worship.

1 In thy courts let peace be found,
Be thy temple full of love;
There we tread on holy ground,
All serene, around, above.

2 While the knee in prayer is bent,
While with praise the heart o'erflows,
Tranquilize the turbulent!
Give the weary one repose!

3 Be the place for worship meet,
Meet the worship for the place;
Contemplation's best retreat,
Shrine of guilelessness and grace!

4 As an infant knows its home,
Lord, may we thy temples know;
Thither for instruction come—
Thence by thee instructed go.

77 Anna L. Waring.

Evening Song.

1 Lord! a happy child of thine,
Patient through the love of thee,
In the light, the life divine,
Lives and walks at liberty.

2 Leaning on thy tender care,
Thou hast led my soul aright;
Fervent was my morning prayer,
Joyful is my song to-night.

3 O my Father, Guardian true!
All my life is thine to keep;
At thy feet my work I do,
In thine arms I fall asleep.

78 Furness.

Eternal Light.

1 Slowly, by God's hand unfurled,
Down around the weary world,
Falls the darkness; oh, how still
Is the working of his will!

2 Mighty Spirit, ever nigh,
Work in me as silently;
Veil the day's distracting sights,
Show me heaven's eternal lights.

3 Living stars to view be brought
In the boundless realms of thought;
High and infinite desires,
Flaming like those upper fires.

4 Holy Truth, Eternal Right,
Let them break upon my sight;
Let them shine serene and still,
And with light my being fill.

79 Anon.

Sabbath Evening.

1 Ere another Sabbath's close,
Ere again we seek repose,
Lord, our song ascends to thee;
At thy feet we bow the knee.

2 For the mercies of the day,
For this rest upon our way,
Thanks to thee alone be given,
Lord of earth, and King of heaven.

3 Whilst this thorny path we tread,
May thy love our footsteps lead!
When our journey here is past,
May we rest with thee at last!

LUTON. L. M.

BURDER.

80

FROTHINGHAM.

Truth and Love.

1 O God, whose presence glows in all,
Within, around us, and above!
Thy word we bless, thy name we call,
Whose word is Truth, whose name is Love.

2 That truth be with the heart believed
Of all who seek this sacred place;
With power proclaimed, in peace received,—
Our spirits' light, thy Spirit's grace.

3 That love its holy influence pour,
To keep us meek, and make us free,
And throw its binding blessing more
Round each with all, and all with thee.

4 Send down its angel to our side—
Send in its calm upon the breast;
For we would know no other guide,
And we can need no other rest.

81

COWPER.

Spiritual Worship.

1 O Lord! where'er thy people meet,
There they behold thy mercy-seat;
Where'er they seek thee, thou art found,
And every place is hallowed ground.

2 For thou, within no walls confined,
Inhabitest the humble mind;
Such ever bring thee where they come,
And, going, take thee to their home.

3 Here may we prove the power of prayer
To strengthen faith and sweeten care;
To teach our faint desires to rise,
And bring all heaven before our eyes.

82

PIERPONT.

Universal Worship.

1 O thou, to whom, in ancient time,
The lyre of Hebrew bards was strung,
Whom kings adored in song sublime,
And prophets praised with glowing tongue;

2 Not now on Zion's height alone
Thy favored worshipper may dwell;
Nor where, at sultry noon, thy Son
Sat weary, by the patriarch's well.

3 From every place below the skies,
The grateful song, the fervent pray'r—
The incense of the heart—may rise
To heaven, and find acceptance there.

4 To thee shall age, with snowy hair,
And strength and beauty bend the knee,
And childhood lisp, with reverent air,
Its praises and its prayers to thee.

5 O Thou, to whom, in ancient time,
The lyre of prophet-bards was strung,
To thee, at last, in every clime
Shall temples rise, and praise be sung.

83

DODDRIDGE.

Subjection to our Father.

1 Eternal Source of life and thought,
Be all beneath thyself forgot:
Whilst thee, great Parent-mind, we own,
In prostrate homage round thy throne.

2 Whilst in themselves our souls survey
Of thee some faint reflected ray,
They, wondering, to their Father rise:
His power how vast! his tho'ts how wise!

BRATTLE STREET. C. M. Double.

84 H. M. WILLIAMS.

Habitual Devotion.

1 While thee I seek, protecting Power,
Be my vain wishes stilled;
And may this consecrated hour
With better hopes be filled.
Thy love the power of tho't bestowed;
To thee my thoughts would soar;
Thy mercy o'er my life has flowed;
That mercy I adore.

2 In each event of life, how clear
Thy ruling hand I see!
Each blessing to my soul more dear,
Because conferred by thee.
In every joy that crowns my days
In every pain I bear,
My heart shall find delight in praise,
Or seek relief in prayer.

3 When gladness wings my favored hour,
Thy love my thoughts shall fill;
Resigned, when storms of sorrow lower,
My soul shall meet thy will.
My lifted eye, without a tear,
The gathering storm shall see:
My steadfast heart shall know no fear;
That heart shall rest on thee.

85 ADDISON.

Providence.

1 When all thy mercies, O my God!
My rising soul surveys,
Transported with the view, I'm lost,
In wonder, love, and praise.
Ten thousand thousand precious gifts
My daily thanks employ;
Nor is the least a cheerful heart,
That tastes those gifts with joy.

2 Through every period of my life,
Thy goodness I'll pursue;
And after death, in distant worlds,
The glorious theme renew.
Through all eternity, to thee
A joyful song I'll raise;
But oh! eternity's too short
To utter all thy praise!

86 ANONYMOUS.

Beneficence.

1 When morning's first and hallowed ray
Breaks, with its trembling light,
To chase the pearly dews away,
Bright tear-drops of the night—
My heart, O Lord! forgets to rove,
But rises gladly free,
On wings of everlasting love,
And finds its home in thee.

CONVENT BELL. 7s Double.

87

BOWRING.

Lowly Praise.

1 LORD, in heaven, thy dwelling-place,
Hear the praises of our race,
And, while hearing, let thy grace
Dews of sweet forgiveness pour;
While we know, benignant King,
That the praises which we bring
Are a worthless offering
Till thy blessing makes it more.

2 More of truth, and more of might,
More of love, and more of light,
More of reason and of right,
From thy pardoning grace be given!
It can make the humblest song
Sweet, acceptable, and strong,
As the strains the angel throng
Pour around the throne of heaven.

88

BOWRING.

Humble Worship.

1 WHEN before thy throne we kneel,
Filled with awe and holy fear,
Teach us, O our God, to feel
All thy sacred presence near.
Check each proud and wandering tho't
When on thy great name we call;
Man is naught—is less than naught—
Thou, our God, art all in all.

2 Weak, imperfect creatures, we
In this vale of darkness dwell,
Yet presume to look to thee
'Midst thy light ineffable.
O, receive the praise that dares
Seek thy heaven-exalted throne;
Bless our offerings, hear our prayers,
Infinite and Holy One!

89

BOWRING.

Morning or Evening—All from God.

1 FATHER! thy paternal care
Has my guardian been, my guide!
Every hallowed wish and prayer
Has thy hand of love supplied;
Thine is every thought of bliss,
Left by hours and days gone by;
Every hope thy offspring is,
Beaming from futurity.

2 Every sun of splendid ray;
Every moon that shines serene;
Every morn that welcomes day;
Every evening's twilight scene;
Every hour which wisdom brings;
Every incense at thy shrine;
These—and all life's holiest things,
And its fairest—all are thine.

3 And for all, my hymns shall rise
Daily to thy gracious throne;
Thither let my asking eyes
Turn unwearied, righteous One!
Through life's strange vicissitude
There reposing all my care,
Trusting still through ill and good,
Fixed and cheered and counselled there.

DEVOTION. 7s.

90

J. TAYLOR.

Preparation for Worship.

1 Lord, before thy presence come,
Bow we down with holy fear;
Call our erring footsteps home,
Let us feel that thou art near.

2 Wandering tho'ts and languid powers
Come not where devotion kneels;
Let the soul expand her stores,
Glowing with the joy she feels.

3 At the portals of thine house,
We resign our earth-born cares;
Nobler thoughts our souls engross,
Songs of praise and fervent prayers.

91

J. TAYLOR.

Acceptable Offerings.

1 Lord! what offering shall we bring,
At thine altars when we bow?
Hearts, the pure, unsullied spring
Whence the kind affections flow:

2 Soft compassion's feeling soul,
By the melting eye expressed;
Sympathy, at whose control
Sorrow leaves the wounded breast;

3 Willing hands, to lead the blind;
Heal the wounded, feed the poor,
Love, embracing all our kind,
Charity, with liberal store.

4 Teach us, O thou heavenly King,
Thus to show our grateful mind,
Thus the accepted offering bring,
Love to thee and all mankind.

92

SALISBURY COLL.

Adoration and Praise.

1 Holy, holy, holy Lord!
Be thy glorious name adored.
Lord, thy mercies never fail:
Hail, celestial Goodness, hail!

2 Though unworthy, Lord, thine ear,
Deign our humble songs to hear;
Purer praise we hope to bring
When around thy throne we sing.

3 While on earth ordained to stay,
Guide our footsteps in thy way;
Then on high we'll joyful raise
Songs of everlasting praise.

4 There no tongue shall silent be;
All shall join in harmony,
That through heaven's capacious round
Praise to thee may ever sound.

5 Lord, thy mercies never fail;
Hail, celestial Goodness, hail!
Holy, holy, holy Lord,
Be thy glorious name adored.

93

KELLY.

A Blessing desired.

1 Father, bless thy word to all;
Quick and powerful let it prove:
Oh, may sinners hear thy call!
Let thy people grow in love.

2 Thine own gracious message bless,—
Follow it with power divine;
Give the gospel great success;
Thine the work, the glory thine.

LENOX. H. M.

94

H. Ballou 2d.

Universal Praise.

1 Ye realms below the skies,
Your Maker's praises sing;
Let boundless honors rise
To heaven's eternal King.
O, bless his name whose love extends
Salvation to the world's far ends.

2 'T is he the mountains crowns
With forests waving wide;
'T is he old ocean bounds,
And heaves her roaring tide;
He swells the tempests on the main,
Or breathes the zephyr o'er the plain.

3 Still let the waters roar
As round the earth they roll:
His praise for evermore
They sound from pole to pole.
'T is nature's wild, unconscious song
O'er thousand waves that floats along.

4 His praise, ye worlds on high,
Display with all your spheres,
Amid the darksome sky,
When silent night appears.
O, let his works declare his name
Through all the universal frame!

95

Watts.

Praise from all Creatures.

1 Ye tribes of Adam, join
With heaven, and earth, and seas,
And offer notes divine
To your Creator's praise:
Ye holy throng of angels bright!
In worlds of light, begin the song.

2 Thou sun with dazzling rays!
And moon that rules the night!
Shine to your Maker's praise,
With stars of twinkling light.
His power declare, ye floods on high!
And clouds that fly in empty air!

3 The shining worlds above
In glorious order stand,
Or in swift courses move,
By his supreme command:
He spake the word, and all their frame
From nothing came, to praise the Lord.

4 Let all the nations fear
The God that rules above;
He brings his people near,
And makes them taste his love:
While earth and sky attempt his praise,
His saints shall raise his honors high.

96

C. Wesley

All Power given to Christ.

1 Rejoice! the Lord is King—
Your God and King adore;
Mortals, give thanks and sing,
And triumph evermore:
Lift up the heart, lift up the voice:
Rejoice aloud, ye saints, rejoice.

2 His kingdom cannot fail,
He rules o'er earth and heaven,
The keys of death and hell
Are to our Jesus given;
Lift up the heart, lift up the voice:
Rejoice aloud, ye saints, rejoice.

COMFORT. 11s & 10s.

97

WHITTIER.

True Worship.

1 OH, he whom Jesus loved has truly spoken!
The holier worship which God deigns to bless
Restores the lost and heals the spirit-broken,
And feeds the widow and the fatherless.

2 Then, brother man, fold to thy heart thy brother!
For where love dwells the peace of God is there;
To worship rightly is to love each other;
Each smile a hymn, each kindly deed a prayer.

3 Follow with reverent steps the great example
Of Him whose holy work was doing good;
So shall the wide earth seem our Father's temple,
Each loving life a psalm of gratitude.

4 Thus shall all shackles fall; the stormy clangor
Of wild war music o'er the earth shall cease;
Love shall tread out the baleful fires of anger,
And in its ashes plant the tree of peace.

98

ANON.

Prayer for Strength.

1 LORD, we have wandered forth through doubt and sorrow,
And thou hast made each step an onward one;
And we will ever trust each unknown morrow, —
Thou wilt sustain us till its work is [done.

2 O Father, now in thy dear presence kneeling, [love;
Our spirits yearn to feel thy kindling
Now make us strong through thine own deep revealing
Of trust and strength and calmness from above.

99

ANON.

The Sorrowing Invited.

1 COME unto me, when shadows darkly gather,
When the sad heart is weary and distressed;
Seeking for comfort from your heavenly Father,
Come unto me, and I will give you rest.

2 Large are the mansions in our Father's dwelling,
Glad are those homes that sorrows never dim;
Sweet are the harps in holy music swelling,
Soft are the tones that raise the heavenly hymn.

OLD HUNDRED. L. M.

100

TATE & BRADY.

Praise to the Great Jehovah.

1 Be thou, O God, exalted high;
And as thy glory fills the sky,
So let it be on earth displayed,
Till thou art here, as there, obeyed.

2 O God, our hearts are fixed and bent
Their thankful tribute to present;
And, with the heart, the voice we'll raise
To thee, our God, in songs of praise.

3 Thy praises, Lord, we will resound
To all the listening nations round;
Thy mercy highest heaven transcends;
Thy truth beyond the clouds extends.

4 Be thou, O God, exalted high;
And as thy glory fills the sky,
So let it be on earth displayed,
Till thou art here, as there, obeyed.

101

H. BALLOU, 2D.

Praise ye the Lord.

1 Praise ye the Lord, around whose throne
All heaven in ceaseless worship waits,
Whose glory fills the worlds unknown—
Praise ye the Lord from Zion's gates.

2 With mingling souls and voices join;
To him the swelling anthem raise;
Repeat his name with joy divine,
And fill the temple with his praise.

3 All-gracious God, to thee we owe
Each joy and blessing time affords,—
Might, life, and health, and all below,
Spring from thy presence, Lord of lords.

4 Thine be the praise, for thine the love
That freely all our sins forgave,
Pointed our dying eyes above,
And showed us life beyond the grave.

102

ANON.

Our Guide and Stay.

1 For mercies past we praise thee, Lord,—
The fruits of earth, the hopes of heaven,
Thy helping arm, thy guiding word,
And answered prayers, and sins forgiven.

2 Whene'er we tread on danger's height,
Or walk temptation's slippery way,
Be still, to lead our steps aright,
Thy word our guide, thine arm our stay.

3 Be ours thy blessèd presence still;
United hearts, unchanging love:
No thought that contradicts thy will;
No wish that centres not above.

103

Mercy of God.

1 Oh, render thanks to God above,
The fountain of eternal love,
Whose mercy firm, through ages past
Hath stood, and shall forever last.

2 Who can his mighty deeds express,
Not only vast, but numberless?
What mortal eloquence can raise
His tribute of immortal praise?

3 Extend to me that favor, Lord,
Thou to thy chosen dost afford;
When thou return'st to set them free,
Let thy salvation visit me.

WILMOT. 8s & 7s M.

104

LIVERPOOL COLL.

Universal Praise.

1 PRAISE the Lord! ye heav'ns adore him;
Praise him, angels in the height;
Sun and moon, rejoice before him;
Praise him, all ye stars of light!

2 Praise the Lord — for he hath spoken;
Worlds his mighty voice obeyed;
Laws which never shall be broken,
For their guidance, he hath made.

3 Praise the Lord — for he is glorious;
Never shall his promise fail;
God hath made his saints victorious,
Sin and death shall not prevail.

4 Praise the God of our salvation,
Hosts on high his power proclaim;
Heaven and earth, and all creation,
Laud and magnify his name.

105

GREGORY NAZIANZEN.

Ancient Hymn.

1 CHRIST, my Lord, I come to bless thee,
Now, when day is veiled in night;
Thou who knowest no beginning,
Light of the Eternal Light!

2 Thou enlightenest man's high reason,
Far above the creatures dumb,
That, light in thy light beholding,
Wholly light he may become.

3 In the night, our wearied nature
Rests from all its toil and tears;
To the works, Lord, that thou lovest,
Thou wilt call when day appears.

106

HOGG.

Praise to the God of Nature.

1 BLESSÉD be thy name for ever,
Thou of life the Guard and Giver:
Thou who slumberest not nor sleepest,
Blest are they thou kindly keepest.

2 God of stillness and of motion,
Of the rainbow and the ocean,
Of the mountain, rock, and river,
Blessed be thy name for ever.

3 God of evening's peaceful ray,
God of every dawning day,
Rising from the distant sea,
Breathing of eternity.

4 Thine the flaming sphere of light,
Thine the darkness of the night:
God of life that fade shall never,
Glory to thy name for ever.

107

LYTE.

Praise for all Blessings.

1 PRAISE the Lord, his glories show,
Saints within his courts below,
Angels round his throne above,
All that see and share his love!

2 Earth to heaven, and heaven to earth,
Tell his wonders, sing his worth;
Age to age, and shore to shore,
Praise him, praise him, evermore!

3 Praise the Lord, his mercies trace;
Praise his providence and grace—
All that he for man hath done,
All he sends us through his Son.

MENDON. L. M.

108

TATE & BRADY.

All Nations exhorted to Adoration and Praise.

1 WITH one consent, let all the earth
To God their cheerful voices raise;
Glad homage pay, with hallowed mirth,
And sing before him songs of praise;

2 Assured that he is God alone, [ceed,—
From whom both we and all pro-
We, whom he chooses for his own,
The flock which he delights to feed.

3 O, enter, then, his temple gate;
Thence to his courts devoutly press;
And still your grateful hymns repeat,
And still his name with praises bless;

4 For he 's the Lord, supremely good;
His mercy is forever sure;
His truth, which always firmly stood,
To endless ages shall endure.

109

ST. AMBROSE.

Worship.

1 BOTH heaven and earth do worship
Thou Father of eternity; [thee
With splendor from thy glory spread
Are heaven and earth replenished.

2 To thee all angels loudly cry,
The heavens and all the powers on high,
The apostles' glorious company,
The prophets' fellowship praise thee.

3 The noble and victorious host
Of martyrs make of thee their boast;
The holy church, in every place
Throughout the earth exalts thy praise.

4 From day to day, O Lord, do we
Highly exalt and honor thee:
Thy name we worship and adore,
World without end, for evermore.

110

WATTS.

The Brightness of God's Glory.

1 Now to the Lord a noble song!
Awake, my soul! awake, my tongue!
Hosanna to th' eternal name,
And all his boundless love proclaim.

2 The spacious earth and spreading flood
Proclaim the wise, the powerful God,
And thy rich glories from afar
Sparkle in every rolling star;

3 But in the gospel of thy Son
Are all thy mightiest works outdone;
The light it pours upon our eyes
Outshines the wonders of the skies.

4 Our spirits kindle in its beam;
It is a sweet, a glorious theme:
Ye angels, dwell upon the sound;
Ye heavens, reflect it to the ground.

111

ANON.

All thy Saints bless Thee.

1 LORD God of Hosts, by all adored!
Thy name we praise with one accord;
The earth and heavens are full of thee,
Thy light, thy love, thy majesty.

2 The holy church in every place
Thro'out the world exalts thy praise;
Both heaven and earth do worship thee,
Thou Father of eternity!

LYONS. 10s & 11s.

112

DODDRIDGE.

Praise and Exultation.

1 OH, praise ye the Lord; prepare a new
song, [join;
And let all his saints in full chorus
With voices united the anthem prolong.
And show forth his praises with
music divine.

2 Let praise to the Lord, who made us,
ascend; [its King;
Let each grateful heart be glad in
The God whom we worship our songs
will attend, [ing we bring.
And view with complacence the offer-

3 Be joyful, ye saints, sustained by his
might, [each morn;
And let your glad song awake with
For those who obey him are still his
delight; [will adorn.
His hand with salvation the meek

4 Then praise ye the Lord; prepare a
glad song, [join;
And let all his saints in full chorus
With voices united the anthem prolong.
And show forth his praises with
music divine.

113

GRANT.

God Glorious.

1 OH, worship the King all glorious above,
And gratefully sing his wonderful love,
Our Shield and Defender, the Ancient
of Days, [praise.
Pavilioned in splendor, and girded with

2 Thy bountiful care what tongue can
recite? [light,
It breathes in the air, it shines in the
It streams from the hills, it descends
to the plain, [rain.
And sweetly distils in the dew and the

3 Frail children of dust, and feeble as
frail, [fail;
In thee do we trust, nor find thee to
Thy mercies how tender! how firm to
the end! [Friend.
Our Maker, Defender, Redeemer, and

114

TATE.

Thanksgiving.

1 OH, praise ye the Lord! prepare your
glad voice,
His praise in the great assembly to sing;
In their great Creator let all men re-
joice, [King.
And heirs of salvation be glad in their

2 Let them his great name devoutly
adore; [express,
In loud swelling strains his praises
Who graciously opens his bountiful
store, [to bless.
Their wants to relieve, and his children

3 With glory adorned, his people shall
sing [plies;
To God, who defence and plenty sup-
Their loud acclamations to him, their
great King,
Through earth shall be sounded, and
reach to the skies.

ST. MARTIN'S. C. M.

115

ANON.

For Sincerity in Worship.

1 LORD! when we bend before thy throne,
And our confessions pour,
O may we feel the sins we own,
And hate what we deplore.

2 Our contrite spirits pitying see;
True penitence impart;
And let a healing ray from thee
Beam hope on every heart.

3 When we disclose our wants in prayer,
O let our wills resign;
And not a thought our bosom share,
Which is not wholly thine.

4 Then, on thy glories while we dwell,
Thy mercies we 'll review;
With love divine transported, tell,—
"Thou, God, art Father too!"

116

JERVIS.

Homage and Devotion.

1 WITH sacred joy we lift our eyes
To those bright realms above,—
That glorious temple in the skies
Where dwells eternal love.

2 Thee we adore, and, Lord, to thee
Our filial duty pay;
Thy service, unconstrained and free,
Conducts to endless day.

3 While in thy house of prayer we kneel
With trust and holy fear,
Thy mercy and thy truth reveal,
And lend a gracious ear.

4 With fervor teach our hearts to pray,
And tune our lips to sing;
Nor from thy presence cast away
The sacrifice we bring.

117

G. BURDER.

God is Love.

1 COME, ye that know and fear the Lord!
And raise your souls above;
Let every heart and voice accord
To sing that—God is love.

2 Behold his loving-kindness waits
For those who from him rove,
And calls of mercy reach their hearts,
To teach them—God is love.

3 Oh! may we all, while here below,
This best of blessings prove;
Till warmer hearts, in brighter worlds
Shall shout that—God is love.

118

BOWRING

Pure Worship.

1 THE off'rings to thy throne which rise,
Of mingled praise and prayer,
Are but a worthless sacrifice,
Unless the heart is there.

2 Upon thine all-discerning ear
Let no vain words intrude;
No tribute but the vow sincere,—
The tribute of the good.

3 My offerings will indeed be blest,
If sanctified by thee;
If thy pure Spirit touch my breast
With its own purity.

AMES. L. M. Dr. L. Mason.

119

BOWRING.

Perpetual Praise.

1 When, wakened by thy voice of power,
The hour of morning beams in light,
My voice shall sing that morning hour,
And thee, who mad'st that hour so bright.

2 The morning strengthens into noon;
Earth's fairest beauties shine more fair,
And noon and morning shall attune
My grateful heart to praise and prayer.

3 When 'neath the evening's western gate
The sun's retiring rays are hid,
My joy shall be to meditate,
E'en as the pious patriarch did.

4 As twilight wears a darker hue,
And gathering night creation dims,
The twilight and the midnight, too,
Shall have their harmonies and hymns.

5 So shall sweet thoughts, and thoughts sublime,
My constant inspirations be;
And every shifting scene of time
Reflect, my God, a light from thee.

120

WATTS.

The Promises sure.

1 Praise, everlasting praise, be paid
To him who earth's foundations laid;
Praise to the God whose strong decrees
Sway all the world as he doth please.

2 Praise to the goodness of the Lord,
Who rules his people by his word;
And there, as strong as his decrees,
Reveals his kindest promises.

3 O for a strong, a lasting faith,
To credit what th' Almighty saith!
To hear the message of his Son,
And call the joys of heaven our own!

4 Then, should the earth's firm pillars shake,
And all the wheels of nature break,
Our steady souls would fear no more
Than solid rocks when billows roar.

121

KEBLE.

"Abide with us, for it is towards Evening, and the Day is far spent."

1 'Tis gone, that bright and orbéd blaze,
Fast fading from our wistful gaze;
Yon mantling cloud has hid from sight
The last faint pulse of quivering light.

2 Sun of my soul! thou Saviour dear,
It is not night if thou be near:
O may no earth-born cloud arise
To hide thee from thy servant's eyes.

3 Abide with me from morn till eve,
For without thee I cannot live;
Abide with me when night is nigh,
For without thee I dare not die.

122

L. BACON.

Light for those who sit in Darkness.

1 Though now the nations sit beneath
The darkness of o'erspreading death;
God will arise with light divine,
On Zion's holy towers to shine.

2 O light of Zion, now arise!
Let the glad morning bless our eyes;
Ye nations, catch the kindling ray,
And hail the splendors of the day.

MARLOW. C. M.

Arr. by Dr. Mason.

123

M. Rayner.

General Praise.

1 Hail! Source of light, of life, and love,
And joys that never end;
In whom all creatures live and move;
Creator, Father, Friend.

2 All space is with thy presence crowned;
Creation owns thy care;
Each spot in nature's ample round,
Proclaims that God is there.

3 Attuned to praise be every voice;
Let not one heart be sad;
Jehovah reigns! Let earth rejoice;
Let all the isles be glad.

4 Then sound the anthem loud and long,
In sweetest, loftiest strains;
And be the burden of the song,
The Lord, Jehovah, reigns!

124

Anon.

Evening Prayer.

1 Thou Lord of life! whose tender care
Hath led us on till now,
We, in this quiet hour of prayer,
Before thy presence bow.

2 Thou, blessed God! hast been our Guide,
Through life our Guard and Friend;
Oh, still on life's uncertain tide,
Preserve us to the end.

3 To thee our grateful praise we bring
For mercies day by day:
Lord, teach our hearts thy love to sing,
Lord, teach us how to pray!

125

Litchfield's Coll.

Evening Hymn.

1 God of the sunlight hours, how sad
Would evening shadows be!
Or night, in deeper shadows clad,
If aught were dark to thee!

2 How mournfully that golden gleam
Would touch the thoughtful heart,
If, with its soft, retiring beam,
We saw thy light depart!

3 Enough, while these dull heavens may lower,
If here thy presence be;
Then midnight shall be morning hour,
And darkness light to me.

126

Spirit of the Psalms

God the only Object of Worship.

1 O God, our strength! to thee the song,
With grateful hearts we raise;
To thee, and thee alone, belong
All worship, love, and praise.

2 In trouble's dark and stormy hour
Thine ear hath heard our prayer;
And graciously thine arm of power
Hath saved us from despair.

3 Led by the light thy grace imparts,
Ne'er may we bow the knee
To idols which our wayward hearts
Set up instead of thee!

4 So shall thy choicest gifts, O Lord!
Thy faithful people bless;
For them shall earth its store afford,
And heaven its happiness.

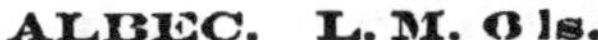

127

C. WESLEY.

Worship in Spirit and in Truth.

1 FATHER of omnipresent grace!
We seem agreed to seek thy face:
But every soul assembled here
Doth naked in thy sight appear;
Thou know'st who only bows the knee,
And who in heart approaches thee.

2 To-day, while it is called to-day,
Awake and stir us up to pray;
The spirit of thy word impart,
And breathe the life into our heart;
Our weakness help, our darkness chase,
And guide us by the light of grace.

128

ANON.

At Evening Time let there be Light.

1 AT evening time, let there be light;
Life's little day draws near its close;
Around me fall the shades of night,
The night of death, the grave's repose:
To crown my joys, to end my woes,
At evening time let there be light.

2 At evening time, there shall be light,
For God hath spoken, — it must be;
Fear, doubt, and anguish take their flight,
His glory now is risen on me;
Mine eyes shall his salvation see;
'T is evening time — and there is light.

129

SIR R. GRANT.

The Morning and Evening Light.

1 WHEN, streaming from the eastern skies,
The morning light salutes mine eyes,
O Sun of righteousness divine,
On me with beams of mercy shine!
Oh! chase the clouds of guilt away,
And turn my darkness into day.

2 When each day's scenes and labors close,
And wearied nature seeks repose,
With pardoning mercy richly blest,
Guard me, my Saviour, while I rest;
And, as each morning sun shall rise,
Oh, lead me onward to the skies!

3 And at my life's last setting sun,
My conflicts o'er, my labors done,
Jesus, thy heavenly radiance shed,
To cheer and bless my dying bed;
And, from death's gloom my spirit raise,
To see thy face, and sing thy praise.

130

C. WESLEY.

Spiritual Needs.

1 I WANT the spirit of power within,
Of love and of a healthful mind,
Of power to conquer every sin,
Of love to God and all mankind;
Of health that pain and death defies,
Most vigorous when the body dies.

2 Oh that the Comforter would come,
Nor visit as a transient guest,
But fix in me his constant home,
And keep possession of my breast,
And make my soul his loved abode,
The temple of indwelling God!

HOLLY. 7s M. Geo. Hews.

131 S. F. Smith.

Sabbath Evening.

1 Softly fades the twilight ray
Of the holy Sabbath day;
Gently as life's setting sun,
When the Christian's course is run.

2 Night her solemn mantle spreads
O'er the earth, as daylight fades;
All things tell of calm repose
At the holy Sabbath's close.

3 Peace is on the world abroad;
'T is the holy peace of God,—
Symbol of the peace within,
When the spirit rests from sin.

4 Still the Spirit lingers near,
Where the evening worshipper
Seeks communion with the skies,
Pressing onward to the prize.

132

God our Shepherd.

1 Lo, my Shepherd's hand divine!
Want shall never more be mine:
In a pasture fair and large
He shall feed his happy charge.

2 When I faint with summer's heat
He shall lead my weary feet
To the streams that, still and slow,
Through the verdant meadows flow.

3 He my soul anew shall frame;
And, his mercy to proclaim,
When through devious paths I stray,
Teach my steps the better way.

4 Constant to my latest end,
Thou my footsteps shalt attend;
And shalt bid thy hallowed dome
Yield me an eternal home.

133 Doane.

Evening Hymn.

1 Softly now the light of day
Fades upon my sight away;
Free from care, from labor free,
Lord, I will commune with thee.

2 Thou, whose all-pervading eye
Naught escapes, without, within,
Pardon each infirmity,
Open fault and secret sin.

3 Soon, for me, the light of day
Shall forever pass away;
Then from sin and sorrow free,
Take me, Lord, to dwell with thee.

134 Anon.

Evening Prayer.

1 Thou from whom we never part,
Thou whose love is everywhere,
Thou who seest every heart,
Listen to our evening prayer.

2 Father, fill our hearts with love,
Love unfailing, full, and free;
Love that no alarm can move;
Love that ever rests on thee.

3 Heavenly Father! through the night
Keep us safe from every ill;
Cheerful as the morning light,
May we wake, to do thy will.

HEBRON. L. M.

Dr. L. Mason.

135 — Anon.

Sabbath Evening.

1 There is a time when moments flow
 More happily than all beside;
It is, of all the times below,
 A Sabbath at the eventide.

2 O then the setting sun shines fair,
 And all below, and all above,
The various forms of Nature, wear
 One universal garb of love.

3 And then the peace that Jesus brought,
 The life of grace eternal beams,
And we, by his example taught,
 Improve the life his love redeems.

4 Delightful scene! a world at rest;
 A God all love; no grief, no fear;
A heavenly hope, a peaceful breast,
 A smile, unsullied by a tear.

136 — Collyer.

Evening Recollections.

1 Another fleeting day is gone;
 Slow o'er the west the shadows rise;
Swift the soft-stealing hours have flown,
And night's dark mantle veils the skies.

2 Another fleeting day is gone
 Swift from the records of the year;
And still, with each successive sun,
 Life's fading visions disappear.

3 Another fleeting day is gone;
 But soon a fairer day shall rise,
A day whose never-setting sun
Shall pour its light o'er cloudless skies.

137 — Watts.

Evening Hymn.

1 Thus far the Lord has led me on,
 Thus far his power prolongs my days'
And every evening shall make known
 Some fresh memorial of his grace.

2 Much of my time has run to waste,
 And I, perhaps, am near my home;
But he forgives my follies past,
He gives me strength for days to come.

3 I lay my body down to sleep;
 Peace is the pillow for my head;
While well-appointed angels keep
Their watchful stations round my bed.

4 Faith in his name forbids my fear:
 O, may thy presence ne'er depart!
And in the morning make me hear
 Thy love and kindness in my heart.

5 And when the night of death shall come,
 Still may I trust Almighty Love,—
The love which triumphs o'er the tomb,
 And leads to perfect bliss above.

138 — E. T. Fitch.

Parting in Peace and Love.

1 Lord, at this closing hour,
 Establish every heart
Upon thy word of truth and power,
 To keep us when we part.

2 Peace to our brethren give;
 Fill all our hearts with love;
In faith and patience may we live,
 And seek our rest above.

LINWOOD. L. M.

MODERN HARP.

139

BREVIARY.

Morning and Evening.

1 GREAT Framer of the earth and sky,
Who dost the light and darkness give,
And all the cheerful change supply
Of alternating morn and eve!

2 Awake us from false sleep profound,
And thro' our senses pour thy light;
Be thy blest name the first we sound
At early dawn, the last at night.

140

LYRA CATH.

Vespers.

1 O thou true Life of all that live!
Who dost, unmoved, all motion sway;
Who dost the morn and evening give,
And thro' its changes guide the day;

2 Thy light upon our evening pour,—
So may our souls no sunset see;
But death to us an open door
To an eternal morning be.

141

EDMESTON.

Sabbath Evening.

1 SWEET is the light of Sabbath eve,
And soft the sunbeams lingering there;
For these blest hours, the world I leave,
Wafted on wings of faith and prayer.

2 Season of rest! the tranquil soul
Feels the sweet calm, and melts to love—
And while these sacred moments roll,
Faith sees the smiling heavens above.

3 Nor will our days of toil be long,
Our pilgrimage will soon be trod:
And we shall join the ceaseless song,—
The endless Sabbath of our God.

142

ANON

The Still Hour.

1 GENTLY the shades of night descend;
Thy temple, Lord, is calm and still;
A thousand lamps of ether blend,
A thousand fires that temple fill.

2 Thou bidd'st the cares of earth depart,
Heaven's peace is wafted from above;
A Sabbath stillness fills the heart,
Devotion's calm and holy love.

143

BREVIARY.

Evening Prayer.

1 O BLEST Creator of the light,
Who dost the dawn from darkness bring,
And, framing nature's depth and height,
Didst with the new-born light begin;

2 Who gently blending eve with morn,
And morn with eve, did'st call them day,—
Thick flows the flood of darkness down:
Oh, hear us as we weep and pray;

3 Teach us to knock at heaven's high door,
Teach us the prize of life to win;
Teach us all evil to abhor,
And purify ourselves within.

144

EDMESTON.

The Close of the Sabbath.

1 THE time how lovely and how still!
Peace shines and smiles on all below;
The plain, the stream, the wood, the hill,
All fair with evening's setting glow.

SALISBURY. L. M. Double.

Arranged from HAYDN, by Dr. MASON.

145 BOWRING.

Evening Worship.

1 How shall we praise thee, Lord of light!
How shall we all thy love declare!
The earth is veiled in shades of night,
But heaven is open to our prayer,—
That heav'n so bright with stars and suns—
That glorious heav'n which has no bound,
Where the full tide of being runs,
And life and beauty glow around.

2 We would adore thee, God sublime!
Whose power and wisdom, love and grace
Are greater than the round of time,
And wider than the bounds of space.
O, how shall thought expression find,
All lost in thine immensity!
How shall we seek thee, glorious Mind,
Amid thy dread infinity!

3 But thou art present with us here,
As in thy glittering, high domain;
And grateful hearts and humble fear
Can never seek thy face in vain.
Help us to praise thee, Lord of light!
Help us thy boundless love declare;
And, here within thy courts to-night,
Aid us, and hearken to our prayer.

146 W. H. BURLEIGH.

Evening Hymn.

1 O HOLY Father! 'mid the calm
And stillness of this evening hour,
We would lift up our solemn psalm,
To praise thy goodness and thy power:
For over us, and over all,
Thy tender mercies still extend,
Nor vainly shall thy children call
On thee, our Father and our Friend!

2 Kept by thy goodness through the day,
Thanksgiving to thy name we pour!
Night o'er us, with its stars,—we pray
Thy love, to guard us evermore!
In grief, console; in gladness, bless;
In darkness, guide; in sickness, cheer;
Till, perfected in righteousness,
Before thy throne our souls appear!

VESPER HYMN. 8s & 7s. RUSSIAN AIR.

Double, by singing small notes.

147 S. LONGFELLOW.

Jubilate.

1 SOFT as fades the sunset splendor,
And the light of day grows dim,
We to thee our praises render;
Sing we thus our vesper hymn:
Jubilate! Amen!
Father, gracious, loving, tender,
O, accept the grateful strain.

2 Day by day comes rich in blessing;
Night by night brings holy calm;
Lord, to thee our praise addressing,
Rises thus our joyful psalm:
Jubilate! Amen!
But, unworthiness confessing,
Into silence fades again.

148 MONTGOMERY.

Vesper Hymn.

1 HARK! the vesper hymn is stealing
O'er the waters soft and clear;
Nearer yet, and nearer pealing,
Now it bursts upon the ear!
Jubilate! Amen!
Farther now, now farther stealing,
Soft it fades upon the ear.

2 Now like moonlight waves retreating
To the shore, it dies along;
Now like angry surges meeting,
Breathes the mingled tide of song.
Jubilate! Amen!
Hush! again like waves retreating
To the shore, it dies along.

ERNAN. 10s M. Dr. Mason.

149 THE INDEPENDENT.

At the Last.

1 The stream is calmest when it nears the tide, [tide,
And flowers are sweetest at the even-
And birds most musical at close of day,
And saints divinest when they pass away.

2 Morning is lovely, but a holier charm
Lies folded close in Evening's robe of balm;
And weary man must ever love her best,
For morning calls to toil, but night to rest.

3 She comes from Heaven, and on her wings doth bear
A holy fragrance, like the breath of prayer;
Footsteps of angels follow in her trace,
To shut the weary eyes of day in peace.

4 O, when our sun is setting, may we glide
Like summer's evening down the golden tide;
And leave behind us, as we pass away,
Sweet, starry twilight round our sleeping clay!

150

Thoughts of Heaven.

1 Often at evening comes a glowing thought [sense;
Of that which lies beyond our present
Of those high scenes whose glories all are wrought [tence.
By God's pure love, and his omnipo-

2 The golden bars that shine behind the sun, [him poured,
The glorious seas that seem beneath
The splendid hues, all melting into one, — [Lord!
These look thy outworks, palace of the

3 Yet not, not here, O city of our God!
Do we thy ageless glories truly see,
As when the souls, submissive 'neath the rod,
Or white in pureness, testify of thee!

4 A holy charity still tells us more [high,
Of thy real beauty, bright, serene and
Where love and faith walk on the emblazoned floor,
And perfect joy doth sing unceasingly.

5 O Son of God! exalted on thy throne,
By whom our pardon, light, and peace are given, [alone,
Impart the grace that comes from thee
And make us feel, that we may see, thy heaven.

151 BEARD'S COLL.

Guidance of the Faith.

1 From soul to soul, quick as the sunbeam's ray,
Let concord spread one universal day;
And faith, by love, lead all mankind to thee,
Parent of peace, and fount of harmony!

FADING, STILL FADING.

152 ANON.

Vespers.

1 FADING, still fading, the last beam is shining,
Father in heaven! the day is declining:
Safety and innocence flee with the light;
Temptation and danger walk forth with the night;
From the fall of the shade till the morning bells chime,
Shield us from danger and keep us from crime!
Father, have mercy, through Jesus Christ our Lord! Amen.

2 Father in heaven, O hear when we call,
Thro' Jesus Christ, who is Saviour of all!
Fainting and feeble, we trust in thy might:
In doubting and darkness, thy love be our light!
Let us sleep on thy breast while the night taper burns,
And wake in thy arms when the morning returns.
Father, have mercy, through Jesus Christ our Lord! Amen.

From the CHIME.

153

ANON.

Evening Prayer.

1 THROUGH the changes of the day
  Kept by thy sustaining power,
Offering of thanks we pay,
  Father, in this evening hour.
Praises to thy name belong,
  Source and Giver of all good;
While we lift our evening song,
  Fill our souls with gratitude!

2 From the dangers which have frowned,
  From the snares in secret set,
We have, through thy mercy, found
  Safety and deliverance yet.
Spirit, who hast been our Light,
  And the Guardian of our way,
Let thy mercy and thy might
  Keep us to another day.

154

MISSIONARY MAG.

Evening Hymn.

1 LORD of glory! King of power!
In this lone and silent hour,
While the shades of darkness rise
And the eve is on the skies,
By thy blessing, as the dews,
Which yon shaded skies diffuse,
Bid our feverish passions cease;
Calm us with thy promised peace.

2 Wheresoe'er the brow of pain
Seeks oblivion's balm in vain,
Or the form of watchful grief
Knows not of the night's relief,
There thy pity, softening pour,
There the spirit's calm restore;
Till each tongue, from murmuring free,
Wakes the hymn of praise to thee.

155

CRABBE.

The Pilgrim's Welcome.

1 PILGRIM, burdened with thy sin,
  Come the way to Zion's gate;
There, till mercy speaks within,
Knock, and weep, and watch, and wait:
Knock — he knows the sinner's cry;
  Weep — he loves the mourner's tears;
Watch, for saving grace is nigh;
  Wait, till heavenly grace appears.

2 Hark! it is the Saviour's voice,
  "Welcome, pilgrim, to thy rest!"
Now within the gate rejoice,
Safe, and owned, and bought, and blest:
Safe, from all the lures of vice;
  Owned, by joys the contrite know;
Bought by love, and life the price;
  Blest, the mighty debt to owe.

156

ANON.

Call to Life.

1 SINNER! rouse thee from thy sleep;
Wake, and o'er thy folly weep;
Raise thy spirit, dark and dead;
Jesus waits his light to shed.
Be not blind and foolish still;
Called of Jesus, learn his will;
Jesus calls from death and night,
Jesus waits to shed his light.

NEWTON. C. M. 6 ls.

JACKSON.

157

ANON.

Eventide.

1 O SHADOW in a sultry land!
We gather to thy breast,
Whose love, enfolding us like night,
Brings quietude and rest;
Glimpse of a fairer life to be,
In foretaste here possessed.

2 From all our wanderings we come,
From drifting to and fro,
From tossing on life's restless deep,
Amid its ebb and flow;
The grander sweep of tides serene
Our spirits yearn to know.

3 That which the garish day has lost,
The twilight vigil brings;—
The breezes from celestial hills,
The draughts from deeper springs,
The sense of an immortal trust,
The touch of angel wings.

158

A. L. WARING.

Lowly Service.

1 I ASK thee for the daily strength
To none that ask denied;
A mind to blend with outward life
While keeping at thy side:
Content to fill a little space,
If thou be glorified.

2 Briers beset my every path,
Which call for patient care;
There is a cross in every lot,
An earnest need for prayer:
But lowly hearts that lean on thee
Are happy anywhere.

3 In service which thy will appoints,
There are no bonds for me;
My inmost heart is taught the truth
That makes thy children free:
A life of self-renouncing love
Is a life of liberty.

159

ANON.

Not Forsaken.

1 AND wilt thou now forsake me, Lord?
I feel it cannot be;
No earthly tongue can ever tell
What thou hast been to me:
Through all the changing scenes of life
Thy love hath sheltered me.

2 And wilt thou now forget thy child?
Thy grace forbids a fear:
Thy love hath been my heritage
Through many a weary year;
I've trusted in thy promises,
And thou hast dried each tear.

3 In life or death, I take my stand
Where I have ever stood,
Beneath the shelter of thy cross,
Still trusting in thy blood,—
E'en when my youth and health and [strength
Shall fail along life's road.

4 And when in all the helplessness
Of death I turn to thee,
Thou wilt not then forsake me, Lord'
I feel it cannot be;
The shades of evening then shall close
Around me peacefully.

WARD. L. M.

Arr. by Dr. Mason.

160

Harris.

Hymn of Night.

1 The stars are sparks of burning sand;
They fall, with measured sound sublime,
From the great hour-glass in God's hand,
And mete the flying years of time.

2 We watch them from our earthly ball;
We hear their faint, mysterious hymn;
From east to west we see them fall
Beyond the blue horizon's rim.

3 O burning hour-glass of the skies;
O sparks from glory's central sun;
Our spirits, while ye fall, arise,
In Love's eternal path to run.

4 From God ye roll in measured flight;
Your glory fails beneath his feet.
To God we tend, from light to light,
And all who love in him shall meet.

161

Breviary.

Night Watches.

1 Throughout the hours of darkness dim,
Still let us watch and raise the hymn;
And in deep midnight's awful calm,
Pour forth the soul in deepest psalm.

2 Amid the silence, else so drear,
Think the Almighty leans to hear;
Well pleased to list at such a time,
The wakeful heart in praise sublime.

3 Still watch and pray and raise the hymn,
Throughout the hours of darkness dim!
God will not spurn the humblest guest,
But give us of his holy rest.

162

Martineau.

"Be still and know that I am God."

1 He who himself and God would know,
Into the silence let him go,
And, lifting off pall after pall,
Reach to the inmost depth of all.

2 Let him look forth into the night;
What solemn depths, what silent might!
Those ancient stars, how calm they roll,
He but an atom 'mid the whole!

3 How small, in that uplifted hour,
Temptation's lure and passion's power!
How weak the foe that made him fall!
How strong the soul to conquer all!

163

From the German.

Blessedness of Love to God.

1 Ah, happy hours! whene'er upsprings
My soul to yon eternal Source,
Whence the glad river downward sings,
Watering with goodness all my course.

2 Can I, with loveless heart, receive
Tokens of love that never cease?
Can I be thankless, Lord, and grieve
Thee, who art all my joy and peace?

3 Forth from thy rich and bounteous store
Life's common blessings daily flow;
More than I dare to ask, far more
Than I deserve, dost thou bestow.

4 Nor here alone: hope pierces far
Through all the shades of earth and time;
Faith mounts beyond the farthest star;
Yon shining heights she fain would climb.

DOANE. L. M. MODERN HARP.

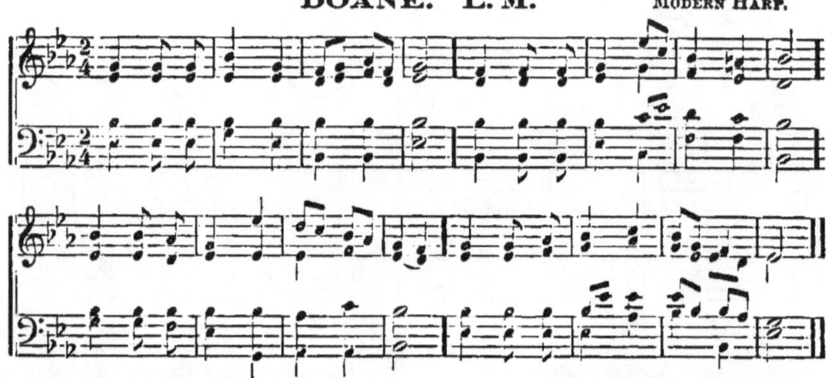

164 BOWRING.

God's sustaining Presence.

1 FATHER and friend, thy light, thy love
Beaming through all thy works we see;
Thy glory gilds the heavens above,
And all the earth is full of thee.

2 Thy voice we hear, thy presence feel,
Whilst thou, too pure for mortal sight,
Involved in clouds, invisible,
Reignest the Lord of life and light.

3 We know not in what hallowed part
Of the wide heav'ns thy throne may be;
But this we know, — that where thou art,
Strength, wisdom, goodness, dwell with thee.

4 Thy children shall not faint nor fear,
Sustained by this delightful thought,
Since thou, their God, art everywhere,
They cannot be where thou art not.

165 ANON.

"In whose Hand are all thy Ways."

1 GOD of my life, whose gracious power
Through varied deaths my soul hath led,
Or turned aside the fatal hour,
Or lifted up my sinking head!

2 In all my ways thy hand I own,
Thy ruling providence I see:
Assist me still my course to run,
And still direct my paths to thee.

3 Whither, O, whither should I fly,
But to my loving Father's breast;
Secure within thine arms to lie,
And safe beneath thy wings to rest!

4 I have no skill the snare to shun,
But thou, O God! my wisdom art;
I ever into ruin run,
But thou art greater than my heart.

166 ANON.

Providence Mysterious.

1 THY ways, O Lord, with wise design,
Are framed upon thy throne above,
And every dark or bending line
Meets in the centre of thy love.

2 With feeble light, and half obscure,
Poor mortals thine arrangements view,
Not knowing that the least are sure,
And the mysterious just and true.

3 They neither know nor trace the way;
But, trusting to thy piercing eye,
None of their feet to ruin stray,
Nor shall the weakest fail or die.

4 My favored soul shall meekly learn
To lay her reason at thy throne;
Too weak thy secrets to discern;
I'll trust thee for my guide alone.

ADMAH. L. M. 6 ls.

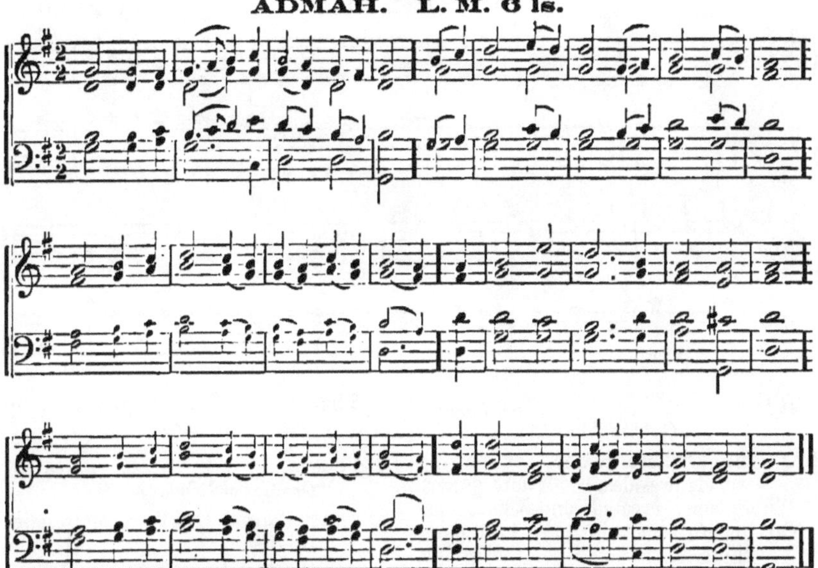

167

W. Ray.

Perfection of God.

1 Thou art, Almighty Lord of all,
From everlasting still the same;
Before thee dazzling seraphs fall,
And veil their faces in a flame,
To see such bright perfections glow, —
Such floods of glory from thee flow.

2 The sun himself is but a gleam,
A transient meteor, from thy throne;
And every frail and fickle beam,
That ever in creation shone,
Is nothing, Lord, compared to thee
In thy own vast immensity.

3 But though thy brightness may create
All worship from the hosts above,
What most thy name must elevate
Is, that thou art a God of love;
And mercy is the central sun
Of all thy glories joined in one.

168

Anon.

Prayer for the Spirit of God's Word.

1 Inspirer of the ancient seers,
Who wrote from thee the sacred page,
The same through all succeeding years!
To us, in our degenerate age,
The spirit of thy word impart,
And breathe its life into our heart.

2 While now thine oracles we read,
With earnest prayer and strong desire,
O, let thy truth from thee proceed
Our souls to waken and inspire;
Our weakness help, our darkness chase,
And guide us by the light of grace.

3 Supplied from out thy treasury,
O, may we always ready stand
To help the souls redeemed by thee,
In what their various states demand;
To teach, convince, correct, reprove,
And build them up in noblest love.

169

Montgomery.

God good and omniscient.

1 How precious are thy thoughts of peace,
O God! to me, — how great the sum!
New every morn, they never cease;
They were, they are, and yet shall come,
In number and in compass more
Than ocean's sand or ocean's shore.

WHITE. 10s. T. B. WHITE.

170 DR. JOHNSON.

God and Man.

1 O THOU, whose power o'er moving worlds presides, [dom guides,
Whose voice created, and whose wis-
On hopeful man in pure effulgence shine, [divine.
And cheer his waiting mind with light

2 'T is thine alone to calm the troubled breast
With silent confidence and holy rest;
From thee, great God! we spring; to thee we tend,
Path, Motive, Guide, Original, and End.

171 JONES VERY.

God's Fatherly Care.

1 FATHER! there is no change to live with thee. [to day,
Save that in Christ I grow from day
In each new word I hear, each thing I see,
I but rejoicing hasten on my way.

2 The morning comes, with blushes over-spread, [within;
And I, new-wakened, find a morn
And in its modest dawn around me shed, [ascending hymn.
Thou hear'st the prayer and the

3 Hour follows hour, the lengthening shades descend, [as me,
Yet they could never reach as far
Did not thy love its kind protection lend,
That I, thy child, might sleep in peace with thee.

172 DERZHAVIN.

"One God and Father of all."

1 O THOU Eternal One! whose presence bright [guide,
All space doth occupy, all motion
Unchanged through time's all-devastating flight, [beside.
Thou only God! there is no God

2 Being above all beings, Mighty One,
Whom none can comprehend and none explore,
Who fill'st existence with thyself alone,
Being whom we call God, and know no more!

3 Thy laws the unmeasured universe surround, [breath;
Upheld by thee, by thee inspired with
Thou the beginning with the end hast bound, [death.
And beautifully mingled life with

4 Father! the effluence of thy light divine,
Pervading worlds, hath reached my bosom too;
Yes; in my spirit doth thy Spirit shine,
As shines the sunbeam in a drop of dew.

5 O thought ineffable! O vision blest!
Though poor be our conceptions all, of thee, [breast,
Yet shall thy shadowed image fill our
And waft its homage to the Deity.

HENDON. 7s. Arr. by Dr. MASON.

173 W. GASKELL.

Omniscience of God.

1 MIGHTY God! the first, the last!
What are ages in thy sight
But as yesterday when past,
Or a watch within the night?

2 All that being ever knew,
Down, far down, ere time had birth,
Stands as clear within thy view,
As the present things of earth.

3 All that being e'er shall know
On, still on, through farthest years,
All eternity can show
Bright before thee now appears.

4 In thine all-embracing sight
Every change its purpose meets,
Every cloud floats into light,
Every woe its glory greets.

5 Whatsoe'er our lot may be,
Calmly in this thought we 'll rest,—
Could we see as thou dost see,
We should choose it as the best.

174 TOPLADY.

God our Life.

1 LORD, it is not life to live,
If thy presence thou deny;
Lord, if thou thy presence give,
'T is no longer death to die.

2 Source and giver of repose,
Singly from thy smile it flows;
Peace and happiness are thine;
Mine they are, if thou art mine.

175 DODDRIDGE.

God's Guardian Care.

1 HEAVENLY Father, gracious name!
Night and day his love the same!
Far be each suspicious thought,
Every anxious care forgot!

2 What if death my sleep invade?
Should I be of death afraid?
While encircled by thine arm,
Death may strike, but cannot harm.

3 With thy heavenly presence blest,
Death is life, and labor rest.
Welcome sleep or death to me,
Still secure,—for still with thee.

176 COX.

Nature's Praise.

1 HEAVEN and earth and sea and air,
God's eternal praise declare:
Up, my soul; awake and raise
Grateful hymns and songs of praise.

2 See the sun, with glorious ray,
Pierce the clouds at opening day;
Moon and stars, in splendor bright,
Praise their God through silent night.

3 See how earth, with beauty decked,
Tells a heavenly Architect;
Woods and fields, with loving kine,
Show their Maker all divine.

4 Through the world, great God, I trace
Wonders of thy power and grace:
Write more deeply on my heart
What I am, and what thou art.

BLENDON. L. M.

F. GIARDINI.

177

KIPPIS.

God Incomprehensible.

1 GREAT God! in vain man's narrow view
Attempts to look thy nature through;
Our laboring powers with reverence own
Thy glories never can be known.

2 Not the high seraph's mighty thought,
Who countless years his God has sought,
Such wondrous height or depth can find,
Or fully trace thy boundless mind.

3 And yet thy kindness deigns to show
Enough for mortal minds to know;
While wisdom, goodness, power divine,
Through all thy works and conduct shine.

4 Oh, may our souls with rapture trace
Thy works of nature and of grace;
Explore thy sacred truth, and still
Press on to know and do thy will.

178

WATTS.

God's Constant Care.

1 MY God! how endless is thy love!
Thy gifts are every evening new;
And morning mercies from above
Gently distil, like early dew.

2 Thou spread'st the curtains of the night,
Great Guardian of my sleeping hours;
Thy sovereign word restores the light,
And quickens all my drowsy powers.

3 I yield my powers to thy command;
To thee I consecrate my days;
Perpetual blessings from thy hand
Demand perpetual songs of praise.

179

SPIRIT OF THE PSALMS.

Eternity of God.

1 ERE mountains reared their forms sublime
Or heaven and earth in order stood,
Before the birth of ancient time,
From everlasting thou art God.

2 A thousand ages, in their flight,
With thee are as a fleeting day;
Past, present, future, to thy sight
At once their various scenes display.

3 But our brief life's a shadowy dream,
A passing thought, that soon is o'er,
That fades with morning's earliest beam,
And fills the musing mind no more.

4 To us, O Lord, the wisdom give,
Each passing moment so to spend,
That we at length with thee may live
Where life and bliss shall never end.

180

WATTS

The Sovereign God.

1 YE nations round the earth, rejoice
Before the Lord, your sovereign King,
Serve him with cheerful heart and voice,
With all your tongues his glory sing.

2 The Lord is God; 't is he alone
Doth life and breath and being give;
We are his work, and not our own,
The sheep that on his pastures live.

3 Enter his gates with songs of joy,
With praises to his courts repair;
And make it your divine employ,
To pay your thanks and honors there.

ACUSHNET. C. M. MODERN HARP.

181 DRENNAN.

The Indwelling God.

1 THE heaven of heavens cannot contain
The universal Lord:
Yet he in humble hearts will deign
To dwell, and be adored.

2 Where'er ascends the sacrifice
Of fervent praise and prayer,
Or on the earth, or in the skies,
The God of heaven is there.

3 His presence is diffused abroad,
Through realms, through worlds unknown:
Who seek the mercies of our God
Are ever near his throne.

182 WHITTIER.

Faith in God's Goodness.

1 THE wrong that pains my soul below
I dare not throne above;
I know not of His hate, — I know
His goodness and his love.

2 I dimly guess from blessings known
Of greater out of sight,
And, with the chastened Psalmist, own
His judgments, too, are right.

3 No offering of my own I have,
Nor works my faith to prove;
I can but give the gifts he gave,
And plead his love for love.

4 O brothers! if my faith is vain,
If hopes like these betray,
Pray for me that my feet may gain
The sure and safer way.

5 And thou, O Lord! by whom are seen
Thy creatures as they be,
Forgive me if too close I lean
My human heart on thee!

183 STERNHOLD.

Majesty of God.

1 THE Lord descended from above,
And bowed the heavens most high,
And underneath his feet he cast
The darkness of the sky.

2 On cherubim and seraphim
Full royally he rode,
And on the wings of mighty winds
Came flying all abroad.

3 He sat serene upon the floods
Their fury to restrain,
And he, as sovereign Lord and King,
For evermore shall reign.

184 WATTS

"Canst thou, by searching, find out God?"

1 How wondrous great, how glorious bright
Must our Creator be,
Who dwells amid the dazzling light
Of an eternal day!

2 Lord, here we bend our humble souls,
In awe and love adore;
For the weak pinions of our mind
Can stretch a thought no more.

3 Thy glories infinitely rise
Above our laboring tongue;
In vain the highest seraph tries
To form an equal song.

ST. PAUL'S. L. M.

Dr. Green.

185

Walker's Coll.

"God, with whom is no Variableness."

1 All-powerful, self-existing God,
Who all creation dost sustain!
Thou wast, and art, and art to come,
And everlasting is thy reign!

2 Fixed and eternal as thy days,
Each glorious attribute divine,
Through ages infinite, shall still
With undiminished lustre shine.

3 Fountain of being! Source of good!
Immutable thou dost remain!
Nor can the shadow of a change
Obscure the glories of thy reign.

4 Earth may, with all her powers, dissolve,
If such the great Creator's will;
But thou forever art the same,—
I AM, is thy memorial still.

186

Doddridge.

Faith in the Invisible God.

1 Almighty and immortal King,
Thy peerless splendors none can bear;
But darkness veils seraphic eyes,
When God with all his glory 's there.

2 Yet faith can pierce the awful gloom,
The great Invisible can see,
And with its tremblings mingle joy,
In fixed regards, great God, to thee.

3 This one petition would it urge,—
To bear thee ever in its sight;
In life, in death, in worlds unknown,
Its only portion and delight.

187

Conder.

The Lord is King.

1 The Lord is King! lift up thy voice,
O earth, and all ye heavens rejoice!
From world to world the joy shall ring;
The Lord Omnipotent is King.

2 The Lord is King! O child of dust,
The Judge of all the earth is just,
Holy and true are all his ways;
Let every creature speak his praise.

3 Come, make your wants, your burdens known;
The contrite soul he'll ne'er disown;
And angel bands are waiting there,
His messages of love to bear.

4 Oh, when his wisdom can mistake,
His might decay, his love forsake;
Then may his children cease to sing
The Lord Omnipotent is King.

188

Tate & Brady.

Eternity and Sovereignty of God.

1 With glory clad, with strength arrayed,
The Lord, that o'er all nature reigns,
The world's foundations strongly laid,
And the vast fabric still sustains.

2 How surely stablished is thy throne,
Which shall no change or period see!
For thou, O Lord! and thou alone,
Art God from all eternity.

3 Thy promise, Lord, is ever sure;
And they that in thy house would dwell,
That happy station to secure,
Must still in holiness excel.

HADDAM. H. M.

189 WATTS.

The Divine Majesty.

1 THE Lord Jehovah reigns;
His throne is built on high;
The garments he assumes
Are light and majesty:
His glories shine
With beams so bright,
No mortal eye
Can bear the sight.

2 The thunders of his hand
Keep the wide world in awe;
His truth and justice stand
To guard his holy law;
And where his love
Resolves to bless,
His truth confirms
And seals the grace.

3 And can this mighty King
Of glory condescend?
And will he write his name
"My Father and my Friend"?
I love his name,
I love his word:
Join, all my powers,
And praise the Lord!

190 WATTS.

God our Preserver.

1 UPWARD I lift mine eyes;
From God is all my aid,—
The God that built the skies,
And earth and nature made:
God is the tower
To which I fly;
His grace is nigh
In every hour.

2 No burning heats by day,
Nor blasts of evening air,
Shall take my health away,
If God be with me there.
Thou art my sun,
And thou my shade,
To guard my head
By night or noon.

3 Hast thou not given thy word,
To save my soul from death?
And I can trust my Lord
To keep my mortal breath.
I'll go and come,
Nor fear to die,
Till from on high
Thou call me home.

191 ANON.

General Praise.

1 OH, spread the joyful sound!
The Saviour's love proclaim;
And publish all around
Salvation through his name;
Till all the world
Take up the strain,
And send the echo
Back again!

PORTUGUESE HYMN. 11s. JOHN READING, 1760.

192 BYROM.

God our Shepherd and Guardian.

1 The Lord is our Shepherd, our Guard-
ian and Guide; [vide:
Whatever we want he will kindly pro-
His care and protection his flock will
surround;
To them will his mercies forever abound.

2 The Lord is our Shepherd; what, then,
shall we fear? [near?
Shall dangers affrighten us while he is
O, no: when he calls us we'll walk
through the vale, [shall not fail.
The shadow of death, but our hearts

3 Afraid, of ourselves, to pursue the dark
way, [and stay;
Thy rod and thy staff be our comfort
We know by thy guidance, when once
it is past,
To life and to glory it brings us at last.

4 The Lord is become our salvation and
song, [life long;
His blessings have followed us all our
His name will we praise, while he lends
to us breath, [our death.
Be joyful through life, and resigned in

193 KIRKHAM.

Ever loving God.

1 How firm a foundation, ye saints of
the Lord! [word!
Is laid for your faith in his excellent
What more can he say than to you he
hath said, — [fled?
To you, who for refuge to Jesus have

2 "Fear not, I am with thee; oh, be not
dismayed, [aid:
For I am thy God, I will still give thee
I'll strengthen thee, help thee, and
cause thee to stand, [hand.
Upheld by my gracious, omnipotent

3 "When through the deep waters I call
thee to go, [flow;
The rivers of sorrow shall not over-
For I will be with thee thy trials to
bless, [tress.
And sanctify to thee thy deepest dis-

4 "When through fiery trials thy path-
way shall lie, [supply,
My grace, all-sufficient, shall be thy
The flame shall not hurt thee; I only
design [refine."
Thy dross to consume, and thy gold to

BELVILLE. L. M. 6 ls. Arr. by Dr. Mason.

194

ADDISON.

God our Shepherd.

1 The Lord my pasture shall prepare,
And feed me with a shepherd's care;
His presence shall my wants supply,
And guard me with a watchful eye;
My noon-day walks he shall attend,
And all my midnight hours defend.

2 When in the sultry glebe I faint,
Or on the thirsty mountains pant,
To fertile vales and dewy meads
My weary, wandering steps he leads,
Where peaceful rivers, soft and slow,
Amid the verdant landscape flow.

3 Though in the paths of death I tread,
With gloomy horrors overspread,
My steadfast heart shall fear no ill,
For thou, O Lord, art with me still.
Thy friendly staff shall give me aid,
And guide me through the dreadful shade.

195

MONTGOMERY'S COLL.

Omnipresence of God.

1 Above, below, where'er I gaze,
Thy guiding finger, Lord, I view,
Traced in the midnight planet's blaze,
Or glist'ning in the morning dew:
Whate'er is beautiful or fair
Is but thine own reflection there.

2 And when the radiant orb of light
Hath tipped the mountain tops with gold,
Smote with the blaze, my weary sight
Shrinks from the wonders I behold;
That ray of glory, bright and fair,
Is but thy living shadow there.

196

MOORE.

All Things are of God.

1 Thou art, O God, the life and light
Of all this wondrous world we see;
Its glow by day, its smile by night,
Are but reflections caught from thee;
Where'er we turn, thy glories shine,
And all things fair and bright are thine.

2 When day, with farewell beam, delays
Among the opening clouds of even,
And we can almost think we gaze
Through golden vistas into heaven,—
Those hues that mark the sun's decline,
So soft, so radiant, Lord, are thine.

3 When night, with wings of starry gloom,
O'ershadows all the earth and skies,
Like some dark, beauteous bird, whose plume
Is sparkling with unnumbered eyes,—
That sacred gloom, those fires divine,
So grand, so countless, Lord, are thine.

DEDHAM. C. M.

197 FABER.

Acknowledgment of Divine Love.

1 How dread are thine eternal years,
O everlasting Lord!
By prostrate spirits day and night
Incessantly adored!

2 Yet I may love thee too, O Lord!
Almighty as thou art,
For thou hast stooped to ask of me
The love of my poor heart.

3 No earthly father loves like thee,
No mother half so mild
Bears and forbears, as thou hast done
With me, thy sinful child.

4 Only to sit and think of God—
Oh what a joy it is!
To think the thought, to breathe the name,
Earth has no higher bliss!

198 BROWN.

Universal Goodness of God.

1 LORD, thou art good! all nature shows
Its mighty Author kind:
Thy bounty through creation flows,
Full, free, and unconfined.

2 It fills the wide extended main,
And heavens which spread more wide:
It drops in gentle showers of rain,
And rolls in every tide.

3 Through the whole earth it pours supplies,
Spreads joy through every part:
O may such love attract my eyes,
And captivate my heart!

4 My highest admiration raise,
My best affections move;
Employ my tongue in songs of praise,
And fill my heart with love.

199 TATE & BRADY.

God Unchangeable.

1 THROUGH endless years thou art the same,
O thou eternal God;
Each future age shall know thy name,
And tell thy works abroad.

2 The strong foundations of the earth
Of old by thee were laid;
By thee the beauteous arch of heaven
With matchless skill was made.

3 Soon may this goodly frame of things,
Created by thy hand,
Be, like a vesture, laid aside,
And changed at thy command.

4 But thy perfections, all divine,
Eternal as thy days,
Through everlasting ages shine,
With undiminished rays.

200 ANON.

God in the Home.

1 HAPPY the home, when God is there,
And love fills every breast;
Where one their wish, and one their prayer,
And one their heavenly rest.

2 Lord! let us in our homes agree,
This blessed peace to gain;
Unite our hearts in love to thee,
And love to all will reign.

SHIRLAND. S. M. STANLEY.

201 MRS. STEELE.

God our Father.

1 My Father! cheering name!
Oh, may I call thee mine?
Give me the humble hope to claim
A portion so divine.

2 Whate'er thy will denies,
I calmly would resign;
For thou art just, and good, and wise:
Oh, bend my will to thine!

3 Whate'er thy will ordains,
Oh, give me strength to bear;
Still let me know a father reigns,
And trust a father's care.

4 Thy ways are little known
To my weak, erring sight;
Yet shall my soul, believing, own
That all thy ways are right.

5 My Father! blissful name!
Above expression dear!
If thou accept my humble claim,
I bid adieu to fear.

202 WATTS.

The Unfailing Power.

1 High as the heavens are raised
Above the ground we tread,
So far the riches of His grace
Our highest thoughts exceed.

2 His power subdues our sins,
And his forgiving love,
Far as the east is from the west,
Doth all our guilt remove.

3 The pity of the Lord,
To those who fear his name,
Is such as tender parents feel:
He knows our feeble frame.

4 Our days are as the grass,
Or like the morning flower:
If one sharp blast sweep o'er the field,
It withers in an hour.

5 But thy compassions, Lord,
To endless years endure;
And children's children ever find,
Thy words of promise sure.

203 WATTS.

Merciful Dealings of God.

1 My soul, repeat his praise,
Whose mercies are so great;
Whose anger is so slow to rise,
So ready to abate.

2 God will not always chide;
And when his wrath is felt,
Its strokes are fewer than our crimes,
And lighter than our guilt.

204 ANON.

"So run that ye may obtain."

1 My soul, it is thy God
Who calls thee by his grace;
Now loose thee from each cumbering load,
And bend thee to the race.

2 Thy crown of life hold fast;
Thy heart with courage stay;
Nor let one trembling glance be cast
Along the backward way.

MARLOW. C. M.

Arr. by Dr. Mason.

205

ANON.

God our Father.

1 Even He who lit the stars of old,
And filled the ocean broad,
Whose works and ways are manifold, —
Our Father is our God.

2 There comes no change upon his years,
No failure to his hand;
His love will lighten all our cares,
His law our steps command.

3 Then as his children we may come,
For he hath called us near,
And bade our souls take courage from
The love that casts out fear.

4 Lord, while on earth we work and pray
For good withheld or given:
Help us in faith and love to say,
Father, who art in heaven!

206

WATTS.

God the Creator.

1 Eternal Wisdom, thee we praise;
Thee all thy creatures sing:
While with thy name, rocks, hills, and seas,
And heaven's high palace, ring.

2 Thy hand, how wide it spread the sky!
How glorious to behold!
Tinged with a blue of heavenly dye,
And decked with sparkling gold.

3 Thy glories blaze all nature round,
And strike the gazing sight,
Through skies, and seas, and solid ground,
With terror and delight.

4 Almighty power, and equal skill,
Shine through the worlds abroad,
Our souls with vast amazement fill,
And speak the builder, God.

207

WHITTIER.

God is Good.

1 I see the wrong that round me lies,
I feel the guilt within;
I hear, with groans and travail-cries,
The world confess its sin!

2 Yet in the maddening maze of things,
And tossed by storm and flood,
To one fixed star my spirit clings:
I know that God is good!

3 Not mine to look where cherubim
And seraphs may not see,
But nothing can be good in him
Which evil is in me.

208

WATTS.

Faithfulness of God.

1 Begin, my tongue, some heavenly theme,
And speak some boundless thing,
The mighty works, or mightier name,
Of our eternal King.

2 Tell of his wondrous faithfulness,
And sound his power abroad;
Sing the sweet promise of his grace,
And the performing God.

3 His very word of grace is strong,
As that which built the skies;
The voice that rolls the stars along
Speaks all the promises.

STOCKWELL 8s & 7s. D. E. JONES.

209

DOWRING.

God is Love.

1 God is love; his mercy brightens
All the path in which we rove;
Bliss he wakes, and woe he lightens;
God is wisdom, God is love.

2 Chance and change are busy ever;
Man decays, and ages move;
But his mercy waneth never;
God is wisdom, God is love.

3 E'en the hour that darkest seemeth
Will his changeless goodness prove,
From the gloom his brightness streameth;
God is wisdom, God is love.

4 He with earthly cares entwineth
Hope and comfort from above:
Everywhere his glory shineth;
God is wisdom, God is love.

210

ANON.

God of Salvation.

1 Hail, the God of our salvation,
Triumph in redeeming love!
Let us all, with exultation,
Imitate the blest above.

2 Light of those whose dreary dwelling
Bordered on the shades of death,
He hath, by his grace revealing,
Scattered all the clouds beneath.

3 Father, Source of all compassion,
Pure, unbounded Love thou art;
Hail, the God of our salvation,
Praise him, every thankful heart!

4 Joyfully on earth adore him,
Till in heaven we take our place;
There, enraptured, fall before him,
Lost in wonder, love and praise.

211

H. BONAR.

The Heavenly Father.

1 Yes, for me, for me he careth,
With a Father's tender care;
Yes, with me, with me he beareth
Every burden, every fear.

2 Yes, in me abroad he sheddeth
Joys unearthly, love and light;
And, to cover me, he spreadeth
His love-brooding wing of might.

3 Yes, in me, in me he dwelleth,
I in him, and he in me;
And my longing soul he filleth,
Here and through eternity.

212

HASTINGS.

God's Presence.

1 Pilgrims in this vale of sorrow,
Pressing onward toward the prize,
Strength and comfort here we borrow
From the Hand that rules the skies.

2 'Mid these scenes of self-denial,
We are called the race to run;
We must meet full many a trial
Ere the victor's crown is won.

3 On the Eternal arm reclining,
We at length shall win the day;
All the powers of earth combining,
Shall not snatch our crown away.

SOUTH STREET. L. M.

HAYDN.

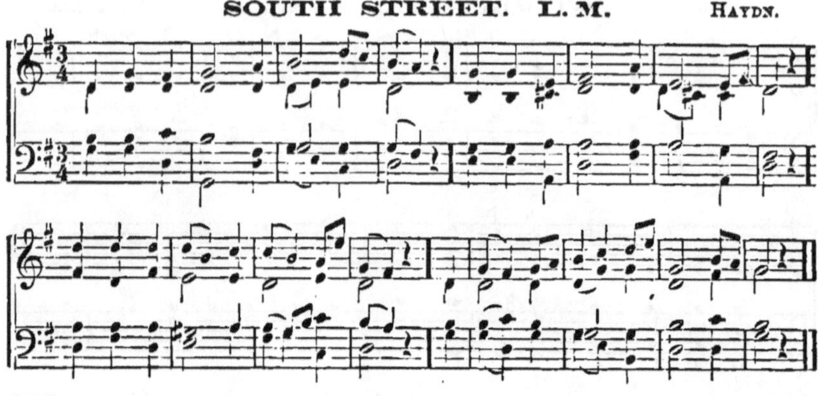

213

HARRIS.

God is Love.

1 FROM all who dwell in heaven above
We hear the anthem, "God is Love!"
While, through the souls of all below,
His tender mercies ever flow.

2 Oh, while this glorious faith we own,
Be love in all our acts made known;
Then blinded eyes shall ope to see
God is not wrath, but charity.

3 He sows the suns, like golden grain,
On the blue ether's boundless plain,
Yet in the soul his mercies are
More vast, more bright than every star.

4 Teach us, O Lord! like thee, to give
To all that love wherein we live;
Till earth below, to heaven above,
Repeats the anthem, "God is Love."

214

MRS. STEELE.

Grace of God's Name.

1 LORD, in thy great, thy glorious name,
I place my hope, my only trust;
Save me from sorrow, guilt, and shame,
Thou ever gracious, ever just.

2 Thou art my rock! thy name alone
The fortress where my hopes retreat;
Oh, make thy power and mercy known;
To safety guide my wandering feet.

3 Blest be the Lord, forever blest,
Whose mercy bids my fears remove;
The sacred walls which guard my rest
Are his almighty power and love.

215

DODDRIDGE.

Praise for Divine Goodness.

1 GOD of my life, through all its days
My grateful powers shall sound thy praise,
The song shall wake with opening light,
And warble to the silent night.

2 When anxious cares would break my rest,
And griefs would tear my throbbing breast,
Thy tuneful praises, raised on high,
Shall check the murmur and the sigh.

3 When death o'er nature shall prevail,
And all its powers of language fail,
Joy through my swimming eyes shall break,
And mean the thanks I cannot speak.

4 But oh! when that last conflict's o'er,
And I am chained to flesh no more,
With what glad accents shall I rise,
To join the music of the skies!

5 Soon shall I learn the exalted strains
Which echo o'er the heavenly plains,
And emulate, with joy unknown,
The glowing seraphs round thy throne.

216

WHITTIER.

The Shadowing Rock.

1 THE path of life we walk to-day
Is strange as that the Hebrews trod;
We need the shadowing rock as they,
We need, like them, the guides of God.

2 God send his angels, Cloud and Fire,
To lead us o'er the desert sand!
God give our hearts their long desire,
His shadow in a weary land!

217

ANON.

God is Love.

1 Earth with her ten thousand flowers,
Air, with all its beams and showers,
Ocean's infinite expanse,
Heaven's resplendent countenance;
All around, and all above,
Hath this record, — God is love.

2 Sounds among the vales and hills,
In the woods and by the rills,
Of the breeze and of the bird,
By the gentle murmur stirred;
All these songs, beneath, above,
Have one burden, — God is love.

3 All the hopes and fears that start
From the fountain of the heart;
All the quiet bliss that lies
In our human sympathies;
These are voices from above,
Sweetly whispering, — God is love.

218

T. T. Lynch.

Prayer for the Spirit.

1 Gracious Spirit, dwell with me;
I myself would gracious be,
And with words that help and heal
Would thy life in mine reveal,
And with actions bold and meek
Would for Christ my Saviour speak.

2 Mighty Spirit, dwell with me;
I myself would mighty be,
Mighty so as to prevail
Where unaided man must fail,
Ever by a mighty hope
Pressing on and bearing up.

3 Holy Spirit, dwell with me;
I myself would holy be;
Separate from sin, I would
Choose and cherish all things good,
And whatever I can be
Give to him who gave me thee.

219

Newton.

Childlike Trust in God.

1 Quiet, Lord, my froward heart;
Make me teachable and mild,
Upright, simple, free from art;
Make me as a weanéd child, —
From distrust and envy free,
Pleased with all that pleases thee.

2 What thou shalt to-day provide,
Let me as a child receive;
What to-morrow may betide,
Calmly to thy wisdom leave:
'T is enough that thou wilt care;
Why should I the burden bear?

3 As a little child relies
On a care beyond his own,
Knows he 's neither strong nor wise,
Fears to stir a step alone;
Let me thus with thee abide,
As my Father, Guard, and Guide.

MANOAH. C. M.

GREATOREX'S COLL.

220 ANCIENT CATH. HYMN.

God's all-embracing Love.

1 THOU Grace divine, encircling all!
A soundless, shoreless sea;
Wherein at last our souls shall fall;
O Love of God, most free.

2 When over dizzy steeps we go,
One soft hand blinds our eyes;
The other leads us safe and slow,
O Love of God most wise!

3 And though we turn as from thy face,
And wander wide and long,
Thou hold'st us still in thine embrace,
O Love of God most strong!

4 The saddened heart, the restless soul,
The toil-worn frame and mind,
Alike confess thy sweet control,
O Love of God most kind!

5 But not alone thy care we claim,
Our wayward steps to win;
We know thee by a dearer name,
O Love of God within!

6 And filled and quickened by thy breath,
Our souls are strong and free;
To rise o'er sin, and fear, and death,
O Love of God, to thee!

221 ANON.

God omnipresent.

1 THERE 's not a place in earth's vast round,
In ocean deep, or air,
Where skill and wisdom are not found,
For God is everywhere.

2 Around, within, below, above,
Wherever space extends,
There heaven displays its boundless love,
And power with mercy blends.

3 Then rise, my soul, and sing his name,
And all his praise rehearse,
Who spread abroad earth's wondrous frame,
And built the universe.

4 Where'er thine earthly lot is cast,
His power and love declare;
Nor think the mighty theme too vast,
For God is everywhere.

222 WATTS.

Power, Wisdom, and Goodness of God.

1 I SING the mighty power of God,
That made the mountains rise,
That spread the flowing seas abroad,
And built the lofty skies.

2 I sing the wisdom that ordained
The sun to rule the day:
The moon shines full at his command,
And all the stars obey.

3 I sing the goodness of the Lord,
That filled the earth with food;
He formed the creatures with his word,
And then pronounced them good.

4 There 's not a plant or flower below,
But makes thy glories known;
And clouds arise and tempests blow
By order from thy throne.

RUSSIAN HYMN. L. M.

223 WATTS.

The Divine Being and Perfections.

1 High in the heavens, eternal God,
Thy goodness in full glory shines;
Thy truth shall break through every cloud,
That veils and darkens thy designs.

2 Forever firm thy justice stands,
As mountains their foundations keep;
Wise are the wonders of thy hands;
Thy judgments are a mighty deep.

3 Thy providence is kind and large:
Both men and beasts thy bounty share:
The whole creation is thy charge;
But saints are thy peculiar care.

4 Life, like a fountain full and free,
Springs from the presence of my Lord;
And in thy light our souls shall see
The glories promised in thy word.

224 WATTS.

Public Adoration.

1 Before Jehovah's awful throne,
Ye nations bow with sacred joy!
Know that the Lord is God alone:
He can create, and he destroy.

2 His sovereign power, without our aid,
Made us of clay, and formed us men;
And when, like wandering sheep, we strayed,
He brought us to his fold again.

3 We are his people, we his care,—
Our souls and all our mortal frame:
What lasting honors shall we rear,
Almighty Maker, to thy name?

4 We'll crowd thy gates: with thankful songs
High as the heavens our voices raise;
And earth, with her ten thousand tongues,
Shall fill thy courts with sounding praise.

5 Wide as the world is thy command,
Vast as eternity thy love;
Firm as a rock thy truth shall stand
When rolling years shall cease to move.

225 BRYANT.

Every Good Gift from the Father.

1 Father, to thy kind love we owe
All that is fair and good below;
Bestower of the health that lies
On tearless cheeks and cheerful eyes!

2 Giver of sunshine and of rain!
Ripener of fruits on hill and plain!
Fountain of light, that, rayed afar,
Fills the vast urns of sun and star!

3 Who send'st thy storms and frosts to bind
The plagues that rise to waste mankind;
Then breathest, o'er the naked scene,
Spring gales, and life, and tender green.

4 Yet deem we not that thus alone,
Thy mercy and thy love are shown;
For we have learned, with higher praise,
And holier names, to speak thy ways.

5 In woe's dark hour, our kindest stay!
Sole trust when life shall pass away!
Teacher of hopes that light the gloom
Of death, and consecrate the tomb!

ST. MARTIN'S. C. M.

226 WATTS.

God's Infinite and Eternal Dominion.

1 GREAT God, how infinite art thou!
How weak and frail are we!
Let the whole race of creatures bow,
And pay their praise to thee.

2 Eternity, with all its years,
Stands present in thy view;
To thee there's nothing old appears—
Great God! there's nothing new.

3 Our lives through various scenes are drawn,
And vexed with trifling cares,
While thine eternal thoughts move on
Thine undisturbed affairs.

227 WATTS.

God our Help.

1 OUR God, our help in ages past,
Our hope for years to come!
Our shelter from the stormy blast,
And our eternal home!

2 Before the hills in order stood,
Or earth received her frame,
From everlasting thou art God,
To endless years the same.

3 A thousand ages in thy sight
Are like an evening gone;
Short as the watch that ends the night,
Before the rising sun.

4 Time, like an ever-rolling stream,
Bears all its sons away;
Then fly, forgotten, as a dream
Dies at the opening day.

5 Our God, our help in ages past,
Our hope for years to come,
Be thou our guard while troubles last,
And our eternal home!

228 TATE & BRADY.

God's Condescension.

1 O THOU, to whom all creatures bow
Within this earthly frame,
Through all the world how great art thou!
How glorious is thy name!

2 When heaven, thy glorious work on high,
Employs my wondering sight,—
The moon that nightly rules the sky,
With stars of feebler light,—

3 Lord, what is man, that he is blessed
With thy peculiar care!
Why on his offspring is conferred
Of love so large a share?

4 O Thou, to whom all creatures bow
Within this earthly frame,
Through all the world how great art thou!
How glorious is thy name!

229 WATTS.

The Everlasting God.

1 GREAT is the Lord, his power unknown,
Oh, let his praise be great!
I'll sing the honors of thy throne;
Thy works of grace repeat.

2 Fathers to sons shall teach thy name,
And children learn thy ways:
Ages to come thy truths proclaim,
And nations sound thy praise.

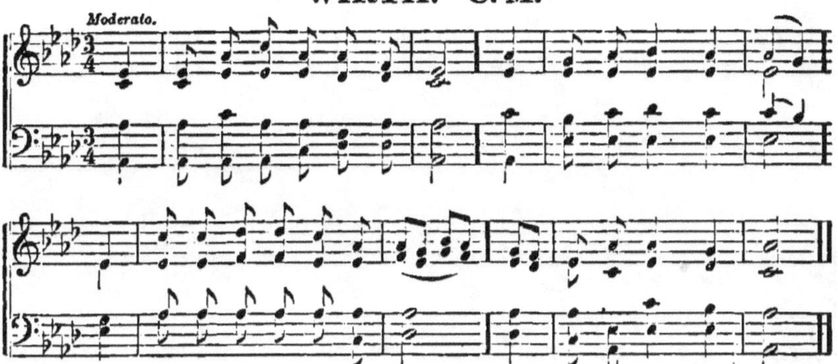

230

WHITTIER.

Divine Goodness.

1 WHO fathoms the Eternal Thought?
Who talks of scheme and plan?
The Lord is God! he needeth not
The poor device of man.

2 I walk with bare, hushed feet the ground
Men tread with boldness shod:
I dare not fix with mete and bound
The love and power of God.

3 They praise his justice; even such
His pitying love I deem;
They seek a king; I fain would touch
The robe that hath no seam.

4 They see the curse which overbroods
A world of pain and loss;
I hear our Lord's beatitudes
And prayer upon the cross.

231

MONTGOMERY.

God's Faithfulness.

1 FAITHFUL, O Lord, thy mercies are,
A rock that cannot move;
A thousand promises declare
Thy constancy of love.

2 Who trusted in thy word of old
Were never put to shame;
And as thy purposes unfold,
Thy truth is still the same.

3 Thou waitest to be gracious still;
Thou dost with sinners bear,
That, saved, we may thy goodness feel,
And all thy grace declare.

4 Its streams the whole creation reach,
So plenteous is the store;
Enough for all, enough for each,
Enough for evermore.

232

The God of Bethel.

1 O GOD of Bethel, by whose hand
Thy people still are fed,
Who, through this weary pilgrimage,
Hast all our fathers led.—

2 Our vows, our prayers, we now present,
Before thy throne of grace:
God of our fathers! be the God
Of their succeeding race.

3 Through each perplexing path of life,
Our wand'ring footsteps guide;
Give us each day our daily bread,
And all we need provide.

4 O spread thy cov'ring wings around,
Till all our wand'rings cease,
And at our Father's loved abode,
Our souls arrive in peace.

233

Ceaseless Praise.

1 THE glorious armies of the sky
To thee, almighty King,
Triumphant anthems consecrate,
And hallelujahs sing.

2 But still their most exalted flights
Fall vastly short of thee;
How distant then must human praise
From thy perfections be!

ECKARDTSHEIM. C. M. ZEUNER.

234 THOMPSON.

All-embracing Providence of God.

1 Jehovah God! thy gracious power
On every hand we see;
O may the blessings of each hour
Lead all our thoughts to thee.

2 If, on the wings of morn, we speed
To earth's remotest bound,
Thy hand will there our footsteps lead,
Thy love our path surround.

3 Thy power is in the ocean deeps,
And reaches to the skies;
Thine eye of mercy never sleeps,
Thy goodness never dies.

4 In all the varying scenes of time,
On thee our hopes depend;
Through every age, in every clime,
Our Father and our Friend!

235 ENG. BAP.

Providence Kind and Bountiful.

1 Thy kingdom, Lord, forever stands,
While earthly thrones decay;
And time submits to thy commands,
While ages roll away.

2 Thy sovereign bounty freely gives
Its unexhausted store;
And universal nature lives
On thy sustaining power.

3 Holy and just in all its ways
Is Providence divine;
In all its works, immortal rays
Of power and mercy shine.

4 The praise of God — delightful theme!
Shall fill my heart and tongue;
Let all creation bless his name,
In one eternal song.

236 SCOTT.

God's Superintendency.

1 God reigns; events in order flow,
Man's industry to guide;
But in a different channel go,
To humble human pride.

2 Weak mortals do themselves beguile,
When on themselves they rest;
Blind is their wisdom, vain their toil,
By thee, O Lord, unblest.

3 'T is ours the furrows to prepare,
And sow the precious grain;
'T is thine to give the sun and air,
And send the genial rain.

4 Evil and good before thee stand,
Their mission to perform;
The sun shines bright at thy command;
Thy hand directs the storm.

5 In all our ways, we humbly own
Thy providential power;
Entrusting to thy care, alone,
The lot of every hour.

237 FAWCETT.

God's Ways.

1 Thy way, O Lord, is in the sea;
Thy paths I cannot trace,
Nor comprehend the mystery
Of thine unbounded grace.

HINGHAM. L. M. Dr. L. Mason.

238 W. Taylor.

The Beneficence of God.

1 God of the universe, whose hand
Hath sown with suns the fields of space,
Round which, obeying thy command,
Unnumbered words fulfil their race;

2 How vast the region where thy will
Existence, form, and order gives,
Pleased the wide cup with joy to fill,
For all that grows, and feels, and lives.

3 Lord! while we thank thee, let us learn
Beneficence to all below:
They praise thee best whose bosoms burn
Thy gifts on others to bestow.

239 Dyer.

God's Care over All.

1 Greatest of Beings! Source of life!
Sovereign of air, of earth, and sea!
All nature feels thy power,— but man
A grateful tribute pays to thee.

2 All, great Creator! all are thine;
All feel thy providential care;
And, through each varying scene of life,
Alike thy constant pity share.

3 And whether grief oppress the heart,
Or whether joy elate the breast,
Or life still keep its little course,
Or death invite the heart to rest;

4 All are thy messengers, and all
Thy sacred pleasure, Lord, obey;
And all are training man to dwell
Nearer to bliss, and nearer thee.

240 Collett.

Providence Kind and Sure.

1 Through all the various passing scene
Of life's mistaken ill or good,
Thy hand, O God! conducts unseen
The beautiful vicissitude.

2 Thou givest with paternal care,
Howe'er unjustly we complain,
To each their necessary share
Of joy and sorrow, health and pain.

3 All things on earth, and all in heaven,
On thy eternal will depend;
And all for greater good were given,
And all shall in thy glory end.

4 Be this my care!— to all beside
Indifferent let my wishes be;
Passion be calm, and dumb be pride,
And fixed my soul, great God, on thee.

241 T. H. Gill.

Desire of Progress.

1 Lord, thou wouldst have us like to thee;
Lord, thou wouldst lift us to thy Son:
Thou biddest us aspirants be,—
Put all divine ambition on.

2 Alas our wrath! alas our pride!
Yet shall they not at last be gone?
Oh may we not each day abide
Still nearer the all-loving One?

3 Would we not grow divinely bright,
Take sweetness in, put glory on,—
Yes, wax more worthy to delight
In thee, first fair, all-glorious One?

JORDAN. C. M. Double. BILLINGS.

242

The Book of Nature. KEBLE.

1 THERE is a book, who runs may read,
Which heavenly truth imparts;
And all the lore its scholars need,
Pure eyes and willing hearts.

2 The works of God above, below,
Within us and around,
Are pages in that book to show
How God himself is found.

3 The glorious sky, embracing all,
Is like the Father's love;
Wherewith encompassed, great and small,
In peace and order move.

4 Thou who hast given us eyes to see
And love this sight so fair,
Give to us hearts to find out thee,
And read thee everywhere.

243

God seen in His Works. WALLACE.

1 THERE'S not a star whose twinkling light
Illumes the distant earth,
And cheers the solemn gloom of night,
But Goodness gave it birth.

2 There's not a cloud whose dews distil
Upon the parching clod,
And clothe with verdure vale and hill,
That is not sent by God.

3 There's not a place in earth's vast round,
In ocean deep, or air,
Where skill and wisdom are not found;
For God is everywhere.

4 Around, within, below, above,
Wherever space extends,
There heaven displays its boundless love,
And power with goodness blends.

244

Nature's Worship. J. G. WHITTIER.

1 THE harp at Nature's advent strung
Has never ceased to play;
The song the stars of morning sung
Has never died away.

2 So nature keeps the reverent frame
With which her years began;
And all her signs and voices shame
The prayerless heart of man.

HENRY. C. M. S. P. Pond.

245 H. K. White.

God over All.

1 The Lord our God is Lord of all;
His station who can find?
I hear him in the waterfall;
I hear him in the wind.

2 If in the gloom of night I shroud,
His face I cannot fly;
I see him in the evening cloud,
And in the morning sky.

3 He lives, he reigns in every land,
From winter's polar snows,
To where, across the burning sand,
The blasting meteor glows.

4 He bids his gales the fields deform,
Then, when his thunders cease,
He paints his rainbow on the storm,
And lulls the winds to peace.

246 Lutheran Coll.

Goodness of God in his Works.

1 Hail, great Creator, — wise and good!
To thee our songs we raise;
Nature, through all her varying scenes,
Invites us to thy praise.

2 Thy glory beams in every star,
Which gilds the gloom of night,
And decks the smiling face of morn
With rays of cheerful light.

3 The lofty hill, the humble lawn,
With countless beauties shine;
The silent grove, the awful shade,
Proclaim thy power divine.

4 Great nature's God! still may these scenes
Our serious hours engage!
Still may our grateful hearts consult
Thy work's instructive page!

247 Anon.

Whispers in the Tempest.

1 Great Ruler of all nature's frame,
We own thy power divine;
We hear thy breath in every storm,
For all the winds are thine.

2 Wide as they sweep their sounding way,
They work thy sovereign will;
And awed by thy majestic voice,
Confusion shall be still.

3 Thy mercy tempers every blast
To those who seek thy face,
And mingles with the tempest's roar
The whispers of thy grace.

4 Those gentle whispers let us hear,
Till all the tumult cease,
And gales of Paradise shall lull
Our weary souls to peace.

248 Hymns of the Spirit.

"His Greatness is Unsearchable."

1 Great God, on whose sustaining power
Unnumbered worlds depend;
Great Spirit, comprehending all,
Whom none can comprehend, —

2 With wondering reverence we adore,
With awe before thee bend,
Whom none, but by thine inward light
And spirit, apprehend.

BOWEN. L. M.

HAYDN.

249

MRS. STEELE.

Being of God.

1 THERE is a God — all nature speaks,
Through earth, and air, and sea, and skies:
See, from the clouds his glory breaks,
When first the beams of morning rise.

2 The rising sun, serenely bright,
O'er the wide world's extended frame
Inscribes, in characters of light,
His mighty Maker's glorious name.

3 The blooming flowers in beauty rise
Above the weak attempts of art;
Their bright, inimitable dyes
Speak sweet conviction to the heart.

4 Ye curious minds, who roam abroad,
And trace creation's wonders o'er,
Confess the footsteps of a God;
Come, bow before him, and adore.

250

MRS. FOLLEN.

Divine Goodness seen in Nature.

1 GOD, thou art good! each perfumed flower,
The waving field, the dark green wood,
The insect fluttering for an hour, —
All things proclaim that God is good.

2 I hear it in each breath of wind:
The hills that have for ages stood,
And clouds with gold and silver lined,
All still repeat that God is good.

3 The countless hosts of twinkling stars,
That sing his praise with light renewed;
The rising sun each day declares,
In rays of glory, God is good.

4 The moon that walks in brightness says
That God is good! and man, endued
With power to speak his Maker's praise,
Doth still repeat that God is good.

251

STERLING.

God's Works.

1 THOU, Lord, who rear'st the mountain's height,
And mak'st the cliffs with sunshine bright,
Oh, grant that we may own thy hand
No less in every grain of sand!

2 With forests huge, of dateless time,
Thy will has hung each peak sublime;
But withered leaves beneath the tree
Have tongues that tell as loud of thee.

3 Teach us that not a leaf can grow
Till life from thee within it flow;
That not a grain of dust can be,
O Fount of being, save by thee.

4 That every human word and deed,
Each flash of feeling, will, or creed,
Hath solemn meaning from above,
Begun and ended all in love.

252

DODDRIDGE.

Divine Goodness.

1 TRIUMPHANT, Lord, thy goodness reigns,
Through all the wide celestial plains;
And its full streams redundant flow
Down to the abodes of men below.

2 Oh, give to every human heart
To taste and feel how good thou art;
With grateful love, and reverent fear,
To know how blest thy children are!

UXBRIDGE. L. M.

L. MASON.

253

J. WESLEY.

"The healthful Spirit of God's Grace."

1 SPIRIT of grace, and health, and power!
Fountain of light and love below!
Abroad thy healing influence shower;
On all thy servants let it flow.

2 Inflame our hearts with perfect love;
In us the work of faith fulfil:
So not heaven's host shall swifter move,
Than we on earth to do thy will.

3 Father! 'tis thine each day to yield
Thy children's wants a fresh supply;
Thou cloth'st the lilies of the field,
And hearest the young ravens cry.

4 On thee we cast our care; we live
Through thee who know'st our every need:
Oh, feed us with thy grace, and give
Our souls this day the living bread!

254

WATTS.

Nature and Scripture compared.

1 THE heavens declare thy glory, Lord;
In every star thy wisdom shines;
But when our eyes behold thy word,
We read thy name in fairer lines.

2 The rolling sun, the changing light,
And nights and days thy power confess;
But, lo! the volume thou hast writ
Reveals thy justice and thy grace.

3 Nor shall thy spreading gospel rest,
Till through the world thy truth has run;
Till Christ has all the nations blest,
That see the light or feel the sun.

255

GRANT.

Permanence of God's word.

1 THE starry firmament on high,
And all the glories of the sky,
Yet shine not to thy praise, O Lord,
So brightly as thy written word.

2 The hopes that holy word supplies,
Its truths divine and precepts wise,
In each a heavenly beam I see,
And every beam conducts to thee.

3 Almighty Lord, the sun shall fail,
The moon forget her nightly tale,
And deepest silence hush on high
The radiant chorus of the sky;—

4 But fixed for everlasting years,
Unmoved, amid the wreck of spheres,
Thy word shall shine in cloudless day,
When heaven and earth have passsed away.

256

WATTS.

"Up to the Hills I lift mine Eyes."

1 UP to the hills I lift mine eyes,
Th' eternal hills beyond the skies;
Thence all her help my soul derives,
There my almighty Refuge lives.

2 He lives—the everlasting God
That built the world, that spread the flood:
The heavens with all their hosts he made,
And the dark regions of the dead.

3 He guides our feet, he guards our way;
His morning smiles bless all the day:
He spreads the evening vail, and keeps
The silent hours, while Israel sleeps.

CEPHAS. L. M. Double. Dr. L. Mason.

257 ADDISON.

The Heavens declare the Glory of God.

1 THE spacious firmament on high,
With all the blue ethereal sky,
And spangled heavens, a shining frame,
Their great original proclaim.
Th' unwearied sun, from day to day,
Doth his Creator's power display;
And publishes to every land
The work of an Almighty hand.

2 Soon as the evening shades prevail,
The moon takes up the wondrous tale,
And nightly to the listening earth
Repeats the story of her birth: [burn,
Whilst all the stars which round her
And all the planets in their turn,
Confirm the tidings as they roll,
And spread the truth from pole to pole.

3 What though, in solemn silence, all
Move round this dark terrestrial ball;
What though no real voice nor sound
Amidst their radiant orbs be found;
In reason's ear they all rejoice,
And utter forth a glorious voice;
Forever singing, as they shine, —
"The hand that made us is divine."

258 T. MOORE.

Nature a Temple.

1 THE turf shall be my fragrant shrine;
My temple, Lord, that arch of thine;
My censer's breath the mountain airs,
And silent thoughts my only prayers.
My choir shall be the moonlit waves,
When murmuring homeward to their caves,
Or when the stillness of the sea,
E'en more than music, breathes of thee.

2 I'll seek, by day, some glade unknown,
All light and silence, like thy throne;
And the pale stars shall be, at night,
The only eyes that watch my rite.
Thy heaven, on which 'tis bliss to look,
Shall be my pure and shining book,
Where I can read in words of flame,
The glories of thy wondrous name.

3 There's nothing bright, above, below,
From flowers that bloom, to stars that glow,
But in its light my soul can see
Some feature of thy Deity.
There's nothing dark, below, above,
But in its gloom I trace thy love,
And meekly wait that moment when
Thy touch shall turn all bright again.

259

MRS. OPIE.

Uniting with Nature in God's Praise.

1 THERE seems a voice in every gale,
A tongue in every opening flower,
Which tells, O Lord, the wondrous tale
Of thine indulgence, love, and power.
The birds that rise on quivering wing
Appear to hymn their Maker's praise,
And all the mingling sounds of Spring
To thee a general pæan raise.

2 And shall my voice, great God, alone
Be mute 'mid Nature's loud acclaim?
No! let my heart, with answering tone,
Breathe forth in praise thy holy name.
And Nature's debt is small to mine —
Thou bad'st her being bounded be;
But (matchless proof of love divine!)
Thou gav'st immortal life to me.

3 The Saviour left his heavenly throne
A ransom for our souls to give;
Man's suffering state he made his own,
And deigned to die that we might live.
But thanks and praise for love so great
No mortal tongue can e'er express;
Then let me bow before thy feet,
In silence love thee, Lord, and bless.

260

ANON.

The Scriptures.

1 LAMP of our feet! whose hallowed beam
Deep in our hearts its dwelling hath,
How welcome is the cheering gleam
Thou sheddest o'er our lowly path!
Light of our way! whose rays are flung
In mercy o'er our pilgrim road,
How blessed, its dark shade among,
The star that guides us to our God.

2 In the sweet morning's hour of prime,
Thy blesséd word our lips engage;
And round our hearths at evening time
Our children spell the holy page;
The waymark through long distant years,
To guide their wandering footsteps on,
Till thy last loveliest beam appears,
Inscribed upon the churchyard stone.

3 Lamp of our feet! which day by day
Are passing to the quiet tomb,
If on it fall thy peaceful ray,
Our last low dwelling hath no gloom.
How beautiful their calm repose
To whom thy blesséd hope is given,
Whose pilgrimage on earth is closed
By the unfolding gates of heaven!

261

STERLING.

The two Temples.

1 WHEN up to nightly skies we gaze,
Where stars pursue their endless ways,
We think we see, from earth's low clod,
The wide and shining home of God.
But could we rise to moon or sun,
Or path where planets duly run,
Still heaven would spread above us far,
And earth, remote, would seem a star.

2 This earth, with all its dust and tears,
Is his no less than yonder spheres;
And rain-drops weak, and grains of sand,
Are stamped by his immediate hand.
But more than this, thou God benign,
Whose rays on us unclouded shine;
Thy breath sustains yon fiery dome,
But man is most thy favored home.

262

W. B. O. PEABODY.

God in Creation.

1 GOD of the rolling orbs above,
Thy name is written clearly bright
In the warm day's unvarying blaze,
Or evening's golden shower of light;
For every fire that fronts the sun,
And every spark that walks alone
Around the utmost verge of heaven,
Were kindled at thy burning throne.

2 God of the world, the hour must come,
And nature's self to dust return;
Her crumbling altars must decay;
Her incense-fires shall cease to burn.
But still her grand and lovely scenes
Have made man's warmest praises flow;
For hearts grow holier as they trace
The beauty of the world below.

263

WATTS.

Goodness of God to Soul and Body.

1 BLESS, O my soul! the living God;
Call home thy tho'ts that rove abroad:
Let all the powers within me join
In work and worship so divine.
Bless, O my soul! the God of grace;
His favors claim thy highest praise:
Why should the wonders he hath wrought
Be lost in silence and forgot?

WOODSTOCK. C. M.

DUTTON.

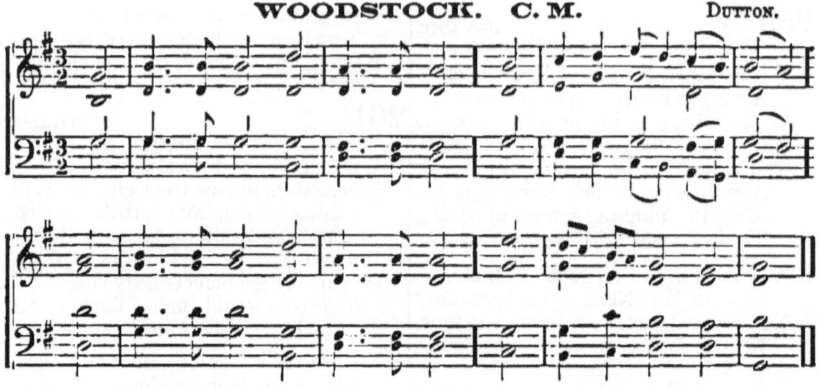

264

BARTON.

Value of the Scriptures.

1 Word of the ever-living God!
Will of his glorious Son!
Without thee how could earth be trod,
Or heaven itself be won?

2 Yet, to unfold thy hidden worth,
Thy mysteries to reveal,
That Spirit which first gave thee forth,
Thy volume must unseal!

3 And we, if we aright would learn
The wisdom it imparts,
Must to its heavenly teaching turn
With simple, childlike hearts!

265

RIPPON'S COLL.

Value of the Bible.

1 How precious is the book divine,
By inspiration given!
Bright as a lamp its doctrines shine,
To lead our souls to heaven.

2 O'er all the straight and narrow way
Its radiant beams are cast;
A light whose never waning ray
Grows brightest at the last.

3 It sweetly cheers our fainting hearts
In this dark vale of tears;
Life, light, and comfort it imparts,
And calms our anxious fears.

4 This lamp through all the dreary night
Of life shall guide our way,
Till we behold the glorious light
Of never-ending day.

266

STEELE.

The Bible suited to our Wants.

1 Father of mercies, in thy word
What endless glory shines!
Forever be thy name adored
For these celestial lines.

2 'T is here the Saviour's welcome voice
Speaks heavenly peace around,
And life, and everlasting joys,
Attend the blissful sound.

3 Oh, may these heavenly pages be
My ever dear delight;
And still new beauties may I see,
And still increasing light.

4 Divine Instructor, gracious Lord,
Be thou forever near;
Teach me to love thy sacred word
And view my Saviour here.

267

COWPER.

Glory of the Word.

1 A glory gilds the sacred page,
Majestic, like the sun;
It gives a light to every age;—
It gives, but borrows none.

2 The hand, that gave it, still supplies
The gracious light and heat;
Its truths upon the nations rise,—
They rise, but never set.

3 Let everlasting thanks be thine,
For such a bright display,
As makes a world of darkness shine
With beams of heavenly day.

PETERBOROUGH. C. M.

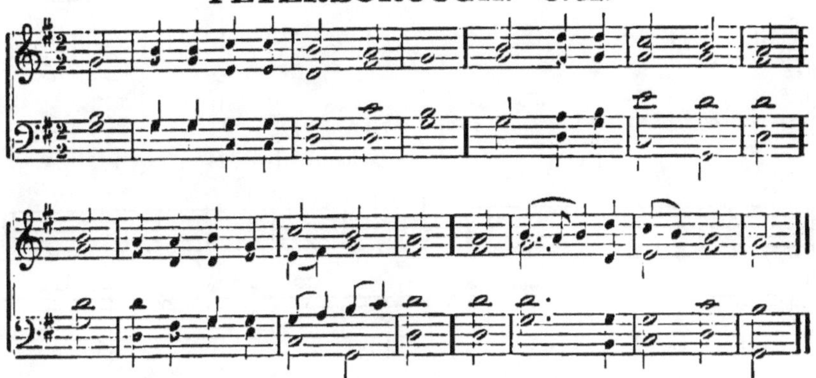

268 WATTS.

Comfort from the Bible.

1 Lord, I have made thy word my choice,
My lasting heritage;
There shall my noblest powers rejoice,
My warmest thoughts engage.

2 I'll read the histories of thy love,
And keep thy laws in sight,
While through the promises I rove,
With ever-fresh delight.

3 'T is a broad land of wealth unknown,
Where springs of life arise,
Seeds of immortal bliss are sown,
And hidden glory lies.

4 The best relief that mourners have,
It makes our sorrows blest;
Our fairest hope beyond the grave,
And our eternal rest.

269 WATTS.

Instruction from the Scriptures.

1 How shall the young secure their hearts,
And guard their lives from sin?
Thy word the choicest rules imparts
To keep the conscience clean.

2 When once it enters to the mind,
It spreads such light abroad,
The meanest souls instruction find,
And raise their thoughts to God.

3 'T is like the sun, a heavenly light
That guides us all the day;
And, through the dangers of the night,
A lamp to lead our way.

4 The starry heavens thy rule obey;
The earth maintains her place;
And these, thy servants, night and day,
Thy skill and power express.

5 But still thy law and gospel, Lord,
Have lessons more divine;
Not earth stands firmer than thy word,
Nor stars so nobly shine.

270 BARTON.

The Bible.

1 Lamp of our feet! whereby we trace
Our path when wont to stray;
Stream from the fount of heavenly grace!
Brook by the traveller's way!

2 Bread of our souls! whereon we feed;
True manna from on high!
Our guide and chart! wherein we read
Of realms beyond the sky.

3 Pillar of fire through watches dark,
And radiant cloud by day! [bark,
When waves would whelm our tossing
Our anchor and our stay!

4 Word of the everlasting God!
Will of his glorious Son!
Without thee how could earth be trod
And heaven itself be won?

5 Lord! grant us all aright to learn
The wisdom it imparts,
And to its heavenly teaching turn
With simple, childlike hearts.

BOYLSTON. S. M.

L. MASON.

271

BEDDOME.

The revealed Word.

1 O LORD, thy perfect word
Direct our steps aright;
Nor can all other books afford
Such profit or delight.

2 Celestial light it sheds,
To cheer this vale below;
To distant lands its glory spreads,
And streams of mercy flow.

3 True wisdom it imparts;
Commands our hope and fear;
Oh, may we hide it in our hearts,
And feel its influence there.

272

ANON.

"Good Tidings of great Joy."

1 SAVIOUR! what gracious words
Are ever, ever thine!
Thy voice is music to the soul,
And life and peace divine.

2 Good, everlasting good —
Glad tidings, full of joy,
Flow from thy lips, the lips of truth,
And flow without alloy.

3 The broken heart, the poor,
The bruised, the deaf, the blind,
The dumb, the dead, the captive wretch,
In thee compassion find.

4 Lord Jesus! speed the day —
The promised day of grace —
To all the poor, the dumb, the deaf,
The dead of Adam's race.

273

E. TAYLOR.

The Bible.

1 IT is the one true light,
When other lamps grow dim,
'T will never burn less purely bright,
Nor lead astray from Him.

2 It is Love's blessed band,
That reaches from the throne
To him —whoe'er he be— whose hand
Will seize it for his own!

3 It is the golden key
Unto celestial wealth,
Joy to the sons of poverty,
And to the sick man, health!

4 The gently proffered aid
Of one who knows and best
Supplies the beings he has made
With what will make them blessed.

5 It is the sweetest sound
That infant years can hear,
Travelling across that holy ground,
With God and angels near.

6 There rests the weary head,
There age and sorrow go;
And how it smooths the dying bed,
Oh! let the Christian show!

274

ANON.

"If God be for us, who can be against us?"

1 HERE I can firmly rest;
I dare to boast of this,
That God, the highest and the best,
My Friend and Father is.

CAMBRIDGE. C. M. Dr. RANDALL.

275 WATTS.

Prayer for Renewal.

1 COME, holy Spirit, heavenly Dove,
With all thy quickening powers,
Kindle a flame of sacred love
In these cold hearts of ours.

2 Look! how we grovel here below,
Fond of these trifling toys!
Our souls can neither fly nor go
To reach eternal joys.

3 In vain we tune our formal songs;
In vain we strive to rise;
Hosannas languish on our tongues,
And our devotion dies.

4 Dear Lord, and shall we ever live
At this poor dying rate —
Our love so faint, so cold to thee,
And thine to us so great!

5 Come, holy Spirit, heavenly Dove,
With all thy quickening powers,
Come, shed abroad a Saviour's love,
And that shall kindle ours.

276 S. F. SMITH.

Spirit of Holiness.

1 SPIRIT of holiness, descend;
Thy people wait for thee;
Thine ear in kind compassion lend;
Let us thy mercy see.

2 Behold thy weary churches wait,
With wistful, longing eyes;
Let us no more lie desolate:
Oh, bid thy light arise!

3 Thy light that on our souls hath shone,
Leads us in hope to thee;
Let us not feel its rays alone —
Alone thy people be.

4 Spirit of holiness, 't is thine
To hear our feeble prayer;
Come,— for we wait thy power divine,—
Let us thy mercy share.

277 COWPER.

Religious Retirement.

1 FAR from the world, O Lord! I flee,—
From strife and tumult far;
From scenes where sin is waging still
Its most successful war.

2 The calm retreat, the silent shade,
With prayer and praise agree,
And seem by thy sweet bounty made
For those who follow thee.

3 There, if thy spirit touch the soul,
And grace her mean abode,
Oh, with what peace, and joy, and love,
She communes with her God!

4 Author and guardian of my life,
Sweet source of light divine,
And all harmonious names in one,—
My Father, thou art mine!

278 LYTE.

Prayer for the Spirit.

1 SPIRIT of purity and grace,
Our weakness pitying see;
Oh, make our hearts thy dwelling-place,
Purer and worthier thee.

GOULD. C. M. MODERN HARP.

279

E. H. SEARS.

Christmas Hymn.

1 CALM on the listening ear of night,
Come heaven's melodious strains,
Where wild Judea stretches far
Her silver-mantled plains.

2 The answering hills of Palestine
Send back the glad reply;
And greet, from all their holy heights,
The dayspring from on high.

3 O'er the blue depths of Galilee
There comes a holier calm,
And Sharon waves, in solemn praise,
Her silent groves of palm.

4 "Glory to God!" the sounding skies
Loud with their anthems ring,—
"Peace to the earth,—good-will to men,
From heaven's eternal King!"

5 Light on thy hills, Jerusalem!
The Saviour now is born!
And bright on Bethlehem's joyous plains
Breaks the first Christmas morn.

280

BULFINCH.

Christ walking on the Sea.

1 LORD, in whose might the Saviour trod
The dark and stormy wave;
And trusted in his Father's arm,
Omnipotent to save;

2 When darkly round our footsteps rise
The floods and storms of life;
Send thou thy Spirit down to still
The dark and fearful strife.

281

MRS. HEMANS

"Peace! Be still!"

1 FEAR was within the tossing bark,
When stormy winds grew loud;
And waves came rolling high and dark,
And the tall mast was bowed.

2 And men stood breathless in their dread,
And baffled in their skill—
But One there was who rose and said
To the wild sea, "Be still!"

3 Thou that didst bow the billow's pride,
Thy mandates to fulfil—
Speak, speak to passion's raging tide,
Speak and say,—"Peace! be still!"

WATCHMAN. 7s, Double. L. MASON.

282

BOWRING.

Advent.

1 WATCHMAN! tell us of the night,
What its signs of promise are;
Traveller! o'er yon mountain's height,
See that glory-beaming star.
Watchman! does its beauteous ray
Aught of hope or joy foretell?
Traveller! yes; it brings the day,
Promised day of Israel.

2 Watchman! tell us of the night,
Higher yet that star ascends;
Traveller! blessedness and light,
Peace and truth, its course portends.
Watchman! will its beams alone
Gild the spot that gave them birth?
Traveller! ages are its own,
See, it bursts o'er all the earth.

3 Watchman! tell us of the night,
For the morning seems to dawn;
Traveller! darkness takes its flight,
Doubt and terror are withdrawn.
Watchman! let thy wanderings cease,
Hie thee to thy quiet home;
Traveller! lo! the Prince of Peace,
Lo! the Son of God is come.

283

ANON.

The Birth of Christ.

1 HARK! the herald-angels sing
Glory to the new-born King!
Peace on earth and mercy mild,
Man to God is reconciled.
Joyful, all ye nations, rise,
Join the triumphs of the skies;
With th' angelic hosts proclaim,
Christ is born in Bethlehem.

2 Mild he lays his glories by;
Born, that man no more may die;
Born, to raise the sons of earth;
Born, to give them second birth.
Hail the heaven-born Prince of Peace!
Hail the Sun of Righteousness!
Light and life to all he brings,
Risen with healing in his wings.

PILGRIM SONG. S. M.

MENDELSSOHN.

284

E. H. CHAPIN.

Christmas Hymn.

1 HARK! hark! with harps of gold,
What anthem do they sing? —
The radiant clouds have backward rolled,
And angels smite the string.
"Glory to God!" — bright wings
Spread glist'ning and afar,
And on the hallowed rapture rings
From circling star to star.

2 "Glory to God!" repeat
The glad earth and the sea;
And every wind and billow fleet
Bears on the jubilee.
Where Hebrew bard hath sung,
Or Hebrew seer hath trod;
Each holy spot has found a tongue:
"Let glory be to God."

3 Soft swells the music now
Along that shining choir,
And every seraph bends his brow
And breathes above his lyre.
What words of heavenly birth
Thrill deep our hearts again,
And fall like dew-drops to the earth?
"Peace and good-will to men!"

4 Soft! — yet the soul is bound
With rapture like a chain:
Earth, vocal, whispers them around,
And heaven repeats the strain.
Sound, harps, and hail the morn
With every golden string;
For unto us this day is born
A Saviour and a King!

285

ANON

Christ ascended.

1 THOU art gone up on high
To mansions in the skies,
And round thy throne unceasingly
The songs of praise arise.
But we are lingering here
With sin and care oppressed;
Lord! send thy promised Comforter,
And lead us to thy rest.

2 Thou art gone up on high!
But thou didst first come down,
Through earth's most bitter misery
To pass unto thy crown:
And girt with griefs and fears
Our onward course must be;
But only let that path of tears
Lead us, at last, to thee!

HARWELL. 8s & 7s Double.

286 CAWOOD.

Song of the Angels of Bethlehem.

1 HARK! what mean those holy voices,
Sweetly sounding through the skies?
Lo! th' angelic host rejoices;
Heavenly hallelujahs rise.
Listen to the wondrous story
Which they chant in hymns of joy;
"Glory in the highest, glory!
Glory be to God most high!

2 "Peace on earth, good-will from heaven,
Reaching far as man is found:
Souls redeemed and sins forgiven:—
Loud our golden harps shall sound.
Christ is born, the great Anointed;
Heaven and earth his praises sing!
Oh, receive whom God appointed
For your Prophet, Priest, and King."

287 ANON.

Praise for a Saviour.

1 LET our songs of praise ascending,
Rise to thee, O God most high;
While before thee, humbly bending,
Glory to thy name we cry.
With the shepherds in the story,
Let our hearts to Bethlehem go,
Where the Lord of life and glory,
In a manger lieth low.

2 Age to age thy glory beareth
On the stream of time abroad;
Race to race thy name declareth,
Son of Mary! Son of God!
Heaven exults and earth rejoices
In the work that thou hast wrought;
Lord, attune our trembling voices,
Let us praise thee as we ought.

288 ELIM.

Christ Risen.

1 ALLELUIA! alleluia!
Hearts to heaven and voices raise;
Sing to God a hymn of gladness,
Sing to God a hymn of praise.
He who on the cross a victim
For the world's salvation bled,—
Jesus Christ, the King of Glory,—
Now is risen from the dead.

2 Now the iron bars are broken,
Christ from death to life is born,—
Glorious life and life immortal,—
On this holy Easter morn.
Christ has triumphed, and we conquer
By his mighty enterprise;
We with Christ to life eternal,
By his resurrection, rise.

3 Christ is risen, we are risen:
Shed upon us heavenly grace,
Rain and dew, and gleams of glory,
From the brightness of thy face.
Grant that we, with hearts in heaven,
Here on earth may fruitful be,
And by angel-hands be gathered,
And be ever safe with thee.

FOLSOM. 11s & 10s. Arr. by Dr. Mason.

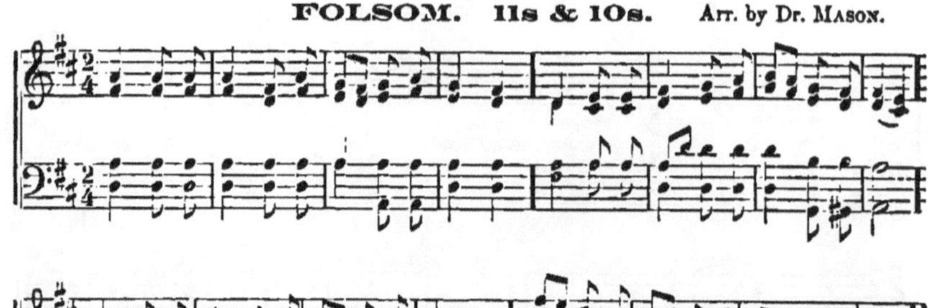

289

Heber.

Star of the East.

1 Brightest and best of the sons of the morning,
Dawn on our darkness and lend us thine aid;
Star of the East, — the horizon adorning, —
Guide where the infant Redeemer is laid.

2 Cold on his cradle the dew-drops are shining;
Low lies his head with the beasts of the stall;
Angels bend o'er him, in slumber reclining, —
Monarch, Redeemer, Restorer of all.

3 Say, shall we yield him in costly devotion,
Odors of Edom, and offerings divine?
Gems of the mountain, and pearls of the ocean,
Myrrh from the forest, or gold from the mine?

4 Vainly we offer each ample oblation,
Vainly with gold would his favor secure;
Richer by far is the heart's adoration,
Dearer to God are the prayers of the poor.

5 Brightest and best of the sons of the morning,
Dawn on our darkness and lend us thine aid;
Star of the East, — the horizon adorning, —
Guide where the infant Redeemer is laid.

290

Anon.

Arise, shine, for thy Light is come.

1 Daughter of Zion! awake from thy sadness;
Wake, for thy foes shall oppress thee no more;
Bright o'er thy hills dawns the daystar of gladness;
Rise! for the night of thy sorrow is o'er.

2 Strong were thy foes, but the arm that subdued them,
Scatt'ring their legions, was mightier far;
Flying like chaff, from the scourge that pursued them;
Vain were their steeds and their chariots of war!

3 Daughter of Zion! the power that hath saved thee,
Praised with the harp and the timbrel should be:
Shout! for the foe is destroyed that enslaved thee,
Tyranny's vanquished, and Zion is free!

TELEMANN'S CHANT. 7s. CH. ZEUNER.

291 HENRY C. LEONARD.

Hymn for Christmas Eve.

1 BELLS, ring out with cheerful might;
Tapers, burn with brilliant flame;
Organs, play glad hymns to-night;
Voices, chant with loud acclaim.

2 Hands, adorn the sacred wall;
Twine the wreath, and braid the vine;
And upraise the fir-tree tall;
Minstrels, sing the glowing line.

3 For the blessed eve has come,
Star-lit, bright as none before;
Magi seek the Saviour's home;
Shepherds find his humble door.

4 With your outward rites and gifts,
Let the heart to Christ be given;
For the heart his power uplifts,
Leading it to truth and heaven.

5 Offering from hand or lip,
Like the ointment Mary poured,
Meaneth inward fellowship
With the Saviour, Christ the Lord.

292 ANCIENT HYMNS.

Rejoicing in Christ.

1 SWEET thy memory, Saviour blest,
In the true believer's breast;
Musing on thy precious name,
Purest joys his heart inflame.

2 By the ear or tuneful tongue
Naught so sweet is heard or sung;
Naught the mind can dwell upon
Sweet as God's belovéd Son.

3 Tongue can speak not their delight,
Nor can pen of man indite;
None can know but they who prove,
What it is their Lord to love.

293 GIBBONS.

The Saviour's Resurrection.

1 ANGELS, roll the rock away;
Death, yield up thy mighty prey:
See! he rises from the tomb —
Rises with immortal bloom.

2 'T is the Saviour; seraphs, raise
Your triumphant shouts of praise;
Let the earth's remotest bound
Hear the joy-inspiring sound.

3 Praise him, all ye heavenly choirs,
Praise him with your golden lyres;
Praise him in your noblest songs;
Praise him from ten thousand tongues.

294 ANON.

Resurrection of Christ.

1 CHRIST, the Lord, is risen to-day,
Our triumphant, holy day;
He endured the cross and grave,
Sinners to redeem and save.

2 Lo! he rises, mighty King!
Where, O death! is now thy sting?
Lo! he claims his native sky!
Grave! where is thy victory?

3 Christ, the Lord, is risen to-day,
Our triumphant holy day;
Loud the song of victory raise:
Shout the great Redeemer's praise.

HAMBURG. L. M.

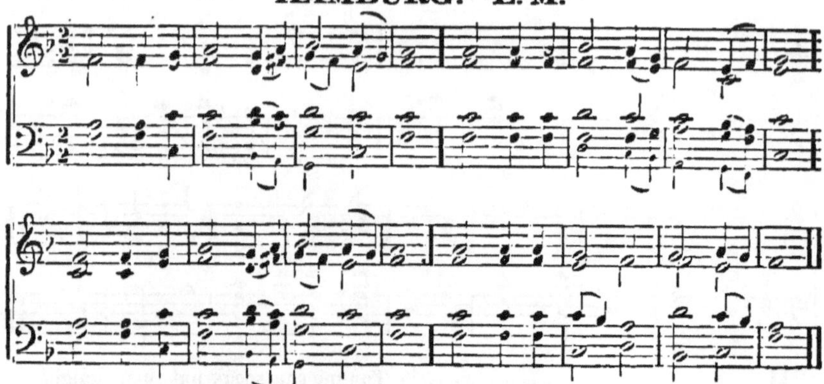

295 BACHE.

"Greater Love hath no Man than this."

1 "See how he loved!" exclaimed the Jews,
As tender tears from Jesus fell;
My grateful heart the thought pursues,
And on the theme delights to dwell.

2 See how he loved, who travelled on,
Teaching the doctrine from the skies;
Who bade disease and pain be gone,
And called the sleeping dead to rise.

3 See how he loved, who, firm yet mild,
Patient endured the scoffing tongue!
Though oft provoked, he ne'er reviled,
Or did his greatest foe a wrong.

4 See how he loved, who never shrank
From toil or danger, pain or death;
Who all the cup of sorrow drank,
And meekly yielded up his breath.

5 Such love can we unmoved survey?
Oh, may our breasts with ardor glow,
To tread his steps, his laws obey,
And thus our warm affections show.

296 BUTCHER.

Miracles of Christ.

1 On eyes that never saw the day
Christ pours the bright celestial ray;
And deafened ears by him unbound
Catch all the harmony of sound.

2 Lameness takes up its bed, and goes
Rejoicing in the strength that flows
Through every nerve; and, free from pain,
Pours forth to God the grateful strain.

3 The shattered mind his word restores,
And tunes afresh the mental powers;
The dead revive, to life return,
And bid affection cease to mourn.

4 Canst thou, my soul, these wonders trace,
And not admire Jehovah's grace?
Canst thou behold thy Prophet's power,
And not the God he served adore?

297 RUSSELL.

"That ye through his Poverty might be Rich."

1 On the dark wave of Galilee
The gloom of twilight gathers fast,
And o'er the waters drearily
Descends the fitful evening blast.

2 The weary bird hath left the air,
And sunk into his sheltered nest;
The wandering beast has sought his lair,
And laid him down to welcome rest.

3 Still, near the lake, with weary tread,
Lingers a form of human kind;
And on his lone, unsheltered head,
Flows the chill night-damp of the wind

4 Why seeks he not a home of rest?
Why seeks he not a pillowed bed?
Beasts have their dens, the bird its nest:
He hath not where to lay his head.

5 Such was the lot he freely chose,
To bless, to save the human race;
And through his poverty there flows
A rich, full stream of heavenly grace.

WARD. L. M. Arr. by Dr. Mason.

298 HEBER.

The Holy Guest.

1 Messiah Lord! who, wont to dwell
In lowly shape and cottage cell,
Didst not refuse a guest to be
At Cana's poor festivity.

2 Oh, when our soul from care is free,
Then, Saviour, would we think on thee;
And, seated at the festal board,
In fancy's eye behold the Lord.

3 Then may we seem, in fancy's ear,
Thy manna-dropping tongue to hear,
And think, — "If now his searching view
Each secret of our spirit knew!"

4 So may such joy, chastised and pure,
Beyond the bounds of earth endure;
Nor pleasure in the wounded mind
Shall leave a rankling sting behind.

299 MILMAN.

Christ's Entry into Jerusalem.

1 Ride on, ride on in majesty!
Hark! all the tribes hosannas cry!
Thy humble beast pursues his road,
With palms and scattered garments strewed.

2 Ride on, ride on in majesty!
In lowly pomp ride on to die!
O Christ! thy triumphs now begin,
O'er captive death and conquered sin.

3 Ride on, ride on in majesty!
The wingéd squadrons of the sky
Look down with sad and wondering eyes,
To see th' approaching sacrifice.

4 Ride on, ride on in majesty!
Thy last and fiercest strife is nigh;
The Father on his sapphire throne
Expects his own anointed Son!

300 MONTGOMERY.

His Submission.

1 Lord! in thy garden agony,
No light seemed on thy soul to break,
No form of seraph lingered nigh,
Nor yet the voice of comfort spake, —

2 Till, by thy own triumphant word,
The victory over ill was won;
Till the sweet, mournful cry was heard,
"Thy will, O God, not mine, be done!"

3 Lord, bring these precious moments back,
When, fainting, against sin we strain;
Or in thy counsels fail to track
Aught but the present grief and pain.

4 In weakness, help us to contend;
In darkness yield to God our will;
And true hearts, faithful to the end,
Cheer by thy holy angels still!

301 CHR. PSALM.ST.

Behold the Man!

1 Behold the man, — how glorious he!
Before his foes he stands unawed;
And, without wrong or blasphemy,
He claims to be the Son of God.

2 Behold the man! though scorned below,
He bears the greatest name above;
The angels at his footstool bow,
And all his royal claims approve.

ASHWELL. L. M.

302

GASKELL.

Christ the Sufferer.

1 DARK were the paths our Master trod,
Yet never failed his trust in God;
Cruel and fierce the wrongs he bore,
Yet he but felt for man the more.

2 Unto the cross in faith he went,
His Father's willing instrument;
Upon the cross his prayer arose
In pity for his ruthless foes.

3 Oh, may we all his kindred be,
By holy love and sympathy;
Still loving man through every ill,
And trusting in our Father's will!

303

LYRA CATH.

Christ Crucified.

1 HAVE we no tears to shed for him,
While soldiers scoff and Jews deride?
Ah! look how patiently he hangs —
Jesus, our love, is crucified!

2 What was thy crime, my dearest Lord?
By earth, by heaven, thou hast been tried,
And guilty found of too much love;
Jesus, our love, is crucified!

3 Found guilty of excess of love,
It was thine own sweet will that tied
Thee tighter far than helpless nails;
Jesus, our love, is crucified!

4 O break, O break, hard heart of mine!
Thy weak self-love and guilty pride
His Pilate and his Judas were;
Jesus, our love, is crucified!

5 A broken heart, a fount of tears —
Ask, and they will not be denied,
A broken heart love's cradle is;
Jesus, our love, is crucified!

304

STENNETT.

Christ Suffering on the Cross.

1 "'T IS finished!" — So the Saviour cried,
And meekly bowed his head and died;
"'T is finished!" — yes, the race is run,
The battle fought, the victory won.

2 "'T is finished!" — all that heaven foretold
By prophets in the days of old;
And truths are opened to our view,
That kings and prophets never knew.

3 "'T is finished!" — Son of God, thy power
Hath triumphed in this awful hour;
And yet our eyes with sorrow see
That life to us was death to thee.

4 "'T is finished!" — let the joyful sound
Be heard through all the nations round;
"'T is finished!" — let the triumph rise,
And swell the chorus of the skies.

305

ANON.

Christ our Strength.

1 WITH tearful eyes I look around,
Life seems a dark and stormy sea;
Yet, 'midst the gloom, I hear a sound,
A heavenly whisper, "Come to Me."

2 Oh, voice of mercy! voice of love!
In conflict, grief, and agony,
Support me, cheer me from above!
And gently whisper, "Come to Me."

ROSEFIELD. 7s, 6 ls. Arr. by Dr. MASON.

306

MONTGOMERY.

Example in Suffering.

1 Go to dark Gethsemane,
Ye that feel temptation's power;
Your Redeemer's conflict see;
Watch with him one bitter hour:
Turn not from his griefs away;
Learn of Jesus Christ to pray.

2 Follow to the judgment-hall;
View the Lord of life arraigned:
Oh, the wormwood and the gall!
Oh, the pangs his soul sustained!
Shun not suffering, shame, or loss;
Learn of him to bear the cross.

3 Calvary's mournful mountain climb;
There, admiring at his feet,
Mark that miracle of time,
God's own sacrifice complete:
"It is finished," hear him cry;
Learn of Jesus Christ to die.

4 Early hasten to the tomb
Where they lay his breathless clay;
All in solitude and gloom:
Who has taken him away?
Christ is risen; he meets our eyes:
Saviour, teach us so to rise!

307

BULFINCH.

It is finished.

1 It is finished, — glorious word
From thy lips, our suffering Lord;
Word of high, triumphant might,
Ere thy spirit takes its flight.
It is finished: all is o'er;
Pain and scorn oppress no more.

2 Now no more foreboding dread
Shades the path thy feet must tread;
No more fear lest, in thine hour,
Pain should patience overpower:
On the perfect sacrifice
Not a stain of weakness lies.

3 Champion, lay thine armor by;
'T is thine hour of victory:
All thy toils are now o'erpast;
Thou hast found thy rest at last;
All hath faithfully been done,
And the world's salvation won.

308

ANON.

Gethsemane.

1 Many woes had Christ endured,
Many sore temptations met,
Patient and to pains inured;
But the sorest trial yet
Was to be sustained in thee,
Gloomy, sad Gethsemane!

2 Came at length the dreadful night;
Sinners, with an iron rod,
Stood, and with collected might,
Bruised the harmless Lamb of God:
See, my soul, thy Saviour see
Prostrate in Gethsemane!

BAILEY. 8s & 7s.

309

BOWRING.

Glorying in the Cross.

1 In the cross of Christ I glory,
Towering o'er the wrecks of time;
All the light of sacred story
Gathers round its head sublime.
When the woes of life o'ertake me,
Hopes deceive, and fears annoy,
Never shall the cross forsake me;
Lo! it glows with peace and joy.

2 When the sun of bliss is beaming
Light and love upon my way,
From the cross the radiance streaming
Adds new lustre to the day.
Bane and blessing, pain and pleasure,
By the cross are sanctified;
Peace is there that knows no measure,
Joys that through all time abide.

310

LYRA CATH.

At the Cross.

1 Sweet the moments, rich in blessing,
Which before the cross I spend;
Life, and health, and peace possessing
From the sinner's dying Friend:
Here alone I find my heaven,
Humbly on the Lamb to gaze;
Feel how much has been forgiven,
To his own eternal praise!

2 Love and grief my heart dividing,
Here I'll spend my latest breath;
Constant still in faith abiding,
Life deriving from his death.
May I still enjoy this feeling,
In all need, to Jesus go,
Prove each day his wounds more healing,
And himself more deeply know!

311

NEVIN.

"I am with you alway."

1 Always with us, always with us,—
Words of cheer and words of love;
Thus the risen Saviour whispers,
From his dwelling-place above.
With us when we toil in sadness,
Sowing much and reaping none;
Telling us that in the future
Golden harvests shall be won.

2 With us when the storm is sweeping
O'er our pathway dark and drear;
Waking hope within our bosoms,
Stilling every anxious fear.
With us in the lonely valley,
When we cross the chilling stream;
Lighting up the steps to glory
With salvation's radiant beam.

TRUMPET. P. M.

312 H. Ware.

Easter Hymn.

1 Lift your glad voices in triumph on high,
For Jesus hath risen, and man cannot die.
Vain were the terrors that gathered around him,
And short the dominion of death and the grave; [that bound him,
He burst from the fetters of darkness
Resplendent in glory, to live and to save.
Loud was the chorus of angels on high,— [shall not die."
"The Saviour hath risen, and man

2 Glory to God, in full anthems of joy;
The being he gave us death cannot destroy. [morrow,
Sad were the life we must part with to-
If tears were our birthright, and death were our end;
But Jesus hath cheered the dark valley of sorrow,
And bade us, immortal, to heaven ascend.
Lift, then, your voices in triumph on high,
For Jesus hath risen, and man shall not die.

NURERMBURG. 7s. Arr. by Dr. Mason.

313
MADAN.

Christ's Resurrection.

1 Hail the day that sees him rise,
Glorious, to his native skies!
Christ, awhile to mortals given,
Enters now the gates of heaven.

2 There the glorious triumph waits;
Lift your heads, eternal gates!
Christ hath vanquished death and sin;
Take the King of glory in.

3 See, the heaven our Lord receives!
Yet he loves the earth he leaves:
Though returning to his throne,
Still he calls mankind his own.

4 What, though parted from our sight,
Far above yon starry height;
Thither our affections rise,
Following him beyond the skies.

314
Louisa, Electress of Brandenburg, 1653.

"I know that my Redeemer liveth."

1 Jesus, my Redeemer, lives,
Christ, my trust, is dead no more;
In the strength this knowledge gives
Shall not all my fears be o'er?

2 Close to him my soul is bound
In the bonds of hope enclasped;
Faith's strong hand this hold hath found,
And the rock hath firmly grasped.

3 Jesus, my Redeemer, lives,
And his life I once shall see:
Bright the hope this promise gives,
Where he is, I, too, shall be.

315
H. C. Leonard.

"The Lord is my Shepherd."

1 Shepherd of the holy hills,
We, thy lambs, with tender feet,
Follow thee beside the rills,
And through pastures green and sweet.

2 Thou dost hear us when we cry;
Thou dost watch us when alone:
When we faint, thou drawest nigh,
Soothing us with winning tone.

3 Thus, through all our earthly day,—
Be our guard and only guide;
Keep us from the evil way;
Keep us ever by thy side.

4 And, when fall the shades of night
On the path we tread below,
Take us to the fields of light,
Where the living waters flow.

316
Collyer.

Resurrection of Christ.

1 Morning breaks upon the tomb,
Jesus dissipates its gloom;
Day of triumph through the skies,
See the glorious Saviour rise!

2 Christians, dry your flowing tears;
Chase those unbelieving fears;
Look on his deserted grave;
Doubt no more his power to save.

3 Ye who are of death afraid,
Triumph in the scattered shade;
Drive your anxious fears away:
See the place where Jesus lay!

HEBER. C. M. GEO. KINGSLEY.

317
ANON.

The Way, the Truth, the Life.

1 Thou art the way;— to thee alone
From sin and death we flee;
And he who would the Father seek
Must seek him, Lord, in thee.

2 Thou art the truth;— thy word alone
True wisdom can impart;
Thou only canst instruct the mind,
And purify the heart.

3 Thou art the life; the rending tomb
Proclaims thy conquering arm;
And those who put their trust in thee,
Not death nor hell shall harm.

4 Thou art the way, the truth, the life;—
Grant us to know that way,
That truth to keep, that life to win,
Which leads to endless day.

318
DODDRIDGE.

The gentle Shepherd.

1 See Israel's gentle Shepherd stand
With all-engaging charms;
Hark, how he calls the tender lambs,
And folds them in his arms.

2 Permit them to approach, he cries,
Nor scorn their humble name;
For 't was to bless such souls as these
The Lord of angels came.

3 Ye little flock, with pleasure hear;
Ye children, seek his face;
And fly with transport to receive
The blessings of his grace.

319
LITCHFIELD'S COLL.

The Shepherd of the Fold.

1 There is a little lonely fold,
Whose flock one Shepherd keeps,
Through summer's heat and winter's cold,
With eye that never sleeps.

2 By evil beast, or burning sky,
Or damp of midnight air,
Not one in all that flock shall die
Beneath that Shepherd's care.

3 For if, unheeding or beguiled,
In danger's path they roam,
His pity follows through the wild,
And guards them safely home.

4 O gentle Shepherd, still behold
Thy helpless charge in me;
And take a wanderer to thy fold,
Who trembling turns to thee.

320
J. G. WHITTIER.

He that hath seen me hath seen the Father.

1 O Love! O Life! our faith and sight
Thy presence maketh one:
As, through transfigured clouds of white,
We trace the noon-day sun,—

2 So, to our mortal eyes subdued,
Flesh-veiled, but not concealed,
We know in thee the fatherhood
And heart of God revealed.

3 We faintly hear, we dimly see,
In differing phrase we pray;
But, dim or clear, we own in thee
The Light, the Truth, the Way.

SHOEL. L. M.

SHOEL.

321

WATTS.

Corner-Stone.

1 Lo, what a precious Corner-Stone
The Jewish builders did refuse!
But God hath built his church thereon,
And bless'd the Gentiles with the Jews.

2 Great God, the work is all divine,
The joy and wonder of our eyes!
This is the day that proves it thine,—
The day that saw our Saviour rise.

3 Sinners, rejoice, and, saints, be glad;
Hosanna! let his name be blest;
A thousand honors on his head,
With peace, and light, and glory rest.

4 In God's own name he comes to bring
Salvation to our sinful race;
Let all on earth address their King,
With hearts of joy and songs of praise.

322

DODDRIDGE.

Knocking at the Door.

1 BEHOLD a stranger at the door!
He gently knocks— has knocked before;
Has waited long — is waiting still;
You treat no other friend so ill.

2 O lovely attitude! — he stands
With melting heart and loaded hands;
O matchless kindness! — and he shows
This matchless kindness to his foes.

3 Rise — touched with gratitude divine,
Turn out his enemy and thine,—
That soul-destroying monster, sin,—
And let the heavenly stranger in.

323

MEDLEY.

Praise for his Loving-Kindness.

1 AWAKE, my soul, in joyful lays,
And sing the great Redeemer's praise:
He justly claims a song from me —
His loving-kindness, oh, how free!

2 He saw me dead in sin and thrall,
Yet loved me, notwithstanding all;
He saved me from my lost estate —
His loving-kindness, oh, how great!

3 When trouble, like a gloomy cloud,
Has gathered thick and thundered loud,
He near my soul has always stood —
His loving-kindness, oh, how good!

4 Soon shall I pass the gloomy vale,
Soon all my mortal powers must fail;
Oh, may my last expiring breath
His loving-kindness sing in death!

324

WATTS.

Example of Christ.

1 MY dear Redeemer, and my Lord,
I read my duty in thy word:
But in thy life the law appears,
Drawn out in living characters.

2 Such was thy truth, and such thy zeal,
Such deference to thy Father's will,
Such love, and meekness so divine,
I would transcribe, and make them mine.

3 Be thou my pattern; may I bear
More of thy gracious image here;
Then God, the Judge, shall own my name
Among the followers of the Lamb.

ROCK OF AGES. 7s, 6 ls. Dr. Hastings.

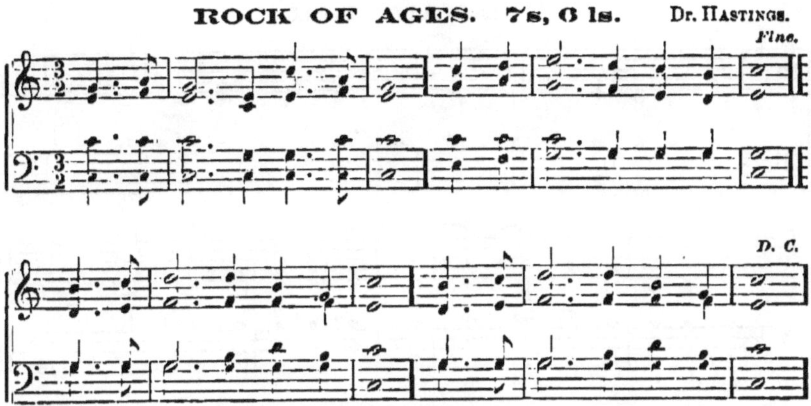

325 C. Wesley.

Sun of Righteousness.

1 Christ, whose glory fills the skies,
Christ, the true, the only light,
Sun of Righteousness, arise,
Triumph o'er the shades of night;
Day-spring from on high, be near,
Day-star, in my heart appear.

2 Dark and cheerless is the morn,
If thy light is hid from me;
Joyless is the day's return,
Till thy mercy's beams I see;
Till thy inward light impart
Warmth and gladness to my heart.

3 Visit, then, this soul of mine;
Pierce the gloom of sin and grief;
Fill me, radiant Sun divine;
Scatter all my unbelief;
More and more thyself display,
Shining to the perfect day.

326 Toplady.

Rock of Ages.

1 Rock of Ages, cleft for me,
Let me hide myself in thee!
Let the water and the blood,
From thy wounded side which flowed,
Be of sin the double cure,
Cleanse me from its guilt and power.

2 Nothing in my hand I bring;
Simply to thy cross I cling;
Naked, come to thee for dress;
Helpless, look to thee for grace;
Sinful, to thy fountain fly;
Wash me, Saviour, or I die!

327 Kelly.

Our King.

1 Glory, glory to our King!
Crowns unfading wreathe his head;
Jesus is the name we sing—
Jesus, risen from the dead;
Jesus, conqueror o'er the grave;
Jesus, mighty now to save.

2 Now behold him high enthroned,
Glory beaming from his face,
By adoring angels owned,
God of holiness and grace:
Oh, for hearts and tongues to sing,
Glory, glory, to our King!

328 Newton.

Christ's Help in Conflicts.

1 Once I thought my mountain strong,
Firmly fixed, no more to move;
Then my Saviour was my song,
Then my soul was filled with love:
Those were happy, golden days,
Sweetly spent in prayer and praise.

2 Saviour! shine and cheer my soul,
Bid my dying hopes revive;
Make my wounded spirit whole;
Far away the tempter drive:
Speak the word, and set me free:
Let me live alone to thee.

ERNAN. L. M.

L. MASON.

329

TENNYSON.

Strong Son of God.

1 STRONG Son of God, immortal Love,
Whom we, that have not seen thy face,
By faith, and faith alone, embrace,
Believing where we cannot prove!

2 Thou seemest human and divine,
The highest, holiest manhood, thou:
Our wills are ours, we know not how,
Our wills are ours, to make them thine.

3 Our little systems have their day;
They have their day and cease to be;
They are but broken lights of thee,
And thou, O Lord, art more than they.

330

S. STREETER.

Our King.

1 A KING shall reign in righteousness,
And all the kindred nations bless;
He's King of Salem, King of peace,
Nor shall his spreading kingdom cease.

2 In him the naked soul shall find
A hiding-place from chilling wind;
Or, when the raging tempests beat,
A covert warm, a safe retreat.

3 In burning sands and thirsty ground,
He like a river shall be found,
Or lofty rock, beneath whose shade
The weary traveller rests his head.

4 The dimness gone, all eyes shall see
His glory, grace, and majesty;
All ears shall hearken, and the word
Of life receive, from Christ the Lord.

331

MASON.

The Image of the invisible God.

1 THOU, Lord! by mortal eyes unseen,
And by thine offspring here unknown,
To manifest thyself to men,
Hast set thine image in thy Son.

2 Though Jews, who granted not his claim,
Contemptuous turned away their face,
Yet those who trusted in his name
Beheld in him thy truth and grace.

3 O thou! at whose almighty word
Fair light at first from darkness shone,
Teach us to know our glorious Lord,
And trace the Father in the Son.

4 While we, thine image there displayed,
With love and admiration view,
Form us in likeness to our Head,
That we may bear thine image too.

332

ANON.

The Lord known to All.

1 MARKED as the purpose of the skies,
This promise meets our anxious eyes,
That heathen lands the Lord shall know,
And warm with faith each bosom glow.

2 Ev'n now the hallowed scenes appear;
Ev'n now unfolds the promised year;
Lo! distant shores thy heralds trace,
And bear the tidings of thy grace.

3 When, worn by toil, their spirits fail,
Bid them the glorious future hail;
Bid them the crown of life survey,
And onward urge their conq'ring way.

EXHORTATION. C. M.

(In singing hymns 333 and 334, repeat last two lines of each verse.)

333 FABER.

Pentecost.

1 No track is on the sunny sky,
No footprints on the air:
Jesus hath gone; the face of earth
Is desolate and bare.

2 That Upper Room is heaven on earth;
Within its precincts lie
All that earth has of faith, or hope,
Or heaven-born charity.

3 He comes! He comes! that mighty breath
From the eternal shores;
His uncreated freshness fills
His church as it adores!

4 One moment—and the Spirit hung
O'er all with dread desire;
Then broke upon the heads of all
In cloven tongues of fire.

334 MRS. STEELE.

Christ's Exaltation.

1 Now with eternal glory crowned,
Our Lord, the conqueror, reigns;
His praise the heavenly choirs resound,
In their immortal strains.

2 Amid the splendors of his throne,
Unchanging love appears;
The names he purchased for his own
Still on his heart he bears.

3 Oh, the rich depths of love divine!
Of bliss, a boundless store;
Dear Saviour, let me call thee mine;
I cannot wish for more.

4 On thee alone, my hope relies;
Beneath thy cross I fall,
My Lord, my Life, my Sacrifice,
My Saviour, and my All.

MIGDOL. L. M.

335

ANON.

"He ever liveth."

1 I KNOW that my Redeemer lives,—
What joy the blest assurance gives!
He lives, he lives, who once was dead;
He lives, my everlasting Head!

2 He lives, to bless me with his love;
He lives, to plead for me above;
He lives, my hungry soul to feed;
He lives, to help in time of need.

3 He lives, and grants me daily breath;
He lives, and I shall conquer death;
He lives, my mansion to prepare;
He lives, to bring me safely there.

4 He lives, all glory to his name;
He lives, my Saviour still the same;
What joy the blest assurance gives,—
I know that my Redeemer lives!

336

H. BALLOU.

Example in Forgiving.

1 TEACH us to feel as Jesus prayed,
When on the cross he bleeding hung;
When all his foes their wrath displayed,
And with their spite his bosom stung.

2 Till death, he loved his foes, and said,
"Father, forgive,"—then groaned and died;
And when arisen from the dead,
His mercy to their souls applied.

3 For such a heart and such a love,
O Lord, we raise our prayer to thee;
Oh, pour thy spirit from above,
That we may like our Saviour be.

337

A. C. COXE.

Christ our Example.

1 How beauteous were the marks divine,
That in thy meekness used to shine;
That lit thy lonely pathway, trod
In wondrous love, O Son of God!

2 Oh, who like thee, so calm, so bright,
So pure, so made to live in light?
Oh, who like thee, did ever go
So patient through a world of woe?

3 Oh, who like thee, so humbly bore
The scorn, the scoffs of men, before?
So meek, forgiving, godlike, high,
So glorious in humility?

4 Oh, in thy light be mine to go,
Illuming all my way of woe!
And give me ever on the road
To trace thy footsteps, Son of God!

338

J. WESLEY

Renouncing all for Christ.

1 COME, Saviour, Jesus, from above,
Assist me with thy heavenly grace;
Empty my heart of earthly love,
And for thyself prepare the place.

2 Oh, let thy sacred presence fill,
And set my longing spirit free;
Which pants to have no other will,
But night and day to live for thee.

3 Henceforth may no profane delight
Divide this consecrated soul;
Possess it thou, who hast the right,
As Lord and Master of the whole.

MARTYN. 7s, Double.

339

WESLEY.

The True Refuge.

1 Jesus, lover of my soul,
Let me to thy bosom fly,
While the billows near me roll,
While the tempest still is high;
Hide me, O my Saviour, hide,
Till the storm of life is past,
Safe into the haven guide;
Oh, receive my soul at last!

2 Other refuge have I none —
Hangs my helpless soul on thee;
Leave, oh! leave me not alone,
Still support and comfort me;
All my trust on thee is stayed,
All my help from thee I bring;
Cover my defenceless head
With the shadow of thy wing.

340

ANON.

Salvation by Redeeming Love.

1 Now begin the heavenly theme,
Sing aloud in Jesus' name:
Ye, who his salvation prove,
Triumph in redeeming love.
Ye, who see the Father's grace
Beaming in the Saviour's face,
As to Canaan on ye move,
Praise and bless redeeming love.

2 Welcome, all by sin oppressed,
Welcome to his sacred rest:
Nothing brought him from above,
Nothing but redeeming love.
When his spirit leads us home,
When we to his glory come,
We shall all the fulness prove
Of our Lord's redeeming love.

341

GERMAN.

Beauty of Christ.

1 Earth has nothing sweet or fair,
Lovely forms or beauties rare,
But before my eyes they bring,
Christ, of beauty, Source and Spring.
When the morning paints the skies,
When the golden sunbeams rise,
Then my Saviour's form I find
Brightly imaged on my mind.

342

ANON.

Nearness of Christ.

1 Mary to the Saviour's tomb,
Hasted at the early dawn,
Spice she brought, and sweet perfume,
But the Lord she loved had gone.
Trembling, while a crystal flood
Issued from her weeping eyes,
For a while she lingering stood,
Filled with sorrow and surprise.

2 But her sorrows quickly fled
When she heard his welcome voice;
Christ had risen from the dead;
Now he bids her heart rejoice;
What a change his word can make,
Turning darkness into day;
Ye who weep for Jesus' sake,
He will wipe your tears away.

COWPER. C. M.

343

WATTS.

Our High Priest.

1 WITH joy we meditate the grace
Of our High Priest above:
His heart is full of tenderness;
His bosom glows with love.

2 Touched with a sympathy within,
He knows our feeble frame;
He knows what sore temptations mean,
For he has felt the same.

3 He, in the days of feeble flesh,
Poured out his cries and tears,
And in his measure feels afresh
What every member bears.

4 Then let our humble faith address
His mercy and his power;
We shall obtain delivering grace
In each distressing hour.

344

COWPER.

A Fountain opened.

1 THERE is a fountain filled with blood,
Drawn from Immanuel's veins;
And sinners, plunged beneath that flood,
Lose all their guilty stains.

2 The dying thief rejoiced to see
That fountain in his day;
Oh, may I there, though vile as he,
Wash all my sins away!

3 Dear, dying Lamb, thy precious blood
Shall never lose its power,
Till all the ransomed church of God
Be saved, to sin no more.

4 E'er since, by faith, I saw the stream
Thy flowing wounds supply,
Redeeming love has been my theme,
And shall be till I die.

5 Then in a nobler, sweeter song
I'll sing thy power to save,
When this poor lisping, stammering tongue
Lies silent in the grave

345

S. JUDD.

Hymn to Jesus.

1 O SON of God! thy children we;
Train us in holiness:
As thou the Father's image bore,
Thine own on us impress.

2 O Bread of God! our natures crave
The lost beatitude:
The Father gave thee meat unknown;
Give us thy flesh and blood.

3 O Vine of God! of thee bereft,
Our virtues wilt and die:
Thou wert the Father's tender care,
Shield us when danger's nigh.

4 O Crucified! we share thy cross;
Thy passion, too, sustain;
We die thy death, to live thy life;
And rise with thee again.

346

Doxology.

To God, before whom angels bow,
The God whom we adore,
Be glory, as it was, is now,
And shall be evermore.

CORONATION. C. M.

347 DUNCAN.

Lord of All.

1 All hail the power of Jesus' name,
Let angels prostrate fall;
Bring forth the royal diadem,
And crown him Lord of all.

2 Ye chosen seed of Israel's race,
A remnant weak and small,
Hail him who saves you by his grace,
And crown him Lord of all.

3 Let every kindred, every tribe
On this terrestrial ball,
To him all majesty ascribe,
And crown him Lord of all.

4 Oh, that with yonder sacred throng
We at his feet may fall!
We'll join the everlasting song,
And crown him Lord of all.

348 WATTS.

The Redeemer's Praise.

1 Oh, for a thousand tongues, to sing
My dear Redeemer's praise,
The glories of my Lord and King,
The triumphs of his grace!

2 Jesus, the name that charms our fears,
That bids our sorrows cease,—
'T is music in the sinner's ears,
'T is life, and health, and peace.

3 He speaks, and, listening to his voice,
New life the dead receive;
The mournful, broken hearts rejoice,
The humble poor believe.

4 Hear him, ye deaf: his praise, ye dumb,
Your loosened tongues employ:
Ye blind, behold your Saviour come,
And leap, ye lame, for joy.

349 KELLY.

A Name above every Name.

1 The head that once was crowned with thorns
Is crowned with glory now;
A royal diadem adorns
The mighty Victor's brow.

2 The highest place that heaven affords
Is his by sovereign right;
The King of kings, and Lord of lords,
He reigns in glory bright.

3 Jesus, the joy of all above!
The joy of all below,
To whom he manifests his love,
And grants his name to know.

4 To them the cross, with all its shame,
With all its grace is given;
Their name—an everlasting name,
Their joy—the joy of heaven.

5 To them the cross is life and health,
Though shame and death to him:
His people's hope, his people's wealth,
Their everlasting theme.

350

Looking to Jesus.

1 In humble notes our faith adores
The great, mysterious King;
While angels strain their nobler powers,
And sweep th' immortal string.

LANGDON. C. M.

GEO. HEWS.

351

FABER.

Jesus.

1 THE light of love is round his feet,
His paths are never dim;
And he comes nigh to us when we
Dare not come nigh to him.

2 Let us be simple with him, then,
Not backward, stiff, or cold,
As though our Bethlehem could be
What Sinai was of old.

3 Poor souls that know not how to love!
They feel not Jesus near;
And they who know not how to love,
Still less know how to fear.

4 They love not, for they have not kissed
The Saviour's outer hem;
They fear not, for the Living God
Is yet unknown to them.

352

DODDRIDGE.

Love to Christ.

1 Do not I love thee, O my Lord?
Behold my heart, and see,
And turn each worthless idol out,
That dares to rival thee.

2 Is not thy name melodious still
To my attentive ear?
Doth not each pulse with pleasure beat
My Saviour's voice to hear?

3 Hast thou a lamb in all thy flock
I would disdain to feed?
Hast thou a foe before whose face
I fear thy cause to plead?

4 Thou know'st I love thee, dearest Lord;
But, oh, I long to soar
Far from the sphere of mortal joys,
And learn to love thee more.

353

WHITTIER.

One Lord.

1 O LORD and Master of us all,
Whate'er our name or sign;
We own thy sway, we hear thy call,
We test our lives by thine.

2 We faintly hear, we dimly see,
In differing phrase we pray;
But, dim or clear, we own in thee,
The Light, the Truth, the Way!

3 Apart from thee all gain is loss,
And labor vainly done;
The solemn shadow of thy cross
Is better than the sun.

4 Alone, O Love ineffable!
Thy saving name is given;
To turn aside from thee is hell,
To walk with thee is heaven.

354

WESLEY.

The Love of Christ.

1 JESUS, thine all-victorious love,
Shed in my heart abroad;
Then shall my feet no longer rove,
Rooted and fixed in God.

2 My steadfast heart, from falling free,
Shall then no longer move;
But God be all the world to me,
And all my heart be love.

PORTUGUESE HYMN. 11s. READING.

355

Looking to Jesus.

1 Oh, eyes that are weary, and hearts
that are sore, [more;
Look off unto Jesus, now sorrow no
The light of his countenance shineth
so bright, [no night.
That here, as in heaven, there need be

2 Looking off unto Jesus, my spirit is
blest; [have rest!
In the world I have turmoil, in him I
The sea of this life all about me may
roar, [more.
While looking to Jesus, I hear it no

3 While looking to Jesus, my heart can-
not fear; [near;
I tremble no more when I see Jesus
I know that his presence my safeguard
will be, [saith unto me.
For, "Why are you troubled?" he

4 Still looking to Jesus, oh, may I be
found, [me round;
When Jordan's dark waters encompass
They bear me away in his presence to
be; [see.
I see him still nearer whom always I

5 Then, then shall I know the full beauty
and grace [to face;
Of Jesus, my Lord, when I stand face
Shall know how his love went before
me each day, [away.
And wonder that ever my eyes turned

356

WHITTIER.

Christ Present in the Spirit.

1 Oh, what though our feet may not tread
where Christ trod,
Our ears hear the dashing of Galilee's
flood, [him to bear,
Our eyes see the cross that he bowed
Our knees press Gethsemane's garden
of prayer!

2 Yet, loved of the Father, thy spirit is
near [here;
The meek and the lowly and penitent
The voice of thy love is the same, even
now, [brow.
As 't Bethany's tomb, or on Olivet's

3 The outward has gone, but in glory and
power [hour;
The Spirit surviveth the things of an
Unchanged, undecaying, its Pentecost
flame [same.
On heart's secret altar is burning the

MISSIONARY HYMN. 7s & 6s. Dr. L. Mason.

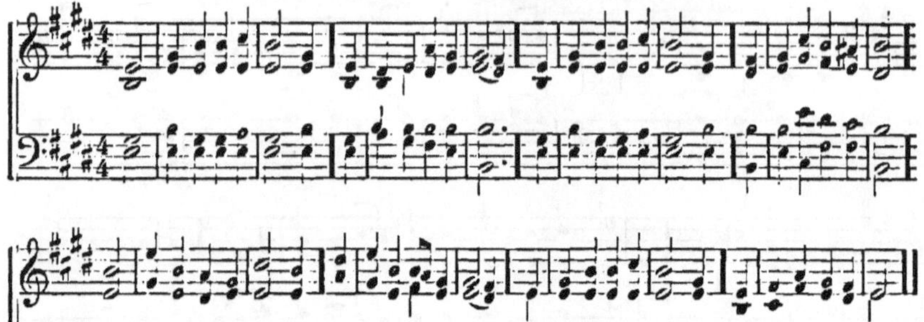

357 Montgomery.

Blessings of Christ's Reign.

1 Hail to the Lord's Anointed!
Great David's greater Son;
Hail, in the time appointed,
His reign on earth begun!
He comes to break oppression,
To set the captive free!
To take away transgression,
And rule in equity.

2 He comes, with succor speedy,
To those who suffer wrong;
To help the poor and needy,
And bid the weak be strong;
To give them songs for sighing,
Their darkness turn to light,
Whose souls, condemned and dying,
Were precious in his sight.

3 O'er every foe victorious,
He on his throne shall rest,
From age to age more glorious,
All blessing, and all blest.
The tide of time shall never
His covenant remove;
His name shall stand forever,—
That name to us is — Love.

358 Hastings.

Universality of Christ's Reign.

1 Now be the gospel banner,
In every land, unfurled;
And be the shout,—"Hosanna!"
Re-echoed through the world;
Till every isle and nation,
Till every tribe and tongue,
Receive the great salvation,
And join the happy throng.

2 Yes,— thou shalt reign forever,
O Jesus, King of kings!
Thy light, thy love, thy favor,
Each ransomed captive sings:
The isles for thee are waiting,
The deserts learn thy praise,
The hills and valleys greeting,
The song responsive raise.

359 Anon.

Fear not, little Flock.

1 In heavenly love abiding,
No change my heart shall fear,
And safe is such confiding,
For nothing changes here:
The storm may roar without me,
My heart may low be laid,
But God is round about me,
And can I be dismayed?

2 Wherever he may guide me,
No want shall turn me back;
My Shepherd is beside me,
And nothing can I lack:
His wisdom ever waketh,
His sight is never dim:
He knows the way he taketh,
And I will walk with him.

HORTON. 7s. Arr. by Dr. Mason.

360 Mrs. Barbauld.

Christ's Invitations.

1 Come, said Jesus' sacred voice,
Come, and make my path your choice;
I will guide you to your home:
Weary pilgrim, hither come.

2 Thou who, houseless, sole, forlorn,
Long hast borne the proud world's scorn,
Long hast roamed the barren waste, —
Weary pilgrim, hither haste.

3 Ye who, tossed on beds of pain,
Seek for ease, but seek in vain;
Ye, whose swollen and sleepless eyes
Watch to see the morning rise; —

4 Ye by fiercer anguish torn,
In remorse for guilt who mourn,
Here repose your heavy care:
Who the stings of guilt can bear?

5 Sinner, come; for here is found
Balm that flows for every wound,
Peace that ever shall endure,
Rest eternal, sacred, sure.

361 Montgomery.

Praise for the Gospel.

1 Songs of praise the angels sang,
Heaven with hallelujahs rang,
When Jehovah's work begun,
When he spake, and it was done.

2 Songs of praise awoke the morn,
When the Prince of Peace was born;
Songs of praise arose, when he
Captive led captivity.

3 Heaven and earth must pass away —
Songs of praise shall crown that day:
God will make new heavens and earth —
Songs of praise shall hail their birth.

4 Saints below, with heart and voice,
Still in songs of praise rejoice;
Learning here, by faith and love,
Songs of praise to sing above.

5 And shall man alone be dumb,
Till that glorious kingdom come?
No; the Church delights to raise
Psalms and hymns and songs of praise.

ORIOLA. C. M. Double.

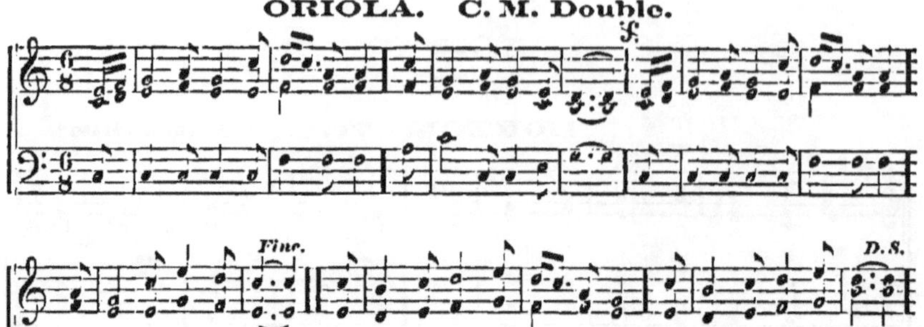

362

WHITTIER.

The Call of Truth.

1 OH! not alone with outward sign,
Of fear, or voice from heaven,
The message of a truth divine,
The call of God, is given;
Awakening in the human heart,
Love for the true and right,
Zeal for the Christian's better part,
Strength for the Christian's fight.

2 Though heralded by naught of fear,
Or outward sign or show;
Though only to the inward ear
It whisper soft and low;
Though dropping as the manna fell,
Unseen yet from above,
Holy and gentle, heed it well,—
The call to truth and love.

363

ANON.

The Gospel.

1 O'ER mountain tops, the mount of God,
In latter days, shall rise
Above the summits of the hills,
And draw the wondering eyes.
To this the joyful nations round,
All tribes and tongues, shall flow;
"Up to the mount of God," they say,
"And to his house we'll go."

2 The beams that shine from Zion's hill
Shall lighten every land;
The King who reigns in Salem's towers
Shall the whole world command.
No war shall rage, nor hostile strife
Disturb those happy years;
To ploughshares men shall beat their swords,
To pruning-hooks their spears.

364

BONAR.

The Voice of Jesus.

1 I HEARD the voice of Jesus say,
"I am this dark world's light:
Look unto me; thy morn shall rise,
And all thy day be bright."
I looked to Jesus and I found
In him my Star, my Sun;
And in that light of life I'll walk
Till all my journey's done.

365

T. MOORE.

Day of Redemption.

1 BUT who shall see the glorious day
When, throned on Zion's brow,
The Lord shall rend that veil away
Which hides the nations now?
When earth no more beneath the fear
Of his rebuke shall lie;
When pain shall cease, and every tear
Be wiped from every eye.

2 Then, Judah, thou no more shalt mourn
Beneath the heathen's chain;
Thy days of splendor shall return,
And all be new again.
The fount of life shall then be quaffed
In peace, by all who come;
And every wind that blows shall waft
Some long-lost exile home.

PILGRIM SONG. S. M.

MENDELSSOHN.

366

EPIS. COLL.

The Spirit's Invitations.

1 THE Spirit, in our hearts,
Is whispering, "Sinner, come:"
The bride, the church of Christ, proclaims
To all his children, "Come!"
Let him who heareth say
To all about him, "Come;"
Let him that thirsts for righteousness
To Christ, the fountain, come.

2 Yes, whosoever will,
Oh, let him freely come,
And freely drink the stream of life;
'T is Jesus bids him come.
Lo! Jesus, who invites,
Declares, "I quickly come:"
Lord, even so; we wait thy hour;
O blest Redeemer, come!

367

Serve God always.

1 COME at the morning hour,
Come, let us kneel and pray;
Prayer is the Christian pilgrim's staff,
To walk with God all day.
At noon, beneath the Rock
Of Ages, rest and pray;
Sweet is that shelter from the sun
In weary heat of day.

2 At evening, in thy home,
Around its altar, pray;
And, finding there the house of God,
With heaven then close the day.
When midnight vails our eyes,
Oh, it is sweet to say,
I sleep, but my heart waketh, Lord!
With thee to watch and pray.

368

DOBELL.

Now is the Day of Salvation.

1 Now is th' accepted time,
Now is the day of grace;
O sinners! come, without delay,
And seek the Saviour's face.
Now is th' accepted time,
The Saviour calls to-day;
To-morrow it may be too late;—
Then why should you delay?

PETERBOROUGH. C. M.

369

S. STREETER.

Blessings of the Gospel.

1 WHAT glorious tidings do I hear
From my Redeemer's tongue!
I can no longer silence bear;
I'll burst into a song:

2 The blind receive their sight with joy;
The lame can walk abroad;
The dumb their loosened tongues employ;
The deaf can hear the word.

3 The dead are raised to life anew
By renovating grace;
The glorious gospel 's preached to you,
The poor of Adam's race.

4 O wondrous type of things divine,
When Christ displays his love,
To raise from woe the sinking mind,
To reign in realms above!

370

WATTS.

Salvation.

1 SALVATION! oh, the joyful sound!
'T is pleasure to our ears;
A sovereign balm for every wound,
A cordial for our fears.

2 Buried in sorrow and in sin,
At death's dark door we lay;
But we arise by grace divine,
To see a heavenly day.

3 Salvation! let the echo fly
The spacious earth around,
While all the armies of the sky
Conspire to raise the sound.

371

NEEDHAM.

Joy over one Sinner that repenteth.

1 OH, how divine, how sweet the joy,
When but one sinner turns,
And, with an humble, broken heart,
His sins and errors mourns.

2 Pleased with the news, the saints below
In songs their tongues employ;
Beyond the skies the tidings go,
And heaven is filled with joy.

3 Nor angels can their joys contain,
But kindle with new fire;—
"The sinner lost is found," they sing,
And strike the sounding lyre.

372

MEDLEY.

The Living Water.

1 OH! what amazing words of grace
Are in the gospel found,
Suited to every sinner's case
Who hears the joyful sound!

2 Come, then, with all your wants and
Your every burden bring; [wounds,
Here love, unchanging love, abounds,—
A deep, celestial spring.

3 This spring with living water flows,
And heavenly joy imparts;
Come, thirsty souls! your wants disclose,
And drink, with thankful hearts.

4 Millions of sinners, vile as you,
Have here found life and peace;
Come then, and prove its virtues too,
And drink, adore, and bless.

BERA. L. M. ROOT & SWEETSER'S COLL.

373

WATTS.

Gospel Invitations.

1 COME hither, all ye weary souls,
Ye heavy-laden sinners, come!
I 'll give you rest from all your toils,
And raise you to my heavenly home.

2 "They shall find rest that learn of me;
I 'm of a meek and lowly mind;
But passion rages like the sea,
And pride is restless as the wind.

3 "Blest is the man whose shoulders take
My yoke, and bear it with delight;
My yoke is easy to his neck,
My grace shall make the burden light."

4 Jesus, we come at thy command;
With faith, and hope, and humble zeal,
Resign our spirits to thy hand,
To mould and guide us at thy will.

374

ANON.

Influence of the Gospel like Rain.

1 As showers on meadows newly mown,
Jesus shall shed his blessings down;
Crowned with whose life-infusing drops,
Earth shall renew her blissful crops.

2 The dews and rains, in all their store,
Drenching the pastures o'er and o'er,
Are not so copious as that grace
Which sanctifies and saves our race.

3 As, in soft silence, vernal showers
Descend, and cheer the fainting flowers,
So, in the secrecy of love,
Falls the sweet influence from above.

4 That heavenly influence let me find
In holy silence of the mind,
While every grace maintains its bloom,
Diffusing wide its rich perfume.

5 Nor let these blessings be confined
To me, but poured on all mankind,
Till earth's wild wastes in verdure rise,
And a young Eden bless our eyes.

375

WHITTIER.

Christianity.

1 O FAIREST born of love and light,
Yet bending brow and eye severe
On all which pains the holy sight,
Or wounds the pure and perfect ear,—

2 The generous feeling, pure and warm,
Which owns the rights of all divine,
The pitying heart, the helping arms,
The prompt self-sacrifice, are thine.

3 Beneath thy broad, impartial eye,
How fade the lines of caste and birth!
How equal in their sufferings lie
The groaning multitudes of earth!

4 In holy words which cannot die,
In thoughts which angels leaned to know,
Christ gave thy message from on high,
Thy mission to a world of woe.

5 That voice's echo hath not died;
From the blue lake of Galilee,
From Tabor's lonely mountain side,
It calls a struggling world to thee.

ANTIOCH. C. M.

L. MASON.

376

A. C. THOMAS.

The Gospel of Peace.

1 JOY to the earth! the Prince of Peace
His banner has unfurled;
Let strife, and sin, and error cease,
And joy pervade the world!

2 Praise ye the Lord! for truth and grace
His word and life display;
Let every soul his love embrace,
And own its gentle sway.

3 Peace on the earth, good-will to men,
Embrace the gospel plan;
Let that sweet strain be heard again,
Which angel tones began.

4 Joy to the isles and lands afar!
Messiah reigns above;
Let every eye behold the star,—
The star of light and love.

377

WATTS.

The Gospel Trumpet.

1 LET every mortal ear attend,
And every heart rejoice;
The trumpet of the gospel sounds,
With an inviting voice.

2 Ho! all ye hungry, starving souls,
Who feed upon the wind,
And vainly strive with earthly toys
To fill th' immortal mind—

3 Eternal wisdom has prepared
A soul-reviving feast;
And bids your longing appetites
The rich provision taste.

4 Ho! ye that pant for living streams,
And pine away and die;
Here you may quench your raging thirst
With streams that never dry.

5 The happy gates of gospel grace,
Stand open night and day;
Lord, we are come to seek supplies,
And drive our wants away.

378

WATTS.

Joy to the World.

1 JOY to the world—the Lord is come!
Let earth receive her King;
Let every heart prepare him room,
And heaven and nature sing.

2 Joy to the earth—the Saviour reigns!
Let men their songs employ;
While fields, and floods, rocks, hills, and plains,
Repeat the sounding joy.

3 No more let sins and sorrows grow,
Nor thorns infest the ground;
He comes to make his blessings flow
Far as the curse is found.

4 He rules the world with truth and grace,
And makes the nations prove
The glories of his righteousness,
And wonders of his love.

379

DODDRIDGE.

Christ coming in Power.

1 HARK, the glad sound! the Saviour [comes,
The Saviour promised long;
Let every heart prepare a throne,
And every voice a song.

ZION. 8s, 7s, & 4. T. HASTINGS.

(In singing hymns 380, 381, and 382, repeat last two lines of each verse.)

380 ALLEN.

Mercy's Plea.

1 HEAR the heralds of the gospel
News from Zion's King proclaim: —
"To each rebel sinner pardon;
Free forgiveness in his name:"
Oh, what mercy!
"Free forgiveness in his name."

2 Sinners, will you scorn the message
Sent in mercy from above;
Every sentence, oh, how tender!
Every line is full of love:
Listen to it;
Every line is full of love.

3 Tempted souls, they bring you succor;
Fearful hearts, they quell your fears;
And with news of consolation
Chase away the falling tears.
Tender heralds —
Chase away the falling tears.

4 O ye angels, hovering round us,
Waiting spirits, speed your way;
Hasten to the court of heaven,
Tidings bear without delay;
Waiting children
Glad the message will obey.

381 KELLY.

Truth spreading.

1 LOOK, ye saints! the day is breaking;
Joyful times are near at hand;
God, the mighty God, is speaking
By his word in every land:
Day advances —
Darkness flies at his command.

2 God of Jacob, high and glorious!
Let thy people see thy power;
Let the gospel be victorious
Through the world for evermore:
Then shall idols
Perish, while thy saints adore.

382 P. WILLIAMS.

Prayer for the Spread of the Gospel.

1 O'ER the gloomy hills of darkness,
Cheered by no celestial ray,
Sun of righteousness! arising,
Bring the bright, the glorious day;
Send the gospel
To the earth's remotest bound.

2 Kingdoms wide that sit in darkness —
Grant them, Lord! the glorious light;
And, from eastern coast to western,
May the morning chase the night:
And redemption,
Freely purchased, win the day.

3 Fly abroad, thou mighty gospel!
Win and conquer, never cease;
May thy lasting, wide dominions,
Multiply and still increase;
Sway thy sceptre,
Saviour! all the world around.

SHIRLAND. S. M. STANLEY.

383 WATTS.

Power of the Gospel.

1 BEHOLD, the morning sun
Begins his glorious way;
His beams through all the nations run,
And life and light convey.

2 But where the gospel comes,
It spreads diviner light;
It calls dead sinners from their tombs,
And gives the blind their sight.

3 How perfect is thy word!
And all thy judgments just!
Forever sure thy promise, Lord,
And we securely trust.

384 JOHNS.

The Kingdom of God.

1 COME, kingdom of our God,
Sweet reign of light and love!
Shed peace, and hope, and joy abroad,
And wisdom from above.

2 Over our spirits first
Extend thy healing reign;
There raise and quench the sacred thirst,
That never pains again.

3 Come, kingdom of our God!
And make the broad earth thine;
Stretch o'er her lands and isles the rod
That flowers with grace divine.

4 Soon may all tribes be blest
With fruit from life's glad tree;
And in its shade like brothers rest,
Sons of one family.

385 C. WESLEY.

The Gospel for All.

1 LORD! send thy servants forth
To call the Hebrews home;
From east, and west, and south, and north,
Let all the wanderers come.

2 Where'er, in lands unknown,
The fugitives remain,
Bid every creature help them on,
Thy holy mount to gain.

3 With Israel's myriads sealed,
Let all the nations meet;
And show the mystery fulfilled —
Thy family complete.

386 H. BALLOU

Universal Redemption.

1 IN God's eternity
There shall a day arise,
When all the race of man shall be
With Jesus in the skies.

2 As night before the rays
Of morning flees away,
Sin shall retire before the blaze
Of God's eternal day.

3 As music fills the grove
When stormy clouds are past,
Sweet anthems of redeeming love
Shall all employ at last.

4 Redeemed from death and sin,
Shall Adam's numerous race
A ceaseless song of praise begin,
And shout redeeming grace.

ALL SAINTS. L. M.

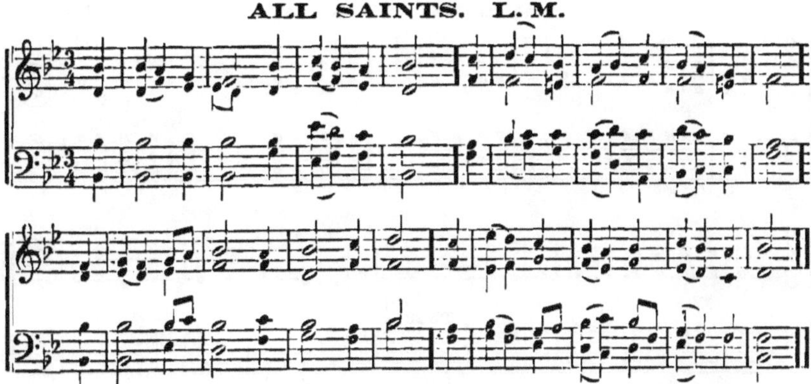

387
WATTS.

Universal Reign of Christ.

1 GREAT God, whose universal sway
The known and unknown worlds obey;
Now give the kingdom to thy Son;
Extend his power, exalt his throne.

2 The heathen lands, that lie beneath
The shades of overspreading death,
Revive at his first dawning light,
And deserts blossom at the sight.

3 The saints shall flourish in his days,
Dressed in the robes of joy and praise;
Peace, like a river, from his throne
Shall flow to nations yet unknown.

388
BOWRING.

Progress of Gospel Truth.

1 UPON the gospel's sacred page
The gathered beams of ages shine:
And, as it hastens, every age
But makes its brightness more divine.

2 Truth, strengthened by the strength of thought,
Pours inexhaustible supplies,
Whence sagest teachers may be taught,
And wisdom's self become more wise.

3 More glorious still as centuries roll,
New regions blest, new powers unfurled,
Expanding with the expanding soul,
Its waters shall o'erflow the world;

4 Flow to restore, but not destroy;
As when the cloudless lamp of day
Pours out its floods of light and joy,
And sweeps each lingering mist away.

389
PRATT'S COLL.

Israel returning from Captivity.

1 WHY, on the bending willows hung,
O Israel, sleeps thy tuneful string?—
Still mute remains thy sullen tongue,
And Zion's song declines to sing?

2 Awake! thy sweetest raptures raise;
Let harp and voice unite their strains:
Thy promised King his sceptre sways;
And Jesus, thy Messiah, reigns.

3 No taunting foes the song require;
No strangers mock thy captive chain,
But friends invite the silent lyre,
And brethren ask the holy strain.

4 Nor fear thy Salem's hills to wrong,
If other lands thy triumph share:
A heavenly city claims thy song;
A brighter Salem rises there.

390
RAY PALMER.

Christ a Conqueror.

1 ETERNAL Father! thou hast said,
That Christ all glory shall obtain;
That he who once a sufferer bled,
Shall o'er the world, a conqueror, reign.

2 We wait thy triumph, Saviour-King!
Long ages have prepared thy way;
Now all abroad thy banner fling,
Set Time's great battle in array.

3 Thy hosts are mustered to the field;
"The Cross! the Cross!" the battle-call;
The old grim towers of darkness yield,
And soon shall totter to their fall.

WEBB. 7s & 6s. G. J. WEBB.

391

S. F. SMITH.

The Light of the Gospel.

1 THE morning light is breaking,
The darkness disappears;
The sons of earth are waking
To penitential tears:
Each breeze that sweeps the ocean
Brings tidings from afar
Of nations in commotion,
Prepared for Zion's war.

2 Rich dews of grace come o'er us
In many a gentle shower,
And brighter scenes before us
Are opening every hour:
Each cry to heaven going,
Abundant answer brings,
And heavenly gales are blowing,
With peace upon their wings.

3 See heathen nations bending
Before the God we love,
And thousand hearts ascending
In gratitude above;
While sinners, now confessing,
The gospel call obey,
And seek the Saviour's blessing,—
A nation in a day.

4 Blest river of salvation;
Pursue thy onward way;
Flow thou to every nation,
Nor in thy richness stay;
Stay not till all the lowly
Triumphant reach their home,
Stay not till all the holy
Proclaim, "The Lord is come."

392

LYTE.

The Salvation of Israel.

1 OH, that the Lord's salvation
Were out of Zion come,
To heal his ancient nation,
To lead his outcasts home!
Let Israel, home returning,
Her lost Messiah see;
Give oil of joy for mourning,
And bind thy church to thee.

393

MRS. COLBURN.

Peace Triumphant.

1 THE morn of peace is beaming —
Its glory will appear;
Behold its early gleaming,
The day is drawing near;
The spear shall then be broken,
And sheathed the glittering sword —
The olive be the token,
And Peace the greeting word.

2 Yes, yes, the day is breaking!
Far brighter joys that beam!
The nations round are waking,
As from a midnight dream:
They see it radiance shedding,
Where all was dark as night;
'T is higher, wider spreading —
A boundless flood of light.

MISSIONARY HYMN. 7s & 6s. Dr. L. Mason.

394 Duffield.

Stand, therefore, having your Loins girt about.

1 Stand up! — stand up for Jesus!
Ye soldiers of the cross;
Lift high his royal banner,
It must not suffer loss:
From vict'ry unto vict'ry
His army shall he lead,
Till every foe is vanquished,
And Christ is Lord indeed.

2 Stand up! — stand up for Jesus!
The trumpet call obey;
Forth to the mighty conflict,
In this his glorious day:
"Ye that are men, now serve him,"
Against unnumbered foes;
Your courage rise with danger,
And strength to strength oppose.

3 Stand up! — stand up for Jesus!
Stand in his strength alone;
The arm of flesh will fail you —
Ye dare not trust your own:
Put on the gospel armor,
And, watching unto prayer,
Whose duty calls, or danger,
Be never wanting there.

4 Stand up! — stand up for Jesus!
The strife will not be long;
This day the noise of battle,
The next the victor's song:
To him that overcometh,
A crown of life shall be;
He with the King of Glory
Shall reign eternally!

395 Heber.

Missionary Hymn.

1 From Greenland's icy mountains,
From India's coral strand,
Where Afric's sunny fountains
Roll down their golden sand;
From many an ancient river,
From many a palmy plain,
They call us to deliver
Their land from error's chain.

2 Shall we, whose souls are lighted
With wisdom from on high,
Shall we to men benighted
The lamp of life deny?
Salvation, O salvation!
The joyful sound proclaim,
Till earth's remotest nation
Has learned Messiah's name.

3 Waft, waft, ye winds, his story,
And you, ye waters, roll,
Till, like a sea of glory,
It spreads from pole to pole;
Till o'er our ransomed nature
The Lamb for sinners slain,
Redeemer, Renovator,
In bliss returns to reign.

PILGRIM. 8s & 7s, Double.

396 HASTINGS.

The Christian Reformer encouraged.

1 He that goeth forth with weeping,
Bearing still the precious seed,
Never tiring, never sleeping,
Soon shall see his toil succeed:
Showers of rain will fall from heaven,
Then the cheering sun shall shine,
So shall plenteous fruit be given,
Through an influence all divine.

2 Sow thy seed, be never weary,
Let not fear thy mind employ;
Though the prospect be most dreary,
Thou may'st reap the fruits of joy:
Lo! the scene of verdure bright'ning,
See the rising grain appear;
Look again! the fields are whit'ning,
Harvest-time is surely near.

397 COWPER.

The Kingdom of Heaven.

1 Hear what God, the Lord, hath spoken;
O my people, faint and few,
Comfortless, afflicted, broken,
Fair abodes I build for you;
Scenes of heartfelt tribulation
Shall no more perplex your ways;
You shall name your walls salvation,
And your gates shall all be praise.

2 There, in undisturbed possession,
Peace and righteousness shall reign;
Never shall you feel oppression,
Never hear of war again;
God shall rise, and, shining o'er you,
Change to day the gloom of night;
He, the Lord, shall be your glory,
God your everlasting light.

398 HOPEDALE COLL.

Reign of Christian Peace.

1 Years are coming — speed them onward!
When the sword shall gather rust,
And the helmet, lance, and falchion,
Sleep at last in silent dust!
Earth has heard too long of battle,
Heard the trumpet's voice too long!
But another age advances,
Seers foretold in ancient song.

2 Years are coming when, forever,
War's dread banner shall be furled,
And the angel Peace be welcomed,
Regent of the happy world.
Hail with song that glorious era,
When the sword shall gather rust,
And the helmet, lance, and falchion,
Sleep at last in silent dust.

399

Christian Effort.

1 'Mid these scenes of self-denial,
We are called the race to run;
We must meet full many a trial
Ere the victor's crown is won.
Love shall every conflict lighten;
Hope shall urge us swifter on;
Faith shall every prospect brighten,
Till the morn of heaven shall dawn

LUTON. L. M. BURDER.

400 WILDE.

The Universal Fold.

1 WHILST far and wide thy scattered sheep,
Great Shepherd, in the desert stray,
Thy love, by some, is thought to sleep,
Unmindful of the wanderer's way.

2 But truth declares, they shall be found,
Wherever now they darkling roam:
Thy voice shall through the desert sound,
And summon every wanderer home.

3 Upon the darkened paths of sin,
Instead of terror's sword of flame,
Shall love descend,—for love can win
Far more than terror can reclaim.

4 And they shall turn their wandering feet,
By grace redeemed, by love controlled,
Till all at last in Eden meet,
One happy, universal fold.

401 ANON.

Gospel Freedom Universal.

1 WE long to see that happy time,
That long-expected, blissful day,
When men of every name and clime
The glorious gospel shall obey.

2 The word of God shall firm abide,
Though earth and hell should dare oppose;
The stone cut from the mountain's side,
To universal empire grows.

3 Afric's emancipated sons
Shall shout to Asia's rapturous song,
Europe, with her unnumbered tongues,
And western climes the strain prolong.

4 From east to west, from north to south,
Immanuel's kingdom shall extend;
And every man, in every face,
Shall meet a brother and a friend.

402 WATTS.

Universal Blessings of Christ's Reign.

1 JESUS shall reign where'er the sun
Does his successive journeys run;
His kingdom stretch from shore to shore,
Till moons shall wax and wane no more.

2 Blessings abound where'er he reigns;
The prisoner leaps to loose his chains;
The weary find eternal rest,
And all the sons of want are blest.

3 Let every creature rise and bring
Peculiar honors to their king;
Angels descend with songs again,
And earth repeat the long Amen.

403 ANON.

Prayer for Christ's Triumph.

1 SOON may the last glad song arise
Through all the millions of the skies,—
That song of triumph which records
That all the earth is now the Lord's!

2 Let thrones and powers and kingdoms be
Obedient, mighty Lord, to thee!
And over land, and stream and main,
Wave thou the sceptre of thy reign!

3 Oh, let that glorious anthem swell,
Let host to host the triumph tell
That not one rebel heart remains,
But over all the Saviour reigns!

BROWN. C. M.

404 H. BALLOU.

The Empire of Christ.

1 Jesus his empire shall extend;
Beneath his gentle sway
Kings of the earth shall humbly bend,
And his commands obey.

2 As clouds descend in gentle showers,
When spring renews her reign;
And call to life the fragrant flowers
O'er forest, hill, and plain; —

3 So Jesus, by his heavenly grace,
Descends on man below,
And o'er the millions of our race
His gentle blessings flow.

4 Long as the sun shall rule the day,
Or moon shall cheer the night,
The Saviour shall his sceptre sway
With unresisted might.

5 All that the reign of sin destroyed,
The Saviour shall restore;
And, from the treasures of the Lord,
Shall give us blessings more.

405 MILTON.

The Kingdom of God on Earth.

1 The Lord will come, and not be slow;
His footsteps cannot err;
Before him righteousness shall go,
His royal harbinger.

2 Mercy and Truth, that long were missed,
Now joyfully are met; [kissed,
Sweet Peace and Righteousness have
And hand in hand are set.

3 The nations all whom thou hast made
Shall come, and all shall frame
To bow them low before thee, Lord,
And glorify thy name.

4 Truth from the earth, like to a flower,
Shall bud and blossom then,
And justice, from her heavenly bower,
Look down on mortal men.

5 Thee will I praise, O Lord, my God,
Thee honor and adore
With my whole heart, and blaze abroad
Thy name for evermore.

406 NOVALIS.

The World restored in Christ.

1 We say to all men far and near
That Christ has risen again;
That he is with us now and here,
And ever shall remain.

2 The way of darkness that he trod
To heaven at last shall come,
And he who hearkens to his word,
Shall reach his Father's home.

3 Now let the mourner grieve no more,
Though his belovéd sleep,
A happier meeting shall restore
Their light to eyes that weep.

4 He lives; his presence hath not ceased
Though foes and fears be rife;
And thus we hail the gospel feast,
A world renewed to life!

TAMWORTH. 8s, 7s, & 4. LOCKHART.

407 KELLY.

Encouraging Prospects.

1 YES, we trust the day is breaking,
Joyful times are near at hand;
God, the mighty God, is speaking,
By his word, in every land:
When he chooses,
Darkness flies at his command.

2 While the foe becomes more daring,
While he enters like a flood,
God, the Saviour, is preparing
Means to spread his truth abroad:
Every language
Soon shall tell the love of God.

3 God of Jacob, high and glorious,
Let thy people see thy hand;
Let the gospel be victorious
Through the world, in every land:
Then shall idols
Perish, Lord, at thy command.

408 MONSELL.

Surely I come quickly.

1 O'ER the distant mountains breaking,
Comes the reddening dawn of day;
Rise, my soul, from sleep awaking,—
Rise, and sing, and watch, and pray:
'T is thy Saviour,
On his bright returning way.

2 O thou long-expected! weary
Waits my anxious soul for thee:
Life is dark and earth is dreary,
Where thy light I do not see:
O my Saviour!
When wilt thou return to me?

3 Nearer is my soul's salvation;
Spent the night, the day at hand:
Keep me in my lowly station,
Watching for thee till I stand,
O my Saviour!
In thy bright and promised land.

409 KELLY.

God's Love for Zion.

1 ZION stands with hills surrounded—
Zion, kept by power divine;
All her foes shall be confounded,
Though the world in arms combine;
Happy Zion,
What a favored lot is thine!

2 Every human tie may perish;
Friend to friend unfaithful prove;
Mothers cease their own to cherish;
Heaven and earth at last remove;
But no changes
Can attend Jehovah's love.

3 In the furnace God may prove thee,
Thence to bring thee forth more bright,
But can never cease to love thee;
Thou art precious in his sight:
God is with thee—
God, thine everlasting light.

CONVENT BELL. 7s, Double.

410

LAMARTINE.

The Victory of Christ.

1 Thou dost come, all-healing Lord,
Thou dost speak, and, lo! thy word
Maketh truth o'er falsehood strong,
Maketh right prevail o'er wrong.
Immortality forth breaks,
Time's best brightness to outglow!
And sweet hope yet briefer makes
Our brief exile here below.

2 Love celestial maketh light,
Lifteth up each burden here;
Lo! the eternal age dawns bright;
No remorse need be despair.
Deeper worth the just soul hath;
Virtue lowlier, loftier grows;
Children know thy humble faith;
Wisdom naught more glorious knows.

411

MONTGOMERY.

Christ's Triumph.

1 Hark! the song of jubilee,
Loud as mighty thunders roar,
Or the fulness of the sea,
When it breaks upon the shore;—
Hallelujah to the Lord!
God omnipotent shall reign;
Hallelujah! let the word
Echo round the earth and main.

2 Hallelujah!—hark! the sound,
Heard through earth, and through the skies,
Wakes above, beneath, around,
All creation's harmonies:
See Jehovah's banner furled,
Sheathed his sword; he speaks,—'t is done!
And the kingdoms of this world
Are the kingdoms of his Son.

412

BAHNMAIER.

Diffusion of the Gospel.

1 Spread, oh, spread, thou mighty word,
Spread the kingdom of the Lord,
Wheresoe'er his breath has given
Life to beings meant for heaven.
Tell them of the spirit given
Now, to guide us up to heaven,
Strong and holy, just and true,
Working both to will and do.

2 Word of life, most pure and strong,
Lo! for thee the nations long;
Spread, till from its dreary night
All the world awakes to light.
Lord of all men, let there be
Joy and strength to work for thee;
Let the nations far and near
See thy light, and learn thy fear.

413

LYTE.

The Gospel's Triumph.

1 Hasten, Lord! the glorious time,
When, beneath Messiah's sway,
Every nation, every clime,
Shall the gospel call obey.
Then shall wars and tumults cease,
Then be banished grief and pain;
Righteousness and joy and peace,
Undisturbed shall ever reign.

SAVANNAH. 10s. PLEYEL.

414 POPE.

Predicted Glory of the Messiah's Kingdom.

1 Rise, crowned with light, imperial Salem, rise!
Exalt thy towering head, and lift thine eyes!
See heaven its sparkling portals wide display,
And break upon thee in a flood of day!

2 See a long race thy spacious courts adorn,
See future sons and daughters yet unborn,
In crowding ranks on every side arise,
Demanding life, impatient for the skies!

3 See barbarous nations at thy gates attend,
Walk in thy light, and in thy temples bend!
See thy bright altars thronged with prostrate kings,
While every land its joyous tribute brings.

4 The seas shall waste, the skies in smoke decay,
Rocks fall to dust, and mountains melt away;
But fixed his word, his saving power remains;
Thy realm shall last, thy own Messiah reigns.

415 EPES SARGENT.

All Souls are Mine.

1 All souls, O Lord, are thine; — assurance blest! —
Thine, not our own to rob of help divine;
Not man's, to doom by any human test,
But thine, O gracious Lord, and only thine!

2 Surely "the soul that sinneth, it shall die,"
Die to the sin that would its life confine!
Evil shall boast not perpetuity,
Since every soul, however fall'n, is thine.

3 Thine, by thy various discipline, to lead
To heights where heavenly truths immortal shine; —
Truths, none eternally shall fail to heed,
For all, O Lord, are thine, forever thine.

4 Forgive the thought, that everlasting ill
To any can be part of thy design;
Finite, imperfect, erring, guilty,— still
All souls, great God, are thine — and mercy thine.

416 ASHWORTH.

Progress of the Gospel.

1 Pour, blessèd gospel, glorious news for man:
Thy stream of life o'er springless deserts roll;
Thy bond of peace the mighty earth can span,
And make one brotherhood from pole to pole.

2 On, piercing gospel, on: of every heart,
In every latitude, thou own'st the key;
From their dull slumbers savage souls shall start,
With all their treasures first unlocked by thee.

AMES. L. M.

Dr. L. Mason.

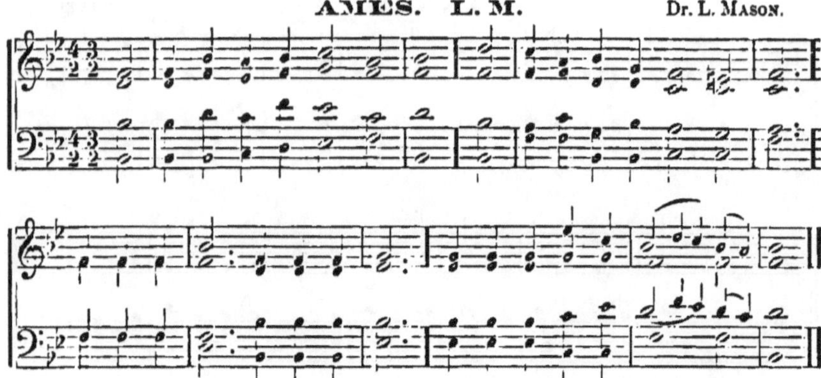

417

H. Ballou.

Blessings of Christ's Universal Reign.

1 When God descends with men to dwell,
And all creation makes anew,
What tongue can half the wonders tell?
What eye the dazzling glories view?

2 Celestial streams shall gently flow;
The wilderness shall joyful be;
Lilies on parchéd ground shall grow;
And gladness spring on every tree;

3 The weak be strong, the fearful bold,
The deaf shall hear, the dumb shall sing.
The lame shall walk, the blind behold,
And joy through all the earth shall ring.

4 Monarchs and slaves shall meet in love;
Old pride shall die, and meekness reign,—
When God descends from worlds above,
To dwell with men on earth again.

418

Richards.

The Cloud and Pillar of Fire.

1 Long as the darkening cloud abode,
So long did ancient Israel rest;
Nor moved they, till the guiding Lord
In brighter garments stood confest.

2 Father of spirits, Light of light,
Lift up the cloud, and rend the veil:
Shine forth in fire, amid that night,
Whose blackness makes the heart to fail.

3 'T is done! to Christ the power is given;
His death has rent the veil away,
Our great forerunner entered heaven,
And oped the gates of endless day.

4 Adoring nations hail the dawn,
All kingdoms bless the noontide beam,
And light, unfolding life's full morn,
Is vast creation's deathless theme.

419

Tennyson.

Good the final Goal of Ill.

1 Oh, yet, we trust that somehow good
Will be the final goal of ill,
To pangs of nature, sins of will,
Defects of doubt, and taints of blood;

2 That nothing walks with aimless feet,
That not one life shall be destroyed,
Or cast as rubbish to the void,
When God hath made the pile complete.

3 That not a worm is cloven in vain;
That not a moth with vain desire
Is shrivelled in a fruitless fire,
Or but subserves another's gain.

4 Behold, we know not anything;
We can but trust that good shall fall
At last — far off — at last, to all,
And every winter change to spring.

420

John Sterling.

Thou, God, wilt hear.

1 Still prayers are strong, and God is good;
Man is not made for endless ill;
Dear spirit! my soul's tormented mood
Has yet a hope thou canst not kill.

2 Thou, God, wilt hear! thy pangs are meant
To heal the spirit, not destroy;
And what may seem for vengeance sent,
When thou commandest, works for joy.

ARIEL. C. P. M.

L. MASON.

421

MEDLEY.

Excellency of Christ.

1 OH, could we speak the matchless worth,
Oh, could we sound the glories forth,
Which in our Saviour shine,
We'd soar, and touch the heavenly strings,
And vie with Gabriel, while he sings,
In notes almost divine.

2 We'd sing the characters he bears,
And all the forms of love he wears,
Exalted on his throne:
In loftiest songs of sweetest praise,
We would, to everlasting days,
Make all his glories known.

3 Well, the delightful days will come,
When our dear Lord will bring us home,
And we shall see his face:
Then, with our Saviour, brother, friend,
A blest eternity we 'll spend,
Triumphant in his grace.

422

M. RAYNER.

Reign of Christ.

1 THE radiant dawn of gospel light,
The prophet saw in vision bright,
And hailed th' auspicious day,
When Christ should all his grace disclose,
And cure the world of all its woes,
By truth's triumphant sway.

2 The blind their eyes shall open wide;
To drink the light's o'erflowing tide,
The deaf sweet music hear;
The lame like bounding hart shall leap;
The dumb no longer silence keep,
But shout Redemption near.

3 And there shall be a holy way,
In which the simple shall not stray,—
The path so plain and bright.
Wayfaring men therein shall walk,
And of their home and kindred talk,
With rapture and delight.

423

ROSCOE.

The Saviour's Mission.

1 OH, let your mingling voices rise
In grateful rapture to the skies,
And hail a Saviour's birth:
Let songs of joy the day proclaim,
When Jesus all-triumphant came
To bless the sons of earth!

NORTHFIELD. C. M.

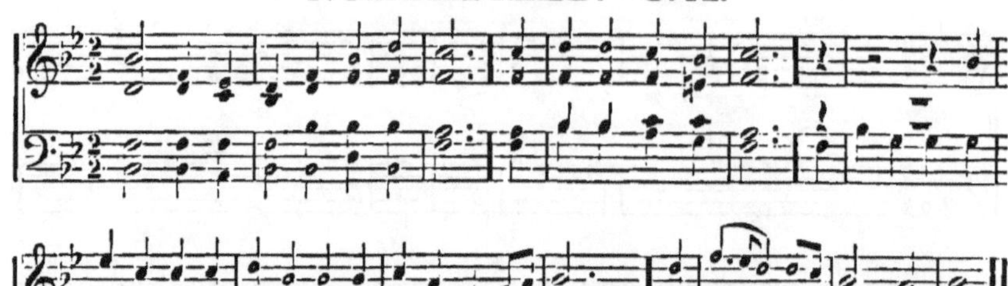

424 WATTS.

Prospect of Universal Blessedness.

1 Lo! what a glorious sight appears
To our believing eyes!
The earth and seas are passed away,
And the old rolling skies.

2 From the third heaven, where God resides,
That holy, happy place,
The new Jerusalem comes down,
Adorned with shining grace.

3 Attending angels shout for joy,
And the bright armies sing,—
"Mortals! behold the sacred seat
Of your descending King:—

4 "The God of glory down to men
Removes his blessed abode;
Men, the dear objects of his grace,
And he, the loving God.

5 "His own soft hand shall wipe the tears
From every weeping eye;
And pains and groans, and griefs and fears,
And death itself shall die."

6 How long, dear Saviour, oh, how long
Shall this bright hour delay?
Fly swifter round, ye wheels of time,
And bring the welcome day.

425 GILL.

God for us.

1 O God! our God! thou shinest here,
Thine own this latter day;
To us thy radiant steps appear;
Here beams thy glorious way!

2 The fathers had not all of thee!
New births are in thy grace;
All open to our souls shall be
Thy glory's hiding-place.

3 On us thy Spirit hast thou poured,
To us thy Word has come;
We feel, we bless thee, quickening Lord,
Thou shalt not find us dumb.

4 Thou comest near; thou standest by;
Our work begins to shine;
Thou dwellest with us mightily;
On speed the years divine!

426 LOGAN.

Latter-Day Glory.

1 In latter days the mount of God
O'er mountain tops shall rise;
Shall be exalted o'er the hills,
And draw the wondering eyes.

2 The beams that shine on Zion's hill
Shall lighten every land;
The King who reigns in Zion's towers
Shall all the world command.

3 The nations, by his justice blest,
Shall give their battles o'er; [swords,
To ploughshares they shall beat their
And learn to war no more.

4 Come, then,—oh, come from every land,
To worship at his shrine;
And, walking in the light of God,
With holy beauty shine.

BANNOCKBURN. 7s & 5s.

427 A. C. THOMAS.

The Reconciliation.

1 THOU, whose wide extended sway
Suns and systems e'er obey!
Thou, our Guardian and our stay,
Evermore adored:
In prospective, Lord, we see
Jew and Gentile, bond and free,
Reconciled in Christ to thee,
Holy, Holy Lord.

2 Thou by all shalt be confessed,
Ever blessing, ever blest,
When to thy eternal rest,
In the courts above,
Thou shalt bring the sore oppressed;
Fill each joy-desiring breast;
Make of each a welcome guest,
At the feast of love.

3 When destroying death shall die,
Hushed be every rising sigh,
Tears be wiped from every eye,
Never more to fall;
Then shall praises fill the sky,
And angelic hosts shall cry,
Holy, Holy Lord, Most High,
Thou art All in All!

428 COLLYER.

The Call to Victory.

1 SAINTS, for whom the Saviour bled,
In your Captain's footsteps tread;
Follow Jesus, and be led
On to victory!
See your foemen take the ground;
While the signal trumpets sound
Hear his accents pour around,
Cheering melody!

2 Christian soldier, on with me!
Soon the enemies must flee;
Your reward before you see
Sparkling from on high!
Boldly take the glorious field;
You may fall — but must not yield;
You shall write upon your shield
Vict'ry, though you die!

3 By the ransom which he gave,
By his triumph o'er the grave,
Trust his mighty power to save;
Firm and faithful be:
And when death's dark hour is nigh,
When the tear-drop dims the eye,
You shall, in the parting sigh,
Grasp the victory.

429 R. C. TRENCH.

The Ministry of Suffering.

1 O LIFE, O death, O world, O time,
O grave, where all things flow,
'T is yours to make our lot sublime,
With your great weight of woe!

2 Though sharpest anguish hearts may wring,
Though bosoms torn may be,
Yet suffering is a holy thing;
Without it, what were we?

430 TOPLADY.

Sweetness of Submission.

1 WHEN languor and disease invade
This trembling house of clay,
'T is sweet to look by faith abroad,
And long to fly away;

2 Sweet to look inward and attend
The whispers of his love;
Sweet to look upward to the place
Where Jesus lives above.

3 Sweet on his faithfulness to rest,
Whose love can never end;
Sweet on his covenant of grace
For all things to depend;

4 Sweet, in the confidence of faith,
To trust his firm decrees;
Sweet to lie passive in his hands,
And know no will but his.

431 WATTS

Human Frailty.

1 TEACH me the measure of my days,
Thou Maker of my frame!
I would survey life's narrow space,
And learn how frail I am.

2 A span is all that we can boast,—
An inch or two of time;
Man is but vanity and dust,
In all his flower and prime.

3 Some walk in honor's gaudy show;
Some dig for golden ore;
They toil for heirs, they know not who,
And straight are seen no more.

4 What should I wish or wait for, then,
From creatures, earth, and dust?
They make our expectations vain,
And disappoint our trust.

CHATHAM. 7s.

WEBER.

432

COWPER.

Trial Profitable.

1 'T is my happiness below,
Not to live without the cross
But the Saviour's power to know,
Sanctifying every loss.

2 Trials must and will befall;
But with humble faith to see
Love inscribed upon them all,
This is happiness to me.

3 Trials make the promise sweet
Trials give new life to prayer;
Bring me to my Father's feet,
Lay me low, and keep me there.

433

J. TAYLOR.

Confession of Sin.

1 God of mercy, God of grace,
Hear our sad, repentant songs;
Oh, restore thy suppliant race,
Thou, to whom our praise belongs.

2 Deep regret for follies past,
Talents wasted, time misspent;
Hearts debased by worldly cares,
Thankless for the blessings lent;—

3 Foolish fears, and fond desires,
Vain regrets for things as vain,
Lips too seldom taught to praise,
Oft to murmur and complain;—

4 These, and every secret fault,
Filled with grief and shame we own;
Humbled at thy feet we lie,
Seeking pardon from thy throne.

434

NEWTON.

Self-Distrust.

1 'T is a point I long to know,—
Oft it causes anxious thought,—
Do I love the Lord or no?
Am I his, or am I not?

2 If I love, why am I thus?
Why this dull and lifeless frame?
Hardly, sure, can they be worse,
Who have never heard his name.

3 If I pray, or hear, or read,
Sin is mixed with all I do;
You that love the Lord, indeed,
Tell me, is it thus with you?

4 Yet I mourn my stubborn will,
Find my sin a grief and thrall;
Should I grieve for what I feel,
If I did not love at all?

435

C. WESLEY.

The Simplicity of Christ.

1 LORD! that I may learn of thee,
Give me true simplicity;
Wean my soul, and keep it low,
Willing thee alone to know.

2 Of my boasted wisdom spoiled,
Docile, helpless as a child;
Only seeing in thy light,
Only walking in thy might.

3 Then infuse the living grace,
Truthful soul of righteousness;
Knowledge, love divine, impart,—
Life eternal to my heart.

CROSS AND CROWN. C. M.

436

BREVIARY.

True Penitence.

1 O SINNER, bring not tears alone,
Or outward form of prayer,
But let it in thy heart be known
That penitence is there.

2 To smite the breast, the clothes to rend,
God asketh not of thee;
Thy secret soul he bids thee bend
In true humility.

3 Oh, let us, then, with heartfelt grief,
Draw near unto our God;
And pray to him to grant relief,
And stay the lifted rod.

4 O righteous One! if thou wilt deign
To grant us what we need,
We pray for time to turn again,
And grace to turn indeed.

437

LUTHER.

Out of the Depths have I called unto Thee.

1 OUT of the depths I cry to thee,
Lord God! oh, hear my prayer,
Incline a gracious ear to me,
And bid me not despair.

2 My hope is ever in the Lord,
My works I count but dust,
I build not there, but on thy word,
And in thy goodness trust.

3 Though thou should'st tarry till the night,
And round again to morn,
My heart shall ne'er mistrust thy might,
Nor count itself forlorn.

4 Though great our sins and sore our wounds,
And deep and dark our fall,
Thy helping mercy hath no bounds;
Thy love surpasseth all.

438

C. WESLEY.

Vain Repentance.

1 TIMES without number have I prayed,
"This only once forgive;"
Relapsing when thy hand was stayed,
And suffered me to live.

2 Yet now the kingdom of thy peace,
Lord, to my heart restore;
Forgive my vain repentances,
And bid me sin no more.

439

ANON.

Prayer for Forgiveness.

1 NOW let our prayers ascend to thee,
Thou great and holy One;
Above the world raise thou our hearts,
In us thy will be done.

2 Oh, let us feel how frail we are,
How much we need thy grace!
Oh, strengthen, Lord, our fainting souls
While here we seek thy face!

3 Our sins, alas! before thee rise;
Thou knowest all our guilt:
Let not our faith, our hope, our trust,
On earthly things be built.

4 Forgive our sins, thy Spirit grant,
Let love our souls refine,
And heavenly peace and holy hope
Assure that we are thine.

440

CHARLOTTE ELLIOT, 1630.

Lo! I come.

1 JUST as I am, without one plea
But that thy blood was shed for me,
And that thou bidd'st me come to thee,
O Lamb of God, I come!

2 Just as I am, though tossed about
With many a conflict, many a doubt,
Fightings and fears within, without,
O Lamb of God, I come!

3 Just as I am, thou wilt receive,
Wilt welcome, pardon, cleanse, relieve!
Because thy promise I believe,
O Lamb of God, I come!

4 Just as I am,— thy love unknown
Hath broken every barrier down;
Now, to be thine, yea, thine alone,
O Lamb of God, I come!

441

WHITTIER.

Man's Works follow him.

1 WE shape ourselves the joy or fear
Of which the coming life is made,
And fill our future's atmosphere
With sunshine or with shade.

2 The tissue of the life to be
We weave with colors all our own,
And in the field of destiny
We reap as we have sown.

3 Still shall the soul around it call
The shadows which it gathered here,
And painted on the eternal wall
The past shall reappear.

4 Ah, yes; we live our life again;
Or warmly touched or coldly dim,
The pictures of the past remain;
Man's works shall follow him.

442

ANON.

There is no Death.

1 THERE is no death! The stars go down
To rise upon some fairer shore;
And bright in heaven's jewelled crown
They shine for evermore.

2 There is no death! The dust we tread
Shall change beneath the summer showers
To golden grain or mellow fruit,
Or rainbow-tinted flowers.

3 The granite rocks disorganize
To feed the hungry moss they bear.
The forest leaves drink daily life
From out the viewless air.

4 There is no death! The leaves may fall,
The flowers may fade and pass away—
They only wait through wintry hours
The coming of the May.

5 There is no death! An angel form
Walks o'er the earth with silent tread,
He bears our best loved things away,
And then we call them "dead."

6 He leaves our hearts all desolate—
He plucks our fairest, sweetest flowers;
Transplanted into bliss, they now
Adorn immortal bowers.

RAPTURE. C. P. M.

Arr. by Dr. Mason.

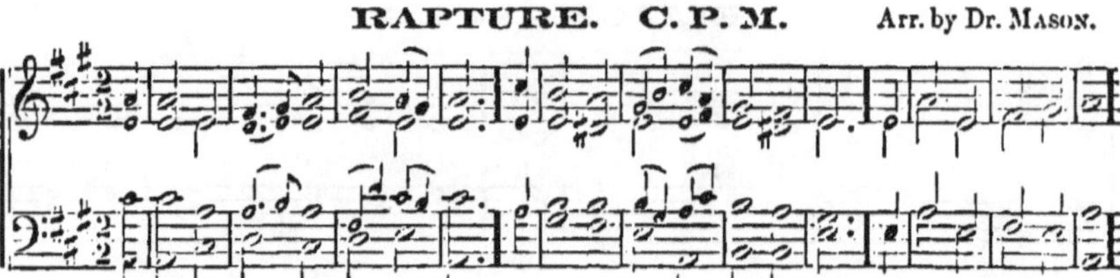

443

Newton.

The Penitent surrendering.

1 Lord, thou hast won—at length I yield;
My heart, by mighty grace compelled,
Surrenders all to thee;
Against thy terrors long I strove,
But who can stand against thy love?—
Love conquers even me.

2 If thou hadst bid thy thunders roll,
And lightnings flash to awe my soul,
I still had stubborn been:
But mercy has my heart subdued,
A bleeding Saviour I have viewed,
And now I hate my sin.

3 Now, Lord, I would be thine alone;
Come, take possession of thine own,
For thou hast set me free;
Released from Satan's hard command,
See all my powers in waiting stand,
To be employed by thee.

444

C. Wesley.

The Sinner turning to Christ.

1 O thou, who hast redeemed of old,
And bidst me of thy strength lay hold,
And be at peace with thee,
Help me thy benefits to own,
And hear me tell what thou hast done,
O dying Lamb! for me.

2 Love, only love, thy heart inclined,
And brought thee, Saviour of mankind,
Down from thy throne above;
Love made my Lord a Man of grief,
Distressed thee sore for my relief:
Oh, mystery of Love!

3 As thou hast loved and died for me,
So grant me, Saviour, love to thee,
And gladly I resign
Whate'er I have, whate'er I am:
My life be all with thine the same,
And all thy death be mine.

445

C. Wesley.

Divine Love.

1 O Love divine, how sweet thou art!
When shall I find my willing heart
All taken up by thee?
I thirst, I faint, I die to prove
The greatness of redeeming love,—
The love of Christ to me.

2 Christ only knows the love of God;
Oh, that it now were shed abroad
In this poor saddened heart!
For love I sigh, for love I pine;
This only portion, Lord, be mine,
Be mine the better part!

3 Oh, that I could, a favored one,
Recline my weary head upon
The dear Redeemer's breast;
From care and sin and sorrow free,
Give me, O Lord! to find in thee
My everlasting rest.

LUTHER'S CHANT. L. M.

CH. ZEUNER.

446

MOORE.

Breathings of Grace.

1 LIKE morning — when her early breeze
Breaks up the surface of the seas,
That, in their furrows, dark with night,
Her hand may sow the seeds of light —

2 Thy grace can send its breathings o'er
The spirit dark and lost before;
And, freshening all its depths, prepare
For truth divine to enter there.

3 Till David touched his sacred lyre,
In silence lay the unbreathing wire;
But when he swept its chords along,
Then angels stooped to hear the song.

4 So sleeps the soul, till thou, O Lord,
Shalt deign to touch its lifeless chord;
Till, waked by thee, its breath shall rise,
In music worthy of the skies.

447

RICHTER.
Translated by J. Wesley.

Devout Penitence.

1 MY soul before thee prostrate lies;
To thee, her source, my spirit flies;
My wants I mourn, my chains I see;
Oh, let thy presence set me free.

2 In life's short day, let me yet more
Of thy enlivening power implore;
My mind must deeper sink in thee,
My foot stand firm from wandering free.

3 Take full possession of my heart;
The lowly mind of Christ impart;
I still will wait, O Lord, on thee,
Till, in thy light, the light I see.

448

COWPER.

Peace after a Storm.

1 WHEN darkness long has veiled my mind,
And smiling day once more appears,
Then, my Creator! then I find
The folly of my doubts and fears.

2 Straight I upbraid my wandering heart,
And blush that I should ever be
Thus prone to act so base a part,
Or harbor one hard thought of thee.

3 Oh! let me then at length be taught,
What I am still so slow to learn,—
That God is love, and changes not,
Nor knows the shadow of a turn.

4 Sweet truth, and easy to repeat!
But when my faith is sharply tried,
I find myself a learner yet,
Unskilful, weak, and apt to slide.

449

JOSEPH B. SMITH.

Afraid to Die.

1 AFRAID to die! Oh, idle fear!
Since God our Father is so near,
With loving arms to clasp the soul
Released from pain and earth's control.

2 Afraid to die! Oh, idle thought!
Since Christ the immortal life hath brought
So clearly to our raptured eyes,
How can we shrink from Paradise!

3 Afraid to die! no, Father, no;
When thou shalt call I'll gladly go;
In death or life I would be thine,
And to thy will my own resign.

LISBON. S. M.

450

HYMNS OF THE UNITY.

The Higher Life.

1 WITHIN thine altar's shade
We bend the shrinking knee,
Knowing our weak humanity
Must strengthened be by thee.

2 With fear that seems like hope,
And hope that seems like fear,
We place thereon a naked heart,
A penitential tear.

3 We know that we are weak,
We know that thou art strong:
Grant us the will to serve the right,
The power to shun the wrong.

4 Act well; for every deed
Will curse you or will bless;
Its influence lingers near the soul,
And makes you more or less.

5 Press on in duty's path;
Press on to nobler life;
Knowing that he who made you men
Is with you in the strife.

451

MONTGOMERY.

Active Effort to do Good.

1 Sow in the morn thy seed,
At eve hold not thy hand;
To doubt and fear give thou no heed,
Broadcast it o'er the land;

2 And duly shall appear,
In verdure, beauty, strength,
The tender blade, the stalk, the ear,
And the full corn at length.

3 Thou canst not toil in vain;
Cold, heat, and moist, and dry,
Shall foster and mature the grain
For garners in the sky.

452

FROTHINGHAM.

Strength.

1 "WHEN I am weak, I'm strong,"
The great apostle cried;
What did not to the earth belong,
The might of heaven supplied.

2 "When I am weak, I'm strong,"
Each Christian heart repeats,
To tune its feeblest breath to song,
And fire its languid beats.

3 O holy strength! whose ground
Is in the heavenly land;
Supporting help alone is found
In God's immortal hand.

4 O blessed! that appears
When fleshly aids are spent,
And girds the mind, when most it fears,
With trust and sweet content.

453

ANON

Peace from Above.

1 LET not your heart be faint,
My peace I give to you,—
Such peace as reason never planned,
Nor sinners ever knew.

2 It tells of joys to come;
It soothes the troubled breast;
It shines, a star amid the storm,—
The harbinger of rest.

LOGAN. C. M.

MODERN HARP.

454

DODDRIDGE.

Brotherly Kindness.

1 FATHER of mercies! send thy grace,
All powerful from above,
To form, in our obedient souls,
The image of thy love.

2 Oh, may our sympathizing breasts
The generous pleasure know,
Kindly to share in others' joy,
And weep for others' woe!

3 When the most helpless sons of grief
In low distress are laid,
Soft be our hearts their pains to feel,
And swift our hands to aid.

455

LOND. INQUIRER.

Encouragement to Christian Effort.

1 SCORN not the slightest word or deed,
Nor deem it void of power;
There's fruit in each wind-wafted seed,
Waiting its natal hour.

2 A whispered word may touch the heart,
And call it back to life;
A look of love bid sin depart,
And still unholy strife.

3 No act falls fruitless; none can tell
How vast its power may be;
Nor what results enfolded dwell
Within it silently.

4 Work, and despair not; bring thy mite,
Nor care how small it be;
God is with all that love the right,
The holy, true, and free.

456

TRENCH.

Giving and Receiving.

1 MAKE channels for the streams of love,
Where they may broadly run;
And love has overflowing streams
To fill them every one.

2 But if at any time we cease
Such channels to provide,
The very fount of love for us
Will soon be parched and dried.

3 For we must share, if we would keep,
That blessing from above;
Ceasing to give, we cease to have;—
Such is the law of love.

457

BREVIARY.

The Reign of Love.

1 SUPREME Disposer of the heart,
Thou, since the world was made,
Hast the blest fruits of holiness
To holy hearts displayed.

2 Here, hope and faith their links unite
With love in one sweet chain;
But, when all fleeting things are past,
Love shall alone remain.

3 'Mid thousand fears and dangers now,
We sow our seed with prayer;
But know that joyful hands shall reap
The shining harvests there.

4 O God of justice, God of power!
Our faith and hope increase;
And crown them, in the future years,
With endless love and peace.

GREENWOOD. S. M.

458 RICHARDS.

Joy and Peace in Christ.

1 O CHRIST, what gracious words,
Are ever, ever thine;
Thy voice is music to the soul,
And life and peace divine.

2 The broken heart, the poor,
The bruised, the deaf, the blind,
The dumb, the dead, the captive wretch,
In thee compassion find.

3 Lord Jesus, speed the day,
The promised day of grace,
To all the poor, the dumb, the deaf,
The dead, of Adam's race.

4 One song shall then employ
The blest, the blessing, whole;
And human nature shout thy name,—
The life of every soul.

459 BULFINCH.

Convert's Joy.

1 How glorious is the hour
When first our souls awake, [power
And through thy spirit's quickening
Of the new life partake!

2 With richer beauty glows
The world, before so fair;
Her holy light religion throws,
Reflected everywhere.

3 Amid repentant tears,
We feel sweet peace within;
We know the God of mercy hears,
And pardons every sin.

4 Born of thy spirit, Lord,
Thy spirit may we share;
Deep in our hearts inscribe thy word,
And place thine image there.

460 JERVIS.

God's Mercy to the Penitent.

1 SWEET is the friendly voice
Which speaks of life and peace;
Which bids the penitent rejoice,
And sin and sorrow cease.

2 No balm on earth like this
Can cheer the contrite heart;
No flattering dreams of earthly bliss
Such pure delight impart.

3 Still merciful and kind,
Thy mercy, Lord, reveal:
The broken heart thy love can bind,
The wounded spirit heal.

4 Thy presence shall restore
Peace to my anxious breast:
Lord, let my steps be drawn no more
From paths which thou hast blessed.

461 WESLEY.

Desire to find God.

1 MY Father bids me come;
Oh, why do I delay?
He calls the wandering spirit home,
And yet from him I stay.

2 Father, the hindrance show,
Which I have failed to see;
And let me now consent to know
What keeps me far from thee.

TAMWORTH. 8s, 7s, & 4. LOCKHART.

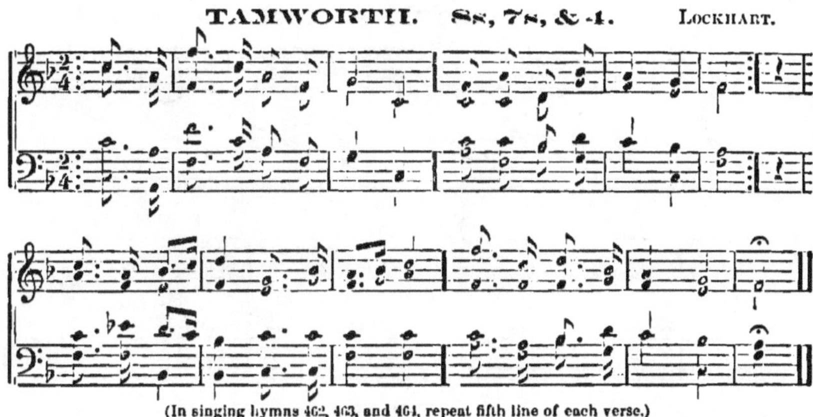

(In singing hymns 462, 463, and 464, repeat fifth line of each verse.)

462 OLIVER.

For Divine Guidance and Sustenance.

1 GUIDE me, O thou great Jehovah!
Pilgrim through this barren land;
I am weak, but thou art mighty;
Hold me with thy powerful hand;
Bread of heaven!
Feed me till I want no more.

2 Open now the crystal fountains
Whence the living waters flow;
Let the fiery, cloudy pillar
Lead me all the journey through.
Strong Deliverer!
Be thou still my strength and shield.

3 When I tread the verge of Jordan,
Bid my anxious fears subside;
Bear me through the swelling current,
Land me safe on Canaan's side.
Songs of praises
I will ever give to thee.

463 ANON.

Divine Presence Requested.

1 KEEP us, Lord, oh, keep us ever!
Vain our hope, if left by thee;
We are thine; oh, leave us never,
Till thy glorious face we see!
Then to praise thee
Through a bright eternity.

2 Precious is thy word of promise,—
Precious to thy people here;
Never take thy presence from us:
Jesus, Saviour, still be near.
Living, dying,
May thy name our spirits cheer.

464 BREVIARY.

Desire for the Heavenly Spirit.

1 HALLELUJAH! best and sweetest
Of the hymns of praise above!
Hallelujah! thou repeatest,
Angel-hosts, these notes of love;
This ye utter,
While your golden harps ye move.

2 Hallelujah! church victorious,
Join the concert of the sky!
Hallelujah! bright and glorious,
Lift, ye saints, this strain on high!
We, poor exiles,
Join not yet your melody.

3 Hallelujah! strains of gladness
Comfort not the faint and worn;
Hallelujah! sounds of sadness
Best become the heart forlorn;
Our offences
We with bitter tears must mourn.

4 But our earnest supplication,
Holy God! we raise to thee;
Visit us with thy salvation,
Make us all thy peace to see!
Hallelujah!
Ours at length this strain shall be.

CHRISTMAS. C. M.

HANDEL.

465

J. WEISS.

Living to Christ.

1 THE world throws wide its brazen gates;
With thee we enter in;
Oh, grant us, in our humble sphere,
To free that world from sin!

2 We have one mind in Christ our Lord,
To stand and point above;
To hurl rebuke at social wrong;
But all, O God, in love.

3 The star is resting in the sky;
To worship Christ we came;
The moments haste; oh, touch our tongues
With thy celestial flame!

4 The truest worship is a life;
All dreaming we resign;
We lay our offering at thy feet,—
Our lives, O Christ, are thine!

466

DODDRIDGE.

The Christian Race.

1 AWAKE, my soul! stretch every nerve,
And press with vigor on;
A heavenly race demands thy zeal,
And an immortal crown.

2 A cloud of witnesses around
Hold thee in full survey:
Forget the steps already trod,
And onward urge thy way.

3 'T is God's all-animating voice
That calls thee from on high;
'T is his own hand presents the prize
To thine aspiring eye;—

4 That prize with peerless glories bright,
Which shall new lustre boast
When victors' wreaths and monarchs' gems,
Must blend in common dust.

467

ANON.

The whole Armor.

1 OH, speed thee, Christian, on thy way,
And to thy armor cling;
With girded loins the call obey
That grace and mercy bring.

2 There is a battle to be fought,
An upward race to run,
A crown of glory to be sought,
A victory to be won.

3 Oh, faint not, Christian, for thy sighs
Are heard before his throne:
The race must come before the prize,
The cross before the crown.

468

T. H. GILL.

Life with God.

1 ALAS the outer emptiness!
What life has it to give?
Oh! shall it God's own fire oppress?
Soul, wilt thou slightly live?

2 Some joy of thine own seeking win;
To thine own strength repair:
Breathe, breathe the awful life within,
Feel all the glory there.

3 Thyself amidst the silence clear,
The world far off and dim,
Thy vision free, the Bright One near,
Thyself alone with him.

MISSIONARY CHANT. L. M.

ZEUNER.

469

WATTS.

The Christian Race.

1 AWAKE, our souls, awake our fears;
Let every trembling thought be gone;
Awake, and run the heavenly race,
And put a cheerful courage on.

2 True, 't is a straight and thorny road,
And mortal spirits tire and faint;
But they forget the mighty God,
That feeds the strength of every saint.

3 From thee, the overflowing spring,
Our souls shall drink a fresh supply;
While such as trust their native strength,
Shall melt away, and droop and die.

4 Swift as an eagle cuts the air,
We'll mount aloft to thine abode;
On wings of love our souls shall fly,
Nor tire amidst the heavenly road.

470

MRS. BARBAULD.

Christian Watchfulness and Life.

1 AWAKE, my soul! lift up thine eyes;
See where thy foes against thee rise,
In long array a numerous host;
Awake, my soul! or thou art lost.

2 Here giant danger threatening stands,
Mustering his pale, terrific bands;
There pleasure's silken banner's spread,
And willing souls are captive led.

3 See where rebellious passions rage,
And fierce desires and lusts engage;
The meanest foe of all the train
Has thousands and ten thousands slain.

4 Thou tread'st upon enchanted ground;
Deceitful snares beset thee round;
Beware of all; guard every part;
But most the traitor in thy heart.

471

DODDRIDGE.

Thy Will be done.

1 THY will be done! In devious way
The hurrying stream of life may run;
Yet still our grateful hearts shall say,
"Our Father, may thy will be done."

2 Thy will be done! If o'er us shine
A glad'ning and a prosperous sun,
This prayer will make it more divine:
"Our Father, may thy will be done."

3 Thy will be done! Though shrouded o'er
Our path with gloom, all prayers in one
Our souls before thy throne shall pour,—
"Our Father, let thy will be done."

4 Thy will be done! The living way
To thine own kingdom is begun,
Continued, ended, when we pray,
"Our Father, let thy will be done."

472

JANE ROSCOE

The Bitter Cup.

1 THY will be done! I will not fear
The fate provided by thy love;
Though clouds and darkness shroud me here,
I know that all is bright above.

2 Father! forgive the heart that clings,
Thus trembling, to the things of time;
And bid the soul, on angel wings,
Ascend into a purer clime.

MORNINGTON. S. M. MORNINGTON.

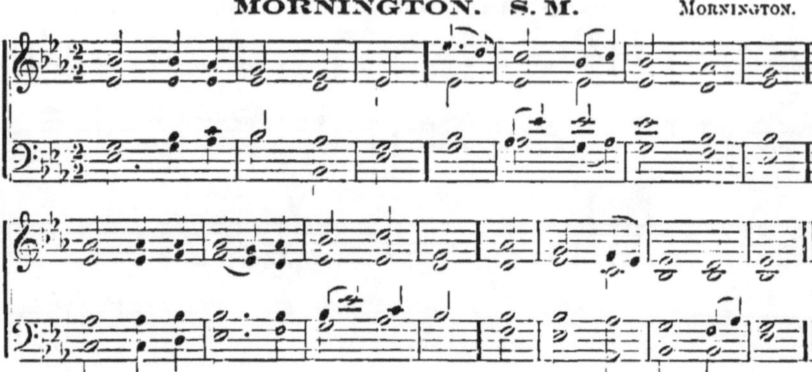

473 HERBERT.

Living to God.

1 TEACH me, my God and King,
Thy will in all to see:
And what I do in anything,
To do it as for thee!

2 To scorn the senses' sway,
While still to thee I tend;
In all I do, be thou the way,
In all, be thou the end.

3 All may of thee partake:
Nothing so small can be,
But draws, when acted for thy sake,
Greatness and worth from thee.

4 If done beneath thy laws,
E'en servile labors shine;
Hallowed is toil, if this the cause;
The meanest work, divine.

474 L. H. SIGOURNEY.

Active Piety.

1 SERVANTS of Christ, arise,
And gird you for the toil;
The dew of promise from the skies
Already cheers the soil.

2 Go where the sick recline,
Where mourning hearts deplore;
And where the sons of sorrow pine,
Dispense your hallowed lore.

3 Urge, with a tender zeal,
The erring child along,
Where peaceful congregations kneel,
And pious teachers throng.

4 Be faith, which looks above,
With prayer, your constant guest,
And wrap the Saviour's changeless love
A mantle round your breast.

5 So shall you share the wealth,
That earth may ne'er despoil,
And the blest gospel's saving health
Repay your arduous toil.

475 SCOTT.

Private Judgment and Accountability.

1 LORD, give the light we need;
Our minds with knowledge fill;
From noxious error guard our creed,
From prejudice our will.

476 BRIGG'S COLL.

The Heavenly Call.

1 COME to the land of peace,
From shadows come away,
Where all the sounds of weeping cease,
And storms no more have sway.

2 Fear hath no dwelling here,
But pure repose and love
Breathe through the bright, celestial air,
The spirit of the dove.

3 Come to the bright and blest,
Gathered from every land;
For here thy soul shall find its rest,
Amidst the shining band.

4 In this divine abode
Change leaves no saddening trace;
Come, trusting spirit, to thy God,
Thy holy resting-place!

MENDON. L. M.

477 GASKELL.

Press on.

1 PRESS on, press on! ye sons of light,
Untiring in your holy fight,
Still treading each temptation down,
And battling for a brighter crown.

2 Press on, press on! through toil and woe,
With calm resolve, to triumph go,
And make each dark and threatening ill
Yield but a higher glory still.

3 Press on, press on! still look in faith
To him who vanquished sin and death:
Then shall ye hear God's word, "Well done!"
True to the last, press on, press on!

478 MONTGOMERY.

The Christian Warrior.

1 THE Christian warrior, see him stand
In the whole armor of his God;
The spirit's sword is in his hand;
His feet are with the gospel shod;

2 In panoply of truth complete,
Salvation's helmet on his head,
With righteousness a breastplate meet.
And faith's broad shield before him spread.

3 With this omnipotence he moves:
From this the alien armies flee;
Till more than conqueror he proves,
Through Christ, who gives him victory.

4 Thus strong in his Redeemer's strength.
Sin, death, and hell he tramples down,—
Fights the good fight; and takes at length,
Through mercy, an immortal crown.

479 STERLING.

Christian Hope and Action.

1 STILL hope! still act! Be sure that life,
The source and strength of every good,
Wastes down in feeling's empty strife,
And dies in dreaming's sickly mood.

2 To toil, in tasks however mean,
For all we know of right and true;
In this alone our worth is seen;
'T is this we were ordained to do.

480 BONAR.

Go work To-day in my Vineyard.

1 Go, labor on; spend and be spent,—
Thy joy to do the Father's will:
It is the way the Master went;
Should not the servant tread it still?

2 Go, labor on; 't is not for naught;
Thine earthly loss is heavenly gain:
Men heed thee, love thee, praise thee not;
The Master praises,— what are men?

3 Go, labor on; enough while here,
If he shall praise thee; if he deign
Thy willing heart to mark and cheer,
No toil for him shall be in vain.

4 Toil on, and in thy toil rejoice;
For toil, comes rest; for exile, home:
Soon shalt thou hear the Bridegroom's voice,
The midnight peal, Behold, I come!

MERTON. C. M.

H. K. OLIVER.

481

HARTFORD SELEC.

Daily Life in God.

1 OH, could I find, from day to day,
A nearness to my God,
Then would my hours glide sweet away,
While leaning on his word.

2 Lord, I desire with thee to live
Anew from day to day,
In joys the world can never give,
Nor never take away.

3. Blest Jesus, come, and rule my heart,
And make me wholly thine,
That I may never more depart,
Nor grieve thy love divine.

482

H B. STOWE.

The other World.

1 IT lies around us like a cloud,—
A world we do not see;
Yet the sweet closing of an eye
May bring us there to be.

2 Sweet hearts around us throb and beat,
Sweet helping hands are stirred,
And palpitates the veil between
With breathings almost heard.

3 The silence — awful, sweet, and calm —
They have no power to break;
For mortal words are not for them
To utter or partake.

4 Scarce knowing if we wake or sleep,
Scarce asking where we are,
We feel all evil sink away,
All sorrow and all care.

483

C. D. STUART.

Attractions of Heaven.

1 As distant lands beyond the sea,
When friends go thence, draw nigh,
So heaven, when friends have thither gone,
Draws nearer from the sky.

2 And as those lands the dearer grow,
When friends are long away,
So heaven itself, through loved ones dead,
Grows dearer day by day.

3 Heaven is not far from those who see,
With the pure spirit's sight,
But near, and in the very hearts
Of those who see aright.

484

W. B. O. PEABODY

Evening Meditations.

1 BEHOLD the western evening light,
It melts in deepening gloom;
So calmly Christians sink away,
Descending to the tomb.

2 The winds breathe low,— the withering
Scarce whispers from the tree; [leaf
So gently flows the parting breath,
When good men cease to be.

3 And now above the dews of night
The yellow star appears;
So faith springs in the hearts of those
Whose eyes are bathed in tears.

4 But soon the morning's happier light
Its glories shall restore;
And eyelids that are sealed in death
Shall wake to close no more.

ARLINGTON. C. M.

Dr. Arne.

485

Watts.

Christian Courage and Self-denial.

1 Am I a soldier of the cross,
A follower of the Lamb,
And shall I fear to own his cause,
Or blush to speak his name?

2 Must I be carried to the skies
On flowery beds of ease,
Whilst others fought to win the prize,
And sailed through bloody seas?

3 Sure I must fight, if I would reign;
Increase my courage, Lord:
I'll bear the toil, endure the pain,
Supported by thy word.

4 Thy saints, in all this glorious war,
Shall conquer though they 're slain:
They view the triumph from afar,
And soon with Christ shall reign.

486

Bath Coll.

Prayer for Faith.

1 Oh, for a faith that will not shrink,
Though pressed by every foe,
That will not tremble on the brink
Of any earthly woe!

2 That will not murmur nor complain
Beneath the chastening rod,
But, in the hour of grief or pain,
Will lean upon its God;—

3 A faith that shines more bright and clear
When tempests rage without;
That when in danger knows no fear,
In darkness feels no doubt.

4 Lord, give us such a faith as this,
And then whate'er may come,
We 'll taste, e'en here, the hallowed bliss
Of our eternal home.

487

Wesleyan.

For Purity of Heart.

1 Oh, for a heart to praise my God,
A heart from sin set free;
A heart that always feels how good,
Thou, Lord, hast been to me.

2 Oh, for a humble, contrite heart,
Believing, true, and clean,
Which neither life nor death can part
From him who dwells within.

3 A heart in every thought renewed,
And full of love divine,
Perfect, and right, and pure, and good,
Conformed, O Lord, to thine.

488

Urwick's Coll.

Prayer for Grace in Trial.

1 Father of all our mercies, thou
In whom we move and live,
Hear us in heaven, thy dwelling, now,
And answer and forgive.

2 When, harassed by ten thousand foes,
Our helplessness we feel,
Oh, give the weary soul repose,
The wounded spirit heal.

3 When dire temptations gather round,
And threaten and allure,
By storm or calm, in thee be found
A refuge strong and sure.

ROCKINGHAM. L. M.

Dr. L. Mason.

489

Watts.

By their Fruits ye shall know them.

1 When Jesus, our great Master, came
To teach us in his Father's name,
In every act, in every thought,
He lived the precepts which he taught.

2 So let our lips and lives express
The holy gospel we profess;
So let our works and virtues shine,
To prove the doctrine all divine.

3 Thus shall we best proclaim abroad
The honors of our Saviour, God,
When the salvation reigns within,
And grace subdues the power of sin.

490

Longfellow.

Steps.

1 We have not wings — we cannot soar —
But we have feet to scale and climb
By slow degrees — by more and more —
The cloudy summits of our time.

2 The heights by great men reached and [kept
Were not attained by sudden flight,
But they while their companions slept
Were toiling upward in the night.

3 Standing on what too long we bore,
With shoulders bent and downcast eyes,
We may discern — unseen before —
A path to higher destinies.

4 Nor deem the irrevocable past
As wholly wasted — wholly vain —
If, rising on its wrecks, at last,
To something nobler we attain.

491

Watts.

We Walk by Faith.

1 'T is by the faith of joys to come
We walk through deserts dark as night;
Till we arrive at heaven, our home,
Faith is our guide, and faith our light.

2 The want of sight she well supplies:
She makes the pearly gates appear;
Far into distant worlds she pries,
And brings eternal glories near.

3 Cheerful we tread the desert through,
While faith inspires a heavenly ray,
Though lions roar, and tempests blow,
And rocks and dangers fill the way.

4 So Abraham, by divine command,
Left his own house to walk with God;
His faith beheld the promised land,
And fired his zeal along the road.

492

Anon.

Self-Sacrifice in the Daily Life.

1 Not by the martyrs' death alone, [won;
The saints in heaven their crowns have
There is a triumph robe on high,
For bloodless fields of victory.

2 What though they were not called to feel
The cross, the flame, the torturing wheel
Yet daily to the world they died,
And sinful passions crucified.

3 Lord, grant us so to thee to turn,
That we to die through life may learn;
And when our earthly toils are o'er,
Rejoice with thee for evermore.

WEBB. 7s & 6s. G. J. WEBB.

493

C. H. TOWNSEND.

Wait!

1 WAIT! for the day is breaking,
Though the dull night be long:
Wait! God is not forsaking
Thy heart. Be strong — be strong!
Wait! and the clouds of sorrow
Shall melt in gentle showers,
And hues from heaven shall borrow,
As they fall amidst the flowers.

2 Wait! 't is the key to pleasure
And to the plan of God;
Oh, tarry thou his leisure,
Thy soul shall bear no load.
Wait! for the time is hasting
When life shall be made clear,
And all who know heart-wasting
Shall feel that God is dear.

494

COWPER.

Joy and Peace in believing.

1 SOMETIMES a light surprises
The Christian while he sings;
It is the Lord, who rises
With healing in his wings;
When comforts are declining,
He grants the soul again
A season of clear shining,
To cheer it after rain.

2 In holy contemplation,
We sweetly then pursue
The theme of God's salvation,
And find it ever new;
Set free from present sorrow,
We cheerfully can say,
"E'en let the unknown morrow
Bring with it what it may."

3 It can bring with it nothing,
But he will bear us through;
Who gives the lilies clothing
Will clothe his people too.
Beneath the spreading heavens,
No creature but is fed;
And he who feeds the ravens
Will give his children bread.

4 Though vine, nor fig-tree neither,
Its wonted fruit should bear;
Though all the field should wither,
Nor flocks nor herds be there;
Yet God the same abiding,
His praise shall tune my voice;
For while in him confiding,
I cannot but rejoice.

495

MONTGOMERY.

Confidence in God.

1 GOD is my strong salvation;
What foe have I to fear?
In darkness and temptation
My light, my help, is near.
Though hosts encamp around me,
Firm to the fight I stand;
What terror can confound me
With God at my right hand?

MOULTON. S. H. M.

496

Excellency of Faith.

1 Faith is the polar star
That guides the Christian's way,
Directs his wanderings from afar
To realms of endless day:
It points the course where'er he roam,
And safely leads the pilgrim home.

2 Faith is the rainbow's form
Hung on the brow of heaven,
The glory of the passing storm,
The pledge of mercy given;
It is a bright, triumphal arch,
Through which the saints to glory march.

497

Montgomery.

Friends die, but to live again.

1 Friend after friend departs;
Who hath not lost a friend?
There is no union here of hearts,
That finds not here an end.
Were this frail world our only rest,
Living or dying, none were blest.

2 Beyond the flight of time,
Beyond this vale of death,
There surely is some blessèd clime,
Where life is not a breath,
Nor life's affections but a fire
Whose sparks fly upward to expire.

3 There is a world above,
Where parting is unknown,—
A whole eternity of love
And blessedness alone;
And faith beholds the dying here
Translated to that happier sphere.

4 Thus, star by star declines
Till all are passed away,
As morning high and higher shines
To pure and perfect day.
Nor sink those stars in empty night —
They hide themselves in heaven's own light.

498

Montgomery.

Burial of Friends.

1 This place is holy ground!
World, with its cares, away!
A holy, solemn stillness, round
This lifeless, mouldering clay;
Nor pain, nor grief, nor anxious fear,
Can reach the peaceful sleeper here.

2 Behold the bed of death,
The pale and mortal clay!
Heard ye the sob of parting breath?
Marked ye the eye's last ray?
No! life so sweetly ceased to be,
It lapsed in immortality.

3 Bury the dead, and weep
In stillness o'er the loss.
Bury the dead! in Christ they sleep
Who bore on earth his cross;
And from the grave their souls shall rise,
In his own image to the skies.

GERMANY. L. M. BEETHOVEN.

499 MONTGOMERY.

The Christian Graces.

1 FAITH, hope, and charity, these three;
Yet is the greatest charity;
Father of lights, these gifts impart
To mine and every human heart.

2 Faith, that in prayer can never fail;
Hope, that o'er doubting must prevail;
And charity, whose name above,
Is God's own name, for God is love.

3 The morning star is lost in light,
Faith vanishes at perfect sight;
The rainbow passes with the storm,
And hope with sorrow's fading form.

4 But charity, serene, sublime,
Beyond the reach of death and time,
Like the blue sky's all-bounding space,
Holds heaven and earth in its embrace.

500 WATTS.

All things Vain without Love.

1 HAD I the tongues of Greeks and Jews,
And nobler speech than angels use,
If love be absent, I am found
Like tinkling brass, an empty sound.

2 Were I inspired to preach and tell
All that is done in heaven and hell;
Or, could my faith the world remove,
Still I am nothing without love.

3 Should I distribute all my store,
To feed the cravings of the poor;
Or give my body to the flame,
To gain a martyr's glorious name;

4 If love to God and love to men
Be absent, all my hopes are vain;
Nor tongues, nor gifts, nor fiery zeal,
The works of love can e'er fulfil.

501 WATTS.

Love to God and our Neighbor.

1 THUS saith the first, the great command,
"Let all thy inward powers unite
To love thy Maker and thy God,
With sacred fervor and delight.

2 "Then shall thy neighbor next in place
Share thine affections and esteem;
And let thy kindness to thyself
Define and rule thy love to him."

502 ANON.

Self-Denial.

1 IF on our daily course our mind
Be set, to hallow all we find,
New treasures still, of countless price,
God will provide for sacrifice.

2 Old friends, old scenes, will lovelier be,
As more of heaven in each we see;
Some softening gleam of love and prayer
Shall dawn on every cross and care.

3 The trivial round, the common task,
Will furnish all we ought to ask;—
Room to deny ourselves, a road
To bring us daily nearer God.

4 Only, O Lord, in thy dear love,
Fit us for perfect rest above;
And help us this and every day
To live more nearly as we pray.

LITANY. 7s. HEROLD.

503 WESLEY'S COLL.

For Brotherly Love.

1 God of love, we look to thee,
Let us in thy Son agree;
Show to us the Prince of Peace;
Bid our jars forever cease.
By thy reconciling love,
Every stumbling block remove;
Each to each unite, endear,
Come, and spread the banner here.

2 Make us of one heart and mind,
Courteous, pitiful, and kind;
Lowly, meek, in thought and word,
Altogether like our Lord.
Let us for each other care;
Each the other's burden bear;
To thy church the pattern give;
Show how true believers live.

504 MRS. HEMANS.

I will that Men pray everywhere.

1 Child, amidst the flowers at play,
While the red light fades away;
Mother, with thine earnest eye
Ever following silently;
Father, by the breeze of eve
Called thy daily work to leave;
Pray! ere yet the dark hours be —
Lift the heart and bend the knee!

2 Traveller, in the stranger's land,
Far from thine own household band;
Mourner, haunted by the tone
Of a voice from this world gone;
Captive, in whose narrow cell
Sunshine hath not leave to dwell;
Sailor, on the darkening sea —
Lift the heart and bend the knee!

505 C. WESLEY

That they also may be one in us.

1 Lord, from whom all blessings flow,
Perfecting the church below!
Steadfast may we cleave to thee:
Love the mystic union be.
Join our faithful spirits, join
Each to each, and all to thine:
Lead us through the paths of peace,
On to perfect holiness.

EVA. C. M. Arr. by Dr. Mason.

506

METHODIST COLL.

Mutual Aid.

1 Help us to help each other, Lord,
Each other's cross to bear;
Let each his friendly aid afford,
And feel his brother's care.

2 Help us to build each other up,
Our little stock improve;
Increase our faith, confirm our hope,
And perfect us in love.

3 Up into thee, our living Head,
Let us in all things grow,
Till thou hast made us free indeed,
And spotless here below.

507

BONAR.

The inner Calm.

1 Calm me, my God, and keep me calm:
Let thine outstretchéd wing
Be like the shade of Elim's palm,
Beside her desert spring.

2 Yes, keep me calm, though loud and rude
The sounds my ear that greet,—
Calm in the closet's solitude,
Calm in the bustling street,—

3 Calm in the hour of buoyant health,
Calm in the hour of pain,
Calm in my poverty or wealth,
Calm in my loss or gain,—

4 Calm in the sufferance of wrong,
Like him who bore my shame,
Calm 'mid the threatening, taunting throng,
Who hate thy holy name.

5 Calm me, my God, and keep me calm,
Soft resting on thy breast;
Soothe me with holy hymn and psalm,
And bid my spirit rest.

508

W. S. LANDOR.

Content.

1 Why, why repine, O pensive friend,
At pleasures slipped away?
Some the stern fates will never lend,
And all refuse to stay.

2 I see the rainbow in the sky,
The dew upon the grass:
I see them, and I ask not why
They glimmer or they pass.

3 With folded arms I linger not
To call them back; 't were vain;
In this, or in some other spot,
I know they 'll shine again.

509

DODDRIDGE.

The Perfect Law of Liberty.

1 Behold that wise, that perfect law,
Which noblest freedom gives:
Oh, may it all our souls refine,
And sanctify our lives!

2 Not with a transient glance surveyed,
And in an hour forgot,
But deep inscribed on every heart,
To reign o'er every thought.

3 Great Author of each perfect gift!
Thy gracious power display,
That our ungrateful, wandering hearts
May hearken and obey.

ERNAN. L. M.

Dr. L. Mason.

510

Whittier.

Mercy and not Sacrifice.

1 O Thou, at whose rebuke the grave
Back to warm life the sleeper gave,
Who, waking, saw with joy, above,
A brother's face of tenderest love;—

2 Thou, unto whom the blind and lame,
The sorrowing and the sin-sick came;
The burden of thy holy faith,
Was love and life, not hate and death.

3 Oh, once again thy healing lay
On the blind eyes which know thee not,
And let the light of thy pure day
Shine in upon the darkened thought!

4 Oh, touch the hearts of men, and show
The power which in forbearance lies;
And let them learn that mercy now
Is better than old sacrifice.

511

Scott.

The Blessing of Meekness.

1 Happy the meek, whose gentle breast
Clear as the summer's evening ray,
Calm as the regions of the blest,
Enjoys on earth celestial day.

2 His heart no broken friendships sting,
No storms his peaceful tent invade;
He rests beneath th' Almighty wing,
Hostile to none, of none afraid.

3 Spirit of grace, all meek and mild,
Inspire our breasts, our souls possess;
Repel each passion rude and wild,
And bless us as we aim to bless.

512

Sir H. Wotton.

The Independent and Happy Man.

1 How happy is he born or taught
Who serveth not another's will!
Whose armor is his honest thought,
And simple truth his highest skill.

2 Whose passions not his masters are;
Whose soul is still prepared for death;
Not tied unto the world with care
Of prince's ear or vulgar breath;

3 Who God doth late and early pray
More of his grace than goods to lend,
And walks with man from day to day,
As with a brother and a friend.

513

Followers of God, as dear Children.

1 We follow, Lord, where thou dost lead,
And, quickened, would ascend to thee,
Redeemed from sin, set free indeed
Into thy glorious liberty.

2 We cast behind fear, sin, and death;
With thee we seek the things above;
Our inmost souls thy Spirit breathe,
Of power, of calmness, and of love:—

3 The power, 'mid worldliness and sin,
To do, in all, our Father's will;
With thee, the victory to win,
And bid each tempting voice be still:

4 The calmness perfect faith inspires,
Which waiteth patiently and long:
The love which faileth not, nor tires,
Triumphant over every wrong.

BALERMA. C. M.

514

MRS. BARBAULD.

Blessed are the Merciful.

1 Blest is the man whose softening heart
Feels all another's pain;
To whom the supplicating eye
Was never raised in vain:—

2 Whose breast expands with generous warmth
A stranger's woes to feel;
And bleeds in pity o'er the wound
He wants the power to heal.

3 To gentle offices of love
His feet are never slow;
He views, through mercy's melting eye,
A brother in a foe.

4 Peace from the bosom of his God
The Saviour's grace shall give;
And when he kneels before the throne,
His trembling soul shall live.

515

LOGAN.

Wisdom.

1 Oh, happy is the man who hears
Instruction's warning voice;
And who celestial wisdom makes
His early, only choice.

2 Her treasures are of more esteem
Than east or west unfold;
And her rewards more precious are
Than all their mines of gold.

3 In her right hand she holds to view
A length of happy days;
Riches with splendid honors joined,
Her left hand full displays.

4 She guides the young with innocence
In pleasure's path to tread;
A crown of glory she bestows
Upon the hoary head.

5 According as her labors rise,
So her rewards increase:
Her ways are ways of pleasantness,
And all her paths are peace.

516

EXETER COLL.

The Influence of Habitual Piety.

1 Blest is the man who fears the Lord!
His well-established mind,
In every varying scene of life,
Shall true composure find.

2 Oft through the deep and stormy sea
The heavenly footsteps lie;
But on a glorious world beyond
His faith can fix its eye.

3 Though dark his present prospects be,
And sorrows round him dwell,
Yet hope can whisper to his soul,
That all shall issue well.

4 Full in the presence of his God,
Through every scene he goes;
And, fearing him, no other fear
His steadfast bosom knows.

517

Doxology.

The grace of Jesus Christ, our Lord,
God's love in boundless store,
The Holy Spirit's fellowship,
Be with us evermore.

COMFORT. 11s & 10s.

518

MRS. H. B. STOWE.

The Calm of the Soul.

1 WHEN winds are raging o'er the upper ocean,
And billows wild contend with angry roar,
'T is said, far down beneath the wild commotion,
That peaceful stillness reigneth, evermore.

2 Far, far beneath, the noise of tempests dieth,
And silver waves chime ever peacefully,
And no rude storm, how fierce soe'er it flieth,
Disturbs the Sabbath of that deeper sea.

3 So to the heart that knows thy love, O Purest!
There is a temple, sacred evermore,
And all the babble of life's angry voices
Dies in hushed stillness, at its peaceful door.

4 Far, far away the roar of passion dieth.
And loving thoughts rise calm and peacefully,
And no rude storm, how fierce soe'er it flieth.
Disturbs the soul that dwells, O Lord, in thee.

5 O rest of rests! O peace serene, eternal!
Thou ever livest, and thou changest never,
And in the secret of thy presence dwelleth
Fulness of joy, forever and forever.

519

W. M. FERNALD.

A Vision of the Eternal Glory.

1 O GOD of glory! when with eye uplifted,
Eye of the soul in visioned wonder clear;
And when by thine eternal spirit gifted,
What deep revealings to the soul appear!

2 Nature recedes; and in the expanse eternal,
Spreading and opening to my raptured sight,
I see the hosts of God, the heights supernal,
The church triumphant crowned in heaven's own light.

3 Ah! there are they who, once among the lowly,
Erst trod the paths of patient virtue here;
And there are they who, in thy presence holy,
Trembled for sin, but knew no other fear.

4 Prophets, reformers,—they who, God revering,
Battled with hoary wrong and ancient might;
Behold them now in triumph reappearing
On all the hills of God, in glory bright!

5 In deepening vision, flames a light before them,
Where a long train of martyrs rise to view;
And lo! a central figure bending o'er them,
The dear Redeemer crowning them anew.

SEASONS. L. M.

PLEYEL.

520

ANON.

Charitable Judgment.

1 OMNISCIENT God, 't is thine to know
The springs whence wrong opinions flow;
To judge from principles within
When frailty errs, and when we sin.

2 Who with another's eye can read,
Or worship by another's creed?
Revering thy command alone,
We humbly seek and use our own.

3 If wrong, forgive; accept, if right,
Whilst, faithful, we obey our light;
And, judging none, are zealous still
To follow as to learn thy will.

4 When shall our happy eyes behold
Thy people fashioned in thy mould?
And charity our kindred prove
Derived from thee, O God of love.

521

G. ROGERS.

Religion.

1 RELIGION! in its blessed ray
All thought of hopeless sorrow flies:
Despair and anguish melt away
Where'er its healing beams arise.

2 How dark our sinful world would be —
A flowerless desert, dry and drear!
Did not this light, O God, from thee,
Its gloom dispel, its aspect cheer.

3 Oh! by it many a heart is soothed,
Which else would be with sorrow crushed,
And many a dying pillow smoothed,
And sob of parting anguish hushed.

4 Across the troubled sky of time
It doth the bow of promise bend,
A symbol of that cloudless clime
That waits the soul when time shall end.

5 Religion! may its holy light
Our footsteps guide to paths of peace!
Our solace in deep sorrow's night,
Our stay as mortal powers decrease.

6 With this our guide, we care not when
Death's signal to depart is given;
Its word shall bring our spirits then
The calm and holy peace of heaven.

522

STEELE.

Christian Resolves.

1 MAY I resolve with all my heart,
With all my powers, to serve the Lord;
Nor from his precepts e'er depart,
Whose service is a rich reward!

2 Be this the purpose of my soul,
My solemn, my determined choice,—
To yield to his supreme control,
And in his kind commands rejoice.

3 Oh, may I never faint nor tire,
Nor, wandering, leave his sacred ways!
Great God, accept my soul's desire,
And give me strength to live thy praise.

523

DODDRIDGE.

Devotion to God.

1 MY gracious God, I own thy right
To every service I can pay;
And call it my supreme delight
To hear thy dictates, and obey.

ARIEL. C. P. M.

L. MASON.

524 COTTON.

Contentment and Resignation.

1 IF solid happiness we prize,
Within our breasts the jewel lies;
Nor need we roam abroad;
The world has little to bestow;
From pious hearts our joys must flow,
Hearts that delight in God.

2 To be resigned when ills betide,
Patient when favors are denied,
And pleased with favors given;
This is the wise, the virtuous part;
This is that incense of the heart,
Whose fragrance reaches heaven.

525 WESLEY'S COLL.

True Wisdom.

1 BE it my only wisdom here
To serve the Lord with filial fear,
With loving gratitude;
Superior sense may I display,
By shunning every evil way,
And walking in the good.

2 Oh, may I still from sin depart!
A wise and understanding heart,
Father, to me be given!
And let me through thy Spirit know
To glorify my God below,
And find my way to heaven.

526 HENRY MOORE.

Holiness is Everlasting.

1 ALL earthly charms, however dear,
Howe'er they please the eye or ear,
Will quickly fade and fly;
Of earthly glory faint the blaze,
And soon the transitory rays
In endless darkness die.

2 The nobler beauties of the just
Shall never moulder in the dust,
Or know a sad decay:
Their honors time and death defy,
And round the throne of heaven on high
Beam everlasting day.

527 C. WESLEY.

Now is the Day of Salvation.

1 O GOD! my inmost soul convert,
And deeply on my thoughtful heart
Eternal things impress:
Give me to feel their solemn weight,
And save me ere it be too late;
Wake me to righteousness.

HEATH. C. M.

L. MASON.

528

FAWCETT.

Importance of Religion.

1 RELIGION is the chief concern
Of mortals here below;
May I its great importance learn,
Its sovereign virtue know.

2 More needful this than glittering wealth,
Or aught the world bestows;
Not reputation, food, or health
Can give us such repose.

3 Religion should our thoughts engage
Amidst our youthful bloom;
'T will fit us for declining age
And for th' approaching tomb.

4 Oh, may my heart, by grace renewed,
Be my Redeemer's throne;
And be my stubborn will subdued,
His government to own.

529

ANON.

The Morning.

1 WE wait in faith, in prayer we wait,
Until the happy hour
When God shall ope the morning gate,
By his almighty power.

2 We wait in faith, and turn our face
To where the daylight springs;
Till he shall come earth's gloom to chase,
With healing on his wings.

3 And even now, amid the gray,
The east is brightening fast,
And kindling to that perfect day,
Which never shall be past.

4 We wait in faith, we wait in prayer,
Till that blest day shall shine,
When earth shall fruits of Eden bear,
And all, O God, be thine!

5 Oh, guide us till our night is done!
Until, from shore to shore,
Thou, Lord, our everlasting sun,
Art shining evermore!

530

M.W. HALE.

The Pure Heart.

1 WHATEVER dims thy sense of truth,
Or stains thy purity,
Though light as breath of summer air,
Count it as sin to thee.

2 Preserve the tablet of thy thoughts
From every blemish free,
While the Redeemer's lowly faith
Its temple makes with thee.

3 And pray of God, that grace be given
To tread time's narrow way:—
How dark soever it may be,
It leads to cloudless day.

531

ANON.

Spirit of Peace.

1 SPIRIT of peace, celestial Dove,
How excellent thy praise!
How rich the gift of Christian love
Thy gracious power displays!

2 Sweet as the dew on hill and flower,
That silently distils,
At evening's soft and balmy hour,
On Zion's fruitful hills.

LABAN. S. M. Dr. L. Mason.

532 Bulfinch.

The Use of present Oportunities.

1 Children of light, awake!
At Jesus' call arise,
Forth with your leader to partake
His toil, his victories.

2 Ye must not idly stand,
His sacred voice who hear;
Arm for the strife the feeble hand,
The holy standard rear.

3 Naught doth the idle world afford,
But toil must be the price;
Wilt thou not, servant of the Lord,
Then toil for paradise?

4 Awake, ye sons of light!
Strive till the prize be won;
Far spent already is the night;
The day comes brightening on.

533 Montgomery.

The Lord's Prayer.

1 Our heavenly Father, hear
The prayer we offer now;
Thy name be hallowed far and near;
To thee all nations bow.

2 Thy kingdom come; thy will
On earth be done in love,
As saints and seraphim fulfil
Thy perfect law above.

3 Our daily bread supply,
While by thy word we live;
The guilt of our iniquity
Forgive, as we forgive.

4 From dark temptation's power
Our feeble hearts defend:
Deliver in the evil hour,
And guide us to the end.

5 Thine, then, forever be
Glory and power divine;
The sceptre, throne, and majesty
Of heaven and earth are thine.

534 C. Wesley.

All Things in Christ.

1 The soul, by faith reclined
On the Redeemer's breast,
'Mid raging storms, exults to find
An everlasting rest.

2 Sorrow and fear are gone,
Whene'er thy face appears;
It stills the sighing orphan's moan,
And dries the widow's tears.

3 It hallows every cross,
It sweetly comforts me;
It makes me now forget my loss,
And lose myself in thee.

4 Jesus, to whom I fly,
Will all my wishes fill;
What though created streams are dry?
I have the fountain still.

5 Stripped of my earthly friends,
I find them all in one,—
And peace, and joy which never ends,
And heaven, in Christ, begun.

HULLAH. 7s, 6 ls.

535 MONTGOMERY.

The Soul panting for God.

1 As the hart, with eager looks,
Panteth for the waterbrooks,
So my soul, athirst for thee,
Pants the living God to see;
When, oh, when with filial fear,
Lord, shall I to thee draw near?

2 Why art thou cast down, my soul?
God, thy God, shall make thee whole:
Why art thou disquieted?
God shall lift thy fallen head,
And his countenance benign
Be the saving health of thine.

536 BOWRING.

The Pilgrimage of Life.

1 LEAD us with thy gentle sway,
As a willing child is led;
Speed us on our forward way,
As a pilgrim, Lord, is sped,
Who with prayers and helps divine
Seeks a consecrated shrine.

2 We are pilgrims, and our goal
Is that distant land whose bourne
Is the haven of the soul;
Where the mourners cease to mourn,
Where the Saviour's hand will dry
Every tear from every eye.

3 Lead us thither! thou dost know
All the way; but wanderers we
Often miss our path below,
And stretch out our hands to thee;
Guide us,— save us,— and prepare
Our appointed mansion there!

537 FRITZ & SCOLETT.

Living Faith.

1 YE who think the truth ye sow
Lost beneath the winter's snow,
Doubt not time's unerring law
Yet shall bring the genial thaw;
God in nature ye can trust,—
Is the God of mind less just?

2 Workers on the barren soil,
Yours may seem a thankless toil;
Sick at heart with hope deferred,
Listen to the cheering word;
Now the faithful sower grieves;
Soon he'll bind his golden sheaves.

538

Consecration.

1 Now, O God, thine own I am!
Now I give thee back thine own:
Freedom, friends, and health and fame,
Consecrate to thee alone:
Thine I live — thrice happy I!
Happy still if thine I die.

2 Take me, Lord, and all my powers;
Tame my mind, and heart, and will;
All my goods and all my hours,
All I know, and all I feel,
All I think, or speak, or do,—
Take my soul and make it new!

MIDDLETON. 8s & 7s, Double.

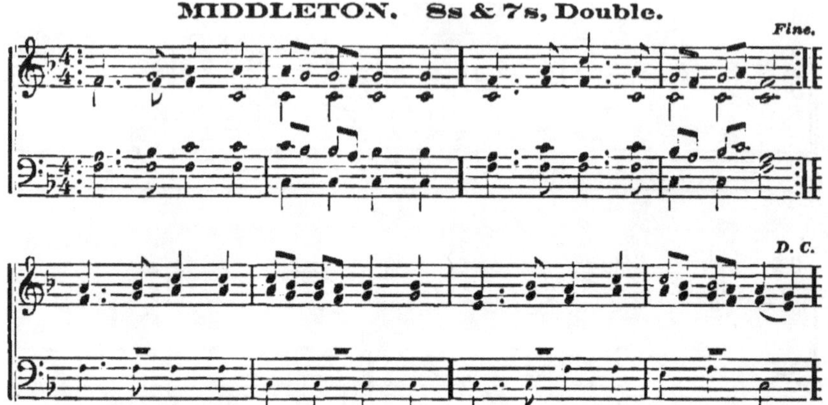

539
WESLEYAN.

Love Divine.

1 Love divine, all love excelling,
Joy of heaven, to earth come down!
Fix in us thy humble dwelling,
All thy faithful mercies crown.
Father! thou art all compassion,
Pure, unbounded love thou art;
Visit us with thy salvation,
Enter every longing heart.

2 Breathe, oh, breathe, thy loving spirit
Into every troubled breast;
Let us all in thee inherit,
Let us find thy promised rest.
Come, almighty to deliver,
Let us all thy life receive;
Graciously come down, and never,
Never more thy temples leave!

540
TOPLADY.

Divine Light Implored.

1 Light of those whose dreary dwelling
Borders on the shades of death!
Rise on us, thyself revealing—
Rise and chase the clouds beneath.
Thou, of heaven and earth Creator!
In our deepest darkness rise;
Scatter all the night of nature,
Pour the day upon our eyes.

2 Still we wait for thine appearing;
Life and joy thy beams impart,
Chasing all our fears, and cheering
Every meek, benighted heart.
By thine all-sufficient merit,
Every burdened soul release;
Every weary, wandering spirit
Guide into thy perfect peace.

541
J. G. BARTHOLOMEW.

Guardian Angels.

1 Is it true that angels hear us,
When we sing our songs of praise?
That bright wings are waving near us,
When to heaven our thoughts we raise?
Is it true that when we're praying
Radiant forms are bending near?
That they know what we are saying,
And our every word can hear?

2 Do they come on holy missions
From our Father's home above,
To return with our petitions,
And our songs of praise and love?
Can we doubt since that bright legion
Came rejoicing to the earth,
Leaving the celestial region
To announce the Saviour's birth?

3 And if men have heard their chorus,
On the earth in days of old,
May they not be bending o'er us,
With their crowns and harps of gold?
Let us listen to their singing,
For it is of heavenly love;
And the very air is ringing
With their praise of God above.

542

ANON.

Rising towards Heaven.

1 Rise, my soul, and stretch thy wings,
Thy better portion trace;
Rise from transitory things,
Towards heaven, thy native place;
Sun, and moon, and stars decay;
Time shall soon this earth remove;
Rise, my soul, and haste away
To seats prepared above.

2 Rivers to the ocean run,
Nor stay in all their course;
Fire ascending, seeks the sun,—
Both speed them to their source;
So a soul that's born of God,
Pants to view his glorious face,
Upward tends to his abode,
To rest in his embrace.

543

Joy in Christ.

1 Joyful let us cast aside
All soul-debasing fear;
Let us hence with thee abide,
And dwell thou with us here.
Thine we are, and would remain,
Whether weal or woe betide;
Let thy favor be our gain,
Thy truth our only guide.

2 Joyful be the hours to-day,
Glad let the seasons be;
Let us sing, for well we may—
Lord, we will sing of thee.
Should thy people silent be,
Then the very stones would sing:
What a debt we owe to thee,
Our Saviour and our King!

3 Joyful are we now to own,—
With rapture now we trace
All the deeds thy love hath done,
The riches of thy grace:
For thy grace alone can save;
Every blessing comes from thee:
All we have and hope to have,
And are, and hope to be.

544

WESLEYAN.

Quiet Religion.

1 Open, Lord, my inward ear,
And bid my heart rejoice;
Bid my quiet spirit hear
The comfort of thy voice;
Never in the whirlwind found,
Or where earthquakes rock the place,
Still and silent is the sound,
The whisper of thy grace.

2 From the world of sin and noise
And tumult I withdraw;
For the small and inward voice
I wait with humble awe;
Silent am I now and still,
Dare not in thy presence move;
To my waiting soul reveal
The secret of thy love.

BETHANY. 6s & 4s. L. MASON.

545 SARAH F. ADAMS.

Nearer to Thee.

1 NEARER, my God, to thee,
Nearer to thee!
E'en though it be a cross
That raiseth me;
Still all my song shall be,
Nearer, my God, to thee,—
Nearer to thee!

2 Though like the wanderer,
The sun gone down,
Darkness be over me,
My rest a stone;
Yet in my dreams I'd be
Nearer, my God, to thee,—
Nearer to thee!

3 There let the way appear,
Steps unto heaven;
All that thou sendest me,
In mercy given;
Angels to beckon me
Nearer, my God, to thee,—
Nearer to thee!

4 Then with my waking thoughts,
Bright with thy praise,
Out of my stony griefs,
Bethel I'll raise;
So by my woes to be
Nearer, my God, to thee,
Nearer to thee!

5 Or if on joyful wing,
Cleaving the sky,
Sun, moon, and stars forgot,
Upward I fly;
Still, all my song shall be,—
Nearer, my God, to thee,
Nearer to thee!

546 T. R. TAYLOR.

Heaven our Home.

1 I'M but a stranger here,
Heaven is my home;
Earth is a desert drear,
Heaven is my home:
Danger and sorrow stand
Round me on every hand;
Heaven is my fatherland,—
Heaven is my home.

2 What though the tempest rage,
Heaven is my home;
Short is my pilgrimage,
Heaven is my home:
Time's cold and wintry blast
Soon will be overpast;
I shall reach home at last;
Heaven is my home.

3 There, at my Saviour's side,
Heaven is my home;
I shall be glorified,
Heaven is my home:
There are the good and blest,
Those I loved most and best,
And there I, too, shall rest;
Heaven is my home!

MARLOW. C. M. Arr. by Dr. Mason.

547 MONTGOMERY.

What is Prayer?

1 Prayer is the soul's sincere desire,
Uttered or unexpressed,
The motion of a hidden fire
That trembles in the breast.

2 Prayer is the burden of a sigh,
The falling of a tear,
The upward glancing of an eye,
When none but God is near.

3 Prayer is the simplest form of speech
That infant lips can try,
Prayer the sublimest strains that reach
The Majesty on high.

4 Prayer is the Christian's vital breath,
The Christian's native air,
The watchword at the gates of death;
He enters heaven with prayer.

5 Prayer is the contrite sinner's voice,
Returning from his ways;
While angels in their songs rejoice,
And cry "Behold he prays!"

548 FABER.

Distraction in Prayer.

1 Had I, dear Lord! no pleasure found
But in the thought of thee;
Prayer would have come unsought, and been
A truer liberty.

2 Yet thou art oft most present, Lord!
In weak, distracted prayer;
A sinner out of heart with self,
Most often finds thee there.

3 And prayer that humbles, sets the soul
From all illusions free;
And teaches it how utterly,
Dear Lord! it hangs on thee.

4 These surface troubles come and go,
Like rufflings of the sea;
The deeper depth is out of reach
To all, my God, but thee!

549 ANON

The still small Voice.

1 Sweet is the prayer whose holy stream
In earnest pleading flows:
Devotion dwells upon the theme,
And warm and warmer glows.

2 Faith grasps the blessing she desires,
Hope points the upward gaze;
And love, untrembling love, inspires
The eloquence of praise.

3 But sweeter far the still small voice,
Heard by no human ear,
When God hath made the heart rejoice,
And dried the bitter tear.

4 Nor accents flow, nor words ascend;
All utterance faileth there;
But listening spirits comprehend,
And God accepts the prayer.

550 MONTGOMERY.

Christ teaches to Pray.

1 O thou by whom we come to God,
The Life, the Truth, the Way!
The path of prayer thyself hast trod;
Lord! teach us how to pray.

HENDON. 7s.

Arr. by Dr. Mason.

551

Methodist Coll.

A Call to Prayer.

1 They who seek the throne of grace
Find that throne in every place;
If we love a life of prayer,
God is present everywhere.

2 In our sickness, in our health,
In our want or in our wealth,
If we look to God in prayer,
God is present everywhere.

3 When our earthly comforts fail,
When the woes of life prevail,
'T is the time for earnest prayer,
God is present everywhere.

4 Then, my soul, in every strait,
To thy Father come and wait;
He will answer every prayer,
God is present everywhere.

552

Conder.

Give us our daily Bread.

1 Day by day the manna fell:
Oh, to learn this lesson well!
Still by constant mercy fed,
Give us, Lord, our daily bread.

2 "Day by day" the promise reads;
Daily strength for daily needs;
Cast foreboding fears away;
Take the manna of to-day!

3 Lord, our times are in thy hand;
All our sanguine hopes have planned,
To thy wisdom we resign,
And would mould our wills to thine.

4 Thou our daily task shalt give;
Day by day to thee we live;
So shall added years fulfil
Not our own, our Father's will.

553

Merrick.

Inward Purity.

1 Blest Instructor, from thy ways,
Who can tell how oft he strays?
Purge me from the guilt that lies
Wrapt within my heart's disguise.

2 Let my tongue, from error free,
Speak the words approved by thee;
To thine all-observing eyes,
Let my thoughts accepted rise.

3 While I thus thy name adore,
And thy healing grace implore;
Blest Redeemer, bow thine ear,
God, my strength, propitious hear!

554

Anon.

A Life hid in God.

1 Let my life be hid in thee,
Life of life, and Light of light!
Love's illimitable sea!
Depth of peace, of power the height:

2 Let my life be hid in thee,
From vexation and annoy;
Calm in thy tranquility,
All my mourning turned to joy.

3 Let my life be hid in thee;
In the world, and yet above;
Hid in thine eternity,
In the ocean of thy love.

DUKE STREET. L. M.

J. HATTON.

555

POPE'S COLL.

The Lord's Prayer.

1 FATHER, adored in worlds above!
Thy glorious name be hallowed still;
Thy kingdom come in truth and love;
And earth, like heaven, obey thy will.

2 Lord, make our daily wants thy care;
Forgive the sins which we forsake;
In thy compassion let us share,
As fellow-men of ours partake.

3 Evils beset us every hour,—
Thy kind protection we implore;
Thine is the kingdom, thine the power,
The glory thine for evermore.

556

MRS. COTTERILL.

For a Life devoted to God's Glory.

1 O THOU, who hast at thy command
The hearts of all men in thy hand!
Our wayward, erring hearts incline
To have no other will but thine.

2 Our wishes, our desires, control;
Mould every purpose of the soul;
O'er all may we victorious be
That stands between ourselves and thee.

3 Thrice blest will all our blessings be,
When we can look through them to thee;
When each glad heart its tribute pays
Of love, and gratitude, and praise.

4 And while we to thy glory live,
May we to thee all glory give,
Until the final summons come,
That calls thy willing servants home.

557

CHRISTIAN PSALMIST.

Prayer for Divine Help.

1 BE with me, Lord, where'er I go;
Teach me what thou would'st have me do;
Show me my weakness,— let me see
I have my power, my all from thee.

2 Enrich me always with thy love;
My kind protection ever prove;
Thy signet put upon my breast,
And let thy spirit on me rest.

3 Assist and teach me how to pray;
Incline my nature to obey;
What thou abhorr'st that let me flee,
And only love what pleases thee.

4 Oh, may I never do my will,
But thine, and only thine, fulfil;
Let all my time and all my ways
Be spent and ended to thy praise.

558

RAY PALMER.

Quiet Devotion.

1 THOU Saviour, from thy throne on high,
Enrobed in light and girt with power,
Dost note the thought, the prayer, the sigh,
Of hearts that love the tranquil hour.

2 Oft thou thyself didst steal away
At eventide, from labor done,
In some still peaceful shade to pray
Till morning watches were begun.

3 Thou hast not, dearest Lord, forgot
Thy wrestlings on Judea's hills;
And still thou lov'st the quiet spot
Where praise the lowly spirit fills.

GEER. C. M. Greatorex's Coll.

559 Wesley's Coll.

Thy Kingdom come.

1 Father of me and all mankind,
And all the hosts above,
Let every understanding mind
Unite to praise thy love.

2 Thy kingdom come, with power and grace
To every heart of man;
Thy peace, and joy, and righteousness,
In all our bosoms reign:

3 The righteousness that never ends,
But makes an end of sin;
The joy that human thought transcends,
Into our souls bring in:

4 The kingdom of established peace,
Which can no more remove;
The perfect power of godliness,
Th' omnipotence of love.

560 Pope.

Prayer for Divine Guidance.

1 Father of all! whose cares extend
To earth's remotest shore,
Through every age let praise ascend,
And every clime adore.

2 Mean though I am, not wholly so,
Since quickened by thy breath;
Lord, lead me whereso'er I go,
Through this day's life or death.

3 Teach me to feel another's woe,
To hide the fault I see;
That mercy I to others show,
That mercy show to me.

4 If I am right, thy grace impart,
Still in the right to stay;
If I am wrong, oh, teach my heart
To find that better way.

5 What conscience dictates to be done,
Or warns me not to do,
This teach me more than hell to shun,
That more than heaven pursue.

561 Montgomery.

For grateful Submission.

1 One prayer I have,—all prayers in one,—
When I am wholly thine;
"Thy will, my God, thy will be done,
And let that will be mine."

2 May I remember that to thee
Whate'er I have I owe;
And back in gratitude from me
May all thy bounties flow.

3 Thy gifts are only then enjoyed,
When used as talents lent;
Those talents only well employed,
When in thy service spent.

4 And though thy wisdom takes away,
Shall I arraign thy will?
No, let me bless thy name, and say,
"The Lord is gracious still."

5 All-wise, almighty, and all-good,
In thee I firmly trust;
Thy ways, unknown or understood,
Are merciful and just.

WEBSTER. 6s, Double. Arr. from WEBER.

562

H. BONAR.

Thy Will be Done.

1 THY way, not mine, O Lord,
However dark it be!
Lead me by thine own hand;
Choose out the path for me.
I dare not choose my lot:
I would not, if I might;
Choose thou for me, my God,
So shall I walk aright.

2 The kingdom that I seek
Is thine: so let the way
That leads to it be thine,
Else I must surely stray.
Take thou my cup, and it
With joy or sorrow fill,
As best to thee may seem;
Choose thou my good and ill.

3 Choose thou for me my friends,
My sickness or my health;
Choose thou my cares for me,
My poverty or wealth.
Not mine, not mine the choice,
In things or great or small;
Be thou my Guide, my Strength,
My Wisdom, and my All.

563

HASTINGS.

Trust in God.

1 BE tranquil, O my soul,
Be quiet every fear!
Thy Father hath control,
And he is ever near.
Ne'er of thy lot complain,
Whatever may befall;
Sickness or care, or pain,
'T is well appointed all.

2 A Father's chastening hand
Is leading thee along;
Nor distant is the land,
Where swells the immortal song.
Oh, then, my soul, be still!
Await heaven's high decree;
Seek but thy Father's will,
It shall be well with thee.

MEDFIELD. C. M.

Wm. Mather.

564

Bryant.

Divine Aid implored.

1 O God! whose dread and dazzling brow
Love never yet forsook,
On those who seek thy presence now,
In deep compassion look.

2 For many a frail and erring heart
Is in thy holy sight,
And feet too willing to depart
From the plain way of right.

3 Yet pleased the humble prayer to hear,
And kind to all that live;
Thou, when thou seest the contrite tear,
Art ready to forgive.

4 Lord! aid us with thy heavenly grace,
Our truest bliss to find;
Nor sternly judge our erring race,
So feeble, and so blind.

565

Merrick.

Dependence and Submission.

1 Author of good, to thee we turn,
Thine ever-watchful eye
Alone can all our wants discern,
Thy hand alone supply.

2 Oh, let thy fear within us dwell,
Thy love our footsteps guide:
That love shall vainer loves expel;
That fear all fears beside.

3 And since, by passion's force subdued,
Too oft, with stubborn will,
We blindly shun the latent good,
And grasp the specious ill,—

4 Not what we wish, but what we want,
Let mercy still supply;
The good, unasked, O Father, grant;
The ill, though asked, deny.

566

H. H. Milman.

Praying for Divine Help.

1 Oh, help us, Lord! each hour of need
Thy heavenly succor give;
Help us in thought, and word and deed,
Each hour on earth we live.

2 Oh, help us, when our spirits bleed,
With contrite anguish sore,
And when our hearts are cold and dead,
Oh, help us, Lord, the more.

3 Oh, help us through the prayer of faith
More firmly to believe;
For still the more the servant hath,
The more shall he receive.

4 Oh, help us, Father! from on high;
We know no help but thee;
Oh! help us so to live and die,
As thine in heaven to be.

567

Cappe's Selection.

Prayer for Divine Direction.

1 Eternal Source of life and light,
Supremely good and wise,
To thee we bring our grateful vows,
To thee lift up our eyes.

2 Our dark and erring minds illume
With truth's celestial rays;
Inspire our hearts with sacred love,
And tune our lips to praise.

SHOEL. L. M. SHOEL.

568

WATTS.

Divine Life sought.

1 My God, permit me not to be
A stranger to myself and thee;
Amid a thousand thoughts I rove,
Forgetful of my highest love.

2 Why should my passions mix with earth,
And thus debase my heavenly birth;
Why should I cleave to things below,
And let my God, my Saviour, go?

3 Call me away from flesh and sense;
One sovereign word can draw me thence;
I would obey the voice divine,
And all inferior joys resign.

4 Be earth, with all her scenes withdrawn;
Let noise and vanity be gone:
In secret silence of the mind,
My heaven, and there my God, I find.

569

SIR WALTER SCOTT.

Divine Guidance implored.

1 When Israel of the Lord beloved,
Out from the land of bondage came,
Her father's God before her moved,
An awful guide in smoke and flame.

2 By day, along th' astonished lands,
The cloudy pillar glided slow;
By night, Arabia's crimsoned sands
Returned the fiery column's glow.

3 Thus present still, though now unseen,
When brightly shines the prosperous day,
Be thoughts of thee a cloudy screen,
To temper the deceitful ray!

570

ANON.

The Light from Above.

1 Eternal God, thou light divine,
Fountain of unexhausted love,
Oh, let thy glories on me shine,
In earth beneath, from heaven above.

2 Thou art the weary wanderer's rest,
Give me the easy yoke to bear;
With steadfast patience arm my breast,
With spotless love and lowly fear.

3 Be thou, O Rock of Ages, nigh!
So shall each murmuring thought be gone,
And grief, and fear, and care shall fly,
As clouds before the midday sun.

4 Speak to my warring passions, "Peace:"
Say to my trembling heart, "Be still;"
Thy power my strength and fortress is,
For all things serve thy holy will.

571

ANON.

Christ's Help in Trouble.

1 Welcome to me the darkest night,
If there the Saviour's presence brigh[t]
Beam forth upon the soul dismayed,
And say, "'T is I! be not afraid!"

2 Welcome the fiercest waves that roll
Their deepening floods to whelm my soul,
If he rebuke the storm of ill,
And bid the tempest, "Peace, be still!"

3 Welcome the thorniest path, if there
The print-marks of his feet appear;
If in his footsteps we may tread,
And follow where our Lord hath led.

HERMON. C. M.

Dr. L. Mason.

572

Cowper.

Walking with God.

1 Oh, for a closer walk with God!
A calm and heavenly frame!
A light to shine upon the road
That leads me to the Lamb!

2 What peaceful hours I once enjoyed!
How sweet their memory still!
But now I find an aching void
The world can never fill.

3 Return, O holy Dove, return,
Sweet messenger of rest;
I hate the sins that made thee mourn,
And drove thee from my breast.

4 The dearest idol I have known,
Whate'er that idol be,
Help me to tear it from thy throne,
And worship only thee.

573

Methodist Coll.

Seeking God.

1 Talk with us, Lord, thyself reveal,
While here o'er earth we rove;
Speak to our hearts, and let us feel
The kindling of thy love.

2 With thee conversing, we forget
All time, and toil, and care:
Labor is rest, and pain is sweet,
If thou, my God, art here.

3 Here, then, my God, vouchsafe to stay,
And bid my heart rejoice;
My bounding heart shall own thy sway,
And echo to thy voice.

574

T. H. Gill.

Serving God.

1 Oh, not to fill the mouth of fame
My longing soul is stirred;
Oh, give me a diviner name!
Call me thy servant, Lord!

2 No longer would my soul be known
As self-sustained and free:
Oh, not mine own! oh, not mine own!
Lord, I belong to thee!

3 In each aspiring burst of prayer,
Sweet leave my soul would ask
Thine every burden, Lord, to bear,
To do thine every task.

4 In life, in death, on earth, in heaven,
No other name for me!
The same sweet style and title given
Through all eternity.

575

Faber.

All Things work together for Good.

1 Ill, that God blesses, is our good,
And unblest good is ill;
And all is right that seems most wrong,
If it be his dear will.

2 Man's weakness, waiting upon God,
Its end can never miss;
For man on earth no work can do
More angel-like than this.

3 He always wins who sides with God
To him no chance is lost;
God's will is sweetest to him when
It triumphs at his cost.

ERNAN. 10s. Dr. L. Mason.

576

Mrs. Stowe.

Abide in Me.

1 That mystic word of thine, O Sovereign Lord! [for me;
Is all too pure, too high, too deep
Weary of striving, and with longing faint, [thee.
I breathe it back again in prayer to

2 Abide in me,—o'ershadow, by thy love,
Each half-formed purpose and dark thought of sin; [desire,
Quench, ere it rise, each selfish, low
And keep my soul as thine,—calm and divine.

3 As some rare perfume in a vase of clay
Pervades it with a fragrance not its own—
So, when thou dwellest in a mortal soul,
All heaven's own sweetness seems around it thrown.

4 The soul alone, like a neglected harp,
Grows out of tune, and needs that hand divine; [the chords,
Dwell thou within it, tune and touch
Till every note and string shall answer thine.

5 Abide in me: there have been moments pure, [thy power;
When I have seen thy face and felt
Then evil lost its grasp, and, passion hushed, [the hour.
Owned the divine enchantment of

6 These were but seasons beautiful and rare; [be;
Abide in me,—and they shall ever
I pray thee now fulfil my earnest prayer,
Come and abide in me, and I in thee.

577

Lyte.

Christ's Presence sought.

1 Abide with me! Fast falls the eventide, [me abide!
The darkness deepens—Lord, with
When other helpers fail, and comforts flee, [me!
Help of the helpless, oh, abide with

2 Swift to its close ebbs out life's little day; [away;
Earth's joys grow dim, its glories pass
Change and decay in all around I see;
O thou who changest not, abide with me!

3 I need thy presence every passing hour:
What but thy grace can foil the tempter's power? [can be?
Who like thyself my guide and stay
Through cloud and sunshine, Lord, abide with me!

4 Not a brief glance I long, a passing word, [Lord,
But as thou dwell'st with thy disciples,
Familiar, condescending, patient, free,
Come, not to sojourn, but abide, with me!

PETERBOROUGH. C. M.

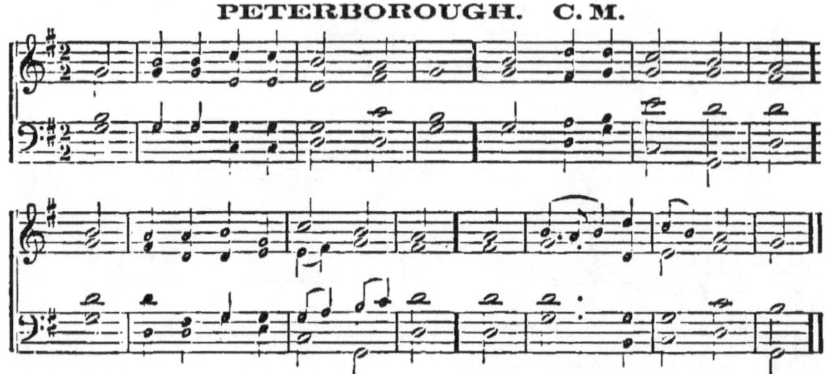

578

WREFORD.

Help Thou my Unbelief.

1 LORD! I believe; thy power I own,
Thy word I would obey;
I wander comfortless and lone,
When from thy truth I stray.

2 Lord! I believe; but gloomy fears
Sometimes bedim my sight;
I look to thee with prayers and tears,
And cry for strength and light.

3 Lord! I believe; but oft, I know,
My faith is cold and weak;
Strengthen my weakness, and bestow
The confidence I seek!

4 Yes, I believe; and only thou
Canst give my soul relief;
Lord! to thy truth my spirit bow,
Help thou my unbelief!

579

B. BARTON.

Walking in the Light.

1 WALK in the light! so shalt thou know
That fellowship of love,
His spirit only can bestow,
Who reigns in light above.

2 Walk in the light! and thou shalt find
Thy heart made truly his,
Who dwells in cloudless light enshrined,
In whom no darkness is.

3 Walk in the light! and thou shalt own
Thy darkness passed away,
Because that light hath on thee shone
In which is perfect day.

4 Walk in the light! thy path shall be
Peaceful, serene, and bright;
For God, by grace, shall dwell in thee,
And God himself is light.

580

LYRA CATH.

Divine Strength invoked.

1 I WORSHIP thee, sweet will of God,
And all thy ways adore;
And every day I live, I long
To love thee more and more.

2 Ill, that God blesses, is our good,
And unblest good is ill;
And all is right that seems most wrong,
If it be his dear will!

3 When obstacles and trials seem
Like prison-walls to be,
I do the little I can do,
And leave the rest to thee.

4 I have no cares, O blessed will!
For all my cares are thine;
I live in triumph, Lord! for thou
Hast made thy triumphs mine.

581

DODDRIDGE.

Walking with God.

1 THRICE happy souls, who, born from heaven,
While yet they sojourn here,
Do all their days with God begin,
And spend them in his fear.

2 'Midst hourly cares, may love present
Its incense to thy throne;
And, while the world our hands employs,
Our hearts be thine alone!

CONVENT BELL. 7s, Double.

582

R. GRANT.

Solemn Litany.

1 FATHER, when in dust to thee
Low we bend the adoring knee;
When, repentant, to the skies
Scarce we lift our weeping eyes;
Oh, by all the pains and woe
Suffered by thy Son below,
Bending from thy throne on high,
Hear our solemn Litany!

2 By his helpless infant years,
By his life of want and tears,
By his days of sore distress
In the savage wilderness;
By the dread mysterious hour
Of the insulting tempter's power;
Turn, oh, turn a favoring eye,
Hear our solemn Litany!

3 By his hour of dire despair;
By his agony of prayer;
By the cross, the nail, the thorn,
Piercing spear, and torturing scorn;
By the gloom that veiled the skies
O'er the dreadful sacrifice;
Listen to our humble cry,
Hear our solemn Litany!

4 By his deep expiring groan;
By the sad sepulchral stone;
By the vault, whose dark abode
Held in vain the Son of God;
By the life to heaven restored,
Reascended Light and Lord;
Father! listen to the cry
Of our solemn Litany!

583

MILMAN

Lord have Mercy.

1 LORD, have mercy when we pray,
Strength to seek a better way;
When our wakening thoughts begin
First to loathe their cherished sin;
Sigh for death, yet fear it still,
From the dread of future ill;
When the dim, advancing gloom
Tells us that our hour is come.

2 Lord, have mercy when we lie
On the restless bed, and sigh,—
Sigh for death, yet fear it still,
From the thought of former ill;
When the dim, advancing gloom
Tells us that our hour has come;
When is loosed the silver cord,—
Then, oh, then! have mercy, Lord.

3 Lord, have mercy, when we know
First how vain this world below;
When its darker thoughts oppress,
Doubts perplex, and fears distress;
When the earliest gleam is given,
Of the bright but distant heaven;
Then thy fostering grace afford,
Then, oh, then! have mercy, Lord!

UXBRIDGE. L. M. Dr. L. Mason.

584 DRUMMOND.

Faith without Works is Dead.

1 As body when the soul has fled,
As barren trees, decayed and dead,
Is faith; a hopeless, lifeless thing,
If not of righteous deeds the spring.

2 One cup of healing oil and wine,
One teardrop shed on mercy's shrine,
Is thrice more grateful, Lord, to thee,
Than lifted eye or bended knee.

3 To doers only of the word,
Propitious is the righteous Lord;
He hears their cries, accepts their prayers,
Binds up their wounds, and soothes their cares.

585 MRS. GILMAN.

Our Sufficiency of God.

1 Is there a lone and dreary hour,
When worldly pleasures lose their power?
My Father! let me turn to thee,
And set each thought of darkness free.

2 Is there a time of racking grief,
Which scorns the prospect of relief?
My Father! break the cheerless gloom,
And bid my heart its calm resume.

3 Is there an hour of peace and joy,
When hope is all my soul's employ?
My Father! still my hopes will roam,
Until they rest with thee, their home.

4 The noontide blaze, the midnight scene,
The dawn, or twilight's sweet serene,
The glow of life, the dying hour,
Shall own my Father's grace and power.

586 LYRA CATH.

Penitential Prayer.

1 HEALTH of the weak, to make them strong!
Refuge of sinners, and their song!
Comfort of each afflicted breast!
Haven of hope in realms of rest!

2 Lord of the patriarchs gone before!
Light of the prophets' learnéd lore!
Deign from thy throne to look on me,
And hear my lowly litany.

3 Lead me, O Spirit, to thy Son,
To taste and feel what he has done;
To lay me low before his cross,
And reckon all beside as dross;

4 To speak, and think, and will, and move,
And love, as thou would'st have me love:
Oh, look upon this bended knee,
And hear my heart's own litany.

587 J. ROSCOE.

Joyful Hope.

1 THE stars of heaven are shining on,
Tho' these frail eyes are dimm'd with tears;
And though the hopes of earth be gone,
Yet are not ours th' immortal years?

2 There shall no doubts disturb its trust,
No sorrows dim celestial love;
But these afflictions of the dust,
Like shadows of the night, remove.

3 That glorious life will well repay
This life of toil and care, and woe:
O Father! joyful on my way,
To drink thy bitter cup, I go.

WOODSTOCK. C. M.

DUTTON.

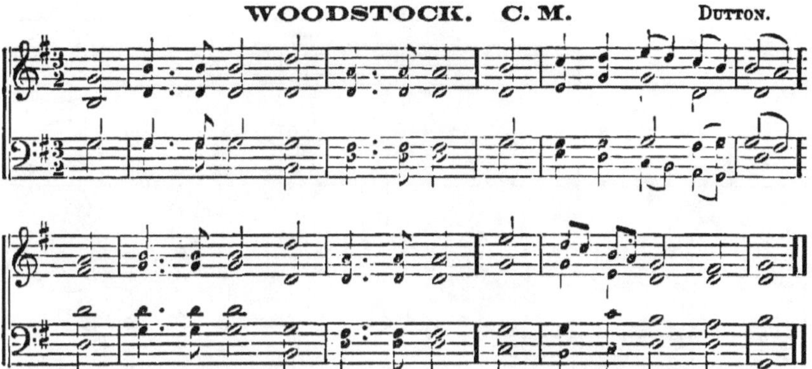

588

HAWEIS, 1792.

Lord, remember Me.

1 O THOU, from whom all goodness flows,
I lift my soul to thee;
In all my sorrows, conflicts, woes,
Good Lord, remember me.

2 When on my aching, burdened heart
My sins lie heavily,
Thy pardon grant, new peace impart;
Good Lord, remember me.

3 When trials sore obstruct my way,
And ills I cannot flee,
Oh, let my strength be as my day;
Good Lord, remember me.

4 And when before thy throne I stand,
And lift my soul to thee,
Then, with the saints at thy right hand,
Good Lord, remember me.

589

SMART.

For Prudence and Wisdom.

1 FATHER of light! conduct my feet
Through life's dark, dangerous road;
Let each advancing step still bring
Me nearer to my God.

2 Let heaven-eyed prudence be my guide;
And when I go astray,
Recall my feet from folly's path
To wisdom's better way.

3 Teach me in every various scene
To keep my end in sight;
And while I tread life's mazy track,
Let wisdom guide me right.

4 That heavenly wisdom from above
Abundantly impart;
And let it guard, and guide, and warm,
And penetrate my heart.

5 Till it shall lead me to thyself,
Fountain of bliss and love!
And all my darkness be dispersed
In endless light above.

590

COWPER.

Purposes of God developed by his Providence.

1 GOD moves in a mysterious way,
His wonders to perform;
He plants his footsteps in the sea,
And rides upon the storm.

2 Ye fearful saints, fresh courage take;
The clouds ye so much dread
Are big with mercy, and shall break
In blessings on your head.

3 Judge not the Lord by feeble sense,
But trust him for his grace;
Behind a frowning providence
He hides a smiling face.

4 His purposes will ripen fast
Unfolding every hour;
The bud may have a bitter taste,
But sweet will be the flower.

5 Blind unbelief is sure to err,
And scan his work in vain;
God is his own interpreter,
And he will make it plain.

MANOAH. C. M.

GREATOREX'S COLL.

591 BOWRING.

Holy Aspirations.

1 THE Saviour now is gone before
To yon blest realms of light:
Oh, thither may our spirits soar,
And wing their upward flight.

2 Lord, make us to those joys aspire,
That spring from love to thee,
That pass the carnal heart's desire,
And faith alone can see.

3 To guide us to thy glories, Lord,
To lift us to the sky,
Oh, may thy spirit still be poured
Upon us from on high.

592 R. BAXTER.

Looking to Christ.

1 CHRIST leads me through no darker rooms
Than he went through before;
He that into God's kingdom comes,
Must enter by the door.

2 Come, Lord, when grace hath made me meet
Thy blessed face to see;
For if thy work on earth be sweet,
What must thy glory be?

3 Then shall I end my sad complaints,
And weary, sinful days,
And join with those triumphant saints,
That sing Jehovah's praise.

4 My knowledge of that life is small,
The eye of faith is dim;
But 't is enough that Christ knows all,
And I shall be with him.

593 FRANCIS XAVIER.

True Love to God and Christ.

1 MY God, I love thee, not because
I hope for heaven thereby:
Nor yet that they who love thee not
Must burn eternally.

2 Not with the hope of gaining aught,
Nor seeking a reward;
But as thyself hast lovéd me,
O ever loving Lord!

3 E'en so I love thee, and will love,
And in thy praise will sing;
Because thou only art my Lord,
And my eternal King.

594 MOORE.

Heaven desired.

1 THE bird let loose in Eastern skies,
Returning fondly home,
Ne'er stoops to earth her wing, nor flies
Where idle warblers roam.

2 But high she shoots through air and [light,—
Above all low delay,
Where nothing earthly bounds her flight,
Nor shadow dims her way.

3 So grant me, God, from every snare
Of sinful passion free,
Aloft through faith's serener air
To hold my course to thee.

4 No sin to cloud, no lure to stay
My soul, as home she springs;
Thy sunshine on her joyful way,
Thy freedom on her wings.

BRADEN. S. M.

595
MME. GUYON.

The Water of Life.

1 THE fountain in its source
No drought of summer fears,
The farther it pursues its course,
The nobler it appears.

2 But shallow cisterns yield
A scanty, short supply;
The morning sees them amply filled,—
At evening they are dry.

3 The cisterns I forsake,
O fount of bliss, for thee!
My thirst with living waters slake,
And drink eternity.

596
MORAVIAN.

Reliance on God.

1 GIVE to the winds thy fears;
Hope, and be undismayed; [tears;
God hears thy sighs, God counts thy
God shall lift up thy head.

2 Through waves, through clouds, and
He gently clears thy way; [storms,
Wait thou his time, so shall the night
Soon end in joyous day.

3 He everywhere hath rule,
And all things serve his might;
His every act pure blessing is,
His path unsullied light.

4 Thou seest our weakness, Lord,
Our hearts are known to thee:
Oh, lift thou up the sinking hand,
Confirm the feeble knee!

5 Let us, in life or death,
Boldly thy truth declare;
And publish, with our latest breath,
Thy love and guardian care.

597
COWPER.

Dependence on God.

1 To keep the lamp alive,
With oil we fill the bowl;
'T is water makes the willow thrive,
And grace that feeds the soul.

2 The Lord's unsparing hand
Supplies the living stream;
It is not at our own command,
But still derived from him.

3 Man's wisdom is to seek
His strength in God alone;
And e'en an angel would be weak,
Who trusted in his own.

4 Retreat beneath his wings,
And in his grace confide;
This more exalts the King of kings
Than all your works beside.

5 In God is all our store,
Grace issues from his throne;
Whoever says, "I want no more,"
Confesses he has none.

598
CH. PS.

The peaceful Death of the Righteous.

1 OH, for the death of those
Who slumber in the Lord!
Oh, be like theirs my last repose,
Like theirs my last reward.

STATE STREET. S. M.

WOODMAN

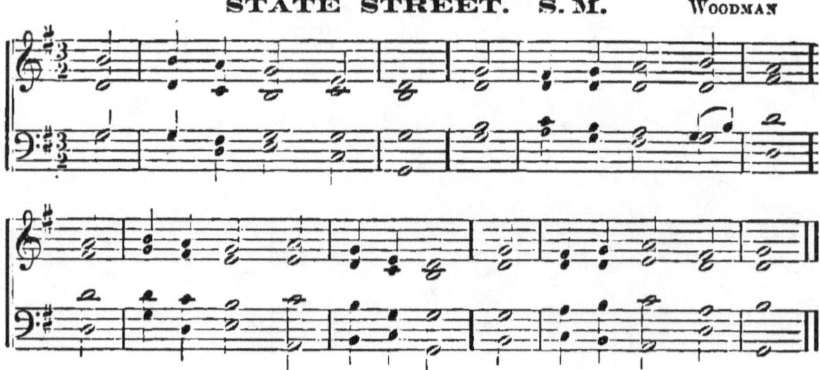

599

DODDRIDGE.

Trust in God.

1 How gentle God's commands!
How kind his precepts are!
"Come, cast your burdens on the Lord,
And trust his constant care."

2 Beneath his watchful eye
His saints securely dwell;
That hand which bears all nature up,
Shall guard his children well.

3 Why should this anxious load
Press down your weary mind?
Haste to your heavenly Father's throne,
And sweet refreshment find.

4 His goodness stands approved,
Through each succeeding day;
I'll drop my burden at his feet,
And bear a song away.

600

PATRICK.

The Fatherly Love of God.

1 GOD, who is just and kind,
Will those who err instruct,
And to the paths of righteousness
Their wandering steps conduct.

2 The humble soul he guides,
Teaches the meek his way,
Kindness and truth he shows to all
Who his just laws obey.

3 Give me the tender heart
That mixes fear with love,
And lead me through whatever path
Thy wisdom shall approve.

4 Oh! ever keep my soul
From error, shame, and guilt;
Nor suffer the fair hope to fail,
Which on thy truth is built.

601

ANON.

My Times are in God's Hands.

1 "My times are in thy hand:"
My God, I'd have them there:
My life, my friends, my soul, I leave
Entirely to thy care.

2 "My times are in thy hand,"
Whatever they may be,—
Pleasing or painful, dark or bright,
As best may seem to thee.

3 "My times are in thy hand:"
Why should I doubt or fear?
My Father's hand will never cause
His child a needless tear.

4 "My times are in thy hand:"
I'll always trust in thee;
And, after death, at thy right hand
May I for ever be

602

FURNESS.

The Want within.

1 I FEEL within a want
For ever burning there:
What I so thirst for, kindly grant,
O thou who hearest prayer!

2 This is the thing I crave,—
A likeness to thy Son;
This boon would I much rather have
Than call the world my own.

GENEVA. C. M.

J. COLE.

603

Watchful Care.

1 How are thy servants blest, O Lord!
How sure is their defence!
Eternal Wisdom is their guide,
Their help, Omnipotence.

2 In foreign realms and lands remote,
Supported by thy care,
Thro' burning climes they pass unhurt,
And breathe in tainted air.

3 In midst of dangers, fears, and death,
Thy goodness we'll adore;
We'll praise thee for thy mercies past,
And humbly hope for more.

4 Our life, while thou preserv'st that life,
Thy sacrifice shall be;
And death, when death shall be our lot,
Shall join our souls to thee.

604

MRS. STEELE.

Trust in the Divine Will.

1 MY God, my Father — blissful name —
Oh, may I call thee mine?
May I with sweet assurance claim
A portion so divine?

2 This only can my fears control,
And bid my sorrows fly;
What harm can ever reach my soul
Beneath my Father's eye?

3 Whate'er thy providence denies,
I calmly would resign;
For thou art good, and just, and wise;
Oh, bend my will to thine.

4 Whate'er thy sacred will ordains,
Oh, give me strength to bear;
And let me know my Father reigns,
And trust his tender care.

605

HYMNS OF THE AGES.

If He is Mine.

1 IF God is mine, then present things
And things to come are mine;
Yea, Christ, his word, and spirit too,
And glory all divine.

2 If he is mine, then from his love
He every trouble sends;
All things are working for my good,
And bliss his rod attends.

3 If he is mine, let friends forsake,
Let wealth and honor flee;
Sure he who giveth me himself
Is more than these to me.

4 Oh, tell me, Lord, that thou art mine!
What can I wish beside?
My soul shall at the fountain live
When all the springs are dried.

606

HEGINBOTHAM.

Constant Care of God.

1 FATHER of mercies! God of love!
My Father and my God!
I'll sing the honors of thy name,
And spread thy praise abroad.

2 In every period of my life
Thy thoughts of love appear;
Thy mercies gild each transient scene,
And crown each passing year.

EFFIELD. 8s & 4s.

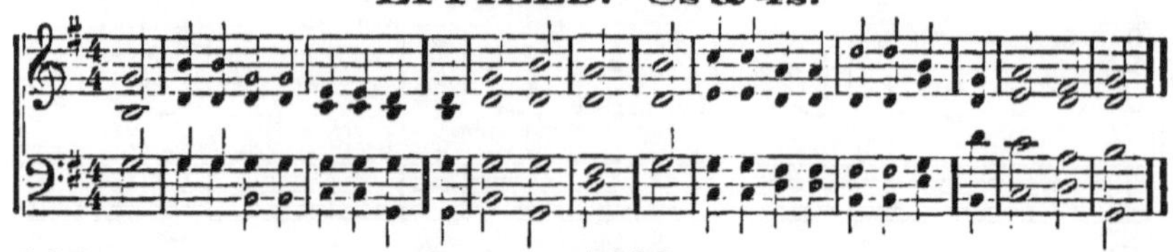

607

ADELAIDE PROCTER.

Trust.

1 FRET not, poor soul: while doubt and
Disturb thy breast, [fear
The pitying angels, who can see,
Say, Trust and rest.

2 Plan not, nor scheme,—but calmly
His choice is best. [wait;
His wisdom sees and judges right,
So trust and rest.

3 Strive not, nor struggle: thy poor
Can never wrest [might
The meanest thing to serve thy will;
Then trust and rest.

4 Desire not: self-love is strong
Within thy breast;
And yet He loves thee better still!
Then trust and rest.

5 What dost thou fear? His wisdom
Supreme confessed; [reigns
His power and love are infinite:
So trust and rest.

608

R. C. TRENCH.

Life's Answer.

1 I KNOW not if the dark or bright
Shall be my lot;
If that wherein my hopes delight
Be best or not.

2 My bark is wafted to the strand
By breath divine:
And on the helm there rests a hand
Other than mine.

3 One who has known in storms to sail,
I have on board;
Above the raving of the gale,
I hear the Lord.

4 He holds me when the billows smite—
I shall not fall;
If sharp, 't is short, if long, 't is light;
He tempers all.

609

LYTE.

Office of the Holy Spirit.

1 OUR blest Redeemer, ere he breathed
His last farewell,
A Guide, a Comforter, bequeathed
With us to dwell.

2 He came in tongues of living flame,
To teach, subdue;
All-powerful as the wind he came,
As viewless too.

3 He comes, his graces to impart,
A willing guest,
While he can find one humble heart
Wherein to rest.

4 He breathes that gentle voice we hear,
As breeze of even; [fear,
That checks each fault, that calms each
And speaks of heaven.

5 And all the good that we possess,
His gift we own;
Yea, every thought of holiness,
And victory won.

6 Spirit of purity and grace!
Our weakness see;
Oh, make our hearts thy dwelling-place,
And worthier thee!

610

J. L. FRANCIS.

Gratitude for Redemption.

1 THE Lord our God has sent his Son
To save our race,
And give us at his glorious throne
A rightful place.

2 He finds us crippled, sick, and poor,
And sunk in sin;
He heals us, opens heav'n's bright door,
And leads us in.

3 Then let us raise our songs of joy
With one accord,
And all our pow'rs henceforth employ
To praise the Lord.

ALFRETON. L. M. W. BEASTALL.

611

O. W. HOLMES.

Hymn of Trust.

1 O LOVE divine, that stooped to share
Our sharpest pang, our bitterest tear,
On thee we cast each earth-born care,
We smile at pain while thou art near!

2 Though long the weary way we tread,
And sorrows crowd each lingering year,
No path we shun, no darkness dread,
Our hearts still whispering, thou art near!

3 When drooping pleasure turns to grief,
And trembling faith is changed to fear,
The murmuring wind, the quivering leaf,
Shall softly tell us, thou art near!

4 On thee we fling our burdening woe,
O Love Divine, forever dear,
Content to suffer, while we know,
Living and dying, thou art near.

612

MONTGOMERY.

Following after God.

1 O GOD, thou art my God alone;
Early to thee my soul shall cry,
A pilgrim in a land unknown,
A thirsty land, whose springs are dry.

2 Yet, through this rough and thorny [maze,
I follow hard on thee, my God;
Thine hand unseen upholds my ways,
I lean upon thy staff and rod.

3 Thee, in the watches of the night,
When I remember on my bed,
Thy presence makes the darkness light,
Thy guardian wings are round my head.

4 Better than life itself thy love,
Dearer than all beside to me;
For whom have I in heaven above,
Or what on earth, compared with thee?

613

ALICE CARY.

The Way.

1 I CANNOT plainly see the way,
So dark my path is; but I know
If I do truly work and pray,
Some good will brighten out of woe.

2 I said I could not see the way,
And yet what need is there to see,
More than to do what good I may,
And trust the great God over me?

614

C. WESLEY.

Enjoyment of Christ's Love.

1 JESUS, thy boundless love to me,
No thought can reach, no tongue declare,
Unite my thankful heart to thee,
And reign without a rival there.

2 Thy love, how cheering is its ray!
All pain before its presence flies;
Care, anguish, sorrow, melt away
Where'er its healing beams arise.

3 Oh, let thy love my soul inflame,
And to thy service sweetly bind;
Transfuse it through my inmost frame,
And mould me wholly to thy mind.

4 Thy love, in sufferings, be my peace:
Thy love, in weakness, make me strong;
And, when the storms of life shall cease,
Thy love shall be in heaven my song.

SESSIONS. L. M.

615
GIBBONS.

Heavenly Life here.

1 Now let our souls on wings sublime,
Rise from the vanities of time,
Draw back the parting veil, and see
The glories of eternity.

2 Born by a new celestial birth,
Why should we grovel here on earth?
Why grasp at transitory toys,
So near to heaven's eternal joys?

3 Shall aught beguile us on the road,
When we are walking back to God?
For strangers into life we come,
And dying is but going home.

616
TENNYSON.

And all is well.

1 Love is and was my Lord and King,
And in his presence I attend
To hear the tidings of my friend,
Which every hour his couriers bring.

2 Love is and was my King and Lord,
And will be, though as yet I keep
Within his court on earth, and sleep
Encompassed by his faithful guard.

3 And hear at times a sentinel
Who moves about from place to place,
And whispers to the worlds of space
In the deep night, that all is well.

4 And all is well, though faith and form
Be sundered in the night of fear;
Well roars the storm to those that hear
A deeper voice across the storm.

617
MRS. WILLARD.

Entire Trust.

1 Rocked in the cradle of the deep,
I lay me down in peace to sleep;
Secure I rest upon the wave,
For thou, O Lord, hast power to save.

2 I know thou wilt not slight my call,
For thou dost mark the sparrow's fall;
And calm and peaceful is my sleep,
Rocked in the cradle of the deep.

3 And such the trust that still were mine,
Though stormy winds swept o'er the brine,
Or though the tempest's fiery breath
Roused me from sleep to wreck and death!

4 In ocean cave still safe with thee,
The germ of immortality;
And calm and peaceful is my sleep,
Rocked in the cradle of the deep.

618
HEGINBOTHAM.

A good Conscience.

1 Sweet peace of conscience, heav'nly guest,
Come, fix thy mansion in my breast;
Dispel my doubts, my fears control,
And heal the anguish of my soul.

2 Come, smiling hope and joy sincere,
Come, make your constant dwelling here;
Still let your presence cheer my heart,
Nor sin compel you to depart.

3 O God of hope and peace divine!
Make thou these secret pleasures mine;
Forgive my sins, my fears remove,
And fill my heart with joy and love.

PLEYEL'S HYMN. 7s. PLEYEL.

619 FURNESS.

Jesus our Leader.

1 FEEBLE, helpless, how shall I
Learn to live and learn to die?
Who, O God, my guide shall be?
Who shall lead thy child to thee?

2 Blessèd Father, gracious One,
Thou hast sent thy holy Son,
He will give the light I need,
He my trembling steps will lead.

3 Thus in deed, and thought, and word,
Led by Jesus Christ the Lord,
In my weakness, thus shall I
Learn to live and learn to die.

4 Learn to live in peace and love,
Like the perfect ones above;—
Learn to die without a fear,
Feeling thee, my Father, near.

620 HYMNS OF THE AGES.

Confidence.

1 WHEN we cannot see our way,
Let us trust and still obey;
He who bids us forward go,
Cannot fail the way to show.

2 Though the sea be deep and wide,
Though a passage seem denied;
Fearless let us still proceed,
Since the Lord vouchsafes to lead.

3 Though it seems the gloom of night,
Though we see no ray of light:
Since the Lord himself is there,
'T is not meet that we should fear.

4 Night with him is never night;
Where he is, there all is light;
When he calls us, why delay;
They are happy who obey.

621 CENNICK.

The Christian rejoicing in Hope.

1 CHILDREN of the Heavenly King,
As ye journey, sweetly sing;
Sing your Saviour's worthy praise,
Glorious in his works and ways.

2 Ye are travelling home to God,
In the way the fathers trod;
They are happy now, and ye
Soon their happiness shall see.

3 Shout, ye little flock, and blest;
You on Jesus' throne shall rest;
There your seat is now prepared,
There your kingdom and reward.

4 Lord, submissive make us go,
Ready, leaving all below;
Only thou our Leader be,
And we still will follow thee.

622 C. WESLEY.

The Christian's Death.

1 Now the Christian's course is run,
Ended is the glorious strife;
Fought the fight, the crown is won,
Death is swallowed up of life.

2 Borne by angels on their wings,
From the earth his spirit flies
To the Lord he loved, and sings,
Triumphing in paradise.

GARDNER. 8s & 7s. From Mornington.

623 Longfellow.

A Psalm of Life.

1 Tell me not in mournful numbers,
"Life is but an empty dream!"
For the soul is dead that slumbers,
And things are not what they seem.

2 Life is real! Life is earnest!
And the grave is not its goal;
"Dust thou art, to dust returnest,"
Was not spoken of the soul.

3 Not enjoyment and not sorrow,
Is our destined end or way;
But to act, that each to-morrow
Find us farther than to-day.

4 Let us then be up and doing,
With a heart for any fate;
Still achieving, still pursuing,
Learn to labor and to wait.

624 Mrs. Hemans.

The greatest of these is Charity.

1 Meek and lowly, pure and holy,
Chief among the blessed three,
Turning sadness into gladness,
Heaven-born art thou, Charity!

2 Pity dwelleth in thy bosom,
Kindness reigneth o'er thy heart;
Gentle thoughts alone can sway thee—
Censure hath in thee no part.

3 Hoping ever, failing never,
Though deceived, believing still;
Long abiding, all confiding,
To thy heavenly Father's will.

4 Never weary of well-doing,
Never fearful of the end;
Claiming all mankind as brothers,
Thou dost all alike befriend.

625 Anon.

Courage.

1 Father, hear the prayer we offer!
Not for ease that prayer shall be,
But for strength that we may ever
Live our lives courageously.

2 Not forever by still waters
Would we idly quiet stay;
But would smite the living fountains
From the rocks along our way.

3 Be our strength in hours of weakness,
In our wanderings, be our guide;
Through endeavor, failure, danger,
Father, be thou at our side!

626 Bonar.

Active Efforts.

1 Like the eagle, upward, onward,
Let my soul in faith be borne:
Calmly gazing, skyward, sunward,
Let my eye unshrinking turn!

2 Where the cross, God's love revealing,
Sets the fettered spirit free,
Where it sheds its wondrous healing,
There, my soul, thy rest shall be!

3 Oh, may I no longer dreaming,
Idly waste my golden day,
But, each precious hour redeeming,
Upward, onward press my way!

FARNHAM. C. M., Double.

627

FABER.

Efficacy of Love.

1 God only is the creature's home,
Though long and rough the road;
Yet nothing less can satisfy
The love that longs for God.
A trusting heart, a yearning eye,
Can win their way above;
If mountains can be moved by faith,
Is there less power in love?

2 Dole not thy duties out to God,
But let thy hand be free:
Look long at Jesus; his sweet blood,
How was it dealt to thee?
Be docile to thine unseen Guide,
Love him as he loves thee;
Time and obedience are enough,
And thou a saint shall be!

628

C. WESLEY.

Watchfulness.

1 I want a principle within
Of jealous, godly fear;
A sensibility of sin,
A pain to find it near.
I want the first approach to feel
Of pride, or fond desire;
To catch the wandering of my will,
And quench the kindling fire.

2 From thee that I no more may part,
No more thy goodness grieve,
The filial awe, the fleshly heart,
The tender conscience give.
Quick as the apple of the eye,
O God, my conscience make!
Awake my soul when sin is nigh,
And keep it still awake.

629

WATTS.

Oh, that my Ways were directed to keep thy Statutes.

1 Oh, that the Lord would guide my ways
To keep his statutes still!
Oh, that my God would grant me grace
To know and do his will!
Oh, send thy spirit down to write
Thy law upon my heart!
Nor let my tongue indulge deceit,
Nor act the liar's part.

2 Order my footsteps by thy word,
And make my heart sincere;
Let sin have no dominion, Lord,
But keep my conscience clear.
Make me to walk in thy commands,—
'T is a delightful road;
Nor let my head, or heart, or hands,
Offend against my God.

630

ANON.

The Seed in good Ground.

1 Almighty God! thy word is cast
Like seed into the ground;
Let now the dew of heaven descend,
And righteous fruits abound.
Let not the world's deceitful cares
The rising plant destroy;
But let it yield, a hundred-fold,
The fruits of peace and joy.

BARBY. C. M.

TANSUR.

631

DODDRIDGE.

Covenant of Grace.

1 My God! the covenant of thy love
Abides forever sure;
And in its matchless grace I feel
My happiness secure.

2 Since thou, the everlasting God,
My Father art become,
Jesus my guardian and my friend,
And heaven my final home;—

3 I welcome all thy sovereign will,
For all that will is love;
And when I know not what thou dost,
I wait the light above.

4 Thy covenant in the darkest gloom
Shall heavenly rays impart,
And when my eyelids close in death,
Sustain my fainting heart.

632

ALICE CARY.

The True Rest.

1 Each fearful storm that o'er us rolls,
Each path of peril trod,
Is but a means whereby our souls
Acquaint themselves with God.

2 Our wants and weakness, shame and sin,
His pitying kindness prove,
And all our lives are folded in
The mystery of his love.

3 His sun is shining, sure and fast,
O'er all our nights of dread;
Our darkness by his light, at last,
Shall be interpreted.

633

ANON.

Our Heaven within.

1 There is a world,— and oh, how blest!
Fairer than prophets told;
And never did an angel guest
One half its peace unfold.

2 Look not abroad, with roving mind,
To seek that fair abode;
It comes where'er the lowly find
The perfect peace of God.

634

ANON.

God's Peace.

1 We bless thee for thy peace, O God!
Deep as the soundless sea,
Which falls like sunshine on the road
Of those who trust in thee.

2 We ask not, Father, for repose
Which comes from outward rest,
If we may have through all life's woes
Thy peace within our breast;—

3 That peace which suffers and is strong,
Trusts where it cannot see,
Deems not the trial way too long,
But leaves the end with thee;—

4 That peace which flows serene and deep,
A river in the soul,
Whose banks a living verdure keep:
God's sunshine o'er the whole!

5 Such, Father, give our hearts such peace,
Whate'er the outward be,
Till all life's discipline shall cease,
And we go home to thee.

SAINT THOMAS. S. M.

A. WILLIAMS.

635

WATTS.

Heavenly Joy on Earth.

1 COME, ye that love the Lord,
And let your joys be known;
Join in a song with sweet accord,
And thus surround the throne.

2 The sorrows of the mind
Be banished from the place!
Religion never was designed
To make our pleasures less.

3 The hill of Zion yields
A thousand sacred sweets,
Before we reach the heavenly fields,
Or walk the golden streets.

4 Then let our songs abound,
And every tear be dry; [ground,
We're marching through Immanuel's
To fairer worlds on high.

636

MONTGOMERY.

The True Rest.

1 OH, where shall rest be found,
Rest for the weary soul?
'T were vain the ocean depths to sound,
Or pierce to either pole:

2 The world can never give
The bliss for which we sigh;
'T is not the whole of life to live,
Nor all of death to die.

3 Beyond this vale of tears,
There is a life above,
Unmeasured by the flight of years,
And all that life is love.

637

MISS FLETCHER.

Where is Heaven?

1 OUR heaven is everywhere,
If we but love the Lord,
Unswerving tread the narrow way,
And ever shun the broad.

2 'T is where the trusting heart
Bows meekly to its grief,
Still looking up with earnest faith
For comfort and relief.

3 Where guileless infancy
In happiness doth dwell,
And where the aged one can say,
"He hath done all things well."

4 Wherever truth abides,
Sweet peace is ever there;
If we but love and serve the Lord,
Our heaven is everywhere.

638

E. R. SILL.

For the Gifts of the Spirit.

1 SEND down thy truth, O God!
Too long the shadows frown;
Too long the darkened way we've trod:
Thy truth, O Lord! send down.

2 Send down thy love, thy life,
Our lesser lives to crown,
And cleanse them of their hate and strife:
Thy living love send down.

3 Send down thy peace, O Lord!
Earth's bitter voices drown
In one deep ocean of accord:
Thy peace, O God! send down.

HAMBURG. L. M.

639 MONTGOMERY.
The Soul returning to God.

1 Return, my soul, unto thy rest,
From vain pursuits and maddening cares,
From lonely woes that wring thy breast,
The world's allurements, toils, and snares.

2 Return unto thy rest, my soul,
From all the wanderings of thy thought;
From sickness unto death made whole;
Safe through a thousand perils brought.

3 Then to thy rest, my soul, return,
From passions every hour at strife;
Sin's works, and ways, and wages spurn,
Lay hold upon eternal life.

4 God is thy rest; — with heart inclined
To keep his word, that word believe;
Christ is thy rest; — with lowly mind,
His light and easy yoke receive.

640 HARRIS.
Peace in Believing.

1 Far from the Lord I wandered long,
Until the Gentle Shepherd came,
And called me to the lowly throng,
Who love his word and own his name.

2 Now in that peaceful fold I dwell,
And hear his voice of love divine:
Oh, for seraphic tongues, to tell
What joys unspeakable are mine.

3 Within my heart a temple stands,
And there the Lord of life comes down:
Soon in a house not made with hands
I shall receive my angel-crown.

641 BULFINCH.
Did not our Hearts burn within us?

1 Hath not thy heart within thee burned
At evening's calm and holy hour,
As if its inmost depths discerned
The presence of a loftier power?

2 As they who once with Jesus trod,
With kindling breast his accents heard,
But knew not that the Son of God
Was uttering every burning word,—

3 Father of Jesus, thus thy voice
Speaks to our hearts in tones divine
Our spirits tremble and rejoice,
But know not that the voice is thine

4 Still be thy hallowed accents near;
To doubt and passion whisper peace.
Direct us on our journey here,
And bid, in heaven, our wanderings cease

642 DODDRIDGE.
Communing with our Hearts.

1 Return, my roving heart, return,
And chase these shadowy forms no more;
Seek out some solitude to mourn,
And thy forsaken God implore.

2 And thou, my God, whose piercing eye
Distinct surveys each deep recess,
In these abstracted hours draw nigh,
And with thy presence fill the place.

3 Through all the mazes of my heart,
My search let heavenly wisdom guide,
And still its radiant beams impart,
Till all be searched and purified.

ZEPHYR. L. M.

643
BEARD'S COLL.

God's Care our Comfort.

1 OH! sweet it is to know, to feel, [here,
In all our gloom, our wanderings
No night of sorrow can conceal
Man from thy notice, from thy care.

2 When disciplined by long distress,
And led through paths of fear and woe,
Say, dost thou love thy children less?
No! ever gracious Father, no!

3 No distance can outstretch thine eye,
No night obscure thy endless day;
Be this my comfort when I sigh,
Be this my safeguard when I stray.

644
MME. GUYON.

The omnipresent Peace of God.

1 O THOU, by long experience tried,
Near whom no grief can long abide;—
My Lord, how full of sweet content
My years of pilgrimage are spent!

2 All scenes alike engaging prove,
To souls impressed with sacred love;
Where'er they dwell, they dwell in thee,
In heaven, in earth, or on the sea.

3 To them remains nor place nor time;
Their country is in every clime;
They can be calm and free from care
On any shore, since God is there.

4 While place we seek, or place we shun,
The soul finds happiness in none;
But with a God to guide our way,
'T is equal joy to go or stay.

645
ANON.

Goodness of God in Affliction.

1 I BLESS thee, Lord, for sorrows sent
To break the dream of human power,
For now my shallow cistern 's spent,
I find thy fount and thirst no more.

2 I take thy hand and fears grow still;
Behold thy face, and doubts remove;
Who would not yield his wavering will
To perfect truth and boundless love!

3 That truth gives promise of a dawn,
Beneath whose light I am to see,
When all these blinding vails are drawn,
This was the wisest path for me.

4 That love this restless soul doth teach
The strength of thy eternal calm;
And tune its sad and broken speech,
To sing ev'n now the angels' psalm.

646
ANON.

Trust in Trouble.

1 No bliss I'll seek, but to fulfil
In life, in death, thy perfect will;
No succor in my woes I want,
But what my Lord is pleased to grant.

2 Our days are numbered: let us spare
Our anxious hearts a needless care;
'T is thine to number out our days;
'T is ours to give them to thy praise.

NAOMI. C. M.

Dr. L. Mason.

647

C. Wesley.

A Rest remaineth.

1 Lord! we believe a rest remains
To all thy people known:
A rest where pure enjoyment reigns;—
For thou art served alone:—

2 A rest where all our soul's desire
Is fixed on things above;
Where fear, and sin and grief expire
Cast out by perfect love.

3 Oh, that we now that rest might know,
Believe and enter in!
Thou Holiest! now the power bestow,
And let us cease from sin.

4 Remove this hardness from our heart,
This unbelief remove:
The rest of perfect faith impart,
The Sabbath of thy love.

648

Rippon's Coll.

Peace with God.

1 Father! whate'er of earthly bliss
Thy sovereign will denies,
Accepted at thy throne of grace,
Let this petition rise:—

2 "Give me a calm, a thankful heart,
From every murmur free;
The blessings of thy grace impart,
And make me live to thee.

3 "Let the sweet hope that thou art mine
My life and death attend;
Thy presence through my journey shine,
And crown my journey's end."

649

Hervey.

Benevolence of God's Decrees.

1 Since all the varying scenes of time
God's watchful eye surveys,
Oh, who so wise to choose our lot,
Or to appoint our ways!

2 Good, when he gives, supremely good;
Nor less when he denies;
Ev'n crosses, from his sovereign hand,
Are blessings in disguise.

3 Why should we doubt a Father's love,
So constant and so kind!
To his unerring, gracious will
Be every wish resigned.

4 In thy fair book of life divine,
My God, inscribe my name;
There let it fill some humble place
Beneath my Lord the Lamb!

650

Mrs. Steele.

The safe Retreat.

1 Dear Father, to thy mercy-seat
My soul for shelter flies:
'T is here I find a safe retreat
When storms and tempests rise.

2 My cheerful hope can never die,
If thou, my God, art near;
Thy grace can raise my comforts high,
And banish every fear.

3 Oh, never let my soul remove
From this divine retreat!
Still let me trust thy power and love,
And dwell beneath thy feet.

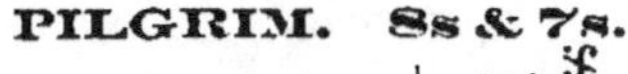

651

GRANT.

Rejoicing in Hope of the Glory of God.

1 KNOW, my soul, thy full salvation;
Rise o'er sin, and fear, and care;
Joy to find in every station
Something still to do or bear;
Think what spirit dwells within thee;
Think what Father's smiles are thine;
Think what Jesus did to win thee;
Child of heaven, canst thou repine?

2 Haste thee on from grace to glory,
Armed by faith and winged by prayer;
Heaven's eternal day 's before thee;
God's own hand shall guide thee there;
Soon shall close thy earthly mission;
Soon shall pass thy pilgrim days;
Hope shall change to glad fruition,
Faith to sight, and prayer to praise.

652

J. G. ADAMS.

Heaven here.

1 HEAVEN is here. Its hymns of gladness
Cheer the true believer's way,
In this world where sin and sadness
Often change to night our day.
Heaven is here; where misery lightened
Of its heavy load is seen,
Where the face of sorrow brightened
By the deed of love hath been:

2 Where the bound, the poor, despairing,
Are set free, supplied and blest;
Where, in others' anguish sharing,
We can find our surest rest.
Where we heed the voice of duty
Rather than man's praise, or rod;
This is heaven,—its peace, its beauty,
Radiant with the smile of God.

653

ANON.

Blessed be the Lord.

1 BLEST be thou, O God of Israel!
Thou, our Father and our Lord!
Majesty is thine for ever;
Ever be thy name adored. [ness;
Thine, O Lord, our power and great-
Glory, victory, are thine own;
All is thine in earth and heaven,
Over all thy boundless throne.

2 Riches come of thee, and honor;
Power and might to thee belong;
Thine it is to make us prosper,
Only thine to make us strong.
Lord, our God, for these, thy bounties,
Hymns of gratitude we raise;
To thy name, for ever glorious,
Ever we address our praise.

654

Doxology.

1 PRAISE the God of our salvation,
Praise the Father's boundless love;
Praise the Lamb, our Great Redeemer;
Praise the Spirit from above;
Praise the fountain of salvation,
Him by whom our spirits live;
Earnest, heartfelt adoration
To the great Jehovah give!

CHINA. C. M.

655

HARRIS.

What is Death?

1 DEATH is the fading of a cloud,
The breaking of a chain;
The rending of a mortal shroud
We ne'er shall find again.

2 Death is the conqueror's welcome home;
The heavenly city's door;
The entrance of the world to come—
'T is life for evermore.

3 Death is the close of life's alarms,—
The watch-light on the shore;—
The clasping in immortal arms
Of loved ones gone before.

4 Death is the gaining of a crown
Where saints and angels meet;
The laying of our burden down
At the Deliverer's feet.

5 Death is the song from seraph lips;—
The dayspring from on high;—
The ending of the soul's eclipse,—
Its transit to the sky.

656

WHITTIER.

God's Love and Care.

1 I LONG for household voices gone,
For vanished smiles I long,
But God hath led my dear ones on,
And he can do no wrong.

2 I know not what the future hath
Of marvel or surprise,
Assured alone that life and death
His mercy underlies.

3 And if my heart and flesh are weak
To bear an untried pain,
The bruiséd reed he will not break,
But strengthen and sustain.

4 And so beside the silent sea
I wait the muffled oar;
No harm from him can come to me
On ocean or on shore.

5 I know not where his islands lift
Their fronded palms in air;
I only know I cannot drift
Beyond his love and care.

657

MONTGOMERY

Christian Hope.

1 THE broken ties of happier days,
How often do they seem
To come before the mental gaze,
Like a remembered dream;

2 And earthly hand can ne'er again
Unite these broken ties,
Around us each dissevered chain
In sparkling ruin lies.

3 Oh, who in such a world as this,
Could bear their lot of pain,
Did not one radiant hope of bliss
Unclouded yet remain?

4 That hope the sovereign Lord has given,
Who reigns above the skies;—
Hope, that unites our souls to heaven,
By faith's endearing ties.

GOTTSCHALK. 7s.

658

MONTGOMERY.

Freedom in Death.

1 "SPIRIT, leave thy house of clay;
 Lingering dust, resign thy breath;
Spirit, cast thy chains away;
 Dust, be thou dissolved in death!"

2 Thus the mighty Saviour speaks,
 While the faithful Christian dies;
Thus the bonds of life he breaks,
 And the ransomed captive flies.

3 Prisoner, long detained below,
 Prisoner, now with freedom blest,
Welcome from a world of woe;
 Welcome to a land of rest.

659

ANON.

Dirge.

1 CLAY to clay, and dust to dust!
Let them mingle — for they must!
Give to earth the earthly clod,
For the spirit's fled to God.

2 Deep the pit, and cold the bed,
Where the spoils of death are laid;
Stiff the curtains, chill the gloom,
Of man's melancholy tomb.

3 Never more shall midnight's damp
Darken round this mortal lamp;
Never more shall noonday's glance
Search this mortal countenance.

4 Look aloft! The spirit's risen —
Death cannot the soul imprison;
'T is in heaven that spirits dwell,
Glorious, though invisible.

660

WESLEY'S COLL.

Blessed are the Dead, that die in the Lord.

1 READY for their glorious crown,—
 Sorrows past and sins forgiven,—
Here they lay their burthen down,
 Hallowed and made meet for heaven.

2 Yes! the Christian's course is run;
 Ended is the glorious strife;
Fought the fight, the work is done;
 Death is swallowed up in life.

661

GASKELL.

Trust in God.

1 WE would leave, O God! to thee
Every anxious care and fear;
Thou the troubled thought canst see,
Thou canst dry the bitter tear.

2 Thou dost care for us, we know,—
Care with all a Father's love;
Thou canst make each earthly woe
Work to higher bliss above.

662

S. F. ADAMS.

Dews and Tears.

1 GENTLY fall the dews of eve,
Raising still the languid flowers;
Sweetly flow the tears that grieve
O'er a mourner's stricken hours,—

2 Blessèd dews and tears, that yet
Lift us nearer unto heaven.
Let us still his praise repeat,
Who in mercy all hath given.

RELIANCE. L. M.

I. B. WOODBURY.

663

MONTGOMERY.

Death, and Entrance on Immortality.

1 O GOD unseen — but not unknown!
Thine eye is ever fixed on me;
I dwell beneath thy secret throne,
Encompassed by thy deity.

2 The moment comes when strength must fail,
When, health and hope and comfort [flown,
I must go down into the vale
And shade of death, with thee alone:

3 Alone with thee: — in that dread strife,
Uphold me through mine agony,
And gently be this dying life
Exchanged for immortality.

4 Then, when th' unbodied spirit lands
Where flesh and blood have never trod,
And in the unveiled presence stands,
Of thee, my Saviour and my God:

5 Be mine eternal portion this,
Since thou wert always here with me,
That I may view thy face in bliss,
And be for evermore with thee.

664

NORTON.

The Fellowship of Christ's Sufferings.

1 FAINT not, poor traveller, though the way
Be rough, like that thy Saviour trod;
Though cold and stormy lower the day:
This path of suffering leads to God.

2 Nay, sink not, though from every limb
Are starting drops of toil and pain:
Thou dost but share the lot of Him
With whom his followers are to reign.

3 Christian, thy Friend, thy Master, prayed
While dread and anguish shook his frame,
Then met his sufferings undismayed:
Wilt thou not strive to do the same?

4 Oh, thinkest thou his Father's love
Shone round him then with fainter rays
Than now, when, throned all height above,
Unceasing voices hymn his praise?

5 Go, sufferer; calmly meet the woes
Which God's own mercy bids thee bear;
Then, rising as thy Saviour rose,
Go, his eternal victory share.

665

HARRIS.

Children borne Home by Angels.

1 "WITH roses crown his baby head;
Close with a kiss his tender eyes;
Strew lilies o'er his cradle bed,
For he shall wake in Paradise."

2 What music fills the silent room?
Oh, list! the guardian angel sings:
"Our spirit rosebud springs to bloom,
Our spirit-bird unfolds its wings."

3 O mother! look with inward eyes;
Dear heart! at once bereaved and blest.
Behold the infant cherub rise;
He smiles upon an angel's breast.

4 Rejoice amid thy sorrow's tears;
Rejoice, for unto thee 't was given
To swell the music of the spheres,
To bear an angel-babe for heaven.

FEDERAL STREET. L. M. H. K. OLIVER.

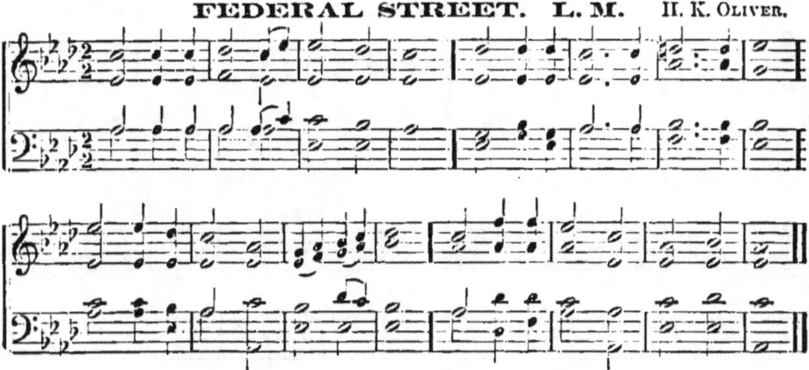

666 MRS. BARBAULD.

Death of the Righteous.

1 SWEET is the scene when virtue dies!
When sinks a righteous soul to rest;
How mildly beam the closing eyes,
How gently heaves th' expiring breast!

2 So fades a summer cloud away,
So sinks the gale when storms are o'er,
So gently shuts the eye of day,
So dies a wave along the shore.

3 Farewell, conflicting hopes and fears,
Where lights and shades alternate dwell;
How bright the unchanging morn appears!
Farewell, inconstant world, farewell!

4 Life's duty done, as sinks the clay,
Light from its load the spirit flies;
While heaven and earth combine to say,
"How blest the righteous when he dies!"

667 WATTS.

Christ's Presence makes Death easy.

1 WHY should we start and fear to die?
What timorous worms we mortals are!
Death is the gate of endless joy,
And yet we dread to enter there.

2 The pains, the groans, the dying strife,
Fright our approaching souls away;
Still we shrink back again to life,
Fond of our prison and our clay.

3 Oh! if my Lord would come and meet,
My soul should stretch her wings in haste,
Fly fearless through death's iron gate,
Nor feel the terrors as she passed.

4 Jesus can make a dying bed
Feel soft as downy pillows are,
While on his breast I lean my head,
And breathe my life out sweetly there.

668 ANON.

Gone before.

1 DEAR is the spot where Christians sleep,
And sweet the strains their spirits pour;
Oh, why should we in anguish weep?—
They are not lost, but gone before.

2 Secure from every mortal care,
By sin and sorrow vexed no more,
Eternal happiness they share
Who are not lost, but gone before.

3 To Zion's peaceful courts above,
In faith triumphant may we soar,
Embracing, in the arms of love,
The friends not lost, but gone before.

4 To Jordan's bank whene'er we come,
And hear the swelling waters roar,
Jesus! convey us safely home,
To friends not lost, but gone before.

669 ANON.

A well-spent Life.

1 How blest is he whose tranquil mind,
When life declines, recalls again
The years that time has cast behind,
And reaps delight from toil and pain.

2 So, when the transient storm is past,
The sudden gloom and driving shower,
The sweetest sunshine is the last;
The loveliest is the evening hour.

HEBRON. L. M.

Dr. L. Mason.

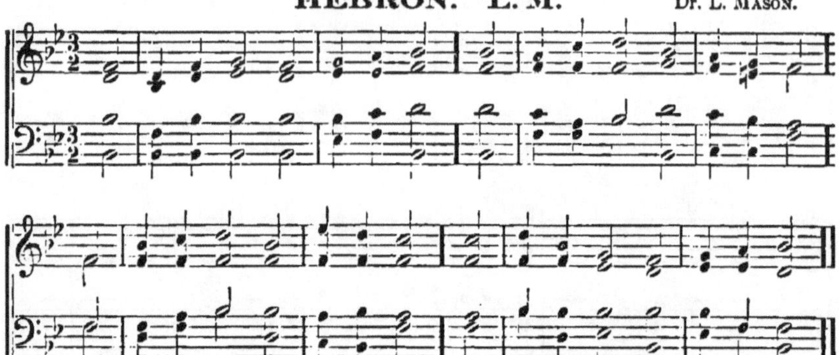

670

Bryant.

Clearing to Earth.

1 Earth's children cleave to earth; her frail,
Decaying children dread decay;
Yon wreath of mist that leaves the vale,
And lessens in the morning ray,—

2 Look, how by mountain rivulet
It lingers as it upward creeps,
And clings to fern and copsewood set
Along the green and dewy steeps.

3 Yet all in vain — it passes still
From hold to hold, it cannot stay;
And in the very beams that fill
The world with glory wastes away.

4 Till, parting from the mountain's brow,
It vanishes from human eye,
And that which sprung of earth is now
A portion of the glorious sky.

671

T. W. Higginson.

I will arise and go unto my Father.

1 To thine eternal arms, O God,
Take us, thy erring children, in;
From dangerous paths too boldly trod,
From wandering thoughts and dreams of sin.

2 Those arms were round our childish ways,
A guard through helpless years to be;
Oh, leave not our maturer days;
We still are helpless without thee.

3 We trusted hope, and pride, and strength;
Our strength proved false, our pride was vain;
Our dreams have faded all at length;
We come to thee, O Lord, again.

4 A guide to trembling steps yet be;
Give us of thine eternal powers;
So shall our paths all lead to thee,
And life smile on like childhood's hours.

672

Mme. Guyon.

How to learn of God.

1 If thou of God wouldst truly learn,
His wisdom, goodness, glory see,
All human arts and knowledge spurn,
Let love alone thy teacher be.

2 Love is my master. When it breaks
The morning light, with rising ray,
To thee, O God! my spirit wakes,
And love instructs it all the day.

673

Anon.

Rest in God.

1 Father, beneath thy sheltering wing,
In sweet security we rest;
And fear no evil earth can bring;
In life, in death, supremely blest.

2 For life is good whose tidal flow
The motions of thy will obeys;
And death is good, that makes us know
The Love Divine that all things sways.

3 And good it is to bear the cross,
And so thy perfect peace to win;
And naught is ill, nor brings us loss,
Nor works us harm, save only sin!

4 Redeemed from sin we ask no more,
But trust the love that saves, to guide;
The grace that yields so rich a store
Will grant us all we need beside.

HOLLEY. 7s. GEO. HEWS.

674

THOMAS HOOD.

Farewell Life! Welcome Life!

1 FAREWELL life! My senses swim,
And the world is growing dim:
Thronging shadows cloud the light,
Like the advent of the night—

2 Colder, colder, colder still,
Upward steals a vapor chill;
Strong the earthy odor grows,—
I smell the mould above the rose.

3 Welcome life! the spirit strives!
Strength returns and hope revives;
Cloudy fears and shapes forlorn
Fly like shadows at the morn;

4 O'er the earth there comes a bloom;
Sunny light for sullen gloom,
Warm perfume for vapor cold—
I smell the rose above the mould!

675

CONDER.

The Just in Heaven.

1 SEE the ransomed millions stand,—
Palms of conquest in their hands!
This before the throne their strain,—
"Hell is vanquished—death is slain!—

2 Blessing, honor, glory, might,
Are the Conqueror's native right!
Thrones and powers before him fall,—
Lamb of God, and Lord of all!"

3 Hasten, Lord! the promised hour;
Come in glory and in power!
Still thy foes are unsubdued:
Nature sighs to be renewed:

4 Time has nearly reached its sum:
All things with the Bride, say, "Come!"
Jesus! whom all worlds adore,
Come,—and reign forevermore!

676

RAFFLES.

God shall wipe away all Tears from their Eyes.

1 HIGH in yonder realms of light,
Dwell the raptured saints above;
Far beyond our feeble sight,
Happy in Immanuel's love:

2 Pilgrims in this vale of tears,
Once they knew, like us below,
Gloomy doubts, distressing fears,
Torturing pain, and heavy woe.

3 But these days of weeping o'er,
Passed this scene of toil and pain,
They shall feel distress no more,—
Never, never weep again:

4 'Mid the chorus of the skies,
'Mid th' angelic lyres above,
Hark, their songs melodious rise,—
Songs of praise to Jesus' love!

5 All is tranquil and serene,
Calm and undisturbed repose;
There no cloud can intervene,
There no angry tempest blows;

6 Every tear is wiped away,
Sighs no more shall heave the breast,
Night is lost in endless day,
Sorrow, in eternal rest.

MOUNT VERNON. 8s & 7s. L. MASON.

677 S. F. SMITH.

Death of a Young Girl.

1 SISTER, thou wast mild and lovely,
Gentle as the summer breeze,
Pleasant as the air of evening,
When it floats among the trees.

2 Peaceful be thy silent slumber—
Peaceful in the grave so low:
Thou no more wilt join our number;
Thou no more our songs shalt know.

3 Dearest sister, thou hast left us;
Here thy loss we deeply feel;
But 't is God that hath bereft us:
He can all our sorrows heal.

4 Yet again we hope to meet thee,
When the day of life is fled,
Then in heaven with joy to greet thee,
Where no farewell tear is shed.

678 HORNE.

Autumn Warnings.

1 SEE the leaves around us falling,
Dry and withered, to the ground;
Thus to thoughtless mortals calling,
In a sad and solemn sound:—

2 "Youth, on length of days presuming,
Who the paths of pleasure tread,—
View us, late in beauty blooming,
Numbered now among the dead.

3 "What though yet no losses grieve you,
Gay with health and many a grace,
Let not cloudless skies deceive you:
Summer gives to autumn place.

4 On the tree of life eternal,
Let our highest hopes be stayed;
This alone, forever vernal,
Bears a leaf that shall not fade.

679 R. C. WATERSTON.

Death of a Female Scholar.

1 ONE sweet flower has drooped and faded,
One sweet infant voice has fled,
One fair brow the grave has shaded,
One dear schoolmate now is dead.

2 But we feel no thought of sadness,
For our friend is happy now;
She has knelt in soul-felt gladness,
Where the blessèd angels bow.

3 She has gone to heaven before us,
But she turns and waves her hand,
Pointing to the glories o'er us,
In that happy spirit land.

4 God, our Father, watch above us,
Keep us from all danger free;
Do thou guard and guide and love us,
Till, like her, we go to thee.

680 ANON.

Death of the Righteous.

1 As the bird with warbling music
Soars above our feeble sight,
Singing still, and still ascending,
Melting in the glorious light,—

2 So the dying saint, departing,
Joyful takes his heavenward way;
Life, and time, and gladness blending
In the light of perfect day.

REST. L. M.

681

BURLEIGH.

Why seek ye the Living among the Dead?

1 AH! why should bitter tears be shed
In sorrow o'er the mounded sod,
When verily there are no dead
Of all the children of our God?

2 They who are lost to outward sense
Have but flung off their robes of clay,
And, clothed in heavenly radiance,
Attend us on our lowly way.

3 And oft their spirits breathe in ours
The hope and strength and love of theirs,
Which bloom as bloom the early flowers
In breath of summer's viewless airs.

4 And silent aspirations start,
In promptings of their purer thought,
Which gently lead the troubled heart
To joys not even Hope had wrought.

682

NORTON.

Blessedness of the pious Dead.

1 OH, stay thy tears; for they are blest,
Whose days are past, whose toil is done:
Here midnight care disturbs our rest;
Here sorrow dims the noonday sun.

2 How blest are they whose transient years
Pass like an evening meteor's flight!
Not dark with guilt, nor dim with tears;
Whose course is short, unclouded, bright.

3 Oh, cheerless were our lengthened way;
But heaven's own light dispels the gloom,
Streams downward from eternal day,
And casts a glory round the tomb.

4 Oh, stay thy tears: the blest above
Have hailed a spirit's heavenly birth,
And sung a song of joy and love;
Then why should anguish reign on earth?

683

MRS. MACKAY.

Asleep in Christ.

1 ASLEEP in Jesus! blessed sleep!
From which none ever wakes to weep;
A calm and undisturbed repose,
Unbroken by the dread of foes.

2 Asleep in Jesus! peaceful rest!
Whose waking is supremely blest;
No fear, no woes shall dim that hour,
Which manifest the Saviour's power!

3 Asleep in Jesus! time nor space
Debars this precious hiding-place;
On Indian plains, or Lapland's snows,
Believers find the same repose.

4 Asleep in Jesus! far from thee
Thy kindred and their graves may be;
But thine is still a blessed sleep,
From which none ever wakes to weep.

684

ANON.

Be ye also Ready.

1 O GOD! thy grace and blessing give,
To us who on thy name attend;
That we this mortal life may live,
Regardful of our journey's end.

2 Then shall not death with terror come;
But welcome as a bidden guest,—
The herald of a better home,
The messenger of peace and rest.

PARK STREET. L. M.

VENUA.

685

ANON.

The Better Land.

1 THERE is a land mine eye hath seen,
In visions of enraptured thought,
So bright that all which spreads between
Is with its radiant glory fraught:—

2 A land upon whose blissful shore
There rests no shadow, falls no stain;
There those who meet shall part no more,
And those long parted meet again.

3 Its skies are not like earthly skies,
With varying hues of shade and light;
It hath no need of suns to rise,
To dissipate the gloom of night.

4 There sweeps no desolating wind
Across that calm, serene abode;
The wanderer there a home may find,
Within the paradise of God.

686

MRS. STEELE.

The glorious World on High.

1 THERE is a glorious world on high,
Resplendent with eternal day;
Faith views the blissful prospect nigh,
And God's own word reveals the way.

2 There shall the servants of the Lord
With never-fading lustre shine;
Surprising honor! large reward,
Conferred on man by love divine!

3 The shining firmament shall fade,
And sparkling stars resign their light;
But these shall know no change nor shade,
Forever fair, forever bright.

4 And shall not these cold hearts of ours
Be kindled at the glorious view?
Come, Lord, awake our active powers,
Our feeble, dying strength renew.

5 On wings of faith and strong desire
Oh, may our spirits daily rise;
And reach at last the shining choir,
In the bright mansions of the skies.

687

ANON.

The World to Come.

1 THERE is a world we have not seen,
That wasting time can ne'er destroy,
Where mortal footsteps have not been,
Nor ear hath caught its sounds of joy.

2 That world to come! and oh, how blest!
Fairer than prophets ever told;
And never did an angel-guest
One half its blessedness unfold.

3 It is all holy and serene,—
The land of glory and repose;
And there, to dim the radiant scene,
No tear of sorrow ever flows.

4 It is not fanned by summer gale;
'T is not refreshed by vernal showers;
It never needs the moonbeam pale,
For there are known no evening hours.

5 There forms unseen by mortal eye,
Too glorious for our sight to bear,
Are walking with their God on high,
And waiting our arrival there.

UNWIN. 8s & 4.

688

MONTGOMERY.

There is a Calm for those who weep.

1 THERE is a calm for those who weep,
A rest for weary pilgrims found;
They softly lie, and sweetly sleep,
Low in the ground.

2 The storm that racks the wintry sky
No more disturbs their deep repose
Than summer evening's latest sigh,
That shuts the rose.

3 I long to lay this painful head
And aching heart beneath the soil;
To slumber in that dreamless bed,
From all my toil.

4 The soul, of origin divine,
God's glorious image, freed from clay,
In heaven's eternal sphere shall shine,
A star of day.

5 The sun is but a spark of fire,
A transient meteor in the sky;
The soul, immortal as its Sire,
Shall never die.

689

ANON.

Love of God in Affliction.

1 I CANNOT always trace the way
Where thou, almighty One, dost move;
But I can always, always say
That God is love.

2 When fear her chilling mantle flings
O'er earth, my soul to heaven above,
As to her native home, upsprings;
For God is love.

3 When myst'ry clouds my darkened path,
I'll check my dread, my doubts reprove;
In this my soul sweet comfort hath,
That God is love.

4 Oh, may this truth my heart employ,
Bid every gloomy thought remove,
And turn all tears, all woes to joy,—
Thou, God, art Love.

690

CHARLOTTE ELLIOTT.

Submission to God's Will.

1 MY God, my Father, while I stray
Far from my home, on life's rough way,
Oh, teach me from my heart to say,
"Thy will be done!"

2 What though in lonely grief I sigh
For friends beloved no longer nigh;
Submissive still would I reply,
"Thy will be done!"

3 If thou shouldst call me to resign
What most I prize,— it ne'er was mine;
I only yield thee what was thine:
"Thy will be done!"

4 Renew my will from day to day;
Blend it with thine, and take away
Whate'er now makes it hard to say,
"Thy will be done!"

5 Then when on earth I breathe no more,
The prayer oft mixed with tears before,
I'll sing upon a happier shore:
"Thy will be done!"

JORDAN. C. M. Double. BILLINGS.

691 WATTS.

A Prospect of the Heavenly Canaan.

1 THERE is a land of pure delight,
Where saints immortal reign;
Infinite day excludes the night,
And pleasures banish pain.

2 There everlasting spring abides,
And never-withering flowers;
Death, like a narrow sea, divides
This heavenly land from ours.

3 Sweet fields, beyond the swelling flood,
Stand dressed in living green;
So, to the Jews, old Canaan stood,
While Jordan rolled between.

4 But timorous mortals start and shrink,
To cross this narrow sea,
And linger shivering on the brink,
And fear to launch away.

5 Oh, could we make our doubts remove,
Those gloomy doubts that rise,
And see the Canaan that we love
With unbeclouded eyes;

6 Could we but climb where Moses stood,
And view the landscape o'er, [flood,
Not Jordan's stream, nor death's cold
Should fright us from the shore.

692 CH. PSALMIST.

The Heavenly Home.

1 JERUSALEM! my happy home!
Name ever dear to me!
When shall my labors have an end
In joy, in peace, and thee?

2 There happier bowers than Eden's
Nor sin nor sorrow know: [bloom,
Blest seats! through bright or stormy
I onward press to you. [scenes

3 Apostles, martyrs, prophets, there
Around my Saviour stand;
And soon my friends in Christ below
Will join the glorious band.

4 Jerusalem! my happy home!
My soul still pants for thee;
Then shall my labors have an end,
When I thy peace shall see.

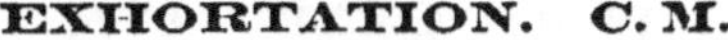

EXHORTATION. C. M.

693 STENNETT.

Prospect of the promised Land.

1 On Jordan's stormy banks I stand,
And cast a wistful eye
To Canaan's fair and happy land,
Where my possessions lie.

2 Oh, the transporting, rapturous scene
That rises to my sight!
Sweet fields, arrayed in living green,
And rivers of delight!

3 All o'er those wide-extended plains
Shines one eternal day;
There God, the sun, forever reigns,
And scatters night away.

4 No chilling winds or poisonous breath
Can reach that healthful shore;
Sickness nor sorrow, pain and death,
Are felt and feared no more.

694 DODDRIDGE.

The Way to the Heavenly City

1 Sing, ye redeeméd of the Lord,
Your great Deliverer sing;
Pilgrims, for Zion's city bound,
Be joyful in your King.

2 A hand divine shall lead you on
Through all the blissful road,
Till to the sacred mount you rise,
And see your Father, God.

3 There garlands of immortal joy
Shall bloom on every head,
While sorrow, sighing, and distress,
Like shadows all are fled.

4 March on in your Redeemer's strength,
Pursue his footsteps still,
And let the prospect cheer your eye
While laboring up the hill.

(In singing hymns 696 and 697, repeat third line of each verse.)

695

W. B. TAPPAN.

Heaven anticipated.

1 THERE is an hour of peaceful rest
To mourning wanderers given;
There is a joy for souls distressed,
A balm for every wounded breast;
'T is found alone in heaven.

2 There is a home for weary souls,
By sins and sorrows driven,
When toss'd on life's tempestu'us shoals,
Where storms arise, and ocean rolls,
And all is drear — 't is heaven.

3 There faith lifts up the tearless eye,
The heart no longer riven,—
And views the tempest passing by,
Sees evening shadows quickly fly,
And all serene in heaven.

4 There fragrant flowers immortal bloom,
And joys supreme are given;
There rays divine disperse the gloom;
Beyond the dark and narrow tomb
Appears the dawn of heaven.

696

WATTS.

Longing for Heaven.

1 FATHER! I long, I faint, to see
The place of thine abode;
I 'd leave thine earthly courts, and flee
Up to thy seat, my God!

2 Here I behold thy distant face,
And 't is a pleasing sight;
But, to abide in thine embrace
Is infinite delight!

3 I 'd part with all the joys of sense
To gaze upon thy throne;
Pleasure springs fresh forever thence,
Unspeakable, unknown.

4 There all the heavenly hosts are seen;
In shining ranks they move;
And drink immortal vigor in,
With wonder and with love.

5 Father! I long, I faint, to see
The place of thine abode;
I 'd leave thine earthly courts to be
Forever with my God!

697

PLYMOUTH COLL.

The Future Life.

1 THERE is a place of sacred rest,
Far, far beyond the skies;
Where beauty smiles eternally,
And pleasure never dies.

2 Beyond the storm, beyond the gloom,
Breaks forth the light of morn;
Bright beaming from the Father's house,
To cheer the soul forlorn.

3 The vision of that heavenly home
Shall cheer the parting soul;
And o'er it, mounting to the skies,
A tide of rapture roll.

4 For there adieus are sounds unknown;
Death frowns not on that scene;
But life and glorious beauty shine,
Untroubled and serene.

698

MONTGOMERY.

Forever with the Lord.

1 "FOREVER with the Lord,"
  Amen. So let it be;
Life from the dead is in that word,
  And immortality.
Here in the body pent,
  Absent from him I roam,
Yet nightly pitch my moving tent
  A day's march nearer home.

2 My Father's house on high,
  Home of my soul, how near,
At times, to faith's aspiring eye,
  Thy golden gates appear!
Yet doubts still intervene,
  And all my comfort flies;
Like Noah's dove, I flit between
  Rough seas and stormy skies.

3 "Forever with the Lord!"
  Father, if 't is thy will,
The promise of thy gracious word,
  E'en here to me fulfil.
Be thou at my right hand,
  So I shall never fail:
Uphold me, and I needs must stand;
  Fight, and I shall prevail.

4 So, when my latest breath
  Shall rend the veil in twain,
By death I shall escape from death,
  And life eternal gain.
Knowing "as I am known,"
  How shall I love that word,
And oft repeat before the throne,
  "Forever with the Lord!"

699

MRS. STEELE.

Heaven.

1 FAR from these scenes of night
  Unbounded glories rise,
And realms of infinite delight,
  Unknown to mortal eyes.
No cloud those regions know,
  Forever bright and fair;
For sin, the source of mortal woe,
  Can never enter there.

2 There night is never known,
  Nor sun's faint, sickly ray;
But glory from th' eternal throne
  Spreads everlasting day.
Oh, may this prospect fire
  Our hearts with ardent love!
And lively faith and strong desire
  Bear every thought above.

MARTYN. 7s, Double. From THE CHIME.

700

TOPLADY.

The Freed Spirit.

1 DEATHLESS principle, arise;
Soar, thou native of the skies;
Pearl of price, by Jesus bought,
To his glorious likeness wrought,
Go to shine before his throne,
Deck his mediatorial crown;
Go, his triumphs to adorn,
Made for God — to God return.

2 Burst thy shackles, drop thy clay,
Sweetly breathe thyself away;
Singing, to thy crown remove,
Swift of wing, and fired with love.
Shudder not to pass the stream;
Venture all thy care on him;
Him, whose dying love and power
Stilled its tossing, hushed its roar.

3 Saints in glory perfect made,
Wait thy passage through the shade;
Ardent for thy coming o'er,
See, they throng the blissful shore;
Mount, their transports to improve,
Join the longing choir above;
Swiftly to their wish be given;
Kindle higher joy in heaven.

701

C. WESLEY.

The faithful Dead.

1 HARK! a voice divides the sky!
Happy are the faithful dead
In the Lord who sweetly die!
They from all their toils are freed.
Yes! the Christian's course is run!
Ended is the glorious strife;
Fought the fight, the work is done;
Death is swallowed up in life!

2 Lo! the prisoner is released —
Lightened of his heavy load;
Where the weary are at rest,
He is gathered unto God!
When from flesh the spirit freed,
Hastens homeward to return,
Mortals cry, "A man is dead!"
Angels sing, "A child is born!"

702

MONTGOMERY.

Christ Lord of All.

1 PALMS of glory, raiment bright,
Crowns that never fade away,
Gird and deck the saints in light;
Priests, and kings, and conquerors, they.
Yet the conquerors bring their palms
To the Lamb amid the throne,
And proclaim, in joyful psalms,
Victory through his cross alone.

2 Kings for harps their crowns resign,
Crying, as they strike the chords,—
"Take the kingdom; it is thine,
King of kings, and Lord of lords."
Round the altar priests confess,
If their robes are white as snow,
'T was their Saviour's righteousness,
And his blood, that made them so.

FREDERICK. 11s. GEO. KINGSLEY.

703 MUHLENBURG.

Longing for Heaven.

1 I WOULD not live alway; I ask not to stay [o'er the way;
Where storm after storm rises dark
The few lucid mornings that dawn on us here
Are followed by gloom or beclouded with fear.

2 I would not live alway thus fettered by sin — [within:
Temptation without and corruption
E'en the rapture of pardon is mingled with fears,
And the cup of thanksgiving with penitent tears.

3 I would not live alway, no — welcome the tomb:
Since Jesus hath lain there, I dread not its gloom;
There sweet be my rest; he will bid me arise,
To share in his joy and his life in the skies.

4 Who, who would live alway away from his God — [abode,
Away from yon heaven, that blissful
Where rivers of pleasure flow bright o'er the plains,
And the noontide of glory eternally reigns?

5 There saints of all ages in harmony meet,
Their Saviour and brethren transported to greet;
While anthems of rapture unceasingly roll,
And the smile of the Lord is the feast of the soul.

704 C. FRY.

Thanks for Trial.

1 FOR what shall I praise thee, my God and my King, [tude bring?
For what blessings the tribute of grati-
Shall I praise thee for pleasure, for health, or for ease,
For the sunshine of youth, for the garden of peace?

2 For this I should praise; but if only for this, [of bliss!
I should leave half untold the donation
I thank thee for sickness, for sorrow, and care,
For the thorns I have gathered, the anguish I bear; —

3 For nights of anxiety, watching, and tears, [fears;
A present of pain, a prospective of
I praise thee, I bless thee, my Lord and my God,
For the good and the evil thy hand hath bestowed

WELTON. L. M. Arr. by Dr. L. Mason.

705 Bowring.

Memory of the Just.

1 Earth's transitory things decay,
Its pomps, its pleasures pass away;
But the sweet memory of the good
Survives in the vicissitude.

2 As 'mid the ever-rolling sea,
The eternal isles established be,
'Gainst which the surges of the main
Fret, dash, and break themselves in vain:—

3 As in the heavens the urns divine
Of golden light forever shine; [rage,
Though clouds may darken, storms may
They still shine on from age to age:—

4 So, through the ocean-tide of years,
The memory of the just appears;
So, through the tempest and the gloom,
The good man's virtues light the tomb.

706 Montgomery.

Preparation for Heaven.

1 Heaven is a place of rest from sin,
But all who hope to enter there
Should here that holy course begin
Which shall their souls for rest prepare.

2 Clean hearts, O God, in us create;
Right spirits in us, Lord, renew;
Commence we now that higher state;
Now do thy will as angels do.

3 In Jesus' footsteps may we tread,
Learn every lesson of his love;
And be from grace to glory led,
From heaven below to heaven above.

707 Anon.

The River of Life.

1 There is a pure and peaceful wave,
That issues from the throne of love,
Whose waters gladden as they lave
The bright and heavenly courts above.

2 The pilgrim faint, who seems to sink
Beneath the sultry sky of time,
May here repose, and freely drink
The waters of that better clime.

3 And every soul may here partake
The blessings of the fount above;
And none who drink will e'er forsake
The crystal stream of boundless love.

708 Kelly.

Love of Earth and Heaven.

1 "We've no abiding city here:"
Sad truth, were this to be our home;
But let this thought our spirits cheer,
"We seek a city yet to come."

2 "We've no abiding city here;"
We seek a city out of sight;
Zion its name, the Lord is there,
It shines with everlasting light.

3 Oh, sweet abode of peace and love,
Where pilgrims freed from toil are blest!
Had I the pinions of the dove,
I'd fly to thee, and be at rest.

4 But hush, my soul! nor dare repine;
The time my God appoints is best:
While here, to do his will be mine,
And his to fix my time of rest.

HELENA. C. M.

709 MOORE.

Consolation.

1 O THOU who driest the mourner's tear,
How dark this world would be,
If, when deceived and wounded here,
We could not fly to thee!

2 But thou wilt heal the broken heart,
Which like the plants that throw
Their fragrance from the wounded part,
Breathes sweetness out of woe.

3 When joy no longer soothes or cheers,
And e'en the hope that threw
A moment's sparkle o'er our tears
Is dimmed and vanished too;

4 Then sorrow, touched by thee, grows bright,
With more than rapture's ray;
As darkness shows us worlds of light
We never saw by day.

710 FABER.

The Eternal Years.

1 How shalt thou bear the cross that now
So dread a weight appears?
Keep quietly to God, and think
Upon the eternal years.

2 Austerity is little help,
Although it somewhat cheers;
Thine oil of gladness is the thought
Of the eternal years.

3 Bear gently, suffer like a child,
Nor be ashamed of tears;
Kiss the sweet cross, and in thy heart
Sing of the eternal years.

4 Death will have rainbows round it, seen
Through calm contrition's tears,
If tranquil Hope but trims her lamp
At the eternal years.

711 BONAR.

Christ's Help in Trouble.

1 JESUS, my sorrow lies too deep
For human ministry;
It knows not how to tell itself
To any but to thee.

2 Thou dost remember still, amid
The glories of God's throne,
The sorrows of mortality,—
For they were once thine own.

3 Jesus! my fainting spirit brings
Its fearfulness to thee!
Thine eye, at least, can penetrate
The clouded mystery.

4 It is enough, my precious Lord,
Thy tender sympathy!
My every sin and sorrow can
Devolve itself on thee.

5 Jesus! thou hast availed to search
My deepest malady;
It freely flows — more freely finds
The gracious remedy.

712

Closing.

1 A BLESSING from thy gracious hand
Our humble prayers implore,—
That thou, the Lord, shalt be our God
And portion evermore.

SAINT PAUL'S. L. M. Dr. Green.

713 Norton.

Trust and Submission.

1 My God, I thank thee! may no thought
  E'er deem thy chastisements severe;
But may this heart, by sorrow taught,
  Calm each wild wish, each idle fear.

2 Thy mercy bids all nature bloom;
  The sun shines bright, and man is gay;
Thine equal mercy spreads the gloom,
  That darkens o'er his little day.

3 Full many a throb of grief and pain
  Thy frail and erring child must know:
But not one prayer is breathed in vain,
  Nor does one tear unheeded flow.

4 Thy various messengers employ;
  Thy purposes of love fulfil;
And 'mid the wreck of human joy,
  Let kneeling faith adore thy will.

714 Bryant.

Blessed are they that mourn.

1 Deem not that they are blessed alone,
  Whose days a peaceful tenor keep;
The God, who loves our race, has shown
  A blessing for the eyes that weep.

2 The light of smiles shall fill again
  The lids that overflow with tears,
And weary hours of woe and pain
  Are earnests of serener years.

3 Oh, there are days of sunny rest
  For every dark and troubled night!
Grief may abide, an evening guest,
  But joy shall come with early light.

4 And thou, who o'er thy friend's low bier
  Sheddest the bitter drops like rain,
Hope that a brighter, happier sphere
  Will give him to thy arms again.

5 For God hath marked each anguished day
  And numbered every secret tear;
And heaven's long age of bliss shall pay
  For all his children suffer here.

715 Elim.

Strangers and Sojourners.

1 We have no home on earth below,
  And time is short and heaven is near:
Oh, that our hearts were weanéd so
  That we could live like strangers here,—

2 Like pilgrims that have paused an hour
  To rest upon some foreign strand;
Like banished men that love to pour
  The praises of their Fatherland!

3 Bright are the flowers that God has lent
  To bloom beneath the traveller's tread;
And beautiful the starry tent
  He spreadeth o'er the pilgrim's head.

4 But in the Land that's far away
  There needs no light of sun or moon;
And flowers that never know decay
  Along its starless shores are strewn.

716 Anon

Right Use of Time.

1 Our days are numbered: let us spare
  Our anxious hearts a needless care;
'T is thine to number out our days;
'T is ours to give them to thy praise.

SCOTLAND. 12s & 11s. Dr. Clarke.

717

HEBER.

Thou art gone to the Grave.

1 Thou art gone to the grave; but we will not deplore thee; [pass the tomb;
Though sorrows and darkness encom-
The Saviour has passed through its portals before thee; [through the gloom.
And the lamp of his love is thy guide

2 Thou art gone to the grave; we no longer behold thee, [by thy side:
Nor tread the rough paths of the world
But the wide arms of mercy are spread to enfold thee, [iour hath died.
And sinners may hope, since the Sav-

3 Thou art gone to the grave; and its mansion forsaking, [lingered long;
Perchance thy weak spirit in doubt
But the sunshine of heaven beamed bright on thy waking,
And the sound thou didst hear was the seraphim's song.

4 Thou art gone to the grave; but we will not deplore thee; [ian, thy Guide;
Since God was thy refuge, thy Guard-
He gave thee, he took thee, and he will restore thee; [iour hath died.
And death has no sting, since the Sav-

718

HEBER.

Lord, save us: we perish.

1 When through the torn sail the wild tempest is streaming,
When o'er the dark wave the red lightning is gleaming,
Nor hope lends a ray, the poor seaman to cherish, [we perish!
We fly to our Maker: help, Lord, or

2 O Jesus, once tossed on the breast of the billow, [thy pillow,
Aroused by the shriek of despair from
Now seated in glory, the mariner cherish, [or we perish!"
Who cries in his danger, "Help, Lord,

3 And, oh! when the whirlwind of passion is raging, [fare is waging,
When sin in our hearts its wild war-
Arise in thy strength, thy redeemèd to cherish! [we perish!
Rebuke the destroyer,—help, Lord, or

WEBSTER. 6s. Arr. from WEBER.

719

ANON.

Death of a faithful Minister.

1 ON Zion's holy walls
Is quenched a beacon light,
In vain the watchman calls,—
"Sentry! what of the night?"
No answering voice is here:
Say — does the soldier sleep?
Oh, yes — upon the bier,
His watch no more to keep.

2 Peace to thee, man of God!
Thine earthly toils are o'er,
The thorny path is trod,
The Shepherd trod before:
Full well he kept his word,—
"I'm with thee to the end;
Fear not! I am the Lord,
Thy never-failing friend."

3 We have no dirge for thee,
It should not call a tear
To know that thou art free;
Thy home — it was not here!
Joy to thee, man of God!
Thy heaven-course is begun,
Unshrinking, thou hast trod
Death's vale,— thy race is run.

720

SCHMOLK.

Submission.

1 MY Jesus, as thou wilt!
Oh, may thy will be mine!
Into thy hand of love
I would my all resign:
Through sorrow, or through joy,
Conduct me as thine own,
And help me still to say,
My Lord, thy will be done!

2 My Jesus, as thou wilt!
Though seen through many a tear,
Let not my star of hope
Grow dim or disappear:
Since thou on earth hast wept,
And sorrowed oft alone,
If I must weep with thee,
My Lord, thy will be done!

3 My Jesus, as thou wilt!
All shall be well for me:
Each changing future scene
I gladly trust with thee:
Then to my home above
I travel calmly on,
And sing, in life or death,
My Lord, thy will be done!

NEARER TO THEE. 6s & 4s.

721 ANN W. HALL.

Prayer in Sorrow.

1 FATHER, oh, hear me now!
Father divine!
Thou, only thou, canst see
The heart's deep agony,—
Help me to say to thee,
Thy will, not mine!

2 O God! be thou my stay
In this dark hour;
Kindly each sorrow hear,
Hush every troubled fear,
And let me still revere
And own thy power.

3 In thee alone I trust,
The Holy One!
Humbly to thee I pray
That, through each troubled day
Of life, I still may say,
Thy will be done.

COME, YE DISCONSOLATE. 11s & 10s. WEBBE.

722 *Come, ye Disconsolate.* MOORE.

1 COME, ye disconsolate, where'er ye languish; [kneel,
Come, at the shrine of God fervently
Here bring your wounded hearts, here tell your anguish; [not heal.
Earth has no sorrow that heaven can-

2 Joy of the desolate, light of the straying, [and pure,
Hope, when all others die, fadeless
Here speaks the Comforter, in God's name saying, [cannot cure.
Earth has no sorrow, that heaven

3 Here see the bread of life; see waters flowing [ing and pure;
Forth from the throne of God, liv-
Come to the feast of love; come, ever knowing [cannot cure.
Earth has no sorrow that heaven

RAMOTH. L. M.

Dr. L. Mason.

723

Anon.

Not lost, but gone before.

1 Why should we weep and mourn for those
Whose places know them here no more;
Released from all life's hurtful foes,
They are not lost, but gone before.

2 How many weary days on earth,
How many griefs, they numbered o'er!
Now they enjoy a heavenly birth:
They are not lost, but gone before.

3 Dear is the spot where Christians sleep,
And sweet the strain which angels pour;
Oh, why should we in anguish weep?
They are not lost, but gone before.

724

Watts.

Death and Burial of a Christian.

1 Unveil thy bosom, faithful tomb!
Take this new treasure to thy trust,
And give these sacred relics room
To seek a slumber in thy dust.

2 Nor pain, nor grief, nor anxious fear
Invade thy bounds; no mortal woes
Can reach the peaceful sleeper here,
While angels watch the soft repose.

3 So Jesus slept; God's dying Son [bed;
Passed through the grave, and blessed the
Then rest, dear saint, for from his throne
Morning shall break, and pierce the shade.

4 Hail! glorious resurrection morn!
Attend, O earth, thy Sov'reign's word!
Not earthly dust, but souls new-born,
Shall live forever with the Lord.

725

Longfellow.

Suspiria.

1 Take them, O death! and bear away
Whatever thou canst call thine own,
Thine image stamped upon this clay
Doth give thee that, but that alone.

2 Take them, O grave! and let them lie
Folded upon thy narrow shelves,
As garments by the soul laid by,
And precious only to ourselves!

3 Take them, O great Eternity!
Our little life is but a gust
That bends the branches of thy tree,
And trails its blossoms in the dust.

726

Hill.

Prayer for a peaceful Death.

1 Gently, my Saviour, let me down,
To slumber in the arms of death;
I rest my soul on thee alone,
E'en till my last expiring breath.

2 Soon will the storm of life be o'er,
And I shall enter endless rest;
There I shall live to sin no more,
And bless thy name, forever blest.

3 Bid me possess sweet peace within;
Let childlike patience keep my heart;
Then shall I feel my heaven begin,
Before my spirit hence depart.

4 Oh, speed thy chariot, God of love!
And take me from this world of woe;
I long to reach those joys above,
And bid farewell to all below.

GORTON. S. M.

Arr. by Dr. Mason.

727

Anon.

Go rest, fair Child.

1 Go to thy rest, fair child!
Go to thy dreamless bed,
While yet so gentle, undefiled,
With blessings on thy head.

2 Ere sin had seared the breast,
Or sorrow woke the tear,—
Rise to thy throne of changeless rest,
In yon celestial sphere.

3 Because thy smile was fair,
Thy lip and eye so bright,
Because thy loving cradle care
Was such a fond delight,—

4 Shall love with weak embrace,
Thy upward wing detain?
No, gentle angel, seek thy place
Amid the cherub train.

728

Now is our Salvation nearer than when we believed.

1 One sweetly solemn thought
Comes to me o'er and o'er,
Nearer my parting hour am I
Than e'er I was before.

2 Nearer my Father's house,
Where many mansions be;
Nearer the throne where Jesus reigns,—
Nearer the crystal sea;

3 Nearer my going home,
Laying my burden down,
Leaving my cross of heavy grief,
Wearing my starry crown;

4 Jesus! to thee I cling:
Strengthen my arm of faith;
Stay near me while my way-worn feet
Press through the stream of death.

729

Montgomery.

On the Death of an aged Christian.

"I have fought a good fight; I have finished my course."

1 Servant of God, well done!
Rest from thy loved employ:
The battle fought, the victory won,
Enter thy Master's joy.

2 The voice at midnight came,
He started up to hear;
A mortal arrow pierced his frame—
He fell, but felt no fear.

3 Tranquil amidst alarms,
It found him on the field,
A veteran slumbering on his arms,
Beneath his red-cross shield.

4 His spirit, with a bound,
Burst its encumbering clay;
His tent, at sunrise, on the ground,
A darkened ruin lay.

5 The pains of death are past,
Labor and sorrow cease,
And life's long warfare closed at last,
His soul is found in peace.

6 Soldier of Christ! well done!
Praise be thy new employ;
And while eternal ages run,
Rest in thy Saviour's joy.

ECKARDTSHEIM. C. M. ZEUNER.

730 MRS. HEMANS.

Death of the Young.

1 CALM on the bosom of thy God,
Young spirit, rest thee now!
E'en while with us thy footsteps trod,
His seal was on thy brow.

2 Dust, to its narrow house beneath!
Soul, to its place on high!
They that have seen thy look in death,
No more may fear to die.

3 Lone are the paths and sad the bowers
Whence thy meek smile is gone;
But, oh, a brighter home than ours,
In heaven is now thine own.

731 WHITTIER.

Death of a young Girl.

1 ANOTHER hand is beckoning us,
Another call is given:
And glows once more with angel steps
The path that leads to heaven.

2 Oh, half we deemed she needed not
The changing of her sphere,
To give to heaven a shining one,
Who walked an angel here.

3 Unto our Father's will alone
One thought has reconciled;
That he whose love exceedeth ours
Hath taken home his child.

4 Fold her, O Father, in thine arms,
And let her henceforth be
A messenger of love between
Our human hearts and thee.

5 Still let her mild rebukings stand
Between us and the wrong,
And her dear memory serve to make
Our faith in goodness strong.

732 DODDRIDGE.

Death of a Minister.

1 WHAT though the arm of conquering
Does God's own house invade; [death
What though our teacher and our friend
Is numbered with the dead;

2 Though earthly shepherds dwell in
The aged and the young; [dust,
The watchful eye in darkness closed,
And dumb th' instructive tongue;

3 Th' eternal Shepherd still survives,
His teaching to impart:
Lord, be our Leader and our Guide,
And rule and keep our heart.

4 Yes, while the dear Redeemer lives,
We have a boundless store,
And shall be fed with what he gives,
Who lives for evermore.

733 DALE.

Death a Release.

1 DEAR as thou wast, and justly dear,
We would not weep for thee;
One thought shall check the starting
It is, that thou art free. [tear,—

3 Gently the passing spirit fled,
Sustained by grace divine:
Oh, may such grace on us be shed,
And make our end like thine!

ZADOC. 6s, 6 ls.

734

CONDER.

The Lord's Supper.

1 Many centuries have fled
Since our Saviour broke the bread,
And this sacred feast ordain'd,
Ever by his church retained;
Those his body who discern,
Thus shall meet till his return.

2 Through the church's long eclipse,
When from priest or pastor's lips,
Truth divine was never heard—
'Mid the famine of the word,
Still these symbols witness gave
To his love who died to save.

3 All who bear the Saviour's name,
Here their common faith proclaim;
Though diverse in tongue or rite,
Here, one body to unite;
Breaking thus one mystic bread,
Members of one common Head.

4 Come, the blessèd emblems share,
Which the Saviour's death declare;
Come, on truth immortal feed,
For his flesh is meat indeed:
Saviour! witness with the sign,
That our ransomed souls are thine.

735

ANON.

Obedience to Christ.

1 Son of God! to thee I cry:
By the holy mystery
Of thy dwelling here on earth,
By thy pure and holy birth,
Hear, oh, hear my lowly plea:
Manifest thyself to me!

2 Lamb of God! to thee I cry:
By thy bitter agony,
By thy pangs to us unknown,
By thy spirit's parting groan,
Hear, oh, hear my lowly plea:
Manifest thyself to me!

3 Lord of glory, Christ most high!
Man exalted to the sky!
With thy love my bosom fill,
Prompt me to perform thy will:
Then thy glory I shall see—
Thou wilt bring me home to thee.

4 Blessèd Saviour! thine am I,
Thine to live, and thine to die;
Height or depth, or earthly power,
Ne'er shall hide my Saviour more:
Ever shall my glory be,
Only, only, only thee!

HENRY. C. M.

S. P. Pond.

736

Anon.

The Jewish and the Christian Zion.

1 With stately towers and bulwarks strong,
Unrivalled and alone,
Loved theme of many a sacred song,
God's holy city shone.

2 Thus fair was Zion's chosen seat,
The glory of all lands;
Yet fairer, and in strength complete,
The Christian temple stands.

3 The faithful of each clime and age
This glorious church compose;
Built on a rock, with idle rage
The threatening tempest blows.

4 In vain may hostile bands alarm,
For God is her defence;
How weak, how powerless is each arm,
Against Omnipotence!

737

A. C. Coxe.

Permanence of the Church.

1 Oh, where are kings and empires now,
Of old that went and came?
But Holy Church is praying yet,
A thousand years the same.

2 Mark ye her holy battlements,
And her foundations strong;
And hear within her solemn voice,
And her unending song.

3 For not like kingdoms of the world
The Holy Church of God:
Though earthquake shocks are rocking her,
And tempests are abroad,—

4 Unshaken as eternal hills,
Immovable she stands,—
A mountain that shall fill the earth,
A fane unbuilt by hands.

738

W. Hunt.

The River of Life.

1 There is a River, deep and broad;
Its course no mortal knows:
It fills with joy the Church of God,
And widens as it flows.

2 Clearer than crystal is the stream,
And bright with endless day;
The waves with every blessing teem,
And life and health convey.

3 Where'er they flow, contentions cease,
And love and meekness reign:
The Lord himself commands the peace,
And foes conspire in vain.

4 Along the shores, angelic bands
Watch every moving wave:
With holy joy their breast expands,
When men the waters crave.

5 To them distressèd souls repair;
The Lord invites them nigh:
They leave their cares and sorrows there;
They drink, and never die.

6 Flow on, sweet stream, more largely flow,
The earth with glory fill;
Flow on, till all the Saviour know,
And all obey his will.

WORTHING. 8s & 7s. Arr. by Dr. Mason.

739

J. Newton.

Glorious Things spoken of Zion.

1 Glorious things of thee are spoken,
Zion, city of our God!
He whose word cannot be broken
Formed thee for his own abode.

2 On the Rock of Ages founded,
What can shake thy sure repose?
With salvation's walls surrounded,
Thou may'st smile at all thy foes.

3 See! the streams of living waters,
Springing from eternal love,
Well supply thy sons and daughters,
And all fear of want remove.

4 Who can faint while such a river
Ever flows, their thirst t' assuage?
Grace, which, like the Lord, the giver,
Never fails from age to age.

5 Round each habitation hovering,
See the cloud and fire appear!
For a glory and a covering,
Showing that the Lord is near.

6 Fading is the worldling's pleasure,
All his boasted pomp and show;
Solid joys and lasting treasure
None but Zion's children know.

740

Newton.

Work in the Vineyard.

1 Saviour, visit thy plantation!
Grant us, Lord, a gracious rain:
All will come to desolation,
Unless thou return again.

2 Keep no longer at a distance,
Shine upon us from on high,
Lest, for want of thine assistance,
Every plant should droop and die.

3 Once, O Lord, thy garden flourished;
Every part looked gay and green;
Then thy word our spirits nourished:
Happy seasons we have seen.

4 But a drought has since succeeded,
And a sad decline we see:
Lord, thy help is greatly needed:
Help can only come from thee.

5 Let our mutual love be fervent:
Make us prevalent in prayer;
Let each one esteemed thy servant
Shun the world's bewitching snare.

6 Break the tempter's fatal power,
Turn the stony heart to flesh,
And begin from this good hour
To revive thy work afresh.

741

Anon.

God our Salvation.

1 Though benighted and forsaken,
Though afflicted and distressed,
God's almighty arm shall waken;
Zion's King shall give thee rest.

2 Cease thy sadness, unbelieving;
Soon his glory shalt thou see!
Joy and gladness, and thanksgiving,
And the voice of melody!

MORNINGTON. S. M.

MORNINGTON.

742

DWIGHT.

Attachment to the Church.

1 I LOVE thy church, O God;
Her walls before thee stand,
Dear as the apple of thine eye,
And graven on thy hand.

2 For her my tears shall fall;
For her my prayers ascend;
To her my cares and toils be given,
Till toils and cares shall end.

3 Beyond my highest joy
I prize her heavenly ways,
Her sweet communion, solemn vows,
Her hymns of love and praise.

4 Sure as thy truth shall last,
To Zion shall be given
The brightest glories earth can yield,
And brighter bliss of heaven.

743

BEDDOME.

Christian Unity.

1 LET party names no more
The Christian world o'erspread;
Gentile and Jew, and bond and free,
Are one in Christ, their Head.

2 Among the saints on earth
Let mutual love be found;
Heirs of the same inheritance,
With mutual blessings crowned:

3 Envy and strife be gone,
And only kindness known;
While all one common Father have,
One common Master own.

4 Thus will the church below
Resemble that above,
Where springs of purest pleasure rise,
And every heart is love.

744

BONAR.

Church Work.

1 FAR down the ages now,
Much of her journey done,
The pilgrim Church pursues her way,
Until her crown be won.

2 No wider is the gate,
No broader is the way,
No smoother is the ancient path,
That leads to life and day.

3 No slacker grows the fight,
No feebler is the foe,
Nor less the need of armor tried,
Of shield and spear and bow.

4 Still faithful to our God,
And to our Captain true,
We follow where he leads the way,
The kingdom in our view.

745

ANON.

Still with Thee.

1 STILL with thee, O my God!
I would desire to be;
By day, by night, at home, abroad,
I would be still with thee;—

2 With thee, in thee, by faith
Abiding I would be:
By day, by night, in life, in death,
I would be still with thee.

HEBER. C. M.

GEO. KINGSLEY.

746

C. WESLEY.

The Church below and above.

1 THE saints on earth and those above,
But one communion make;
Joined to the Lord in bonds of love,
All of his grace partake.

2 One family, we dwell in him:
One church above, beneath;
Though now divided by the stream,
The narrow stream of death.

3 One army of the living God,
To his command we bow;
Part of the host have crossed the flood,
And part are crossing now.

4 O God, be thou our constant guide!
Then, when the word is given,
Bid death's cold flood its waves divide,
And land us safe in heaven.

747

SCHMOLCK.

Death and Life in Christ.

1 LORD, let thy conquering banner wave
O'er hearts thou makest free,
And point the path that from the grave
Leads heavenward up to thee.

2 We bury all our sin and crime
Deep in our Saviour's tomb,
And seek the treasures there that time
Nor change can e'er consume.

3 We die with thee: oh, let us live
Henceforth to thee aright;
The blessings thou hast died to give,
Be daily in our sight.

4 Fearless we lay us in the tomb,
And sleep the night away,
If thou art there to break the gloom,
And call us back to day.

748

S. F. SMITH.

One in Christ.

1 PLANTED in Christ, the living Vine,
This day, with one accord,
Ourselves, with humble faith and joy,
We yield to thee, O Lord!

2 Joined in one body may we be;
One inward life partake;
One be our heart, one heavenly hope
In every bosom wake.

3 In prayer, in effort, tears, and toils,
One wisdom be our guide;
Taught by one spirit from above,
In thee may we abide.

4 Then, when among the saints in light
Our joyful spirits shine,
Shall anthems of immortal praise,
O Lamb of God, be thine.

749

MONTGOMERY.

This do in Remembrance of Me.

1 ACCORDING to thy gracious word,
In meek humility,
This will I do, my dying Lord,—
I will remember thee.

2 Thy body, broken for my sake,
My bread from heaven shall be;
Thy testamental cup I take,
And thus remember thee.

WARD. L. M.

Arr. by Dr. Mason.

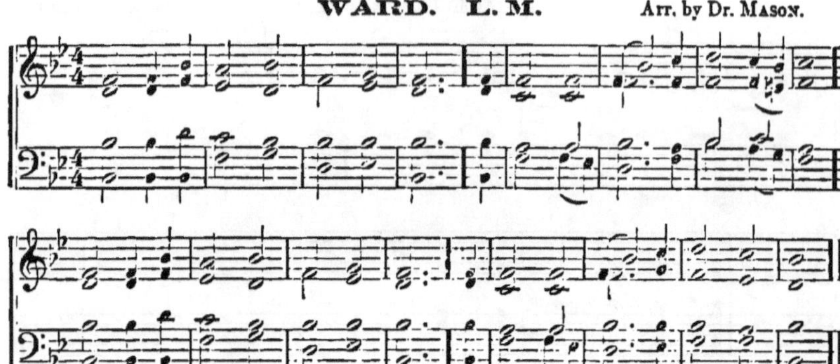

750

DODDRIDGE.

Uniting with the Church.

1 O HAPPY day, that fixed my choice
On thee, my Saviour, and my Lord!
Well may this glowing heart rejoice,
And tell its raptures all abroad.

2 Oh, happy bond that seals my vows
To him who merits all my love!
Let cheerful anthems fill the house,
While to his altar now I move.

3 'T is done — the great transaction 's done;
I am my Lord's, and he is mine;
He drew me, and I followed on,
Charmed to confess the voice divine.

4 Now rest, my long-divided heart!
Fixed on this blissful centre, rest;
Here have I found a nobler part,
Here heavenly pleasures fill my breast.

5 High heaven, that hears the solemn vow,
That vow renewed shall daily hear,
Till in life's latest hour I bow,
And bless in death a bond so dear.

751

GASKELL.

Bearing with us the Dying of Jesus.

1 NOT in this simple rite alone
May Calvary's cross to us be shown,
But may we turn, in many an hour,
To feel its soul-constraining power.

2 When indolence would have its will,
And selfish ease would keep us still,
Then to the Saviour may we look,
And meet his eye's serene rebuke.

3 When men have done us cruel wrong,
And angry thoughts are rising strong,
May we with softened hearts turn there,
And learn the Lord's forgiving prayer.

4 When sin looks tempting in our eyes,
May Jesus on the cross arise,
And ask if we will him forsake,
And wear the chains he died to break.

5 When pain, or sickness, or distress,
Our fainting souls would overpress,
To him on Calvary looking still,
May we find strength to hear God's will.

752

STENNETT.

Commemoration of Christ's Death.

1 THUS we commemorate the day
On which our dearest Lord was slain:
Thus we our pious homage pay,
Till he appear on earth again.

2 Come, great Redeemer, open wide
The curtains of the parting sky;
On a bright cloud in triumph ride,
And on the wind's swift pinions fly.

753

MONTGOMERY.

Welcome to Christian Fellowship.

1 COME in, thou blessèd of our God,
In Jesus' name we bid thee come;
No more thy feet shall roam abroad,
Henceforth a brother,— welcome home.

2 Those joys which earth cannot afford,
We'll seek in fellowship to prove,
Joined in one spirit to our Lord,
Together bound by mutual love.

PLEYEL'S HYMN. 7s.

PLEYEL.

754 MONTGOMERY.

Joined to God's People.

1 PEOPLE of the living God,
I have sought the world around,
Paths of sin and sorrow trod,
Peace and comfort nowhere found.

2 Now to you my spirit turns,—
Turns, a fugitive unblest;
Brethren, where your altar burns,
Oh, receive me into rest.

3 Lonely I no longer roam,
Like the cloud, the wind, the wave;
Where you dwell shall be my home,
Where you die shall be my grave.

755 RAY PALMER.

Gratitude for the Church.

1 FOUNT of everlasting love!
Rich thy streams of mercy are;
Flowing purely from above,
Beauty marks their course afar.

2 Lo! thy Church, athirst and faint,
Drinks the full, refreshing tide;
Thou hast heard her sad complaint;
Floods of grace are sweeping wide!

3 God of mercy, to thy throne
Now our fervent thanks we bring;
Thine the glory, thine alone,
Joyous praise to thee we sing.

4 While we lift our grateful song,
Let thy Spirit still descend;
Roll the tide of grace along,
Widening, deepening, to the end!

756 BOWRING.

A Communion Hymn.

1 NOT with terror do we meet
At the board by Jesus spread;
Not in mystery drink and eat
Of the Saviour's wine and bread.

2 'T is his memory we record,
'T is his virtues we proclaim;
Grateful to our honored Lord,
Here we bless his sacred name.

3 Yes, we will remember thee,
Friend and Saviour; and thy feast
Of all services shall be
Holiest and welcomest.

757 CONDER

The Symbols of Spiritual Food.

1 BREAD of heaven, on thee we feed,
For thy flesh is meat indeed;
Ever let our souls be fed
With this true and living bread.

2 Vine of heaven, thy blood supplies
This blest cup of sacrifice;
Lord, thy wounds our healing give;
To thy cross we look and and live.

3 Day by day with strength supplied,
Through the life of Him who died;
Lord of life, oh, let us be
Rooted, grafted, built on thee.

ARLINGTON. C. M.

Dr. Arne.

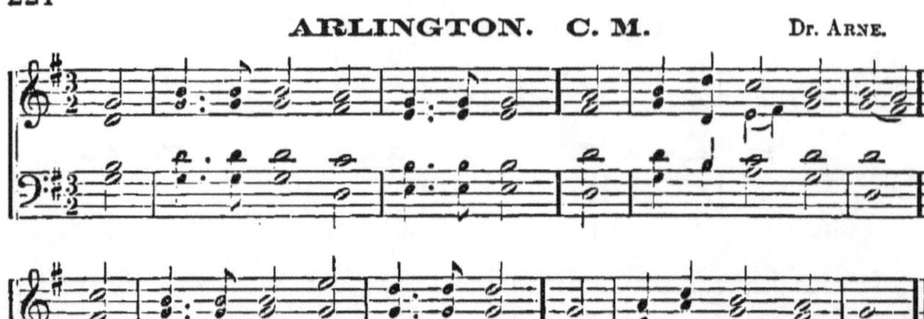

758

Anon.

Christ's Law of Love.

1 Ye followers of the Prince of peace,
Who round his table draw!
Remember what his spirit was,
What his peculiar law.

2 The love which all his bosom filled
Did all his actions guide;
Inspired by love, he lived and taught,
Inspired by love, he died.

3 And do you love him? do you feel
Your warm affection move?
This is the proof which he demands,—
That you each other love.

759

Anon.

Union with Christ in Sorrow.

1 Who, when beneath affliction's rod,
Can inward rest attain,
And bless the chastening love of God
In some remembered strain?

2 Who, when in pain he lies apart,
And powers of life decay,
Can muse with holy joy of heart
On some familiar lay?

3 He can suffice for these good things
Whose mind with Christ's is one;
Who closely in communion clings
To God's most faithful Son.

4 O Saviour! Fount of wondrous might!
Let me this gift receive:
Thus, Lord, in sorrow's darkest night
Thy servant's grief relieve.

5 Let songs of Zion, known of old
Within the hallowed place,
My spirit cheer, my faith uphold
Through thine all-strengthening grace.

760

E. Taylor.

Thoughts at the Communion.

1 Oh, here, if ever, God of love!
Let strife and hatred cease;
And every thought harmonious move,
And every heart be peace.

2 Not here, where met to think on him
Whose latest thoughts were ours,
Shall mortal passions come to dim
The prayer devotion pours.

3 "Thy kingdom come;" we watch, we
To hear thy cheering call; [wait,
When heaven shall ope its glorious gate,
And God be all in all.

761

S. Gilman.

Faithfulness to Christ.

1 O God, accept the sacred hour
Which we to thee have given;
And let this hallowed scene have power
To raise our souls to heaven.

2 Still let us hold till life departs,
The precepts of thy Son,
Nor let our thoughtless, thankless hearts,
Forget what he has done.

3 His true disciples may we live,
From all corruption free,
And humbly learn like him to give
Our powers, our wills to Thee.

BOYLSTON. S. M. Dr. L. Mason.

762 Doddridge.

Communion with God and Christ.

1 My heavenly Father calls,
And Christ invites me near;
With both my friendship shall be sweet,
And my communion dear.

2 God pities all my griefs;
He pardons every day;
Almighty to protect my soul,
And wise to guide my way.

3 Jesus, my living Head,
I bless thy faithful care;
My Advocate before the throne,
And my Forerunner there.

4 Here fix my roving heart;
Here wait my warmest love,
Till the communion be complete,
In nobler scenes above.

763 Furness.

The Communion.

1 Here, in the broken bread,
Here, in the cup we take,
His body and his blood behold,
Who suffered for our sake.

2 O thou, who didst allow
Thy Son to suffer thus, [done,
Father, what more couldst thou have
Than thou hast done for us?

3 We are persuaded now
That nothing can divide
Thy children from thy boundless love,
Displayed in Him who died;—

4 Who died to make us sure
Of mercy, truth, and peace,
And from the power and pains of sin
To bring a full release.

764 Sigourney.

Active Effort.

1 Laborers of Christ, arise,
And gird you for the toil!
The dew of promise from the skies
Already cheers the soil.

2 Go where the sick recline,
Where mourning hearts deplore;
And where the sons of sorrow pine,
Dispense your hallowed store.

3 Be faith, which looks above,
With prayer, your constant guest;
And wrap the Saviour's changeless love
A mantle round your breast.

4 So shall you share the wealth
That earth may ne'er despoil,
And the blest gospel's saving health
Repay your arduous toil.

765 Eng. Bap. Coll.

Obeying Christ.

1 Here, Saviour, we would come,
In thine appointed way;
Obedient to thy high commands,
Our solemn vows we pay.

2 Oh, bless this sacred rite,
To bring us near to thee;
And may we find that as our day
Our strength shall also be.

DEDHAM. C. M.

766 STEELE.

Yet there is Room.

1 Ye wretched, hungry, starving poor,
Behold a royal feast,
Where Mercy spreads her bounteous store
For every humble guest.

2 There Jesus stands with open arms;
He calls — he bids you come:
Though guilt restrains, and fear alarms,
Behold, there yet is room.

3 Oh, come, and with his children taste
The blessings of his love;
While hope expects the sweet repast
Of nobler joys above.

4 There, with united heart and voice,
Before th' eternal throne,
Ten thousand thousand souls rejoice,
In songs on earth unknown.

5 And yet ten thousand thousand more
Are welcome still to come:
Ye longing souls, the grace adore,
Approach, there yet is room.

767 DODDRIDGE.

Room at the Lord's Table.

1 Millions of souls, in glory now,
Were fed and feasted here;
And millions more, still on the way,
Around the board appear.

2 Yet is his house and heart so large
That millions more may come:
Nor could the whole assembled world
E'er fill the spacious room.

3 All things are ready; come away,
Nor weak excuses frame;
Crowd to your places at the feast,
And bless the Founder's name.

768 LUTHERAN COLL.

Close of Communion Service.

1 Pity the nations, O our God,
Constrain the earth to come;
Send thy victorious word abroad,
And bring the strangers home.

2 We long to see thy churches full,
That all thy faithful race
May with one voice, and heart, and soul,
Sing thy redeeming grace.

769 NOEL.

Remembering Christ.

1 If human kindness meets return,
And owns the grateful tie;
If tender thoughts within us burn,
To feel that friends are nigh,—

2 Oh, shall not warmer accents tell
The gratitude we owe
To Him who died our fears to quell,
And save from sin and woe?

3 While yet his anguished soul surveyed
Those pangs he would not flee,
What love his latest words displayed! —
"Meet and remember me."

4 Remember thee! thy death, thy shame,
The griefs which thou didst bear!
Oh, memory! leave no other name
But his recorded there.

BERA. L. M. Root & Sweetser's Coll.

770 J. Lombard.

That they may all be one.

1 When death was on the path he trod,
And Jesus saw his work was done,
He raised his eyes and prayed to God,
That his disciples might be one.

2 This, Father, is our prayer to-day,
That we may one in spirit be,
Through Christ, who came to teach the way,
And all united, God, in thee!

3 One in the Faith that works by love
And purifies the heart and life;
One in the Hope that looks above,
And sees an end of sin and strife:

4 One in the Love that warms the heart
And makes it thy most worthy shrine;
And one in thee, O God, who art
The Giver of these gifts divine;

5 Through life, and till we reach its goal,
When what we have to do is done,
Heart linked to heart, and soul to soul.
And all, through Christ, in thee be one.

771 St. Bernard.

Jesus the joy of the Heart.

1 Jesus, thou joy of loving hearts!
Thou fount of life! Thou light of men!
From the best bliss that earth imparts,
We turn unfilled to thee again.

2 Thy truth unchanged hath ever stood;
Thou savest those that on thee call;
To them that seek thee, thou art good,
To them that find thee thou art all.

3 We taste thee, O thou living bread,
And long to feast upon thee still!
We drink of thee, the fountain head,
And thirst our souls from thee to fill.

4 Our restless spirits yearn for thee,
Where'er our changeful lot is cast;
Glad, when thy gracious smile we see,
Blest, when our faith can hold thee fast.

5 O Jesus, ever with us stay!
Make all our moments calm and bright!
Chase the dark night of sin away,
Shed o'er the world thy holy light!

772 Collyer.

The Baptism of a Household.

1 United prayers ascend to thee,
Eternal Parent of mankind!
Smile on this waiting family;
Thy blessing let thy servants find.

2 Let the dear pledges of their love,
Like tender plants, around them grow;
Thy present grace, and joys above,
Upon their little ones bestow.

3 Receive at their believing hand
The charge which they devote as thine,
Obedient to their Lord's command;
And seal, with power, the rite divine.

4 To every member of their house,
Thy grace impart, thy love extend;
Grant every good that time allows,
With heavenly joys that never end.

HOLLEY. 7s. Geo. Hews.

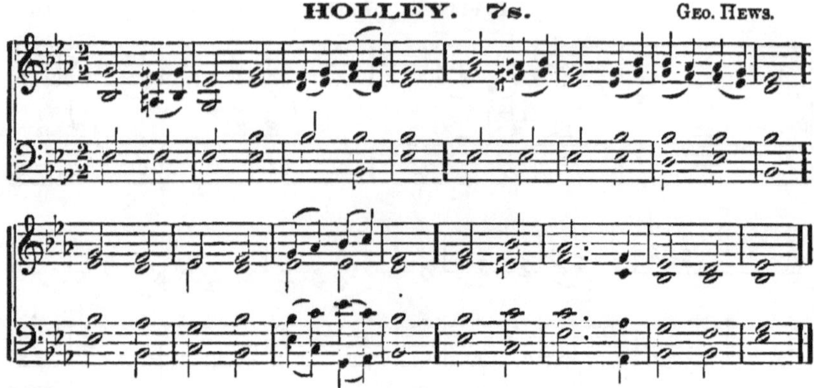

773 C. Wesley.

The Harmony of Love.

1 Lord! subdue our selfish will:
Each to each our tempers suit,
By thy modulating skill,
Heart to heart, as lute to lute.

2 Sweetly on our spirits move;
Gently touch the trembling strings;
Make the harmony of love,
Music for the King of kings!

774 Bowring.

Infant Baptism.

1 Drop the limpid waters now
On the infant's sinless brow;
Dedicate the unfolding gem
Unto Him, who blessed the stem.

2 Let our aspirations be
Innocent as infancy;
Pure the prayers that force their way,
As the child for whom we pray.

3 In the Christian garden we
Plant another Christian tree;
Be its blossoms and its fruit
Worthy of the Christian root.

4 To that garden now we bring
Waters from the living spring;
Bless the tree, the waters bless,
Holy One, with holiness.

5 When life's harvests all are past,
Oh, transplant the tree at last,
To the fields where flower and tree
Blossom through eternity.

775 Anon.

Love for Christ.

1 Saviour! teach me, day by day,
Love's sweet lesson to obey,
Sweeter lesson cannot be,
Loving him who first loved me.

2 With a child-like heart of love,
At thy bidding may I move;
Prompt to serve and follow thee,
Loving him who first loved me.

3 Teach me all thy steps to trace,
Strong to follow in thy grace;
Learning how to love from thee,
Loving him who first loved me.

4 Love in loving finds employ—
In obedience all her joy;
Ever new that joy will be,
Loving him who first loved me.

5 Thus may I rejoice to show
That I feel the love I owe;
Singing, till thy face I see,
Of his love who first loved me.

776 Newton

Christ the Shepherd.

1 Now may he who from the dead
Brought the Shepherd of the sheep,
Jesus Christ, our king and head,
All our souls in safety keep.

2 May he teach us to fulfill
What is pleasing in his sight;
Make us perfect in his will,
And preserve us day and night!

STOCKWELL. 8s & 7s. D. E. JONES.

777 ANON.

Desires after Christian Obedience.

1 FROM the table now retiring,
Which for us the Lord hath spread,
May our souls, refreshment finding,
Grow in all things like our Head.

2 His example by beholding,
May our lives his image bear;
Him our Lord and Master calling,
His commands may we revere.

3 Love to God and man displaying,
Walking steadfast in his way,
Joy attend us in believing:
Peace from God, through endless day.

778 ANON.

Children commended to Christ.

1 SAVIOUR! who thy flock art feeding
With the shepherd's kindest care,
All the feeble gently leading,
While the lambs thy bosom share;

2 Now, these little ones receiving,
Fold them in thy gracious arm;
There we know — thy word believing —
Only there, secure from harm.

3 Never, from thy pasture roving,
Let them be the lion's prey;
Let thy tenderness, so loving,
Keep them all life's dangerous way:

4 Then within thy fold eternal
Let them find a resting-place;
Feed in pastures ever vernal,
Drink the rivers of thy grace.

779 ROBINSON.

Mercies gratefully acknowledged.

1 COME, thou Fount of every blessing,
Tune my heart to sing thy grace;
Streams of mercy, never ceasing,
Call for songs of loudest praise.

2 Teach me some melodious measure,
Sung by raptured saints above;
Fill my soul with sacred pleasure,
While I sing redeeming love.

3 By thy hand sustained, defended,
Safe through life, thus far, I've come;
Safely, Lord, when life is ended,
Bring me to my heavenly home.

780 ANON.

Christ's Table.

1 JESUS spreads his banner o'er us,
Cheers our famished souls with food;
He the banquet spreads before us,
Of his mystic flesh and blood.

2 Precious banquet; bread of heaven;
Wine of gladness, flowing free;
May we taste it, kindly given,
In remembrance, Lord, of thee!

3 Though unseen, now be thou near us,
With the still small voice of love;
Whispering words of peace to cheer us —
Every doubt and fear remove.

ORTONVILLE. C. M.

781

S. F. SMITH.

Self-Consecration in Baptism.

1 While in this sacred rite of thine,
We yield our spirits now,
Shine o'er the waters, Dove divine,
And seal the cheerful vow.

2 All glory be to him whose life
For ours was freely given,
Who aids us in the spirit's strife,
And makes us meet for heaven.

3 To thee we gladly now resign
Our life and all our powers;
Accept us in this rite divine,
And bless these hallowed hours.

4 Oh, may we die to earth and sin,
Beneath the mystic flood;
And when we rise, may we begin
To live anew for God.

782

JAS. NEWTON.

After Baptism.

1 Let plenteous grace descend on those,
Who, hoping in thy word,
This day have solemnly declared
That Jesus is their Lord.

2 With cheerful feet may they advance,
And run the Christian race,
And, through the troubles of the way,
Find all-sufficient grace.

3 Lord, plant us all into thy death,
That we thy life may prove,—
Partakers of thy cross beneath,
And of thy crown above.

783

Christ's Baptism.

1 Buried beneath the yielding wave
The great Redeemer lies;
Faith views him in the watery grave,
And thence beholds him rise.

2 Thus do believers here to-day,
Their ardent zeal express,
And, in the Lord's appointed way,
Fulfill all righteousness.

3 With joy we in his footsteps tread,
And would his cause maintain —
Like him be numbered with the dead,
And with him rise and reign.

4 His presence oft revives our hearts,
And drives our fears away; [parts,
When he commands, and strength im-
We cheerfully obey.

784

Christ's Baptism.

1 "I come," the great Redeemer cries,
"To do thy will, O Lord!"
At Jordan's flood, behold, he seals
The sure prophetic word.

2 "Thus it becomes us to fulfil
All righteousness," he said;
He spake obedient, and beneath
The yielding wave was laid.

3 Hark! a glad voice; the Father speaks
From heaven's exalted height:
"This is my Son, my well-beloved,
My joy, my chief delight."

PARAH. S. M.

Dr. L. Mason.

785

J. F. Clarke.

Baptism of a Child.

1 To thee, O God, in heaven,
This little one we bring,
Giving to thee what thou hast given,
Our dearest offering.

2 Into a world of toil
These little feet will roam,
Where sin its purity may soil,
Where care and grief may come.

3 Oh, then, let thy pure love,
With influence serene,
Come down, like water, from above,
To comfort and make clean.

786

Anon.

Consecration of Children.

1 Our children thou dost claim,
O Lord, our God, as thine:
Ten thousand blessings to thy name
For goodness so divine!

2 Thee let the fathers own,
Thee let the sons adore;
Joined to the Lord in solemn vows,
To be forgot no more.

3 How great thy mercies, Lord!
How plenteous is thy grace,
Which, in the promise of thy love,
Includes our rising race!

4 Our offspring, still thy care,
Shall own their fathers' God!
To latest times thy blessings share,
And sound thy praise abroad.

787

Fellows.

Baptism of Children.

1 Great God, now condescend
To bless our rising race;
Soon may their willing spirits bend,
The subjects of thy grace.

2 Oh, what a pure delight
Their happiness to see;
Our warmest wishes all unite
To lead their souls to thee.

3 Now bless, thou God of love,
This ordinance divine;
Send thy good Spirit from above,
And make these children thine.

788

J. F. Clarke.

Dedication of Children.

1 To him who children blest,
And suffered them to come,
To him who took them to his breast,
We bring these children home.

2 To thee, O God, whose face
Their spirits still behold,
We bring them praying that thy grace
May keep, thine arms enfold.

3 And as this water falls
On each unconscious brow,
Thy holy spirit grant, O Lord,
To keep them pure as now.

MARLOW. C. M.

Arr. by Dr. L. Mason.

789

Bryant.

Dedication Hymn.

1 O thou, whose own vast temple stands
Built over earth and sea,
Accept the walls that human hands
Have raised to worship thee.

2 Lord, from thine inmost glory send,
Within these courts to bide,
The peace that dwelleth, without end,
Serenely by thy side.

3 May erring minds that worship here
Be taught the better way,
And they who mourn, and they who fear,
Be strengthened as they pray!

4 May faith grow firm, and love grow [warm,
And pure devotion rise,
While round these hallowed walls the [storm
Of earth-born passion dies!

790

H. Bacon.

Ordination.

1 Not for the prophet tongue of fire,
Nor voice of trumpet tone,
We lift our prayer, Immortal Sire,
For him before thy throne.

2 Lord, bless him now! by holy rite,
We consecrate to thee!
Make to his eye the chief delight
Christ's prospering work to see.

3 Bold let him be for truth and man,
For God and righteousness!
Free let him speak the gospel plan,
And the whole truth confess.

4 Be cloud and fire about his way,
Till Canaan's land is trod!
Then o'er his grave thy church shall say,
He led us to our God!

791

Miss L. T. Caswell.

Ordination.

1 "I am the way, the truth, the life,"
Our blessed Master said;
And whoso to the Father comes,
Must in my pathway tread.

2 A way it is, not hedged with forms,
A truth, too large for creeds,
A life, indwelling, deep and broad,
That meets the soul's great needs.

3 To point that living way, to speak
That truth "which makes men free,"
To bring that quickening life from [heaven,
Is highest ministry.

4 God give thee so to teach and lead,
Our brother in the faith!
God give thee to be strong and true,
And steadfast unto death.

792

Anon.

Dedication.

1 God of the universe, to thee
This sacred fane we rear,
And now, with songs and bended knee,
Invoke thy presence here.

2 Here let thy love, thy presence dwell;
Thy glory here make known;
Thy people's home, oh, come and fill,
And seal it as thine own.

LUTON. L. M.

BURDER.

793

WILLIS.

Dedication Hymn.

1 The perfect world by Adam trod,
Was the first temple,—built by God;
His fiat laid the corner-stone,
And heaved its pillars, one by one.

2 He hung its starry roof on high,—
The broad, illimitable sky;
He spread its pavement, green and bright,
And curtained it with morning light.

3 The mountains in their places stood,—
The sea, the sky,—and "all was good:"
And when its first pure praises rang,
The "morning stars together sang."

4 Lord! 't is not ours to make the sea
And earth and sky a house for thee;
But in thy sight our offering stands,
A humbler temple, "made with hands."

794

MRS. PAGE.

Dedication of a Church.

1 O God! ere heaven and earth were planned,
Adoring silence worshipped thee;
Now the vast universe doth stand
The temple of thy majesty.

2 Its walls are wrought of sapphire bright;
Its countless spires are starry flame:
Suns on the boundless ether write
The sovereign beauty of thy name.

3 An earthly temple, by thy grace,
This day we dedicate to thee;
Deign to make here thy dwelling-place,
O thou that fill'st immensity.

4 Fold us beneath thy sheltering wings,
As here we worship at thy shrine:
Ours be the peace thy presence brings,
The glory and the praise be thine.

795

MONTGOMERY.

Laying of a Corner-Stone.

1 This stone to thee in faith we lay,—
We build the temple, Lord, to thee,
Thine eye be open night and day,
To keep this house from error free.

2 Here, when thy people seek thy face,
And dying sinners pray to live,
Hear thou, in heaven, thy dwelling-place,
And when thou hearest, Lord, forgive.

3 Here, when thy messengers proclaim
The blesséd gospel of thy Son,
Still by the power of his great name
Be mighty signs and wonders done.

4 Thy glory never hence depart!
Yet choose not, Lord, this house alone;
Thy kingdom come to every heart;
In every bosom fix thy throne.

796

ANON.

Dedication.

1 Oh, bow thine ear, Eternal One!
On thee our heart adoring calls;
To thee the followers of thy Son
Have raised, and now devote these walls.

2 Here let thy holy days be kept;
And be this place to worship given,
Like that bright spot where Jacob slept,
The house of God, the gate of heaven.

LITANY. 7s.

HEROLD.

797 E. H. CHAPIN.

Dedication of a Church.

1 Father, lo! we consecrate
  Unto thee this house and shrine,
Oh! may Jesus visit here,
  As he did in Palestine.
Here may blind eyes see his light,
  Deaf ears hear his accents sweet,
And we, like those groups of old,
  Sit and linger at his feet.

2 And to learn of faith and love,
  Strong in sorrow, pain and loss,
May we come and find them here,
  In the garden, on the cross.
Like the spices that enfold
  Him we love in rich perfume,
May our thoughts embalm him here,
  While he slumbers in the tomb.

3 When we watch by shrouded hopes,
  Weeping at death's marble door,
May the angels meet us here,—
  Lo! your Christ has gone before!
And while we stand "looking up,"
  In our faith and wonder lost,
Here send down thy spirit's power,
  Like the tongues of Pentecost.

798 MONTGOMERY.

God's Deliverance.

1 Thank and praise Jehovah's name;
  For his mercies, firm and sure,
From eternity the same,
  To eternity endure.
Let the ransomed thus rejoice,
  Gathered out of every land;
As the people of his choice,
  Plucked from the destroyer's hand.

2 In the wilderness astray,
  Hither, thither, while they roam,
Hungry, fainting by the way,
  Far from refuge, shelter, home;—
Then unto the Lord they cry;
  He inclines a gracious ear,
Sends deliverance from on high,
  Rescues them from all their fear.

3 To a pleasant land he brings,
  Where the vine and olive grow;
Where, from flowery hills, the springs
  Through luxuriant valleys flow.
Oh, that men would praise the Lord,
  For his goodness to their race;
For the wonders of his word,
  And the riches of his grace!

799*

MRS. E. M. BARSTOW.

Dedication of a Church.

1 GREAT God, our king! to thee
We come on bended knee,
Our gift to bring;
Our suppliant prayer we raise,
That this, our house of praise,
Accepted be.

2 And to this sacred place,
Oh, turn thy gracious face
By night and day;
Here hearken to our prayers,
Here lift the heavy cares
From burdened hearts.

3 Here may the erring come;
Here wanderers find a home
In thy great love;
Here may the sinning bring—
Thy favorite offering—
A contrite heart;

4 Here sing the wondrous grace
Which saves our guilty race
From sin's dark stain,
Till in thy courts above,
Raised by redeeming love,
New songs we bring.

* Repeat fifth line of this hymn to music.

800

GOODE.

Praise at the Altar.

1 PRAISE ye Jehovah's name,
Praise through his courts proclaim;
Rise and adore;
High o'er the heavens above,
Sound his great acts of love,
While his rich grace we prove,
Vast as his power.

2 Now let the trumpet raise
Sounds of triumphant praise,
Wide as his fame;
There let the harp be found;
Organs, with solemn sound,
Roll your deep notes around,
Filled with his name.

3 While his high praise you sing,
Shake every sounding string;
Sweet the accord!
He vital breath bestows;
Let every breath that flows,
His noblest fame disclose;
Praise ye the Lord.

801

ANON

Worthy the Lamb.

1 COME, all ye saints of God,
Wide through the earth abroad
Spread Jesus' fame:
Tell what his love hath done;
Trust in his name alone;
Shout to his lofty throne,
"Worthy the Lamb!"

MIGDOL. L. M.

802

PIERPONT.

Ordination of a Minister.

1 O THOU, who art above all height!
Our God, our Father, and our friend!
Beneath thy throne of love and light,
Let thine adoring children bend.

2 Since thy young servant now hath given
Himself, his powers, his hopes, his youth,
To the great cause of truth and heaven,
Be thou his guide, O God of truth!

3 Here may his doctrine drop like rain,
His speech like Hermon's dew distil,
Till green fields smile, and golden grain,
Ripe for the harvest, waits thy will.

4 And when he sinks in death,—by care,
Or pain, or toil, or years oppressed,—
O God! remember then our prayer,
And take his spirit to thy rest.

803

MRS. L. C. MYRICK.

Ordination Hymn.

1 WITH willing feet thy servant stands,
Dear Lord, within thy vineyard's gate,
He fain would join the laboring bands;
Help him to work, and watch, and wait.

2 Grant him thy grace, that he may see
The truth with pure, far-reaching sight,
And give it utterance, calm and free,
Fearless forever for the right.

3 Move him that he may others move;
Bless him that he may others bless;
Crown him with self-forgetting love,
And clothe him with thy righteousness.

4 The winter of delay is gone, [near;
The spring-time's promised bloom is
Make beautiful, O blessed One!
The footsteps of thy messenger.

804

H. WARE, JR.

Ordination or Installation.

1 O THOU, who on thy chosen Son
Didst send thy spirit like a dove,
To mark the long-expected one,
And seal the messenger of love;

2 And when the heralds of his name
Went forth his glorious truth to spread,
Didst send it down in tongues of flame
To hallow each devoted head;

3 So, Lord, thy servant now inspire
With holy unction from above;
Give him the tongue of living fire,
Give him the temper of the dove.

4 Lord, hear thy suppliant church to-day;
Accept our work, our souls possess;
'T is ours to labor, watch, and pray;
Be thine to cheer, sustain, and bless.

805

NORTON.

Temple Worship.

1 WHERE ancient forests widely spread,
Where bends the cataract's ocean-fall,
On the lone mountain's silent head,—
There are thy temples, God of all!

2 All space is holy, for all space
Is filled by thee; but human thought
Burns clearer in some chosen place,
Where thine own words of love are taught.

HAMDEN. 8s, 7s, & 4. Dr. L. Mason.

806

E. H. Chapin.

Ordination.

1 Father! at this altar bending, [free;
Set our hearts from world-thoughts
Prayer and praise their incense blending,
May our rites accepted be:
Father, hear us,
Gently draw our souls to thee.

2 Deign to smile upon this union
Of a pastor and a flock;
Sweet and blest be their communion:
May he sacred truths unlock,—
And this people
Plant their feet on Christ the Rock.

3 Be his life a living sermon,
Be his thoughts one ceaseless prayer:
Like the dews that fell on Hermon,
Making green the foliage there,
May his teachings
Drop on souls beneath his care.

4 Here may sin repent its straying,
Here may grief forget to weep,
Here may hope, its light displaying,
And blest faith, their vigils keep,
And the dying
Pass from hence in Christ to sleep.

5 When his heart shall cease its motion,
All its toils and conflicts o'er:
When they for an unseen ocean,
One by one, shall leave the shore;
Pastor, people, there — in heaven,
May they meet to part no more.

807

Kelly.

The Church Encouraged.

1 On the mountain's top appearing,
Lo! the sacred herald stands,
Welcome news to Zion bearing,—
Zion, long in hostile lands:
Mourning captive!
God himself shall loose thy bands.

2 Has thy night been long and mournful?
Have thy friends unfaithful proved?
Have thy foes been proud and scornful,
By thy sighs and tears unmoved?
Cease thy mourning;
Zion still is well beloved.

3 God, thy God, will now restore thee;
He himself appears thy friend;
All thy foes shall flee before thee;
Here their boasts and triumphs end:
Great deliverance
Zion's King will surely send.

4 Peace and joy shall now attend thee;
All thy warfare now is past;
God thy Saviour will defend thee;
Victory is thine at last;
All thy conflicts
End in everlasting rest.

HEBRON. L. M.

Dr. L. Mason.

808

Montgomery.

A Pastor Welcomed.

1 We bid thee welcome in the name
Of Jesus, our exalted Head;
Come as a servant; so he came;
And we receive thee in his stead.

2 Come as an angel, hence to guide
A band of pilgrims on their way;
That, safely walking at thy side,
We never fail, nor faint, nor stray.

3 Come as a teacher sent from God,
Charged his whole counsel to declare;
Lift o'er our ranks the prophet's rod,
While we uphold his hands with prayer.

4 Come as a messenger of peace,
Filled with the spirit, fired with love;
Live to behold our large increase,
And die to meet us all above.

809

G. T. Flanders.

Installation of a Minister.

1 The harvest-fields are broad and white,
And ready for the reaper's hand,
Within the realm of fading night
The heralds of the morning stand.

2 The gardens blush with fragrant flowers.
Whence is the gard'ner's long delay?
He comes with morning's rosy hours
And joins us in our joy to-day.

3 The reaper where the harvest shines;
The gard'ner with his floral crown;
The dresser midst the purple vines:
Father, install him as thine own.

4 His heart, and mind, and voice, inspire
With truth and wisdom from above:
Give to his speech angelic fire:
Breathe o'er his spirit perfect love.

5 Great Shepherd, may he lead thy sheep
Through pastures ever green and fair,
To worship at Messiah's feet,
And dwell with God, the Father, there.

810

C. H. Fay.

Installation.

1 Another pastor hast thou given,
Our Father, to this flock of thine,
To feed them with the bread of heaven,
And guide them to the life divine.

2 Oh, make him here we humbly pray,
So faithful to the trust he bears,
That from his fold no lamb may stray,
Or fall within the tempter's snares.

3 And when the dying need his aid,
Then may he speak those truths sublime,
Which lift from death its fearful shade,
And ope to view yon better clime.

4 Where death has been, in homes of grief,
And sorrow's lowest depths are stirred;
There may he offer sweet relief,
Through Christ, the life and living word.

5 Here may he labor while 't is day,
That when night's gloom comes deep'ning on,
Like his loved Master, he may say,
The work thou gavest me is done.

(In singing hymns 812 and 813, repeat third line of each verse.)

811

S. F. SMITH.

Benefits of the Ministry.

1 BLEST is the hour when cares depart,
And earthly scenes are far, —
When tears of woe forget to start,
And gently dawns upon the heart
Devotion's holy star.

2 Blest is the place where angels bend
To hear our worship rise,
Where kindred thoughts their musings blend,
And all the soul's affections tend
Beyond the veiling skies.

3 Blest are the hallowed vows that bind
Man to his work of love, —
Bind him to cheer the humble mind,
Console the weeping, lead the blind,
And guide to joys above.

4 Sweet shall the song of glory swell,
Spirit divine, to thee,
When they whose work is finished well,
In thy own courts of rest shall dwell,
Blest through eternity.

812

WHITTIER.

All as God wills.

1 ALL as God wills! who wisely heeds
To give or to withhold,
And knoweth more of all my needs
Than all my prayers have told.

2 Enough, that blessings undeserved
Have marked my erring track;
That, wheresoe'er my feet have swerved,
Thy chastening turned me back;

3 That more and more a providence
Of love is understood,
Making the springs of time and sense
Bright with eternal good;

4 That death seems but a covered way
Which opens into light,
Wherein no blinded child can stray
Beyond the Father's sight.

5 No longer forward or behind
I look, in hope or fear,
But grateful take the good I find,
God's blessing, now and here.

813

W. B. TAPPAN.

The Peace and Repose of Heaven.

1 THERE is an hour of hallowed peace
For those with cares oppressed,
When sighs and sorrowing tears shall cease,
And all be hushed to rest.

2 'T is then the soul is freed from fears
And doubts that here annoy;
Then they that oft had sown in tears
Shall reap again in joy.

3 There, purity with love appears,
And bliss without alloy;
There, they, who oft have sown in tears,
Shall reap again in joy.

4 There is a home of sweet repose,
Where storms assail no more:
The stream of endless pleasure flows
On that celestial shore.

DUKE STREET. L. M. J. HATTON.

814

H. BALLOU.

At an Annual Convention.

1 DEAR Lord, behold thy servants, here,
From various parts, together meet,
To tell their labors through the year,
And lay the harvest at thy feet.

2 In thy wide fields and vineyards, Lord,
We've toiled and wrought with watchful care;
Thy wheat hath flourished by thy word,
Thy love consumed the choking tare.

3 The reapers cry, "Thy fields are white,
All ready to be gathered in,
And harvests wave, in changing light,
Far as the eye can trace the scene."

4 Lord, bless us while we here remain;
With holy love our bosoms fill;
Oh, may thy doctrine drop like rain,
And like the silent dew distil.

5 While we attend thy churches' care,
Oh, grant us wisdom from above;
With prudent thought and humble prayer,
May we fulfil the works of love.

815

MONTGOMERY.

Meeting of Ministers.

1 POUR out thy spirit from on high;
Lord! thine assembled servants bless;
Graces and gifts to each supply, [ness.
And clothe thy priests with righteous-

2 Within thy temple where we stand,
To teach the truth as taught by thee,
Saviour! like stars in thy right hand,
The angels of the churches be!

3 Wisdom and zeal and faith impart,
Firmness with meekness from above,
To bear thy people on our heart,
And love the souls whom thou dost love:—

4 To watch and pray, and never faint;
By day and night strict guard to keep;
To warn the sinner, cheer the saint,
Nourish thy lambs, and feed thy sheep.

5 Then, when our work is finished here,
In humble hope, our charge resign;
When the chief Shepherd shall appear,
O God! may they and we be thine.

816

S. C. BEACH.

For Inspiration.

1 MYSTERIOUS Presence, Source of all,—
The world without, the soul within;
Fountain of life, oh, hear our call,
And pour thy living waters in!

2 Thou breathest in the rushing wind,
Thy spirit stirs in leaf and flower;
Nor wilt thou from the willing mind
Withhold thy light and love and power.

3 Thy hand unseen, to accents clear
Awoke the Psalmist's trembling lyre;
And touched the lips of holy seer
With flame from thine own altar fire.

4 That touch Divine still, Lord, impart,
Still give the prophet's burning word;
And, vocal in each waiting heart,
Let living psalms of praise be heard.

MANOAH. C. M. GREATOREX'S COLL.

817 LYRA CATH.

God at Work in his Ministry.

1 GOD'S glory is a wondrous thing,
Most strange in all its ways,
And, of all things on earth, least like
What men agree to praise.

2 Oh, bless'd is he to whom is given
The instinct that can tell
That God is on the field when he
Is most invisible!

3 Workmen of God! oh, lose not heart,
But learn what God is like;
And in the darkest battle-field
Thou shalt know where to strike.

4 And bless'd is he who can divine
Where real right doth lie,
And dares to take the side that seems
Wrong to man's blindfold eye!

5 Oh, learn to scorn the praise of man!
Oh, learn to lose with God!
For Jesus won the world through shame,
And beckons thee his road.

818 SELECT HYMNS.

Opening of a Conference Meeting.

1 WITHIN these doors assembled now,
We wait thy blessing, Lord!
Appear within the midst, we pray,
According to thy word.

2 May some sweet promise be applied,
When we attempt to read:
For this alone can give support
In every time of need.

3 Oh, breathe upon our lifeless souls,
And raise each drooping heart!
That we may see thy smiling face
Before we hence depart.

4 And now, O blessed Spirit, come!
We long to see thee move;
Strengthen our faith, revive our zeal,
And fill us all with love.

819 BARTON.

The Dead.

1 THE dead are like the stars by day,
Withdrawn from mortal eye,
Yet holding unperceived their way
Through the unclouded sky.

2 By them, through holy hope and love,
We feel, in hours serene,
Connected with a world above,
Immortal and unseen.

3 For death his sacred seal hath set
On bright and bygone hours;
And they we mourn are with us yet,
Are more than ever ours;—

4 Ours, by the pledge of love and faith,
By hopes of heaven on high;
By trust, triumphant over death,
In immortality.

820 J. NEWTON.

Christian Perseverance.

1 REJOICE, believer, in the Lord,
Who makes your cause his own:
The hope that's built upon his word
Can ne'er be overthrown.

WOODSTOCK. C. M. DUTTON.

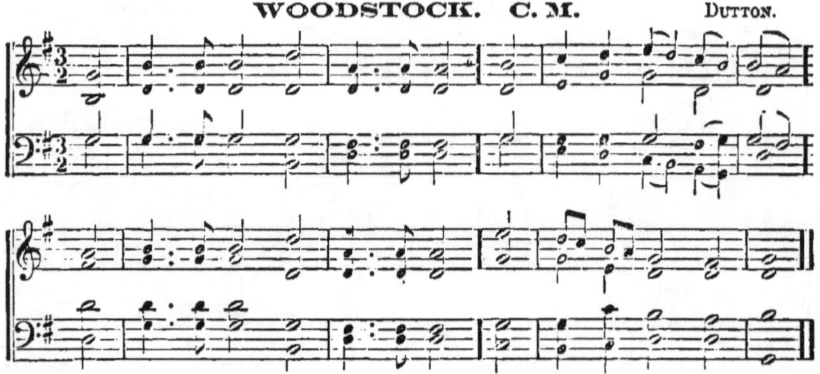

821 WATTS.

Triumph in the Assurance of Heaven.

1 When I can read my title clear
To mansions in the skies,
I bid farewell to every fear,
And wipe my weeping eyes.

2 Should earth against my soul engage,
And hellish darts be hurled,
Then I can smile on Satan's rage,
And face a frowning world.

3 Let cares, like a wild deluge, come,
And storms of sorrow fall;
May I but safely reach my home,
My God, my heaven, my all.

4 There shall I bathe my weary soul
In seas of heavenly rest;
And not a wave of trouble roll
Across my peaceful breast.

822 SUTTON.

Christian Hope.

1 Hail, sweetest, dearest tie, that binds
Our glowing hearts in one!
Hail! sacred hope! that tunes our minds
To sing what God hath done.

2 What though the northern wint'ry blast
Shall howl around our cot;
What though beneath an eastern sun
Be cast our distant lot;

3 No lingering look, no parting sigh,
Our future meeting knows;
There friendship beams from every eye,
And love immortal glows.

4 O sacred hope! O blissful hope!
Which Jesus' grace has given,—
The hope, when days and years are past,
We all shall meet in heaven.

823 MRS. BROWN.

Secret Prayer.

1 I love to steal awhile away
From every cumbering care,
And spend the hours of setting day
In humble, grateful prayer.

2 I love to think on mercies past,
And future good implore,
And all my cares and sorrows cast
On him whom I adore.

3 I love by faith to take a view
Of brighter scenes in heaven;
The prospect doth my strength renew,
While here by tempests driven.

4 Thus, when life's toilsome day is o'er,
May its departing ray
Be calm as this impressive hour,
And lead to endless day.

824 WATTS.

The New Birth.

1 When God revealed his gracious name,
And changed my mournful state,
My rapture seemed a pleasing dream,
The grace appeared so great.

2 The world beheld the glorious change,
And did thy hand confess;
My tongue broke out in unknown strains,
And sung surprising grace.

ALETTA. 7s.

825 *The Prodigal.* J. F. CLARKE.

1 BROTHER, hast thou wandered far
From thy Father's happy home,
With thyself and God at war?
Turn thee, brother, homeward come!

2 Hast thou wasted all thy powers
God for noble uses gave?
Squandered life's most golden hours!
Turn thee, brother, God can save!

3 Is a mighty famine now
In thy heart and in thy soul?
Discontent upon thy brow?
Turn thee, God will make thee whole!

4 He can heal thy bitterest wound,
He thy gentlest prayer can hear;
Seek him, for he may be found;
Call upon him; he is near.

SILVER STREET. S. M.

826 *Worship of God.* WATTS

1 COME, sound his praise abroad,
And hymns of glory sing;
Jehovah is the sovereign God,
The universal king.

2 He formed the deeps unknown;
He gave the seas their bound;
The watery worlds are all his own,
And all the solid ground.

3 Come, worship at his throne;
Come, bow before the Lord:
We are his work, and not our own;
He formed us by his word.

4 To-day attend his voice,
Nor dare provoke his rod;
Come like the people of his choice
And own your gracious God.

GREENVILLE. 8s & 7s, Double.

827

Blessings of Christ. HART.

1 Come, thou long-expected Jesus,
Born to set thy people free,
From our fears and sins release us;
Let us find our rest in thee:
Israel's strength and consolation,
Hope of all our souls thou art;
Dear desire of every nation,
Joy of every longing heart.

2 Born thy people to deliver,
Born a child and yet a king;
Born to reign in us forever,
Now thy precious kingdom bring:
By thine own eternal spirit,
Rule in all our hearts alone;
By thine all-sufficient merit,
Raise us to thy glorious throne.

SICILIAN HYMN. 8s, 7s, & 4.

(In singing, repeat fifth line.)

828

Gently lead us. ANON.

1 Gently, Lord, oh, gently lead us
Through this lowly vale of tears,
And, O Lord, in mercy give us
Thy rich grace in all our fears.
Oh, refresh us,—
Oh, refresh us with thy grace.

2 Though ten thousand ills beset us,
From without and from within,
Jesus says he 'll ne'er forget us,
He will save from every sin.
Therefore praise him—
Praise the great Redeemer's name.

3 Though distresses now attend thee,
And thou tread'st the thorny road;
His right hand shall still defend thee;
Soon he 'll bring thee home to God!
Therefore praise him—
Praise the great Redeemer's name.

RETREAT. L. M.

Dr. Hastings.

829 Stowell.

The Mercy-Seat.

1 From every stormy wind that blows,
From every swelling tide of woes,
There is a calm, a sure retreat;
'T is found before the mercy-seat.

2 There is a place where Jesus sheds
The oil of gladness on our heads,—
A place of all on earth most sweet;
It is the heavenly mercy-seat.

3 There is a scene where spirits blend,
Where friend holds fellowship with friend;
Though sundered far, by faith they meet
Around one common mercy-seat.

4 There, there, on eagle wings we soar,
And sin and sense molest no more;
And heaven comes down our souls to greet,
And glory crowns the mercy-seat.

830 Watts.

Retirement from the World.

1 Far from my thoughts, vain world! be gone,
Let my religious hours alone:
Fain would mine eyes my Saviour see;
I wait a visit, Lord! from thee.

2 My heart grows warm with holy fire,
And kindles with a pure desire;
Come, my dear Jesus! from above,
And feed my soul with heavenly love.

SESSIONS. L. M.

831 *Seeking Refuge.* Heber.

1 Forth from the dark and stormy sky,
Lord, to thine altar's shade we fly;
Forth from the world, its hope and fear,
Father, we seek thy shelter here:
Weary and weak, thy grace we pray;
Turn not, O Lord, thy guests away.

2 Long have we roamed in want and pain,
Long have we sought thy rest in vain;
Wildered in doubt, in darkness lost,
Long have our souls been tempest-tost;
Low at thy feet our sins we lay;
Turn not, O Lord, thy guests away.

CONVERT'S HYMN. P. M.

832 *Convert's Hymn.* C. WESLEY.

1 OH! how happy are they
Who the Saviour obey,
And have laid up their treasures above!
Oh, what tongue can express
The sweet comfort and peace
Of a soul in its earliest love!

2 It was heaven below
My Redeemer to know!
And the angels could do nothing more,
Than to fall at his feet,
And the story repeat,
And the lover of sinners adore.

3 Oh, the rapturous height
Of that holy delight,
Which I felt in the life-giving blood!
Of my Saviour possess'd
I was perfectly blest,
As if filled with the fulness of God.

4 Jesus all the day long
Was my joy, and my song, [name
Was redemption through faith in his
Oh, that all might believe,
And salvation receive,
And their song and their joy be the same.

CORONATION. C. M.

833 *Praising the Lamb.* WATTS.

1 COME, let us join our cheerful songs
With angels round the throne;
Ten thousand thousand are their tongues,
But all their joys are one.

2 "Worthy the Lamb that died," they cry,
"To be exalted thus;"
"Worthy the Lamb," our lips reply,
"For he was slain for us."

ALL SAINTS. L. M.

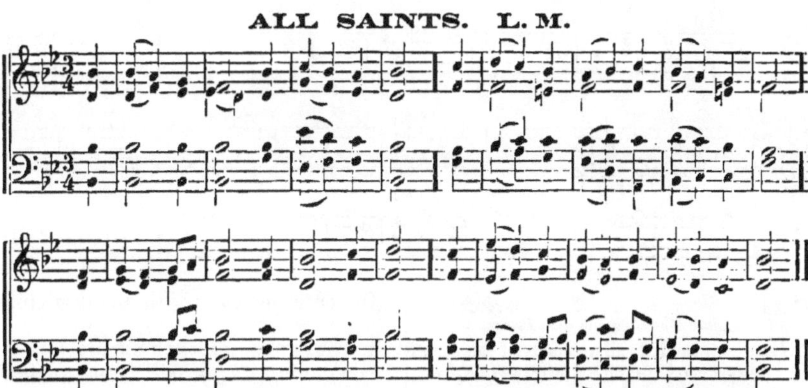

834 DYER.

Public Humiliation.

1 GREAT Framer of unnumbered worlds,
And whom unnumbered worlds adore!
Whose goodness all thy creatures share,
While nature trembles at thy power,—

2 Thine is the hand that moves the spheres,
That wakes the wind, and lifts the sea;
And man, who moves the lord of earth,
Acts but the part assigned by thee.

3 While suppliant crowds implore thine
To thee we raise the humble cry; [aid,
Thine altar is the contrite heart,
Thine incense a repentant sigh.

4 This day we deeply mourn our sins,
Confess thy power, and bless thy rod;
Oh, let us know thy pardoning love,
And find in thee a guardian God.

835 WHITTIER.

Thanksgiving.

1 O HOLY Father! just and true [ways;
Are all thy works, and words, and
And unto thee alone are due
Thanksgiving and eternal praise.

2 As children of thy gracious care,
We veil the eye, we bend the knee;
With broken words of praise and prayer,
Father and God, we come to thee.

3 The laborer sits beneath his vine;
The soul is glad, the hand is free,
Thanksgiving! for the work is thine!
Praise, for the blessing is of thee!

836 L. BACON.

Our Pilgrim Fathers.

1 O GOD, beneath thy guiding hand,
Our exiled fathers crossed the sea;
And when they trod the wintry strand,
With prayer and psalm they worshipped thee.

2 Thou heard'st, well-pleased, the song,
the prayer,— [power
Thy blessing came; and still its
Shall onward, through all ages, bear
The memory of that holy hour.

3 Laws, freedom, truth, and faith in God
Came with those exiles o'er the waves,
And where their pilgrim feet have trod,
The God they trusted guards their graves.

ORD. 11s & 8s.

837 MONTGOMERY.

Call to Thanksgiving and Praise.

1 Be joyful in God, all ye lands of the earth,
Oh, serve him with gladness and fear;
Exult in his presence with music and mirth,
With love and devotion draw near.

2 Jehovah is God, and Jehovah alone,
Creator and ruler o'er all; [own;
And we are his people, his sceptre we
His sheep, and we follow his call.

3 Oh, enter his gates with thanksgiving and song;
Your vows in his temple proclaim;
His praise with melodious accordance prolong,
And bless his adorable name.

4 For good is the Lord, inexpressibly good,
And we are the work of his hand;
His mercy and truth from eternity stood,
And shall to eternity stand.

NASHVILLE. L. P. M.

838 *Thanksgiving for National Prosperity.* KIPPIS.

1 How rich thy gifts, almighty King!
From thee our public blessings spring:
Th' extended trade, the fruitful skies,
The treasures liberty bestows,
Th' eternal joys the gospel shows,—
All from thy boundless goodness rise.

2 With grateful hearts, with joyful tongues,
To God we raise united songs;
Here still may God in mercy reign;
Crown our just counsels with success,
With peace and joy our borders bless,
And all our sacred rights maintain.

UXBRIDGE. L. M.

Dr. L. Mason.

839

Flint.

We have a goodly Heritage.

1 In pleasant lands have fallen the lines
That bound our goodly heritage,
And safe beneath our sheltering vines
Our youth is blest, and soothed our age.

2 What thanks, O God, to thee are due,
That thou didst plant our fathers here,
And watch and guard them as they grew,
A vineyard, to the planter dear.

3 The toils they bore, our ease have wrought;
They sowed in tears — in joy we reap;
The birthright they so dearly bought
We 'll guard till we with them shall sleep.

4 Thy kindness to our fathers shown,
In weal and woe through all the past,
Their grateful sons, O God, shall own,
While here their name and race shall last.

840

Tennyson.

The dying Year.

1 Ring out, wild bells, to the wild sky,
The flying cloud, the frosty light;
The year is dying to the night;
Ring out wild bells, and let him die.

2 Ring out the old, ring in the new;
Ring, happy bells, across the snow;
The year is going; let him go;
Ring out the false, ring in the true.

3 Ring out the grief that saps the mind,
For those that here we see no more;
Ring out the feud of rich and poor;
Ring in redress to all mankind.

4 Ring out a slowly dying cause,
And ancient forms of party strife;
Ring in the nobler modes of life,
With sweeter manners, purer laws.

5 Ring out false pride in place and blood,
The civic slander and the spite;
Ring in the love of truth and right,
Ring in the common love of good.

6 Ring in the valiant man and free,
The larger heart, the kindlier hand;
Ring out the darkness of the land,
Ring in the Christ that is to be.

841

Doddridge.

The Year crowned with Goodness.

1 Eternal Source of every joy!
Well may thy praise our lips employ,
While in thy temple, we appear,
Whose goodness crowns the circling year.

2 The flowery spring, at thy command,
Embalms the air and paints the land;
The summer rays, with vigor, shine
To raise the corn, and cheer the vine.

3 Thy hand, in autumn, richly pours,
Through all our coasts, redundant stores;
And winters softened by thy care,
No more a face of horror wear.

4 Seasons, and months, and weeks, and days,
Demand successive songs of praise;
Still be the cheerful homage paid,
With morning light and evening shade.

FARNHAM. C. M., Double.

842

WATTS.

The Works of God recounted to Posterity.

1 Let children hear the mighty deeds,
Which God performed of old;
Which in our younger years we saw,
And which our fathers told.
He bids us make his glories known,—
His work of power and grace;
And we'll convey his wonders down,
Through every rising race.

2 Our lips shall tell them to our sons,
And they again to theirs,
That generations yet unborn,
May teach them to their heirs.
Thus shall they learn, in God alone
Their hope securely stands;
That they may ne'er forget his works,
But practice his commands.

843

MRS. MILES.

Summer.

1 The earth, all light and loveliness,
In summer's golden hours,
Shines, in her bridal vesture clad,
And crowned with festal flowers,—
So radiantly beautiful,
So like to heaven above, [world
We scarce can deem more fair that
Of perfect bliss and love.

2 Is this a shadow faint and dim
Of that which is to come?
What shall the unveiled splendor be,
Of our celestial home,
Where waves the glorious tree of life,
Where streams of bliss gush free,
And all is glowing in the light
Of immortality?

844

WATTS.

The Seasons ordained by God.

1 With songs and honors sounding loud,
Address the Lord on high;
Over the heavens he spreads his cloud,
And waters vail the sky.
He sends his showers of blessings down
To cheer the plains below;
He makes the grass the mountains crown,
And corn in valleys grow.

845

WREFORD.

For our Country.

1 Oh, guard our shores from every foe,
With peace our borders bless,
With prosperous times our cities crown,
Our fields with plenteousness!
Unite us in the sacred love
Of knowledge, truth, and thee;
And let our hills and valleys shout
The songs of liberty.

2 Here may religion pure and mild
Smile on our Sabbath hours,
And piety and virtue bless
The home of us and ours.
Lord of the nations, thus to thee
Our country we commend:
Be thou her refuge and her trust,
Her everlasting friend.

BENEVENTO. 7s, 8 lines. S. WEBBE.

846

NEWTON.

New Year's Day.

1 WHILE, with ceaseless course, the sun
  Hasted through the former year,
Many souls their race have run,
  Never more to meet us here:
Fixed in an eternal state,
  They have done with all below:
We a little longer wait,
  But how little none can know.

2 As the wingéd arrow flies,
  Speedily the mark to find,
As the lightning from the skies
  Darts, and leaves no trace behind;—
Swiftly thus our fleeting days
  Bear us down life's rapid stream:
Upward, Lord, our spirits raise;
  All below is but a dream.

3 Thanks for mercies past receive;
  Pardon of our sins renew;
Teach us henceforth how to live,
  With eternity in view;
Teach us, as we pass along
  In the shining of thy face,
Many a sweet thanksgiving-song,
  Even in the dreary place.

847

HARTFORD COLL.

Thanksgiving.

1 SWELL the anthem, raise the song;
Praises to our God belong;
Saints and angels! join to sing
Praises to the heavenly King.
Blessings from his liberal hand
Flow around this happy land,
Guarded by his watchful eye
Peace and freedom we enjoy.

2 Here, beneath a virtuous sway,
May we cheerfully obey,
Never feel oppression's rod,
Ever own and worship God.
Hark! the voice of nature sings
Praises to the King of kings;
Let us join the choral song,
And the grateful notes prolong.

CARTHAGE. 8s & 7s.

848 ANON.

National Thanksgiving and Prayer.

1 Lord of heaven, and earth, and ocean,
Hear us from thy bright abode,
While our hearts with deep devotion,
Own their great and gracious God:

2 Now with joy we come before thee;
Seek thy face, thy mercies sing:
Lord of life, and light, and glory,
Guard thy church, thou heavenly King.

3 Health, and every needful blessing,
Are thy bounteous gifts alone;
Comforts undeserved possessing,
Here we bend before thy throne:

4 Thee, with humble adoration,
Lord, we praise for mercies past;
Still to this most favored nation
May those mercies ever last.

849 PIERPONT.

Temperance Vows.

1 Pillows wet with tears of anguish,
Couches pressed in sleepless woe,
Where the sons of Belial languish,
Father, may we never know.

2 For the maddening cup shall never
To our thirsting lips be pressed,
But our draught shall be, forever,
The cold water thou hast blessed.

3 This shall give us strength to labor,
This make all our stores increase;
This, with thee and with our neighbor,
Bind us in the bonds of peace.

4 For the lake, the well, the river,
Water-brook and crystal spring,
Do we now, to thee, the Giver,
Thanks, our daily tribute, bring.

850

Brother's Keeper.

1 Blessèd angels, high in heaven
O'er the penitent rejoice;
Hast thou for thy brother striven
With an importuning voice?

2 Art thou not thy brother's keeper?
Canst thou not his soul obtain?
He that wakes his brother sleeper
Double light himself shall gain.

851 ANON.

Dedication to God.

1 Holy Father, thou hast taught me
I should live to thee alone;
Year by year thy hand hath brought me
On through dangers oft unknown.

2 When I wandered, thou hast found me;
When I doubted, sent me light;
Still thine arm has been around me,
All my paths were in thy sight.

3 I would trust in thy protecting,
Wholly rest upon thine arm;
Follow wholly thy directing,
Thou mine only guard from harm.

4 Keep me from mine own undoing,
Help me turn to thee when tried;
Still my footsteps, Father, viewing,
Keep me ever at thy side.

BERA. L. M. Root & Sweetser's Coll.

852 — Heginbotham.

The God of the Seasons.

1 Great God! let all our tuneful powers
Awake and sing thy mighty name;
Thy hand rolls on our circling hours,
The hand from which our being came.

2 Seasons and moons revolving round
In beauteous order, speak thy praise,
And years with smiling mercy crowned,
To thee successive honors raise.

3 Each changing season on our souls
Its sweetest, kindest influence sheds;
And every period, as it rolls,
Showers countless blessings on our heads.

4 Our lives, our health, our friends, we owe
All to thy vast, unbounded love;
Ten thousand precious gifts below,
And hopes of nobler joys above.

853 — Doddridge.

A Song for the opening Year.

1 Great God! we sing that mighty hand,
By which supported still we stand;
The opening year thy mercy shows,—
Let mercy crown it till it close.

2 By day, by night,— at home, abroad,
Still we are guarded by our God;
By his incessant bounty fed,
By his unerring counsel led.

3 With grateful hearts the past we own;
The future — all to us unknown —
We to thy guardian care commit,
And peaceful leave before thy feet.

4 In scenes exalted or depressed,
Be thou our joy, and thou our rest;
Thy goodness all our hopes shall raise,
Adored, through all our changing days.

5 When death shall close our earthly songs,
And seal, in silence, mortal tongues,
Our helper, God, in whom we trust,
Shall keep our souls, and guard our dust.

854 — Doddridge.

Redeeming the Time.

1 God of eternity! from thee
Did infant Time its being draw:
Moments and days, and months, and years,
Revolve by thine unvaried law.

2 Silent and swift they glide away;
Steady and strong the current flows;
Lost in Eternity's wide sea,
The boundless gulf whence it arose.

3 With it the thoughtless sons of men
Before the rapid stream are borne
On to their everlasting home,
Whence not one soul can e'er return.

4 Yet, while the shore on either side
Presents a gaudy, flattering show,
We gaze, in fond amusement lost,
Nor think to what a world we go.

5 Great Source of wisdom! teach our hearts
To know the price of every hour,
That Time may bear us on to joys
Beyond its measure and its power.

NUREMBURG. 7s. Arr. by Dr. L. Mason.

855

Mrs. Barbauld.

God's Goodness in the Seasons.

1 Praise to God, immortal praise,
For the love that crowns our days;
Bounteous Source of every joy,
Let thy praise our tongues employ:

2 For the flocks spread o'er the plain,
Yellow sheaves of ripened grain,
Clouds that drop their fattening dews,
Suns that temperate warmth diffuse;

3 All that spring, with bounteous hand,
Scatters o'er the smiling land;
All that liberal autumn pours
From her rich o'erflowing stores;—

4 For the blessings of the field,
For the stores the gardens yield,
For the joy which harvests bring,
Grateful praises now we sing.

5 These to thee, our God, we owe,
Source whence all our blessings flow;
And for these our souls shall raise
Grateful vows and solemn praise.

856

Anna L. Waring.

The entered Year.

1 Sunlight of the heavenly day,
Mighty to revive and cheer,
Bless our yet untrodden way,
Lead us through the entered year.

2 Open thou beneath our tread
Springs the distance could not show;
From the holy Fountain-Head
Let them rise where'er we go.

3 Teach us, as we pass along
In the shining of thy face,
Many a sweet thanksgiving-song,
Even in the dreary place.

4 Bold in thy protecting care,
Through the desert or the sea,
Sure to prove thee faithful there,
On! to reign in life with thee.

857

Anon

The Flight of Time.

1 Time by moments steals away,
First the hour, and then the day:
Small the daily loss appears,
Yet it soon amounts to years.

2 Thus another year is flown;
Now it is no more our own,
If it brought or promised good,
Than the years before the flood.

3 But may none of us forget
It has left us much in debt;
Who can tell the vast amount
Placed to every one's account!

4 Favors from the Lord received,
Sins that have his spirit grieved,
Marked by an unerring hand,
In his book recorded stand.

5 If we see another year,
May thy blessings meet us here;
Sun of righteousness, arise,
Warm our hearts and bless our eyes!

AMERICA. 6s & 4s.

858

S. F. SMITH.

National Hymn.

1 My country, 't is of thee,
Sweet land of liberty,
Of thee I sing;
Land where my fathers died,
Land of the pilgrims' pride,
From every mountain side
Let freedom ring.

2 My native country, thee —
Land of the noble, free —
Thy name I love;
I love thy rocks and rills,
Thy woods and templed hills;
My heart with rapture thrills
Like that above.

3 Our fathers' God, to thee,
Author of liberty,
To thee we sing:
Long may our land be bright
With freedom's holy light;
Protect us by thy might,
Great God, our King.

859

ANON.

The same.

1 God bless our native land!
Firm may she ever stand,
Through storm and night:
When the wild tempests rave,
Ruler of winds and wave,
Do thou our country save,
By thy great might.

2 For her our prayer shall rise
To God above the skies!
On him we wait;
Thou who hast heard each sigh,
Watching each weeping eye,
Be thou forever nigh; —
God save the State!

860

PIERPONT.

The Fathers remembered.

1 Gone are those great and good
Who here in peril stood
And raised their hymn:
Peace to the reverend dead!
The light, that on their head
The glorious past has shed,
Shall ne'er grow dim.

2 Ye temples, that to God
Rise where our fathers trod,
Guard well your trust,—
The faith that dared the sea,
The truth that made them free,
Their cherished purity,
Their garnered dust.

3 Thou high and holy One,
Whose care for sire and son
All nature fills;
While day shall break and close,
While night her crescent shows,
Oh, let thy light repose
On these thy hills!

PARK STREET. L. M.

VENUA.

861

O. W. HOLMES.

Army Hymn.

1 O LORD of Hosts! Almighty King!
Behold the sacrifice we bring:
To every arm thy strength impart,
Thy spirit shed through every heart!

2 Wake in our breasts the living fires,
The holy faith that warmed our sires;
Thy hand hath made our nation free;
To die for her is serving thee.

3 Be thou a pillared flame to show
The midnight snare, the silent foe;
And when the battle thunders loud
Still guide us in its moving cloud.

4 God of all nations! Sovereign Lord!
In thy dread name we draw the sword;
We lift the starry flag on high
That fills with light our stormy sky.

5 No more its flaming emblems wave
To bar from hope the trembling slave;
No more its radiant glories shine
To blast with woe a child of thine.

6 From treason's rent, from murder's stain,
Guard thou its folds till peace shall reign;
Till fort and field, till shore and sea,
Join our loud anthem, Praise to Thee!

862

AIKIN.

In Time of War.

1 WHILE sounds of war are heard around,
And death and ruin strow the ground,
To thee we look, on thee we call,
The Parent and the Lord of all.

2 Thou, who hast stamped on human kind
The image of a heaven-born mind,
And in a Father's wide embrace
Hast cherished all the kindred race,—

3 Great God, whose powerful hand can bind
The raging waves, the furious wind,
Oh, bid the human tempest cease,
And hush the maddening world to peace.

4 With reverence may each hostile land
Hear and obey that high command,
Thy Son's blest errand from above,—
"My creatures, live in mutual love!"

863

W. R. WALLACE.

National Anthem.

1 GOD of the free! upon the breath
Our flag is for the right unrolled,
As broad and brave as when its stars
First lit the hallowed time of old.

2 For duty still its folds shall fly;
For honor still its glories burn,
Where truth, religion, valor, guard
The patriot's sword and martyr's urn.

3 God of the free! our nation bless
In its strong manhood as its birth;
And make its life a star of hope
For all the struggling of the earth.

4 Then shout beside thine oak, O North!
O South! wave answer with thy palm;
And in our Union's heritage
Together sing the nation's psalm!

KNOX. C. M.

864

PEABODY.

Who is my Neighbor?

1 Who is thy neighbor? He whom thou
Hast power to aid or bless;
Whose aching heart or burning brow
Thy hand may soothe or press.

2 Thy neighbor? he who drinks the cup
When sorrow drowns the brim;
With words of high sustaining hope,
Go thou and comfort him.

3 Thy neighbor? 't is the weary slave,
Fettered in mind and limb;
He hath no hope this side the grave;
Go thou and ransom him.

4 Thy neighbor? 'T is the fainting poor,
Whose eye with want is dim:
Oh, enter thou his humble door,
With aid and peace for him!

5 Thy neighbor? pass no mourner by,
Perhaps thou canst redeem
A breaking heart from misery;
Go, share thy lot with him.

865

ANON.

The Widow's Prayer.

1 Though faint and sick, and worn away
With poverty and woe,
My widowed feet are doomed to stray
'Mid thorny paths below.

2 Be thou, O Lord, my Father still,
My confidence and guide:
I know that perfect is thy will,
Whate'er that will decide.

3 I know the soul that trusts in thee,
Thou never wilt forsake;
And though a bruiséd reed I be,
That reed thou wilt not break.

4 Then keep me, Lord, where'er I go,
Support me on my way,
Though worn with poverty and woe,
My widowed footsteps stray.

5 To give my weakness strength, O God,
Thy staff shall yet avail;
And though thou chasten with thy rod,
That staff shall never fail.

866

ANON.

The Orphan's Hymn.

1 Where shall the child of sorrow find
A place of calm repose?
Thou Father of the fatherless,
Pity the orphan's woes!

2 What friend have I in heaven or earth,
What friend to trust but thee?
My father's dead — my mother's dead;
My God, remember me!

3 Thy gracious promise now fulfil,
And bid my trouble cease;
In thee the fatherless shall find
Pure mercy, grace, and peace.

4 I've not a secret care or pain
But he that secret knows;
Thou Father of the fatherless,
Pity the orphan's woes!

CESAREA. 8s & 7s, or 7s. Arr. by Dr. Mason.

867

ANON.

Give to the Poor.

1 Give as God hath given thee,
With a bounty full and free:
If he hath with liberal hand,
Given wealth to thy command,
For the fulness of thy store,
Give thy needy brother more.

2 If the lot his love doth give
Is by earnest toil to live,
If with nerve and sinew strong
Thou dost labor hard and long;
Then e'en from thy slender store
Give, and God shall give thee more.

3 Hearts there are with grief oppressed;
Forms in tattered raiment dressed;
Homes where want and woe abide;
Dens where vice and misery hide;
With a bounty large and free,
Give, as God hath given thee.

4 Wealth is thine to aid and bless,
Strength to succor and redress;
Bear thy weaker brother's part,
Strong of hand and strong of heart;
Be thy portion large or small,
Give, for God doth give thee all.

868

ANON.

Active Benevolence.

1 In the morning sow thy seed,
Nor at eve withhold thy hand;
Who can tell which may succeed,
Or, if both alike should stand,
And a glorious harvest bear,
To reward the sower's care?

2 Sow it 'mid the haunts of vice,—
Scenes of infamy and crime;
Suddenly, may Paradise
Burst, as in the northern clime
Spring, with all its verdant race,
Starts from Winter's cold embrace.

3 Sow it with unsparing hand;
'T is the kingdom's precious seed,
'T is the Master's great command,
And his grace shall crown the deed,
He hath said, the precious grain
Never should be sowed in vain.

869

ANON.

Benevolent Efforts.

1 Cast thy bread upon the waters,
Thinking not 't is thrown away;
God himself saith, thou shalt gather
It again some future day.
Cast thy bread upon the waters;
Wildly though the billows play,

2 As the seed, by billows floated
To some distant island lone,
So to human souls benighted,
That thou flingest may be borne.
Cast thy bread upon the waters;
Why wilt thou still doubting stand?

3 Bounteous shall God send the harvest,
If thou sow'st with liberal hand.
Give, then, freely of thy substance—
O'er this cause the Lord doth reign;
Cast thy bread, and toil with patience,
Thou shalt labor not in vain.

DENFIELD. C. M.

GLASER.

870

CROSSWELL.

To do Good and to Communicate forget not.

1 LORD, lead the way the Saviour went,
By lane and cell obscure,
And let our treasures still be spent,
Like his, upon the poor.

2 Like him, through scenes of deep distress,
Who bore the world's sad weight,
We, in their gloomy loneliness,
Would seek the desolate.

3 For thou hast placed us side by side
In this wide world of ill;
And that thy followers may be tried,
The poor are with us still.

4 Small are the offerings we can make;
Yet thou hast taught us, Lord,
If given for the Saviour's sake,
They lose not their reward.

871

ANON.

Words and Deeds.

1 BENEATH the thick but struggling
We talk of Christian life; [clouds,
The words of Jesus on our lips,
Our hearts with man at strife.

2 Traditions, forms, and selfish aims,
Have dimmed the inner light;
Have closely veiled the spirit-world
And angels from our sight.

3 Strong souls and willing hands we need,
Our temple to repair;
Remove the gathering dust of years,
And show the model fair.

4 We slumber while the present calls,
But darkness grows with rest;
Wouldst thou see truth? To action
Do the divine behest. [wake,—

872

HAMPSON.

Compassion.

1 OUR offering is a willing mind
To comfort the distressed;
In others' good our own to find,
In others' blessings blessed.

2 Go to the pillow of disease,
Where night gives no repose,
And on the cheek where sickness preys,
Bid health to plant a rose.

3 Go where the friendless stranger lies,
To perish in his doom,
Snatch from the grave his closing eyes,
And bring his blessing home.

4 Thus what our heavenly Father gave
Shall we as freely give;
Thus copy him who lived to save,
And died that we might live.

873

Help one another.

1 HOW sweet, how heavenly is the sight,
When those who love the Lord
In one another's peace delight,
And so fulfill his word!

2 When each can feel his brother's sigh,
And with him bear a part!
When sorrow flows from eye to eye,
And joy from heart to heart!

CONVENT BELL. 7s, Double. SPANISH.

874 J. TAYLOR.

Acceptable Offering.

1 FATHER of our feeble race,
Wise, beneficent, and kind!
Spread o'er nature's ample face,
Flows thy goodness unconfined.
Musing in the silent grove,
Or the busy walks of men,
Still we trace thy wondrous love,
Claiming large returns again.

2 Lord, what offering shall we bring,
At thine altars when we bow?
Hearts, the pure unsullied spring
Whence the kind affections flow;
Soft compassion's feeling soul,
By the melting eye expressed;
Sympathy, at whose control
Sorrow leaves the wounded breast.

3 Willing hands to lead the blind,
Bind the wounded, feed the poor;
Love, embracing all our kind;
Charity, with liberal store;—
Teach us, O thou heavenly King,
Thus to show our grateful mind,
Thus the accepted offering bring,
Love to thee and all mankind.

875 MILMAN.

And he arose and rebuked the Winds and Sea.

1 LORD! thou didst arise and say,
To the troubled waters, "Peace,"
And the tempest died away;
Down they sank, the foaming seas,
And a calm and heaving sleep
Spread o'er all the glassy deep,
All the azure lake serene
Like another heaven was seen!

2 Lord! thy gracious word repeat
To the billows of the proud!
Quell the tyrant's martial heat,
Quell the fierce and changing crowd!
Then the earth shall find repose,
From oppressions and from woes;
And another heaven appear
On our world of darkness here!

876 ALFORD.

Harvest-Hymn.

1 COME, ye thankful people! come,
Raise the song of Harvest-Home!
All is safely gathered in
Ere the winter storms begin;
God our Maker doth provide
For our wants to be supplied;
Come to God's own temple, come!
Raise the song of Harvest-Home!

2 Then, thou Church triumphant! come,
Raise the song of Harvest-Home!
All are safely gathered in,
Free from sorrow, free from sin,
There forever, purified,
In God's garner to abide:
Come, ten thousand angels, come,
Raise the glorious Harvest-Home!

877

STEELE.

Spring.

1 When verdure clothes the fertile vale,
And blossoms deck the spray,
And fragrance breathes in every gale,
How sweet the vernal day!

2 Hark! how the feathered warblers sing!
'T is nature's cheerful voice;
Soft music hails the lovely spring,
And woods and fields rejoice.

3 O God of nature and of grace,
Thy heavenly gifts impart;
Then shall my meditation trace
Spring, blooming in my heart.

4 Inspired to praise, I then shall join
Glad nature's cheerful song,
And love and gratitude divine
Attune my joyful tongue.

878

WHITTIER.

Spring.

1 The snow-plumed angel of the North
Has dropped his icy spear;
Again the mossy earth looks forth,
Again the streams gush clear.

2 "Bear up, O mother nature!" cry
Bird, breeze, and streamlet free;
Our winter voices prophesy
Of summer days to thee.

3 So in these winters of the soul,
By bitter blasts and drear
O'erswept from memory's frozen pole,
Will sunny days appear.

4 The night is mother of the day,
The winter of the spring,
And ever upon old decay,
The greenest mosses cling.

5 Behind the cloud the starlight lurks,
Through showers the sunbeams fall;
For God, who loveth all his works,
Has left his hope for all.

879

CHR. PSALMIST.

Thanks for an abundant Harvest.

1 Fountain of mercy, God of love,
How rich thy bounties are!
The rolling seasons, as they move,
Proclaim thy constant care.

2 When in the bosom of the earth
The sower hid the grain,
Thy goodness marked its secret birth,
And sent the early rain.

3 The spring's sweet influence, Lord, was [thine:
The plants in beauty grew;
Thou gav'st refulgent suns to shine,
And mild, refreshing dew.

4 These various mercies from above
Matured the swelling grain;
A kindly harvest crowns thy love,
And plenty fills the plain.

5 We own and bless thy gracious sway;
Thy hand all nature hails;
Seed-time nor harvest, night nor day,
Summer nor winter, fails.

MILTON. L. M.

HAYDN.

880

H. WARE, JR.

The God of our Fathers.

1 LIKE Israel's host to exile driven,
Across the flood the pilgrims fled;
Their hands bore up the ark of heaven,
And heaven their trusting footsteps led,
Till on these savage shores they trod,
And won the wilderness for God.

2 Then, when their weary ark found rest,
Another Zion proudly grew;
In more than Judah's glory dressed,
With light that Israel never knew,
From sea to sea her empire spread,
Her temple heaven, and Christ her Head.

3 Then let the grateful Church to-day
Its ancient rite with gladness keep;
And still our fathers' God display
His kindness, though the fathers sleep,
Oh, bless as thou hast blest the past,
While earth, and time, and heaven shall last!

881

COLLINS.

Dirge for the heroic Dead.

1 How sleep the brave who sink to rest
By all their country's wishes blest!
When spring, with dewy fingers cold,
Returns to deck their hallowed mould,
She there shall dress a sweeter sod
Than Fancy's feet have ever trod.

2 By fairy hands their knell is rung,
By forms unseen their dirge is sung;
There Honor comes, a pilgrim gray,
To bless the turf that wraps their clay,
And Freedom shall awhile repair,
To dwell a weeping hermit there.

882

PRATT'S COLL.

The Blessedness of considering the Poor.

1 BLEST who with generous pity glows,
Who learns to feel another's woes:
Bows to the poor man's wants his ear,
And wipes the helpless orphan's tear!
In every want, in every woe,
Himself thy pity, Lord, shall know.

2 Thy love his life shall guard, thy hand
Give to his lot the chosen land;
Nor leave him, in the troubled day,
To unrelenting foes a prey.
In sickness thou shalt raise his head,
And make with tenderest care his bed.

HENRY. C. M. S. P. POND.

883 WATTS.

The Seasons of the Year.

1 'TIS by thy strength the mountains
God of eternal power! [stand,
The sea grows calm at thy command;
And tempests cease to roar.

2 Thy morning light and evening shade
Successive comforts bring;
Thy plenteous fruits make harvest glad,
Thy flowers adorn the spring.

3 Seasons and times, and moons and hours,
Heaven, earth, and air are thine;
When clouds distil in fruitful showers,
The author is divine.

4 Those wandering cisterns in the sky,
Borne by the winds around,
With watery treasures well supply
The furrows of the ground.

884 ANON.

Hymn of Peace.

1 THE dwellings of the free resound
With songs of victory;
And countless hearts, the land around,
For peace are blessing thee.

2 By thee we raised the conquering sign
That led the victor band;
Thine was the power, the peace is thine;
We see in all, thy hand.

3 Still let that conquering banner wave
O'er souls thou hast made free,
And fold the hearts which through the grave
Have heavenward passed to thee.

4 In joyful songs thy name we bless,
Who makest wars to cease; [ness,
Oh, grant our land, through righteous-
A never broken peace.

885 ANON.

New Year.

1 OUR Father! through the coming year
We know not what shall be;
But we would leave, without a fear,
Its ordering all to thee.

2 It may be we shall toil in vain
For what the world holds fair;
And all the good we thought to gain
Deceive, and prove but care.

3 It may be it shall darkly blend
Our love with anxious fears,
And snatch away the valued friend,
The tried of many years.

4 It may be it shall bring us days
And nights of lingering pain;
And bid us take a farewell gaze
Of these loved haunts of men.

5 But calmly, Lord, on thee we rest;
No fears our trust shall move;
Thou knowest what for each is best,
And thou art Perfect Love.

COME, LET US ANEW. P. M.

886

The New Year.

C. WESLEY.

1 COME, let us anew Our journey pursue,
Roll round with the year,
And never stand still till the Master appear;
His adorable will Let us gladly fulfil,
And our talents improve,
By the patience of hope and the labor of love.

2 Our life is a dream; Our time, as a stream,
Glides swiftly away,
And the fugitive moment refuses to stay.
The arrow is flown,—The moment is gone;
The millenial year
Rushes on to our view, and eternity's here.

3 Oh, that each, day by day To his Saviour may say,—
I have fought my way through:
I have finish'd the work thou didst give me to do.
Oh, that each from his Lord May receive the glad word,—
Well and faithfully done!
Enter into my joy, and sit down on my throne.

LUTHER'S CHANT. L. M.

ZEUNER.

887

MONTGOMERY.

For a Female Friendly Society.

1 Our soul shall magnify the Lord,
In him our spirit shall rejoice;
Assembled here with sweet accord,
Our hearts shall praise him with our voice.

2 Since he regards our low estate, [pray,
And hears his handmaids when they
We humbly plead at mercy's gate,
Where none are ever turned away.

3 The poor are his peculiar care,
To them his promises are sure;
His gifts the poor in spirit share:
Oh, may we always thus be poor!

4 God of our hope, to thee we bow,
Thou art our refuge in distress:
The husband of the widow, thou,
The father of the fatherless.

5 May we the law of love fulfil;
To bear each other's burdens here;
Suffer and do thy righteous will,
And walk in all thy faith and fear.

888

MRS. MAYO.

Reclaiming Love.

1 Oh, shut not out sweet pity's ray
From souls now clouded o'er by sin;
Touch their deep springs, and let the
Of Christian love flow freely in. [day

2 Send them kind missions, though their feet
No more again the world may tread;
Some pulse of better life may beat
In hearts that seem unmoved and dead.

3 'T is just that they should bear the pain
Of keen remorse and guilty shame;
But scorn may drive to crime again—
'T is only love that can reclaim.

889

MISS FLETCHER.

For the Prisoner.

1 Father! we pray for those who dwell
Within the prison's gloomy cell!
For those whose souls are bending low
Beneath the weight of guilt and woe!

2 Thy love hath kept our thorny way,
And saved us from sin's iron sway;
Our brethren in a weaker hour
Have yielded to temptation's power.

3 Teach us with humble hearts to feel,
How darkly on our brows the seal
Of guilt might now perchance be set,
Had we the same temptation met.

4 Then while the error we would shun,
We still would aid the erring one
To turn from sin's unpitying sway,
To virtue's fair and pleasant way.

890

GIBBONS.

Liberality.

1 Teach us, O Lord, to keep in view
Thy pattern, and thy steps pursue;
Let alms bestowed, let kindness done,
Be witnessed by each rolling sun.

2 For he who marks, from day to day,
In generous acts his radiant way,
Treads the same path his Saviour trod,
The paths to glory and to God.

GERMANY. L. M.

BEETHOVEN

891

MRS. SIGOURNEY.

For a Temperance Anniversary.

1 WE praise thee, if one rescued soul,
While the past year prolonged its flight,
Turned, shuddering, from the poisonous bowl,
To health, and liberty, and light.

2 We praise thee, if one clouded home,
Where broken hearts despairing pined,
Beheld the sire and husband come
Erect and in his perfect mind.

3 No more a weeping wife to mock,
Till all her hopes in anguish end;
No more the trembling child to shock,
And sink the father in the fiend.

4 Still give us grace, almighty King!
Unwavering at our posts to stand,
Till grateful to thy shrine we bring
The tribute of a ransomed land.

892

WHITTIER.

For an Agricultural Festival.

1 O MAKER of the fruits and flowers!
We thank thee for thy wise design,
Whereby these human hands of ours
In nature's garden work with thine.

2 And thanks that from our daily need
The joy of simple faith is born,
That he who smites the summer weed
May trust thee for the autumn corn.

3 For he who blesses most is blest,
And God and man shall own his worth
Who toils to leave, as his bequest,
An added beauty to the earth.

4 And soon or late, to all that sow,
The time of harvest shall be given;
The flower shall bloom, the fruit shall grow,
If not on earth, at last in heaven.

893

ANON

The Hope of Man.

1 THE past is dark with sin and shame,
The future dim with doubt and fear;
But, Father, yet we praise thy name,
Whose guardian love is always near.

2 For man has striven, ages long,
With faltering steps to come to thee,
And in each purpose high and strong
The influence of thy grace could see.

3 He could not breathe an earnest prayer,
But thou wast kinder than he dreamed,
As age by age brought hopes more fair,
And nearer still thy kingdom seemed.

4 But never rose with his breast
A trust so calm and deep as now;—
Shall not the weary find a rest?
Father, Preserver, answer thou!

5 'T is dark around, 't is dark above,
But through the shadow streams the sun;
We cannot doubt thy certain love;
And man's true aim shall yet be won!

SILVER STREET. S. M.

894 M. W. HALL.

For a Temperance Anniversary.

1 PRAISE for the glorious light,
Which crowns this joyous day;
Whose beams dispel the shades of night,
And wake our grateful lay!

2 Praise for the mighty band,
Redeemed from error's chain,
Whose echoing voices, through our land,
Join our triumphant strain!

3 Ours is no conquest gained
Upon the tented field;
Nor hath the flowing life-blood stained
The victor's helm and shield.

4 But the strong might of love,
And truth's all-pleading voice,
As angels bending from above,
Have made our hearts rejoice.

5 Lord! upward to thy throne
Th' imploring voice we raise;
The might, the strength, are thine alone!
Thine be our loftiest praise.

895 MISS MARTINEAU.

Come, Lord Jesus.

1 LORD Jesus, come! for here
Our path through wilds is laid;
We watch, as for the day-spring near,
Amid the breaking shade.

2 Lord Jesus, come! for hosts
Meet on the battle plain;
Our holiest hopes seem vainest boasts,
And tears are shed like rain.

3 Lord Jesus, come! the slave
Still bears his heavy chains;
Their daily bread the hungry crave,
While teem the fruitful plains.

4 Hark! herald voices near
Lead on thy happier day;
Come, Lord, and our hosannas hear!
We wait to strew thy way.

896

Reform.

1 MOURN for the thousands slain,
The youthful and the strong;
Mourn for the wine-cup's fearful reign,
And the deluded throng.

2 Mourn for the tarnished gem—
For reason's light divine,
Quenched from the soul's bright diadem,
Where God had bid it shine.

3 Mourn for the lost; but call,
Call to the strong, the free:
Rouse them to shun that dreadful fall,
And guard their liberty.

4 Mourn for the souls who pray,
Pray to our God above,
To break the fell destroyer's sway,
And show his saving love.

ALETTA. 7s.

897

P. H. SWEETSER.

Temperance Hymn.

1 Hark! the voice of choral song
Floats upon the breeze along,
Chanting clear, in solemn lays,—
"Man redeemed—to God the praise!"

2 Angels, strike the golden lyre!
Mortals, catch the heavenly fire!
Thousands ransomed from the grave,
Millions yet our pledge shall save!

3 Save from sin's destructive breath,
Save from sorrow, shame, and death—
From intemperance and strife,
Save the husband, children, wife!

4 Courage! let no heart despair—
Mighty is the truth we bear!
Forward, then, baptized in love,
Led by wisdom from above!

898

MONTGOMERY.

The Liberty of the Sons of God.

1 God made all his creatures free;
Life itself is liberty;
God ordained no other bands
Than united hearts and hands.

2 Sin the primal charter broke,—
Sin, itself earth's heaviest yoke;
Tyranny with sin began,
Man o'er brute, and man o'er man.

3 But a better day shall be,
Life again be liberty,
And the wide world's only bands
Love-knit hearts and love-linked hands.

4 So shall every slavery cease,
All God's children dwell in peace,
And the new-born earth record
Love, and Love alone, is Lord.

899

The Prodigal's Confession.

1 Come, ye weary souls, oppressed,
Answer to the Saviour's call;
"Come, and I will give you rest;
Come, and I will save you all."

2 Jesus, full of truth and love,
We thy kindest call obey,
Faithful let thy mercies prove,
Take our load of guilt away.

3 Weary of this war within,
Weary of this endless strife,
Weary of ourselves and sin,
Weary of a wretched life;—

4 Burdened with a world of grief,
Burdened with our sinful load,
Burdened with this unbelief,
Burdened in life's weary road;—

5 Lo, we come to thee for ease,
True and gracious as thou art;
Now our weary souls release,
Write forgiveness on our heart.

ORIOLA. C. M., Double.

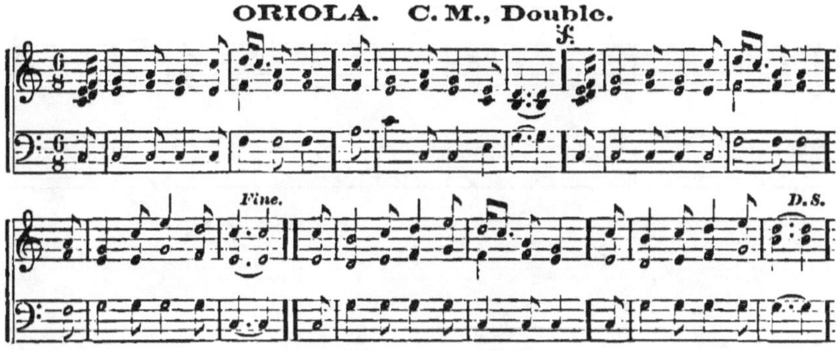

900 *Compassion for the Sinning.* MISS FLETCHER.

1 THINK gently of the erring!
Lord, let us not forget,
However darkly stained by sin,
He is our brother yet.
Heir of the same inheritance!
Child of the self-same God!
He hath but stumbled in the path,
We have in weakness trod.

2 Speak gently to him, brother;
Thou yet mayst lead him back,
With holy words and tones of love,
From misery's thorny track.
Forget not thou hast often sinned,
And sinful yet must be:
Deal gently with the erring one,
As God hath dealt with thee.

ERNAN. 10s. Dr. L. MASON.

901 ANON.

Compassion for the Erring.

1 BREATHE thoughts of pity o'er a brother's fall,
But dwell not with stern anger on his fault;
The grace of God alone holds thee, holds all;
Were that withdrawn, thou, too, wouldst swerve and halt.

2 Send back the wand'rer to the Saviour's fold;
That were an action worthy of a [saint;
But not in malice let the crime be told,
Nor publish to the world the evil taint.

3 Rebuke the sin, and yet in love rebuke;
Feel as one member in another's pain;
Win back the soul that his fair path forsook,
And mighty and rejoicing is thy [gain!

BOWEN. L. M.

HAYDN.

902

MRS. LIVERMORE.

Reclaiming Power of Love.

1 JESUS, what precept is like thine,
"Forgive, as ye would be forgiven!"
If heeded, oh, what power divine
Would then transform our earth to heaven.

2 Not by the harsh or scornful word,
Should we our brother seek to gain;
Not by the prison or the sword,
The shackle, or the clanking chain;

3 But from our spirits there must flow
A love that will his wrong outweigh;
Our lips must only blessings know,
And wrath and sin shall die away.

903

WHITTIER.

Old and New.

1 OH, sometimes gleams upon our sight,
Through present wrong, the Eternal Right!
And step by step, since time began,
We see the steady gain of man;—

2 That all of good the past has had
Remains to make our own time glad,
Our common daily life divine,
And every land a Palestine.

3 We lack but open eye and ear
To find the Orient's marvels here,
The still small voice in autumn's hush,
Yon maple wood the burning bush.

4 For still the new transcends the old,
In signs and tokens manifold;
Slaves rise up men; the olive waves
With roots deep set in battle graves.

5 Through the harsh noises of our day
A low, sweet prelude finds its way;
Through clouds of doubt and creeds of fear
A light is breaking, calm and clear.

6 Henceforth my heart shall sigh no more
For olden time and holier shore;
God's love and blessing, then and there,
Are now, and here, and everywhere.

904

J. F. CLARKE.

The Protestant Reformation.

1 FOR all thy gifts we praise thee, Lord,
With lifted song and bended knee;
But now our thanks are chiefly poured
For those who taught us to be free.

2 For when the soul lay bound below
A heavy yoke of forms and creeds,
And none thy word of truth could know,
O'ergrown with tares and choked [with weeds;

3 The monarch's sword, the prelate's pride,
The church's curse, the empire's ban,
By one poor monk were all defied,
Who never feared the face of man.

4 Half-battles were the words he said,
Each born of prayer, baptized in tears;
And routed by them, backward fled
The errors of a thousand years.

5 With lifted song and bended knee,
For all thy gifts we praise thee, Lord;
But chief for those who made us free,
The champions of thy holy word.

905 ANON.

He maketh all Things new.

1 ALMIGHTY Spirit, now behold
A world by sin destroyed!
Creative Spirit, as of old,
Move on the formless void!

2 Give thou the word,— the healing sound
Shall quell the deadly strife,
And earth again, like Eden crowned,
Bring forth the tree of life.

3 If sang the morning stars for joy
When nature rose to view,
What strains shall angel harps employ,
When thou shalt all renew?

906 DRENNAN.

Law of Love.

1 ALL nature feels attractive power,
A strong embracing force;
The drops that sparkle in the shower,
The planets in their course.

2 Thus, in the universe of mind,
Is felt the law of love;
The charity both strong and kind,
For all that live and move.

3 In this fine sympathetic chain
All creatures bear a part;
Their every pleasure, every pain,
Linked to the feeling heart.

4 More perfect bond, the Christian plan
Attaches soul to soul;
Our neighbor is the suffering man,
Though at the farthest pole.

5 To earth below, from heaven above,
The faith in Christ professed,
More clearly shows that God is love,
And whom he loves is blessed.

907 H. MARTINEAU.

All Men are Equal.

1 ALL men are equal in their birth,
Heirs of the earth and skies;
All men are equal when that earth
Fades from their dying eyes.

2 God meets the throngs who pay their vows
In courts that hands have made,
And hears the worshipper who bows
Beneath the plantain shade.

3 'T is man alone who difference sees,
And speaks of high and low,
And worships those, and tramples these,
While the same path they go.

4 Oh, let man hasten to restore
To all their rights of love;
In power and wealth exult no more;
In wisdom lowly move.

5 Ye great, renounce your earth-born pride,
Ye low, your shame and fear;
Live, as ye worship, side by side;
Your brotherhood revere.

NAUL. 6s & 10s.

908 *The Prince of Peace.* MILTON, GARDNER, AND DWIGHT.

1 No war nor battle's sound
Was heard the world around,—
No hostile chiefs to furious combat ran;
But peaceful was the night
In which the Prince of light
His reign of peace upon the earth began.

2 Unwilling kings obeyed,
And sheathed the battle blade,
And called their bloody legions from the field;
In silent awe they wait,
And close the warrior's gate,
Nor know to whom their homage thus they yield.

3 The peaceful Conqueror goes,
And triumphs o'er his foes,
His weapons drawn from armories above;
Behold the vanquished sit
Submissive at his feet,
And strife and hate are changed to peace and love.

COMFORT. 11s & 10s.

909 *Past, Present, and Future.* HARRIS.

1 O EARTH! thy Past is crowned and consecrated
With its reformers, speaking yet, though dead;
Who unto strife and toil and tears were fated,
Who unto fiery martyrdoms were led.

2 O Earth! the Present too is crowned with splendor
By its reformers battling in the strife;
Friends of humanity, stern, strong, and tender,
Making the world more hopeful with their life.

3 O Earth! thy Future shall be great and glorious
With its reformers, toiling in the van;
Till truth and love shall reign o'er all victorious,
And earth be given to freedom and to man.

PEARL STREET. C. M. STANLEY.

910

ANON.

We are all Brethren.

1 HUSHED be the battle's fearful roar,
The warrior's rushing call! [gore?
Why should the earth be drenched with
Are we not brothers all?

2 Want, from the starving poor depart!
Chains, from the captives fall!
Great God, subdue the oppressor's heart!
Are we not brothers all?

3 Sect, clan, and nation, oh, strike down
Each mean partition-wall!
Let love the voice of discord drown!
Are we not brothers all?

4 Let grace, and truth, and peace, alone
Hold human hearts in thrall,
That heaven at length its work may own,
And men be brothers all.

911

R. NICOLL.

Honor all Men.

1 I MAY not scorn the meanest thing
That on the earth doth crawl:
The slave who would not burst his chain,
The tyrant in his hall.

2 The vile oppressor, who hath made
The widowed mother mourn,
Though worthless, soulless, he may stand,
I cannot, dare not scorn.

3 The darkest night that shrouds the sky,
Of beauty hath a share;
The blackest heart hath sighs to tell
That God still lingers there.

912

ANON

Break every Yoke.

1 "BREAK every yoke," the gospel cries,
"And let the oppressed go free;"
Let every burdened captive rise,
And taste sweet liberty.

2 Lord! when shall man thy voice obey,
And rend each iron chain?
Oh! when shall love its golden sway
O'er all the earth maintain?

913

CHR. PSALMIST.

The Prince of Peace.

1 THE race that long in darkness pined
Have seen a glorious light;
The people dwell in day, who dwelt
In death's surrounding night.

2 To hail thy rise, thou better Sun,
The gathering nations come,
Joyous as when the reapers bear
The harvest treasures home.

3 To us a child of hope is born;
To us a Son is given;
Him shall the tribes of earth obey,—
Him, all the hosts of heaven.

4 His name shall be the Prince of Peace,
Whose rule shall stretch abroad;
The Wonderful, the Counsellor,
The great and mighty Lord.

5 His power increasing still shall spread;
His reign no end shall know;
Justice shall guard his throne above,
And peace abound below.

GRATITUDE. L. M. MENDELSSOHN COLL.

914

SCOTT.

Domestic Worship.

1 WHERE'ER the Lord shall build my house,
An altar to his name I'll raise;
There, morn and evening, shall ascend
The sacrifice of prayer and praise.

2 With duteous mind, the social band
Shall search the records of thy law;
There learn thy will, and humbly bow
With filial reverence and awe.

3 Here may God fix his sacred seat,
And spread the banner of his love;
Till ripened for a happier state,
We meet the family above.

915

DODDRIDGE & MERRICK.

Family Worship.

1 To Him who condescends to dwell
With men in their obscurest cell,
Be our domestic altars raised,
And daily let his name be praised.

2 Then shall the charms of wedded love
Still more delightful blessings prove;
And parents' hearts shall overflow
With joy that parents only know.

3 When nature droops, our aged eyes
Shall see our children's children rise;
Till pleased and thankful we remove,
And join the family above.

916

ANON.

Sunday School Teacher's Hymn.

1 WHILE yet the youthful spirit bears
The image of its God within,
And uneffaced that beauty wears,
So soon to be destroyed by sin;

2 Then is the time for faith and love
To take in charge their precious care,
Teach the young eye to look above,
Teach the young knee to bend in prayer.

3 The world will come with care and crime,
And tempt too many a heart astray;
Still, the seed sown in early time
Will not be wholly cast away.

4 The infant prayer, the infant hymn,
Within the darkened soul will rise,
When age's weary eye is dim,
And the grave's shadow round us lies.

5 Lord, grant our hearts be so inclined,
Thy work to seek, thy will to do;
And while we teach the youthful mind,
Our own be taught thy lessons too.

MARTYN. 7s, Double. THE CHIME.

917 CAMPBELL'S COLL.

Prayer for Children.

1 GOD of mercy, hear our prayer
For the children thou hast given;
Let them all thy blessings share—
Grace on earth and bliss in heaven.

2 In the morning of their days,
May their hearts be drawn to thee:
Let them learn to lisp thy praise,
In their earliest infancy.

3 When we see their passions rise,
Sinful habits unsubdued,
Then to thee we lift our eyes,
That their hearts may be renewed.

4 For this mercy, Lord, we cry;
Bend thy ever-gracious ear;
While on thee our souls rely,
Hear our prayer,—in mercy hear.

918 ANON.

Silent Worship.

1 WOULD'ST thou in thy lonely hour,
Praises to the Eternal pour?
I will teach thy soul to be
Temple, hymn, and harmony.

2 Sweeter songs than poets sing,
Thou shalt for thine offering bring;
Softly murmured hymns, that dwell
In devotion's deepest cell.

3 Know that music's holiest strain
Loves to linger, loves to reign,
In that calm of quiet thought,
Which the passions trouble not.

4 Wouldst thou, in thy lonely hour,
Praises to th' Eternal pour?
Thus thy soul may learn to be,
Temple, hymn, and harmony.

919 BOYLSTON.

Leaving School for Church.

1 To thy temple I repair;
Lord, I love to worship there;
Abba! Father! give me grace
In thy courts to seek thy face.

2 While thy glorious praise is sung,
Touch my lips, unloose my tongue,
While the prayer of saints ascend,
God of love, to mine attend.

3 While thy ministers proclaim
Peace and pardon in thy name,
While I hearken to thy law,
Fill my heart with humble awe.

4 From thy house when I return,
May my heart within me burn;
And at evening let me say,
"I have walked with God to-day."

920 SPIRIT OF THE PSALMS

Safety in God.

1 THEY who on the Lord rely,
Safely dwell, though danger 's nigh;
Lo! his shelt'ring wings are spread
O'er each faithful servant's head.

2 When they wake, or when they sleep,
Angel-guards their vigils keep;
Death and danger may be near,—
Faith and love have naught to fear.

HEBER. C. M.

GEO. KINGSLEY.

921

DODDRIDGE.

Sickness and Recovery.

1 LORD, in thy service I would spend
The remnant of my days;
Why was this fleeting breath renewed,
But to renew thy praise?

2 Thy own almighty power and love
Did this weak frame sustain;
When life was hovering o'er the grave,
And nature sunk with pain.

3 Back from the borders of the grave,
At thy command I come;
Nor would I urge a speedier flight
To my celestial home.

4 Where thou appointest mine abode,
There would I choose to be;
For in thy presence death is life,
And earth is heaven with thee.

922

FABER.

Childhood looking to Jesus.

1 DEAR Jesus! ever at my side,
How loving must thou be,
To leave thy throne in heaven, to guard
A little child like me.

2 I cannot feel thee touch my hand
With pressure light and mild,
To check me, as my mother did,
When I was but a child.

3 But I have felt thee in my thoughts,
Fighting with sin for me;
And when my heart loves God, I know
The sweetness is from thee.

4 And when, dear Saviour! I kneel down
Morning and night to prayer,
Something there is within my heart,
Which tells me thou art there.

5 Yes! when I pray, thou prayest too,--
The prayer is all for me:
But when I sleep, thou sleepest not,
But watchest patiently.

923

ANON.

A Child's Prayer.

1 LORD, teach a little child to pray,
And, oh, accept my prayer;
Thou canst hear all the words I say,
For thou art everywhere.

2 A little sparrow cannot fall
Unnoticed, Lord, by thee;
And though I am so young and small,
Thou dost take care of me.

3 Teach me to do whate'er is right,
And, when I sin, forgive;
And make it still my chief delight
To serve thee while I live.

924

ANON.

Family Worship.

1 HERE let thy peace, O Father, rest,
Here let thy love abide!
Our every joy in thee more blest,
Each sorrow sanctified.

2 Teach us, with hearts made one in love,
To do thy pure commands;
And give us, in thy time, above,
A house not made with hands.

HOUR OF PRAYER. L. M.

Wm. B. Bradbury

925 S. S. Cutting.

Family Hymn.—Evening.

1 Father, we bless the gentle care
That watches o'er us day by day,
That guards us from the tempter's snare,
And guides us in the heavenward way:
We bless thee for the tender love,
That mingles all our hearts in one,—
The music of the soul;—above
'T is purer spirits' unison.

2 Father, 't is evening's solemn hour,
And cast we now our cares on thee;
Darkly the storm may round us lower,—
Peace is within,— Christ makes us free;
And when life's toil and joy are o'er,
And evening gathers on its sky,
Our circle broke,— we sing no more,—
Oh, may we meet and sing on high.

926 Songs in the Night.

Detained from the Sanctuary.

1 Sweet Sabbath bells! I love your voice,
You call me to the house of prayer;
Oft have you made my heart rejoice,
When I have gone to worship there.
But now a prisoner of the Lord,
His hand forbids, I cannot go;
Yet may I here his love record,
And here the sweets of worship know.

2 Each place alike is holy ground,
Where prayer from humble souls is poured,
Where praise awakes its silver sound,
Or God is silently adored.
His sanctuary is the heart,—
There, with the contrite, will he rest;
Lord, come, a Sabbath frame impart,
And make thy temple in my breast.

927 Pierpont.

Evening Hymn.

1 Another day its course hath run,
And still, O God, thy child is blest,
For thou hast been by day my sun,
And thou wilt be by night my rest.
Sweet sleep descends my eyes to close,
And now when all the world is still
I give my body to repose,—
My spirit to my Father's will.

928 Anon.

Prayer for Children.

1 Dear Saviour, if these lambs should stray
From thy secure enclosure's bound,
And, lured by worldly joys away,
Among the thoughtless crowd be found,--
Remember still that they are thine,
That thy dear sacred name they bear;
Think that the seal of love divine,
The sign of cov'nant grace they wear.

GREENWOOD. S. M.

929

ANON.

Domestic Affection.

1 How pleasing, Lord! to see,
How pure is the delight,
When mutual love, and love to thee,
A family unite!

2 From these celestial springs
Such streams of comfort flow,
As no increase of riches brings,
Nor honors can bestow.

3 No bliss can equal theirs,
Where such affections meet;
While mingled praise and mingled prayers
Make their communion sweet.

4 'T is the same pleasure fills
The breast in worlds above;
There joy like morning dew distills,
And all the air is love.

930

WATTS.

Early Instruction.

1 The praises of my tongue
I offer to the Lord,
That I was taught and learned so young,
To read his holy word.

2 Dear Lord! this book of thine
Informs me where to go,
For grace to pardon all my sin,
And make me holy too.

3 Oh! may thy Spirit teach,
And make my heart receive,
Those truths which all thy servants preach,
And all thy saints believe.

4 Then shall I praise the Lord
In a more cheerful strain,
That I was taught to read his word,
And have not learned in vain.

931

DODDRIDGE.

Christ calling Children to Himself.

1 The Saviour gently calls
Our children to his breast;
He folds them in his gracious arms;
Himself declares them blest.

2 "Let them approach," he cries,
"Nor scorn their humble name;
The heirs of heaven are such as these;—
For such as these I came."

3 Gladly we bring them, Lord,
Devoting them to thee:
Imploring, that, as we are thine,
Thine may our offspring be.

932

ANON.

Invoking God's Mercy on Children.

1 Thou God of Sov'reign grace,
In mercy now appear;
We long to see thy smiling face,
And feel that thou art near.

2 To-day in love descend;
Oh, come, this precious hour;
In mercy now their spirits bend
By thy resistless power.

3 Low bending at thy feet,
Our offspring we resign:
Thine arm is strong, thy love is great,
And high thy glories shine.

I. B. Woodbury.

933

William Cutter.

Youthful Example.

1 What if the little rain should say,
So small a drop as I
Can ne'er refresh these thirsty fields,
I'll tarry in the sky?

2 What if a shining beam of noon
Should in its fountain stay,
Because its feeble light alone
Cannot create a day?

3 Doth not each rain-drop help to form
The cool, refreshing shower,
And every ray of light to warm
And beautify the flower?

4 Go thou, and strive to do thy share,—
One talent — less than thine —
Improved with steady zeal and care,
Would gain rewards divine.

934

Watts.

Advantage of early Piety.

1 When children give their hearts to God
'T is pleasing in his eyes;
A flower, when offered in the bud,
Is no vain sacrifice.

2 It saves us from a thousand fears,
To mind religion young;
With joy it crowns succeeding years,
And renders virtue strong.

3 To thee, Almighty God! to thee
May we our hearts resign;
'T will please us to look back and see
That our whole lives were thine.

935

Early Religion.

1 By cool Siloam's shady rill
How sweet the lily grows!
How sweet the breath beneath the hill
Of Sharon's dewy rose!

2 Lo, such the child whose early feet
The paths of peace have trod;
Whose secret heart, with influence sweet,
Is upward drawn to God!

3 By cool Siloam's shady rill
The lily must decay;
The rose that blooms beneath the hill
Must shortly fade away.

4 And soon, too soon, the wintry hour
Of man's maturer age
Will shake the soul with sorrow's power,
And stormy passion's rage!

5 O thou, who giv'st us life and breath,
We seek thy grace alone,
In childhood, manhood, age, and death,
To keep us still thine own!

936

Early Devotion to God.

1 Deep in thy soul, before its powers
Are yet by vice enslaved,
Be thy Creator's glorious name
And character engraved,

2 Ere yet the shades of sorrow cloud
The sunshine of thy days,
And cares and toils, in endless round,
Encompass all thy ways.

STOCKWELL. 8s & 7s. JONES.

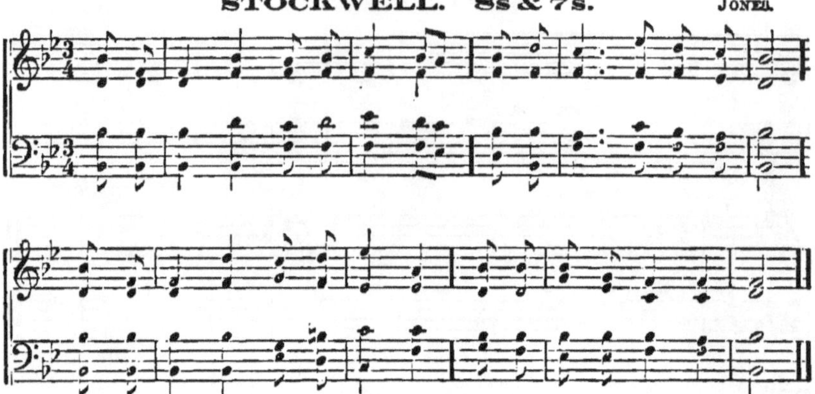

937

Children's Hymn. ANON.

1 LORD, a little band and lowly,
We are come to sing to thee;
Thou art great, and high, and holy,—
Oh, how solemn should we be!

2 Fill our hearts with thoughts of Jesus,
And of heaven where he is gone;
And let nothing ever please us
He would grieve to look upon.

3 Let our sins be all forgiven:
Make us fear whate'er is wrong;
Lead us on our way to heaven,
There to sing a nobler song.

WEBB. 7s & 6s. G. J. WEBB.

938

Remember thy Creator. S. F. SMITH.

1 "REMEMBER thy Creator"
While youth's fair spring is bright,
Before thy cares are greater,
Before comes age's night;
While yet the sun shines o'er thee,
While stars the darkness cheer,
While life is all before thee,
Thy great Creator fear.

BERA. L. M. ROOT & SWEETSER'S COLL.

939

We are but Young.

1 We are but young,—yet we may sing
The praises of our heavenly King;
He made the earth, the sea, the sky,
And all the starry worlds on high.

2 We are but young,—we need a guide;
Jesus, in thee we would confide;
Oh, lead us in the path of truth,
Protect and bless our helpless youth.

3 We are but young,—yet God has shed
Unnumbered blessings on our head;
Then let our youth in riper days
Be all devoted to his praise.

940 ANON.

A Child's Hymn for Christmas.

1 Thou holy Jesus, kind and dear,
Who for us children camest here,
That blest and purified by thee,
God's little children we might be.

2 God sent thee down, a light divine,
Through all this darkened world to shine,
A heavenly child, a heavenly ray,
To guide us all the heavenly way.

3 O holy Jesus, kind and dear,
Because thy birthday now is near,
For every child, in every clime,
It is a happy, joyful time.

4 Then bless me too, and from thy throne,
Look down, Lord, on thy little one;
Make thou my heart all pure and white,
In heavenly fountains clear and bright.

5 Lord, make me like the angels mild,
A loving, humble, grateful child;
That thine I evermore may be,
Thou holy Jesus, grant to me!

941 PIERPONT.

Morning Hymn for a Child.

1 O God, I thank thee that the night
In peace and rest hath passed away,
And that I see, in this fair light,
My Father's smile, that makes it day.

2 Be thou my guide, and let me live
As under thine all-seeing eye;
Supply my wants, my sins forgive,
And make me happy when I die.

942 DODDRIDGE.

Family Worship.

1 Father of men! thy care we bless,
Which crowns our families with peace,
From thee they sprung, and by thy hand
Their root and branches are sustained.

2 To God, most worthy to be praised,
Be our domestic altars raised,
Who, Lord of heaven, scorns not to dwell
With saints in their obscurest cell.

3 To thee may each united house,
Morning and night, present its vows;
Our servants here and rising race
Be taught thy precepts and thy grace.

4 Oh, may each future age proclaim
The honors of thy glorious name;
While, pleased and thankful, we remove
To join the family above.

SOMETHING IN HEAVEN TO DO.

BRADBURY.

943

R. S. TAYLOR.

Something in Heaven to do.

1 THERE'LL be something in heaven for children to do:
None are idle in that blessed land;
There'll be loves for the heart, there'll be thoughts for the mind,
And employment for each little hand.
CHORUS — There'll be something to do;
There'll be something to do;
There'll be something for children to do;
On the bright shining shore,
Where there's joy evermore,
There'll be something for children to do.

2 There'll be lessons to learn of the wisdom of God,
As they wander the green meadows o'er:
And they'll have for their teachers in that blest abode, [before.
All the good that have gone there
CHO. — There'll be something to do, etc.

3 There'll be errands of love from the mansions above,
To the dear ones that linger below;
And it may be our Father the children will send
To be angels of mercy in woe.
CHORUS — There'll be something to do;
There'll be something to do;
There'll be something for children to do;
On the bright shining shore,
Where there's joy evermore,
There'll be something for children to do.

NUREMBURG. 7s. Arr. by Dr. MASON.

944

NEWTON.

Parting Hymn.

1 FOR a season called to part,
Let us then ourselves commend
To the gracious eye and heart
Of our ever-present Friend.

2 Father, hear our humble prayer!
Tender Shepherd of thy sheep,
Let thy mercy and thy care
All our souls in safety keep.

3 In thy strength may we be strong;
Sweeten every cross and pain;
Give us, if we live, e'er long,
Here to meet in peace again.

945

SALISBURY COLL.

Supplication.

1 GLORIOUS in thy saints appear;
Plant thy heavenly kingdom here;
Light and life to all impart;
Shine on each believing heart;—

2 And, in every grace complete,
Make us, Lord, for glory meet;
Till we stand before thy sight,
Partners with the saints in light.

946

ANON.

All Things from God.

1 HOMAGE pay to God above,—
God, whose nature all is love;
In his praise your breath employ,—
Gracious source of every joy.

2 All our hopes of life and heaven
Through thy grace alone are given;
Bliss eternal, pure, divine,—
Every gift, O God, is thine.

947

ANON

Praise.

1 PRAISE the Lord,—his glory bless;
Praise him in his holiness;
Praise him as the theme inspires;
Praise him as his fame requires.

2 Let the trumpet's lofty sound
Spread its loudest notes around;
Let the harp unite in praise
With the sacred minstrel's lays.

3 Let the organ join to bless
God, the Lord, our righteousness;
Tune your voice to spread the fame
Of the great Jehovah's name.

LISCHER. H. M. Arr. by Dr. L. Mason.

948 E. TURNER.

Thanks at the Close of Service.

1 Kind Lord, before thy face,
Again with joy we bow;
For all the gifts and grace
Thou dost on us bestow;
Our tongues would all thy love proclaim,
And chant the honors of thy name.

2 Here, in thine earthly house,
Our joyful souls have met;
Here paid our solemn vows,
And felt our union sweet.
For this our tongues thy love proclaim,
And chant the honors of thy name.

3 Now may we dwell in peace,
Till here again we come:
And may our love increase,
Till thou shalt bring us home.
Then shall our tongues thy love proclaim,
And chant the honors of thy name.

SICILIAN HYMN. 8s, 7s, & 4.

(In singing, repeat fifth line.)

949 *Dismission.* TOPLADY'S COLL.

1 Lord! dismiss us with thy blessing,
Fill our hearts with joy and peace;
Let us all, thy love possessing,
Triumph in redeeming grace;
Oh! refresh us—
Travelling through this wilderness.

2 Thanks we give and adoration,
For thy gospel's joyful sound;
May the fruits of thy salvation
In our hearts and lives abound;
May thy presence
With us evermore be found.

VESPER. 8s & 7s. Arr. from FLOTOW.

950

NEWTON.

Closing Prayer.

1 MAY the grace of Christ, our Saviour,
And the Father's boundless love,
With the holy Spirit's favor,
Rest upon us from above!

2 Let us thus abide in union
With each other, and the Lord;
And possess, in sweet communion,
Joys which earth cannot afford.

951

BICKERSTETH.

Closing Hymn.

1 ISRAEL'S Shepherd, guide us, feed us,
Through our pilgrimage below,
And beside the waters lead us,
Where thy flock rejoicing go.

2 Lord, thy guardian presence ever,
Meekly kneeling, we implore;
We have found thee, and would never,
Never wander from thee more.

952

C. ROBBINS.

Close of the Sabbath.

1 Lo! the day of rest declineth,
Gather fast the shades of night;
Yet the sun that ever shineth
Fills our souls with heavenly light.

2 While, thine ear of love addressing,
Thus our parting hymn we sing,
Father, with thine evening blessing
Rest we safe beneath thy wing.

953

ANON.

Go in Peace.

1 Go in peace! — serene dismission,
To the loving heart made known;
When it pours, in deep contrition,
Prayer before the eternal throne.

2 Go in peace! thy sins forgiven,
Christ has healed thee, set thee free;
Every spirit-fetter riven,
Go in peace, and liberty!

3 Saviour! breathe this benediction
O'er our spirits while we pray;
Let us part in sweet conviction
Thou hast blessed our souls to-day.

954

S. F. ADAMS.

Peace be with you.

1 PART in peace! is day before us?
Praise his name for life and light;
Are the shadows lengthening o'er us?
Bless his care who guards the night.

2 Part in peace! with deep thanksgiving,
Rendering, as we homeward tread,
Gracious service to the living,
Tranquil memory to the dead.

3 Part in peace! such are the praises,
God, our Maker, loveth best;
Such the worship that upraises
Human hearts to heavenly rest.

DARWELL. H. M.

DARWELL.

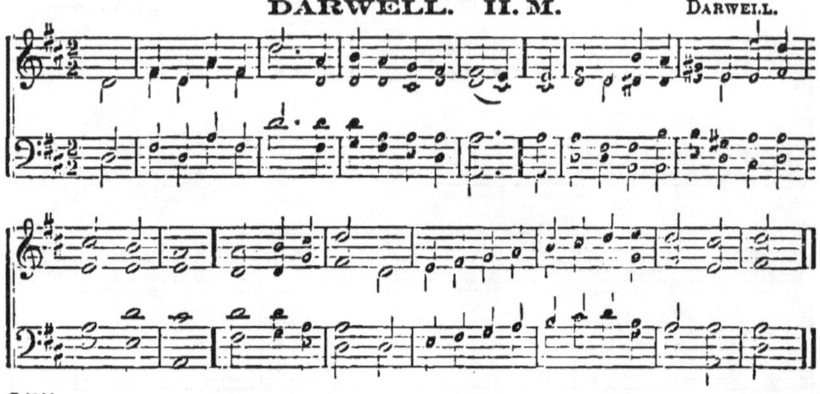

955 *A Blessing sought on Worship.* BREVIARY.

1 HERE, gracious God, do thou
In mercy now draw nigh;
Accept each faithful prayer,
And mark each suppliant sigh;
In copious shower, | This holy day,
On all who pray, | Thy blessings pour.

2 Here may we find from heaven,
The grace which we implore;
And may that grace once given,
Be with us evermore,—
Until that day | To endless rest
When all the blest | Are called away.

WOODSTOCK. C. M.

DUTTON.

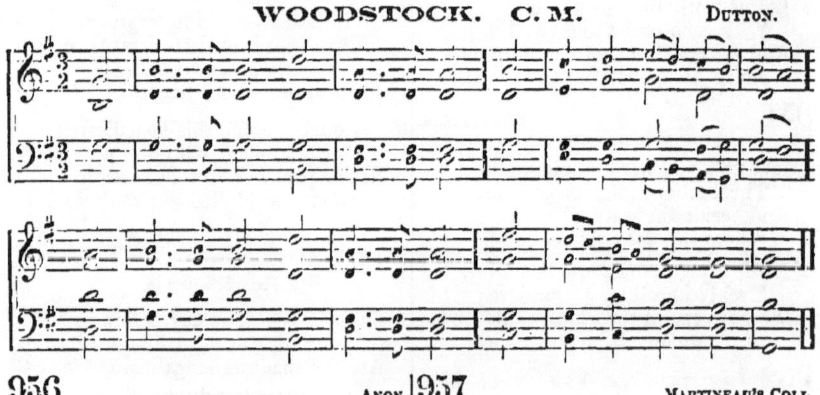

956 ANON.

Doxology.

1 THOU art the first, and thou the last,
Time centres all in thee,
The Almighty God who was, and is,
And evermore shall be.

2 To thee let every tongue be praise,
And every heart be love;
All grateful honors paid on earth,
And nobler songs above.

957 MARTINEAU'S COLL.

Closing Hymn.

3 O THOU great Spirit, who along
The waters first didst move
And straight from warring chaos sprung
Light, harmony, and love;
Upon our waiting spirits brood,
Bid all their discord cease,
And breathe upon the troubled soul
Thy last, best gift of peace.

SHAWMUT. S. M.

Dr. L. Mason.

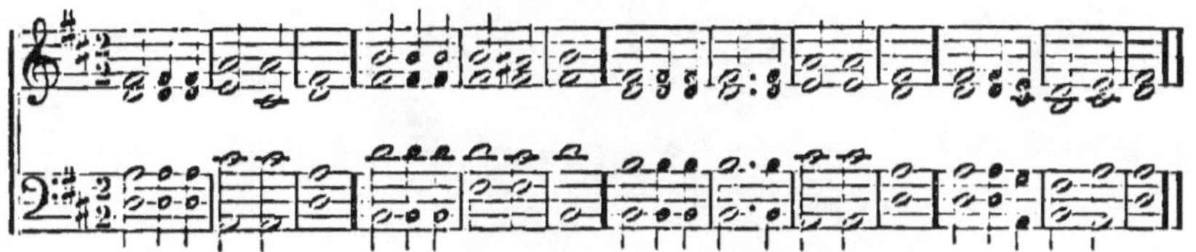

958

Praise to the Name of the Lord.

Watts.

1 Thy name, almighty Lord,
Shall sound through distant lands:
Great is thy grace, and sure thy word;
Thy truth forever stands.

2 Far be thine honor spread,
And long thy praise endure,—
Till morning light and evening shade
Shall be exchanged no more.

WARSAW. H. M.

T. Clark.

959

Rippon's Coll.

Doxology.

Glory to God on high;
Forever bless his name;
Let earth, and seas, and sky,
His wondrous love proclaim;
To him be praise and glory given
By all on earth and all in heaven.

960

Doxology.

To God, from day to day,
Whose Spirit ever blest
Has lightened up our way,
All worship be addrest;
As heretofore it was, is now,
And shall be so for evermore.

AUTUMN. 8s & 7s. Double.

961 ANON.

Supplication.

1 Gracious Source of every blessing,
Guard our breast from anxious fears;
Let us, each thy care possessing,
Peaceful reach the vale of years;
All our hopes on thee reclining,
Peace, companion of our way,
May our sun, in smiles declining,
Rise in everlasting day.

962 ANON.

Prayer for Peace.

1 Peace of God, which knows no measure,
Heavenly sunlight of the soul,
Peace beyond all earthly treasure,
Come and all our hearts control!
Come, almighty to deliver!
Naught shall make us then afraid;
We will trust in thee forever,
Thou on whom our hope is stayed!

OLD HUNDRED. L. M.

963 WATTS.

Doxology.

1 From all that dwell below the skies,
Let the Creator's praise arise;
Let the Redeemer's name be sung,
Through every land, by every tongue.

2 Eternal are thy mercies, Lord!
Eternal truth attends thy word;
Thy praise shall sound from shore to shore,
Till suns shall rise and set no more.

964 KENN.

Doxology.

1 Praise God, from whom all blessings flow!
Praise him, all creatures here below!
Praise him above, ye heavenly throng!
Praise God, our Father, in your song!

965

God our Guardian. WESLEY.

1 GOD shall bless thy going out,
Shall bless thy coming in;
Kindly compass thee about,
Till thou art saved from sin:
Lean upon thy Father's breast;
It is he thy spirit keeps;
Rest in him, securely rest;
Thy guardian never sleeps.

PLEYEL'S HYMN. 7s. PLEYEL.

966

GASKELL.

Glory to the Father.

1 FATHER! glory be to thee,
Source of all the good we see!
Glory for the blessèd light,
Rising on the ancient night!

2 Glory for the hopes that come
Streaming through the dreary tomb!
Glory for the counsel given,
Guiding us in peace to heaven!

967

ANON.

Divine Blessing Implored.

1 THANKS for mercies, Lord, receive;
Pardon of our sins renew:
Teach us henceforth how to live
With eternity in view.

2 Bless thy word to old and young;
Grant us, Lord, thy peace and love;
And, when life's short race is run,
Take us to thy house above.

968

ANON.

The Father's Care Implored.

1 FATHER, hear our humble prayer!
Tender Shepherd of thy sheep,
Let thy mercy and thy care
All our souls in safety keep.

DUKE STREET. L. M.

J. Hatton.

969

Doddridge.

Christian Farewell.

1 Thy presence, ever-living God!
Wide through all nature spreads abroad;
Thy watchful eyes, which never sleep,
In every place thy children keep.

2 While near each other we remain,
Thou dost our lives and powers sustain;
When separate, we rejoice to share
Thy counsels and thy gracious care.

3 To thee we now commit our ways,
And still implore thy heavenly grace;
Still cause thy face on us to shine,
And guard and guide us still as thine.

4 Give us within thy house to raise
Again united songs of praise;
Or, if that joy no more be known,
Give us to meet around thy throne.

970

Montgomery.

Sabbath Evening.

1 Millions within thy courts have met;
Millions, this day, before thee bowed;
Their faces Zionward were set, [vowed.
Vows with their lips to thee they

2 And not a prayer, a tear, a sigh,
Hath failed this day some suit to gain;
To those in trouble thou wert nigh;
Not one hath sought thy face in vain.

3 Yet one prayer more!—and be it one
In which both heaven and earth accord,
Fulfil thy promise to thy Son;
Let all that breathe call Jesus Lord!

971

Shrubsole.

Awake, put on Thy Strength.

1 Arm of the Lord, awake! awake!
Put on thy strength, the nations shake;
Now let the world adoring see
Triumphs of mercy wrought by thee.

2 Almighty God, thy grace proclaim
Through every clime, of every name;
Let adverse powers before thee fall,
And crown the Saviour Lord of all.

972

Heber.

Close of Service.

1 Lord, now we part, in thy blest name,
In which we here together came:
Grant us our few remaining days
To work thy will and spread thy praise.

2 Teach us in life and death to bless
The Lord our strength and righteousness;
And grant us all to meet above,
Then shall we better sing thy love.

973

Anon.

Close of Worship.

1 Ere to the world again we go,
Its pleasures, cares, and idle show,
Thy grace, once more, O God, we crave,
From folly and from sin to save.

2 May the great truths we here have heard,
The lessons of thy holy word,
Dwell in our inmost bosoms deep,
And all our souls from error keep.

UXBRIDGE. L. M. L. MASON.

974

MRS. COUNTRYMAN.

Close of the Sabbath.

1 ANOTHER Sabbath, Lord, has gone,
Another day of peace and rest:
Swiftly its precious hours have flown —
Hours which thy sacred presence blest.

2 The portals of a week of care,
Stand open for our weary feet;
Oh! give us strength to enter there,
Grant us thy grace its toils to meet.

3 May the pure joys this day hath brought,
Shed gladness o'er the coming hours,—
The cheering truths thy word hath taught,
Give strength to all our faltering powers.

4 May faith's bright angel be our guide
Across the stream of toil and care,
Whose troubled waters so divide
These Sabbath times of praise and prayer.

975

HEBER.

Manna.

1 THY bounteous hand with food can bless
The bleak and barren wilderness;
And thou hast taught us, Lord, to pray
For daily bread from day to day.

2 And, oh, when through the wilds we roam,
That part us from our heavenly home;
When, lost in danger, want, and woe,
Our faithless tears begin to flow,—

3 Do thou thy gracious comfort give,
By which alone the soul can live;
And grant thy children, Lord, we pray,
The bread of life from day to day.

976

H. BALLOU.

Dismission.

1 FROM worship, now, thy church dismiss,—
But not without thy blessing, Lord;
Oh, grant a taste of heavenly bliss,
And seal instruction from thy word.

2 Oft may these pleasant scenes return,
When we shall meet to worship thee;
Oft may our hearts within us burn,
To hear thy word, thy goodness see.

977

MONTGOMERY.

Pastoral Benediction.

1 NOW may the Lord, our Shepherd, lead
To living streams his little flock;
May he in flowery pastures feed,
Shade us at noon beneath the rock!

2 Now may we hear our Shepherd's voice,
And gladly answer to his call;
Now may our hearts for him rejoice,
Who knows, and names, and loves us all.

978

WATTS.

Closing Prayer.

1 COME, dearest Lord! descend and dwell
By faith and love in every breast;
Then shall we know, and taste, and feel
The joys that can not be expressed.

2 Come, fill our hearts with inward strength,
Make our enlargéd souls possess,
And learn the height, and breadth, and [length,
Of thine immeasurable grace.

ARLINGTON. C. M.

Dr. Arne.

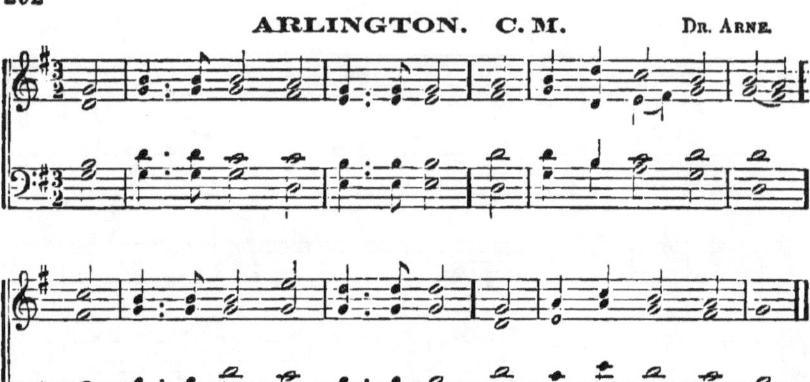

979

Moses Ballou.

Closing Hymn.

1 We now invoke thy blessing, Lord,
On this day's worship here:
Help us to lean upon thy word,
And find our comfort there.

2 Hallow the hours that unto thee,
In faith and love we've given;
And daily help our souls to see,
More of the bliss of heaven.

980

Anon.

At close of Day.

1 The twilight falls, the night is near;
I fold my work away;
And kneel to Him who bends to hear
The story of the day.

2 The old, old story! yet I kneel
To tell it at His call;
And cares grow lighter as I feel
That Jesus knows them all.

3 Yes, all! the morning and the night,
The joy, the grief, the loss,
The roughened path, the sunbeam bright,
The hourly thorn and cross.

4 And Jesus loves me! all my heart
With answering love is stirred;
And every anguish, every smart,
Finds healing in the Word.

5 So then I lay me down to rest,
As nightly shadows fall;
And lean, confiding, on His breast
Who knows and pities all.

981

Anon.

Rest in the Father.

1 Oh, wondrous depth of grace divine,
My soul would fain adore:
Dear Father, let me call thee mine,
And I will ask no more.

2 By thee in all things richly blest,
Low at thy feet I fall;
Thou art my Hope, my Life, my Rest,
My Father and my all!

982

Heber

The Seed of the Word.

1 O God, by whom the seed is given,
By whom the harvest blest,
Whose word, like manna showered from heaven,
Is planted in our breast;

2 Preserve it from the passing feet,
And plunderers of the air;
The sultry sun's intenser heat,
And weeds of worldly care.

3 Though buried deep, or thinly strewn,
Do thou thy grace supply;
The hope in earthly furrows sown,
Shall ripen in the sky.

MARLOW. C. M. Arr. by Dr. MASON.

983 ANON.

Sun of Righteousness.

1 ETERNAL Sun of Righteousness,
Display thy beams divine,
And cause the glory of thy face
On all our hearts to shine.

2 Light in thy light, oh, may we see,
Thy grace and mercy prove; [thee,
Revived, and cheered, and blessed by
The God of pardoning love.

984 ANON.

Bless God in the Sanctuary.

1 BLESS God, ye servants that attend
Upon his solemn state,—
That in his temple's hallowed courts
With humble reverence wait.

2 Within his house lift up your hands,
And bless his holy name;
From Zion bless thy Israel, Lord,
Who earth and heaven didst frame.

985 ANON.

Honor to the Saviour.

1 To Him that loved the souls of men,
And shed for us his blood,
To royal honors raised our head,
And made us priests to God:

2 To Him let every tongue be praise,
And every heart be love!
All grateful honors paid on earth,
And nobler songs above!

986 WATT.

Universal Praise.

1 O ALL ye nations! praise the Lord,
Each with a different tongue;
In every language learn his word,
And let his name be sung.

2 His mercy reigns through every land,—
Proclaim his grace abroad;
Forever firm his truth shall stand,—
Praise ye the faithful God!

987

Doxology.

1 Now hallelujah, power and praise,
To God in Christ be given,
By all who tread these earthly ways,
And all the blest in heaven.

988 WARDLAW.

Thanks at close of Service.

1 LIFT up to God the voice of praise,
Whose breath our souls inspired;
Loud and more loud the anthem raise,
With grateful ardor fired.

2 Lift up to God the voice of praise,
Whose goodness, passing thought,
Loads every minute, as it flies,
With benefits unsought.

3 Lift up to God the voice of praise,
For hope's transporting ray, [death,
Which lights, through darkest shades of
To realms of endless day.

MISCELLANEOUS.

LUTHER'S CHANT L. M. ZEUNER.

989 J. G. ADAMS.

For a Christian Festival.

1 THOU God of years and seasons all,
Of light, and peace, and love, and power;
Once more on thy great name we call,
In this our holy festal hour.

2 We praise thee for thy presence here,
For prayer, and speech, and cheerful song:
For guardian care, that year by year
Attends us all life's ways along:

3 For what we hope, and what we see
Of human progress in our time;
But gleams of freedom though they be,
Yet dawning of its day sublime!

990 BRYANT.

The Mother's Hymn.

1 LORD, who ordainest for mankind,
Benignant toils and tender cares,
We thank thee for the ties that bind
The mother to the child she bears.

2 We thank thee for the hopes that rise
Within her heart, as, day by day,
The dawning soul from those young eyes
Looks with a clearer, steadier ray.

3 And grateful for the blessing given,
With that dear infant on her knee,
She strains the eye to look to heaven,
The voice to lisp a prayer to thee.

4 All Gracious! grant to those who bear
A mother's charge the strength and light,
To guide the feet that own their care
In ways of love and truth and right.

991 MONTGOMERY.

Opening of an Organ.

1 THE morning stars in concert sang,
When God created heaven and earth;
And earth and heaven with music rang,
When angels hailed Messiah's birth.

2 Nor ever, since his sabbath-rest,
When the great Maker from the skies,
His finished works beheld and bless'd,
Have songs of glory ceased to rise.

3 Now, with all instruments in one,
All spirits tuned to one accord,
Our prayer be this, "Thy will be done;"
And this our anthem, "Praise the Lord!"

MANOAH. C. M. GREATOREX'S COLL.

992 S. W. LIVERMORE.

The Western Churches.

1 OUR pilgrim brethren dwelling far,—
O God of truth and love,
Light thou their path with thine own star,
Bright beaming from above.

2 Wide as their mighty rivers flow,
Let thine own truth extend;
Where prairies spread and forests grow,
O Lord, thy gospel send.

3 Then will a mighty nation own
A union firm and strong;—
The sceptre of th' eternal throne
Shall rule its councils long.

993 L. H. SIGOURNEY.

Marriage Hymn.

1 NOT for the summer's hour alone,
When skies resplendent shine,
And youth and pleasure fill the throne,
Our hearts and hands we join;

2 But for those stern and wintry days
Of sorrow, pain, and fear,
When Heaven's wise discipline doth make
Our earthly journey drear;—

3 Not for this span of life alone,
Which like a blast doth fly,
And as the transient flowers of grass
Just blossom, droop, and die;—

4 But for a being without end
This vow of love we take;
Grant us, O God, one home at last,
For thy great mercy's sake.

994 ANCIENT HYMN.

The Noble Army of Martyrs.

1 THE triumphs of the martyred saints
The joyous lay demand;
The heart delights in song to dwell
On that victorious band,—

2 Those whom the senseless world ab- [horred,
Who cast the world aside,
Deeming it worthless, for the sake
Of Christ, their Lord and guide.

3 For him they braved the tyrant's rage,
The scourge's cruel smart;
The wild beast's fang their bodies tore,
But vanquished not the heart;

4 Like lambs before the sword they fell,
Nor cry nor plaint expressed;
For patience kept the conscious mind,
And armed the fearless breast.

5 What tongue can tell the crown prepared
The martyr's brow to grace?
His shining robe, his joys unknown,
Before thy glorious face?

6 Vouchsafe us, Lord, if such thy will,
Clear skies and seasons calm;
If not the martyr's cross to bear,
And win the martyr's palm.

MARTYRS. 10s & 8. T. B. White.

995 *Of many Martyrs.* Breviary.

1 Sing we the peerless deeds of martyred saints, [tion blest;
Their glorious merits and their por-
Of all the conquerors the world has seen,
The greatest, bravest, and the best.

2 They trod beneath them every threat of man, [through;
And came victorious all torments
The iron hooks that piecemeal tore their flesh,
Could not their val'rous souls subdue.

3 What tongue those joys, O Jesus, can disclose, [dost prepare!
Which for thy martyred saints thou
Happy who in thy pains, thrice happy those
Who in thy endless glory share!

WEBSTER. 6s, Double. Arr. from Weber.

996

(To tune "Webster," opposite.)

LUTHER.

The Death of Martyrs.

1 Flung to the heedless winds,
Or on the waters cast,
Their ashes shall be watched,
And gathered at the last:
And from that scattered dust,
Around us and abroad,
Shall spring a plenteous seed
Of witnesses for God.

2 The Father hath received
Their latest living breath;
Yet vain is Satan's boast
Of victory in their death:
Still, still, though dead, they speak,
And trumpet-tongued proclaim
To many a wakening land
The one availing name.

AUTUMN. 8s & 7s, Double.

997

PIERPONT.

Anniversary Hymn.

1 God of mercy, do thou never
From our offering turn away,
But command a blessing ever
On the memory of this day.
Light and peace do thou ordain it;
O'er it be no shadow flung;
Let no deadly darkness stain it,
And no clouds be o'er it hung.

2 May the song this people raises
And its vows to thee addrest,
Mingle with the prayers and praises
That thou hearest from the blest.
When the lips are cold that sing thee,
And the hearts that love thee dust,
Father, then our souls shall bring thee
Holier love and firmer trust.

998

ANON.

Call of the Age.

1 We are living, we are dwelling
In a grand and awful time;
In an age on ages telling,
To be living is sublime:
Will ye play, then, will ye dally
With your music and your wine?
Up! it is th' Almighty's rally!
God's own arm hath need of thine!

999

MONTGOMERY.

Martyr Spirit.

1 Call Jehovah thy salvation;
Rest beneath th' Almighty's shade;
In his secret habitation
Dwell, and never be dismayed!
There no tumult can alarm thee;
Thou shalt dread no hidden snare;
Guile nor violence can harm thee,
In eternal safeguard there.

2 He shall charge his angel legions
Watch and ward o'er thee to keep;
Though thou walk thro' hostile regions,
Though in desert wilds thou sleep;
Thou shalt call on him in trouble,
He will hearken, he will save;
Here, for grief reward thee double,
Crown with life beyond the grave.

CESAREA. 7s, 61. Arr. by Dr. Mason.

1000

Ancient Hymn to the Saviour.

1 Holy Saviour! Lord of light!
From thy clear celestial height,
Thy pure beaming radiance give.
Come, thou lover of the poor!
Come, with treasures which endure!
Come, thou Light of all that live!

2 Thou of all consolers best,
Visiting the troubled breast,
Dost refreshing peace bestow;
Thou in toil art comfort sweet,
Pleasant coolness in the heat,
Solace in the midst of woe.

3 Light immortal! Light divine!
Visit thou these hearts of thine,
And our inmost being fill:
If thou take thy grace away,
Nothing pure in man will stay;
All his good is turned to ill.

4 Heal our wounds, our strength renew;
On our dryness pour thy dew;
Wash the stains of guilt away:
Bend the stubborn heart and will;
Melt the frozen, warm the chill;
Guide the steps that go astray.

5 Thou, on those who evermore
Thee confess, and thee adore,
In thy heavenly gifts, descend;
Give them comfort when they die;
Give them life with thee on high;
Give them joys which never end.

1001

Schenck.

All Saints Day.

1 Who are those before God's throne,
What the crownéd host I see?
As the sky with stars thick strown
Is their shining company;
Hallelujahs, hark! they sing;
Solemn praise to God they bring.

2 Who are those arrayed in light,
Clothed in righteousness divine,
Wearing robes most pure and white,
That unstained shall ever shine,
That can nevermore decay?—
Whence came all this bright array?

3 They are those who much have borne,
Trial, sorrow, pain, and care;
Who have wrestled night and morn
With the mighty God in prayer;
Now their strife hath found its close;
God hath turned away their woes.

4 They are those who hourly here
Served as priests before their Lord,
Offering up with gladsome cheer
Soul and body at his word;
Now within the holy place,
They behold him face to face.

MILTON. L. M.

HAYDN.

1002

Saturday Evening.

ANON.

1 SWEET to the soul the parting ray,
That ushers placid evening in,
When with the still, expiring day,
The Sabbath's peaceful hours begin;
How grateful to the anxious breast
The sacred hours of holy rest!

2 Hushed is the tumult of this day,
And worldly cares and business cease;
While soft the vesper breezes play,
To hymn the glad return of peace.
O season blest! O moment given
To turn the vagrant thoughts to heaven!

COMFORT. 11s & 10s.

1003

Spiritual Blessings.

ANON.

1 ALMIGHTY Father! thou hast many a blessing
In store for every erring child of thine;
For this I pray,—Let me, thy grace possessing,
Seek to be guided by thy will divine.

2 Not for earth's treasures, for her joys the dearest,
Would I my supplications raise to thee;
Not for the hopes that to my heart are nearest,
But only that I give that heart to thee.

TRUMPET. P. M.

Fine.

D. C.

1004 EPISCOPAL COLL.

The City of God.

1 SHOUT the glad tidings, exultingly sing;
Jerusalem triumphs, Messiah is king!
Zion, the marvellous story be telling,
The Son of the highest, how lowly
his birth!
The highest archangel in glory excelling,
He stoops to redeem thee, he reigns
upon earth.—Shout, etc.

2 Tell how he cometh; from nation to
nation, [echo round;
The heart cheering news, let the earth
How free to the faithful he offers sal-
vation, [are crowned.
How his people with joy everlasting
Shout the glad tidings, etc.

3 Mortals, your homage be gratefully
bringing, [arise;
And sweet let the gladsome hosanna
Ye angels the full hallelujah be singing;
One chorus resound through the
earth and the skies.—Shout, etc.

1005 MOORE.

Miriam's Song.

1 SOUND the loud timbrel o'er Egypt's
dark sea, [are free.
Jehovah has triumphed, his people
Sing, for the pride of the tyrant is
broken, [did and brave;
His chariots, his horsemen, all splen-
How vain was their boasting! the Lord
hath but spoken, [in the wave.
And chariots and horsemen are sunk
Sound the loud timbrel, etc.

2 Praise to the Conqueror, praise to the
Lord; [was our sword.
His word was our arrow, his breath
Who shall return to tell Egypt the
story [of her pride?
Of those she sent forth in the hour
For the Lord hath looked out from
his pillar of glory,
And all her brave thousands are
dashed in the tide.
Sound the loud timbrel, etc.

ALPHABETICAL INDEX OF HYMNS.

[Figures refer to the numbers of the hymns.]

INDEX OF SUBJECTS.

[Figures refer to the numbers of the hymns.]

ALPHABETICAL INDEX OF TUNES.

[Numbers refer to pages.]

METRICAL INDEX OF TUNES.

[Numbers refer to pages.]

www.ingramcontent.com/pod-product-compliance
Lightning Source LLC
Chambersburg PA
CBHW021217270326
41929CB00010B/1162
* 9 7 8 3 3 3 7 2 4 2 7 6 3 *